The Complexity of Identity and Interaction in Language Education

PSYCHOLOGY OF LANGUAGE LEARNING AND TEACHING
Series Editors: Sarah Mercer, *Universität Graz, Austria* and Stephen Ryan, *Waseda University, Japan*

This international, interdisciplinary book series explores the exciting, emerging field of Psychology of Language Learning and Teaching. It is a series that aims to bring together works which address a diverse range of psychological constructs from a multitude of empirical and theoretical perspectives, but always with a clear focus on their applications within the domain of language learning and teaching. The field is one that integrates various areas of research that have been traditionally discussed as distinct entities, such as motivation, identity, beliefs, strategies and self-regulation, and it also explores other less familiar concepts for a language education audience, such as emotions, the self and positive psychology approaches. In theoretical terms, the new field represents a dynamic interface between psychology and foreign language education and books in the series draw on work from diverse branches of psychology, while remaining determinedly focused on their pedagogic value. In methodological terms, sociocultural and complexity perspectives have drawn attention to the relationships between individuals and their social worlds, leading to a field now marked by methodological pluralism. In view of this, books encompassing quantitative, qualitative and mixed methods studies are all welcomed.

All books in this series are externally peer-reviewed.

Full details of all the books in this series and of all our other publications can be found on http://www.multilingual-matters.com, or by writing to Multilingual Matters, St Nicholas House, 31–34 High Street, Bristol BS1 2AW, UK.

PSYCHOLOGY OF LANGUAGE LEARNING AND TEACHING: 7

The Complexity of Identity and Interaction in Language Education

Edited by
Nathanael Rudolph, Ali Fuad Selvi and Bedrettin Yazan

MULTILINGUAL MATTERS
Bristol • Blue Ridge Summit

DOI https://doi.org/10.21832/RUDOLP7420
Library of Congress Cataloging in Publication Data
A catalog record for this book is available from the Library of Congress.
Names: Rudolph, Nathanael- editor. | Selvi, Ali Fuad, editor. | Yazan, Bedrettin, editor.
Title: The Complexity of Identity and Interaction in Language Education/ Edited by Nathanael Rudolph, Ali Fuad Selvi and Bedrettin Yazan.
Description: Blue Ridge Summit: Multilingual Matters, 2020. | Series: Psychology of Language Learning and Teaching: 7 | Includes bibliographical references and index. | Summary: "This book brings together critical approaches to identity and experience, with attention to the complexity of identity and interaction in and beyond the classroom, within language education. The chapters, written by professionals from a diverse array of backgrounds and contexts, have a particular focus on teacher education and classroom practice"—Provided by publisher. Identifiers: LCCN 2019044360 (print) | LCCN 2019044361 (ebook) | ISBN 9781788927413 (paperback) | ISBN 9781788927420 (hardback) | ISBN 9781788927437 (pdf) | ISBN 9781788927444 (epub) | ISBN 9781788927451 (kindle edition) Subjects: LCSH: Second language acquisition—Study and teaching. | Second language acquisition—Psychological aspects. | Language and languages—Study and teaching.
Classification: LCC P118.2 .C648 2020 (print) | LCC P118.2 (ebook) | DDC 418.0071—dc23 LC record available at https://lccn.loc.gov/2019044360 LC ebook record available at https://lccn.loc.gov/2019044361

British Library Cataloguing in Publication Data
A catalogue entry for this book is available from the British Library.

ISBN-13: 978-1-78892-742-0 (hbk)
ISBN-13: 978-1-78892-741-3 (pbk)

Multilingual Matters
UK: St Nicholas House, 31–34 High Street, Bristol BS1 2AW, UK.
USA: NBN, Blue Ridge Summit, PA, USA.

Website: www.multilingual-matters.com
Twitter: Multi_Ling_Mat
Facebook: https://www.facebook.com/multilingualmatters
Blog: www.channelviewpublications.wordpress.com

The policy of Multilingual Matters/Channel View Publications is to use papers that are natural, renewable and recyclable products, made from wood grown in sustainable forests. In the manufacturing process of our books, and to further support our policy, preference is given to printers that have FSC and PEFC Chain of Custody certification. The FSC and/or PEFC logos will appear on those books where full certification has been granted to the printer concerned.

Typeset by Nova Techset Private Limited, Bengaluru and Chennai, India.
Printed and bound in the UK by the CPI Books Group Ltd.
Printed and bound in the US by NBN.

Contents

Contributors

Sedat Akayoğlu is an assistant professor at the Department of Foreign Language Education, Abant İzzet Baysal University, in Bolu, Turkey. His research interests include Computer Assisted Language Learning, English Language Teacher Education, Culture in English Language Teaching and Discourse Analysis. He has recent publications in *CALICO Journal* and *Ilkogretim Online.* His current projects include designing and implementing telecollaboration initiatives to enhance preservice teachers' intercultural communicative competence.

Elena Andrei, EdD, is an assistant professor of TESOL and TESOL Program Coordinator at Cleveland State University. She is interested in classroom-based research, studying both the pre-K-12 classroom where ELs learn and her own post-secondary EL teacher education classrooms. She speaks English as her additional language and Romanian as her first language.

Adolfo Arrieta is an associate professor at the University of Sucre in Colombia. He holds a PhD in Education from Universidad Del Atlántico and a Master's Degree in Education from Universidad del Norte. His main research interests are learners' motivation, classroom interaction, critical pedagogy and teacher identity.

Lobat Asadi is a PhD candidate in Curriculum and Instruction, Texas A&M University, and lecturer of Foundations of Multicultural Education. At the crossroads of teacher education in multicultural education and TESOL, Lobat highlights social justice and intersectionality in linguistics, race, culture, gender and sexuality. Research interests include borderland studies, Gloria E. Anzaldúa, postcolonialism, translanguaging, linguistic and cultural imperialism, Middle Eastern studies, multicultural education and arts-based education.

Melanie J. Baker Robbins is the Academic Coordinator of the Intensive English Program at Western Carolina University. She holds a Master's degree in TESOL from Seattle Pacific University and is a doctoral candidate of International Education Policy at the University of Maryland. Her research focuses on teachers and the teaching profession.

Liaquat Ali Channa holds a PhD degree in Applied Linguistics. He presently serves as Associate Professor in the Department of English, Balochistan University of IT, Engineering & Management Sciences (BUITEMS), Quetta, Pakistan. His research work has been published in prestigious research journals.

Maya Khemlani David holds a PhD degree in Sociolinguistics. She is an Adjunct Professor in the Jaipuria Institute of Management, Lucknow, India, and a Research Associate in the Asia Europe Institute, University of Malaya. She is a widely published scholar in sociolinguistics and language policy and planning.

Francisco Perlas Dumanig holds a PhD in Sociolinguistics. He is an Assistant Professor of English at the University of Hawaii at Hilo. He used to be a Senior Lecturer at the Faculty of Languages and Linguistics, University of Malaya, Kuala Lumpur, Malaysia.

Jeremy R. Gombin-Sperling is a PhD candidate in the International Education Policy program and a Research Associate in the Education Abroad office at the University of Maryland-College Park. His research looks at issues of social identity and inclusion in international education programming, and how social justice-informed pedagogies can reshape student learning.

Eliana Hirano is an Associate Professor of Teacher Education and the Coordinator of the Teaching English as a Foreign Language minor at Berry College. Her research explores the intersection between identity and language learning, academic literacies in higher education with a focus on refugee-background students, and L2 teacher education.

Sarah Hopkyns is a faculty member in the College of Education, Zayed University, Abu Dhabi. She holds a PhD in Educational Research in the discipline of Applied Linguistics from the University of Leicester, UK. She has presented and published widely on the areas of sociolinguistics, globalization, culture and identity.

Shinji Kawamitsu is an assistant professor at Kansai Gaidai University. His research interests include systemic functional linguistics (SFL), SFL-informed language teaching, post-structuralist understanding of identity and investment, and critical discourse analysis. Kawamitsu is interested in teaching reading and writing (particularly elementary Japanese) through an SFL perspective and making opportunities for language learners to negotiate meaning-making practices.

Véronique Lemoine-Bresson is a Junior Lecturer at the Institute of Teacher Education (INSPE), University of Lorraine (France). Her main research interests include intercultural teaching practices, academic literacy, and comparative education. She has also worked as a teacher trainer focused on pedagogical development in language teaching and learning at the primary level.

Syed Abdul Manan holds PhD degree in Applied Linguistics. He presently serves as an Associate Professor in the Graduate School of Education, Nazarbayev University, in Nur-Sultan (Astana) Kazakhstan. His work on sociolinguistics, language policy and planning, multilingual/plurilingual education, and linguistic landscape has been published in a number of impact factor (ISI-indexed) journals.

Naashia Mohamed is a Lecturer at the University of Auckland. Her research focuses on language learning and teaching, addressing practices, pedagogies and policies that best facilitate language development and the maintenance of indigenous languages. Her work draws on the fields of second language acquisition, teacher education, language policy and sociolinguistics.

Stephanie Moody has over a decade of experience teaching elementary ESL, and is currently a PhD candidate at Texas A&M University. Her research focuses on translanguaging as a literacy strategy, the impact of writing on vocabulary development, and preservice teacher preparation for ELL writing instruction.

Yolanda N. Padrón is a Professor in the Bilingual Education Program, in the College of Education & Human Development at Texas A&M University. She also serves as Director of Faculty Development for the College. Her research interests focus on improving classroom instruction for English Language Learners and effective teacher training for teachers of second language students.

Caroline Payant is an Associate Professor at the Université du Québec à Montréal. Her research with bi/multilingual learners examines first and second language mediation during task-based interactions. Her most recent work can be found in the *Canadian Journal of Applied Linguistics*, *Journal of English for Academic Purposes* and *Critical Multilingual Studies*.

Nayibe Rosado is a language teacher and teacher educator at Universidad del Norte in Colombia. Her research interests reside in the intersection of students and teacher learning and how language affects the construction of reality in contexts such as classrooms and in other institutions that surround us.

Nathanael Rudolph is an associate professor of sociolinguistics and language education at Kindai University in Higashiosaka, Japan. His research interests include critical approaches to language teacher and learner identity, and (in)equity in (and beyond) language education.

April S. Salerno is an assistant professor of ESL teacher education at the University of Virginia. Her work focuses on better preparing and supporting preservice and in-service teachers to work with multilingual learners. Her work has appeared in *TESOL Quarterly, Linguistics and Education*, and other publications.

Ali Fuad Selvi is an Assistant Professor of TESOL and Applied Linguistics and the Chair of the Teaching English as a Foreign Language Program at Middle East Technical University, Northern Cyprus Campus. His research interests include Global Englishes; (in)equity, professionalism, marginalization and discrimination in TESOL; and second language teacher education.

Glenn Toh has for 30 years taught English in schools and tertiary institutions as well as lectured on teacher education programs in Australia, Hong Kong, Singapore, Thailand and Japan. He has published in the areas of ideology, power and language education and maintains an interest in ongoing developments in these areas.

Şeyma Toker is a PhD student in Applied Linguistics at Georgetown University. Her research interests include L2 teacher education, language socialization, identity, critical multilingualism, and migration. She is particularly interested in the intersection of L2 learning and L2 teacher development with race, ethnicity, gender and social class in migration contexts.

Alfredo Urzúa is an Associate Professor of Applied Linguistics at San Diego State University. He received his MA in TESOL from UCLA and his PhD in Applied Linguistics from the University of Northern Arizona. He has worked as a language teacher educator, researcher, and program coordinator in Mexico and the US.

Babürhan Üzüm is an associate professor at the Department of Language, Literacy, and Special Populations at Sam Houston State University. His research interests include language teacher identity, reflective practice, and preparing teachers for linguistically and culturally diverse educational contexts. His recent work has appeared in *Language Teaching Research* and *Teaching and Teacher Education* journals. His current projects focus on telecollaboration initiatives to prepare preservice teachers for multicultural educational contexts.

Meike Wernicke is an Assistant Professor in the Department of Language and Literacy Education at the University of British Columbia. Building on an extensive background in L2 teaching, her research in French second language teacher education has focused on study abroad and teacher identity with research interests in intercultural education, bi-/multilingual language policy and pedagogies, and discourse analytic research methodologies. Her current research examines pre- and in-service second language teacher professional learning and the development of professional support programs. She is also involved in an international project on multilingualism and teacher education in the European context.

Bedrettin Yazan is an assistant professor of educational linguistics at the University of Alabama, Tuscaloosa. His research focuses on language teacher learning and identity, teacher collaboration, World Englishes, and language policy and planning. His recent work has appeared in *Teacher Education Quarterly*, *TESOL Journal*, *Language Teaching Research* and *Critical Inquiry in Language Studies*.

Introduction: The Complexity of Identity and Interaction in Language Education

Nathanael Rudolph, Ali Fuad Selvi and Bedrettin Yazan

Every day in our dynamic world, people negotiate being and belonging in interaction with each other and with the settings in which they live, work and study. Such contextualized interaction can be richly multimodal, occurring via spoken and written discourse, and through contact with images, other humanmade artefacts and the environment (natural, manipulated and/or artificial), inscribed with and interpreted as having 'meaning' (e.g. Boix-Fuster, 2015; Pennycook & Otsuji, 2015; Pennycook, 2017, 2018). Identity and interaction are characterized by motion, diversity and complexity (Blommaert, 2010; Makoni & Pennycook, 2012).

The negotiation of identity and community membership in interaction is not neutral. It is a struggle over positionality: who individuals, and others around them, 'are/are not,' and 'can' and/or 'should' be or become (e.g. Davies & Harré, 1990; Martin-Jones *et al.*, 2012; Rudolph, 2016; Rudolph *et al.*, 2018). This struggle includes individuals and groups defining and patrolling, and/or problematizing and destabilizing, essentialized and idealized notions of 'language,' 'culture,' 'identity' and 'place,' which can afford people validity, authority and agency, and/or strip it away from them (e.g. Doerr, 2009; McCarty & May, 2017).

'Language' education, as with interaction, is inseparably bound to identity negotiation (Higgins, 2011), shaping and reflecting contextualized, sociohistorical delineations of 'truth,' 'correctness,' 'normativity' and 'value' and 'change.' What may appear to superficially be 'linguistic' or 'cultural,' in teaching, is, on a deeper level, ontological, axiological and epistemological. Language education can impose, affirm, problematize, challenge, transform and reify essentialized and idealized notions of being and becoming (e.g. Kramsch, 2014; McCarty & May, 2017). Language teaching and learning can thus create, limit and/or eliminate space for identity, both in and beyond the classroom.

The 'language/s' we promote and teach, neglect or Other purposefully and otherwise, represent a prioritization, and therefore privileging and marginalization (past and present), of ways of being and becoming. This can be due to the (ongoing) epistemic and actualized violence of colonialism, the influences of nationalism and neoliberalism and/or the drive to reclaim identity and community membership. Language education, and its underpinning policies, can therefore empower, emancipate, revitalize, unite, and/or control and destroy.

In the interest of framing the nature and purpose of this volume, we first begin by reviewing scholarship exploring the negotiation of identity and interaction in (and transcending) communities, followed by work attending to language education. Our intent is neither to provide an exhaustive sociohistorical account nor attempt an explanation of the countless terms and concepts proliferating in academia. Instead, our goal is to illuminate key themes and issues shaping (and shaped by) conceptual and inquiry-based approaches to language education, and to identify the dialogue to which this volume contributes. Furthermore, we hope to inspire readers to reflect upon how the themes and issues in this introduction, and the chapters that follow, manifest in their own contexts.

The Negotiation of 'Identity' and 'Interaction': An Academic Survey

Transdisciplinary, critically oriented scholarship, in 'domains' (Pennycook, 2018) including applied linguistics, sociolinguistics, history, geography, cultural anthropology, and language policy and planning, has increasingly examined sociohistorical 'flows' of people, information, goods, finances and technology (Appadurai, 1996). In doing so, such work has sought to explore and apprehend the complexity of negotiated identity and community membership within and transcending linguistic, cultural, ethnic, socioeconomic, religious, political, geographic, gendered and sexual 'borders' (Canagarajah, 2013, 2017). Scholars have examined topics including individuals' negotiations of bi- and multilingual identities, resistance to and advocacy for mono-, bi- and multilingualism in education, local and national bi- and multilingual policy and the complexity of multimodal, multilingual interaction (e.g. García *et al.*, 2017; May, 2013). Scholarship has additionally documented linguistic diversity emergent from colonialism and imperialism, including English*es* (Kachru, 1986, 1992; Kirkpatrick, 2010; Schneider, 2014), Spanish*es* (e.g. Mar-Molinero, 2010; Mar-Molinero & Paffey, 2011; Niño-Murcia *et al.*, 2008; Paffey, 2012) and French*es* (e.g. Avalos & Augustin, 2018).

Scholars have additionally examined how language policy and planning can create and/or eliminate space for different ways of being in a given community or society. Guerrero (2008) and Guerrero and Quintero (2009), for instance, note how national language policies in Colombia have equated bilingualism with 'Spanish' and 'English,' while marginalizing the language and identities of diverse indigenous peoples around the country. In

Haiti, language policy and education generally privilege French over local Haitian Kreyol, the everyday language of the population (Avalos & Augustin, 2018). Thus, within Haitian society, discourses of essentialized and idealized 'Frenchness' privilege and marginalize individuals personally and professionally. The situation has further been complicated by the increasing introduction of English education, and Haitian emigration. Exploring transnational policy, Flores (2013) notes how 'English' is positioned at the center of conversations about multilingualism, trans-/multi-/plurilingual policy and practice in the European Union.

McCarty *et al.* (2006), McCarty *et al.* (2015) and Wiley *et al.* (2014) explore the history of language loss and revitalization pertaining to the language of Native Americans in the United States. Additional work has examined language policy and the language rights of linguistic minorities, for example, in India (e.g. Benedikter, 2009; Sridhar, 1996), and the language and lived experiences of immigrants to regions including Europe (e.g. Extra & Gorter, 2001; Extra & Yağmur, 2004). Others have researched the lived experiences of refugees and asylum seekers, and their ongoing negotiations of identity and community membership. Warriner (2007), for example, examines the experiences of Sudanese women wrestling with identity and belonging in the United States, while McNamara (2014) unpacks the role of Language Analysis for Determining Origin (LADO) in validating asylum claims in different countries around the globe.

Further work has explored 'lingua franca' interaction (e.g. Jenkins *et al.*, 2017). Scholarship examining the use of English as a lingua franca (ELF), originally treating ELF as code used between 'non-native speakers,' has passed through conceptual phases. ELF scholars are increasingly exploring the function of English employed as a (multi)lingua franca (Jenkins, 2015), in acknowledgement of the linguistic and cultural complexity of such interaction. In Estonia, for example, Estonians, comprising more than 2/3 of the population, speak Estonian and increasingly pursue English in line with a sociocultural and educational pivot toward the West, while Russians, representing around 25% of the population, speak Russian and have increasingly prioritized the Estonian language socially and educationally, followed by English (Soler-Carbonell, 2014). This has resulted in a linguascape in which there has been a marked shift from Russian towards the use of Estonian and, increasingly, the use of ELF, in interethnic interaction (particularly among youth), though sociohistorical tensions remain in Estonia and the region (Soler-Carbonell, 2011, 2014). Jenkins (2014) and Galloway and Rose (2015) describe 'native Englishes,' 'new (postcolonial) Englishes' and English used as a lingua franca, as 'global Englishes,' a term increasingly employed to describe work seeking to attend to movement, change, diversity and hybridity. Scholarship pertaining to the use of 'lingua francas' is not limited to 'English,' including the use of Spanish between different indigenous peoples in Peru (Steckbauer, 1997), Japanese as a lingua franca between individuals in and beyond Japan (e.g. Kubota, 2013; Rudolph, 2018), Arabic (see Meierkord, 2008), Bahasa Indonesia and *putonghua* ('standard' Chinese) (see Kirkpatrick, 2010; Pennycook, 2012).

Further work, informed by postmodern (and poststructural) theory, has both implicitly and explicitly problematized the use of named and bounded language/s, culture/s, identity/ies and places in conceptualizing and approaching the negotiation of identity and community membership in interaction (e.g. Blommaert, 2010; Rubdy & Alsagoff, 2013). Work by Vertovec (2007), Blommaert (2010, 2015) and Arnaut *et al.* (2015), explores the notion of *superdiversity*, or the complexity of (a diversification of) diversity stemming from a great degree of transnational movement and resultant hybridity. Otsuji (2011), Otsuji and Pennycook (2010) and Pennycook and Otsuji (2015, 2019), conceptualize and explore individuals' (often urban), trans-border negotiations of identity and interaction, and the complexity of (non-bounded) language (practices) shaping and emergent from such interaction, as *metrolingualism*. Canagarajah (2012, 2013) presents the concept of *translingual practice* as an umbrella term for lenses such as *translanguaging* (Creese & Blackledge, 2010), that conceptualize communication as the transcending of individual, bounded languages, and the employing of diverse, multimodal semiotic resources in each context in which a person interacts (Canagarajah, 2012: 6–7). Additionally, and notably, Canagarajah (2013) problematizes the binaries of mono-/multi- and uni-/plurilingual, contending that monolingualism itself is a construct:

> 'Communities and communication have always been heterogeneous. Those who are considered monolingual are typically proficient in multiple registers, dialects, and discourses of a given language. Even when they speak or write in a single 'language,' they still have to communicate in relation to diverse other codes in the environment. That very 'language' is constituted by resources from diverse places'. (2013: 8)

The edited volume by Canagarajah (2017) addresses many of these topics in its thematic exploration of language and migration: the negotiation of identity and community membership, entailing the transcending of and wrestling with borders (e.g. linguistic, sociocultural cultural, educational, ethnic, national, religious, geographical) (see also Yazan *et al.*, 2019).

There has been additional focus on language ideologies, or beliefs people negotiate and hold, that shape how they view 'language' itself (Pennycook, 2017), as well as notions such as ownership and use (e.g. Woolard, 1998), and teaching (e.g. Mirhosseini, 2018). McCarty (2014) notes that ideologies are about identity, power, and notions of community membership (2014: 14). Scholarship has been engaged both implicitly and explicitly with notions of 'Self' and 'Otherness.' Charalambous *et al.* (2016), for example, looking at Greek-Cypriot identity and education, examine how sociohistorical events and language ideologies, grounded in the equation of language with nation, give shape to the construction and maintenance of ethnonationalist identities. Such events and ideologies, they argue, potentially serve as a catalyst for resistance to the valuing and incorporation of translanguaging practices in education in a 'superdiverse' setting plagued by conflict. Exploring ideologies, and the equation of language, culture and ethnicity with nation, Heinrich (2012) and Morris-Suzuki (1997) unpack the historical construction of Japan as a site of homogeneity, which occurred during a process of nation-building commencing near the beginning of the Meiji Era (1868–1912), from which sprang the idea of Japan as a 'monolingual,' 'monocultural' and 'mono-ethnic' society. Bilingualism is, at present, imagined as entailing the use of Japanese and English (Kubota, 1998, 2002). Heinrich *et al.* (2015) and Anderson and Heinrich (2014) have examined how the political, social and educational making of 'monolingual Japan' has endangered the six distinct languages of the Ryukyus (present-day Okinawa prefecture and a portion of Kagoshima prefecture in Japan), a formerly independent region annexed by Japan during the Meiji Era. Their work highlights local and international efforts at language revitalization, despite the national government classifying these 'languages' as 'dialects of Japanese' for socio-political and ideological reasons (see also Shimoji & Pellard, 2010). Rudolph (2019a) examines how divergent narratives of 'identity,' 'place,' 'language' and 'culture' – Japan as a sociohistorical site of homogeneity vs as a site of movement, change, diversity and hybridity – give rise to competing views of Japaneseness/not-Japaneseness within Japanese society, Japaneseness-Otherness in terms of the 'world beyond,' and Japan's connections to 'elsewhere.' In a similar fashion, Horner (2007) examines competing historical narratives of 'purity' and 'hybridity' giving shape to approaches to language and national identity in Luxembourgish society. Such work highlights how certain ways of being and belonging are valued, while other individuals find their identities and lived experiences devalued, denigrated and erased, stripping them of a voice (Yazan & Rudolph, 2018). Hua and Wei (2014) discuss the promotion of Chinese as a global language by the government-sponsored Confucius Institutes, and how such education involves the perpetuation of essentialized and idealized Chineseness. Hua and Wei note the effect this has upon students of 'Chinese' ancestry, whose linguistic, cultural and ethnic identities are devalued and ignored.

An edited collection by Springer *et al.* (2016) explores the discourse of *neoliberalism*, which they define as, 'the extension of competitive markets into all areas of life, including the economy, politics and society… Key to this process is an attempt to instill a series of values and social practices in subjects' (2016: 2). De Costa *et al.* (2016) examine how neoliberalism gives shape to 'linguistic entrepreneurship' in language learning, while De Costa (2019) highlights how the discourse of neoliberalism is implicated in the construction and maintenance of '*elite multilingualism*.'

Neoliberalism, in interaction with ideologies of Self-Otherness, can additionally give shape to how individuals and groups imagine what to expect regarding interaction with 'others' (e.g. who others 'are,' and how we might connect with 'them'), something which education can and does play a role in perpetuating (see the special issue by Shin & Park, 2016). Kubota (2013) illuminates how Japanese professionals stationed in China are confronted with the linguistic diversity of their workplace, as Chinese, Japanese and English are used, which challenged their beliefs that English was the global key to unlocking the doors of communication.

Transdisciplinary conversations regarding ideologies discussing and problematizing constructions of 'Self-Other,' focus attention on essentialized and idealized being and belonging, which includes the concept of 'nativeness' (and, by proxy, 'not- and non-nativeness'). Scholars have documented the privilege-marginalization that individuals experience as they position themselves and are positioned, for instance, as 'native' and 'non-native' language users, resulting in them being afforded or stripped of value and authority as (in)authentic community members (e.g. Doerr, 2009). Wernicke-Heinrichs (2013) and Wernicke (2017), for instance, explores individuals' experiences negotiating positionality as teachers of French, as professionals whose identities do not correspond with essentialized and idealized nativeness. Valdés (1997), Train (2007), Mar-Molinero (2010), Mar-Molinero and Paffey (2011) and Paffey (2012) explore the ideological construction of nativeness in Spanish, and the othering of identities and varieties of Spanish that do not correspond with dominant, globalized discourses of nativeness and language ownership. Hashimoto (2018), Houghton *et al.* (2018) and Rudolph (2012, 2016, 2019b) explore the construction of idealized nativeness in Japanese. The famous debate between World Englishes scholar Braj Kachru and Sir Randolph Quirk (see Quirk, 1990 and Kachru, 1991), is an example of the centrality of 'nativeness' and ideas such as 'purity' and 'correctness,' to discussions of language, community membership, movement and change. Quirk argued for a universal standard English as necessary to maintain 'correctness,' while Kachru contended critically and practically for the need to acknowledge history, and both account for and celebrate the ongoing emergence of diverse ways of being and belonging.

Some scholars are problematizing critical discourses seeking to account for the negotiated complexity of identity and interaction. Hall (2002), for instance, takes issue with the notion of the 'post' in 'postcolonial,' contending that colonialism and imperialism continue undiminished. Horner (2007) and Makoni (2012) assert that the ideologies of naming and boundary drawing pertaining to language are dominant within the domains of historical linguistics (Horner, 2007) and sociolinguistics (Makoni, 2012). O'Rourke and Pujolar (2013) note that critical attention to language revitalization is largely predicated on the identities of localized, native speakers, and therefore upon essentialized and idealized 'nativeness.' O'Rourke and Pujolar assert that many users of endangered and minority language are 'new speakers,' whose identities and lived experiences are marginalized and even discounted, unintentionally or not. Sewell (2019) and O'Regan (2014, 2015) note the persistence of naming and boundary drawing within 'ELF scholarship' (e.g. 'ELF users'; 'ELF communication'; English as a *multi*lingua franca; 'native speakers'; 'non-native speakers') despite such work engaging with post-modern movement, complexity, diversity and hybridity. Work by scholars including Rivers and Zotsmann (2017), Rudolph *et al.* (2019) and Yazan and Rudolph (2018) has addressed naming/labeling and boundary drawing pertaining to the use of essentializing categories to apprehend identity, experience and (in)equity. This scholarship contends that the universalized, categorical assignment ('native'/ 'non-native'; 'native speaker teacher'/'non-native speaker teacher'; Western/not-Western) of knowledge and skills (e.g. monolingual/multilingual) and assumption of experiences (privileged/marginalized) fails to capture the complexity of identity and the fluidity of individuals' negotiation of privilege-marginalization across 'borders.' We will expand the discussion regarding nativeness, as it relates to language education, in the next section.

Other work has taken issue with concepts and corresponding terminology proposed by scholarship purporting to move beyond naming and boundary drawing. Makoni (2012) and Pavlenko (2018) question, for instance, the term *superdiversity*. Makoni (2012), speaking about the African continent, notes that movement (and resultant interaction and diversity) are not new; they were simply labeled with different terminology (e.g. nomadism) (2012: 193). Makoni additionally expresses concern that use of the term 'superdiversity' masks the inequity manifesting in the contexts so described. Pavlenko (2018) questions whether superdiversity is a theoretical lens or a phenomenon, and wonders whether the term is describing something new, or something that has existed from time immemorial. In referring to a move within sociolinguistic scholarship toward a break from naming and boundary drawing pertaining to language, Makoni (2012) questions the term *translanguaging*, asserting, 'You can only translanguage, perform a form of languaging, if you assume in the first instance that there are codes called languages' (Makoni, 2012: 192). Otheguy *et al.* (2015), and Pennycook (2017) alternately propose conceptualizations of 'translanguaging' that move beyond the notion of named and bounded languages and semiotic resources. It is important to note here, that 'translanguaging' can refer to transcending 'bounded languages,' or transcending the notion of 'language*s*' itself (as with Pennycook, 2017). This is a (potentially) confusing conceptual issue that affects ontological and epistemological clarity (see, for example, Cenoz, 2019, discussing translanguaging, multilingualism and ELF).

Within the above-mentioned scholarship, dialogue is inscribed with concern relating to identity and community membership, (in)equity and inclusivity. Critically, scholars are shedding light on the privilege-marginalization individuals experience in their ongoing negotiations of being and belonging. Practically, scholars are drawing attention to the complexity characterizing our world and the contexts therein, in order to educate and transform the spaces in which people live. We also see a tension within such scholarship, pertaining to naming/labeling and boundary-drawing, in terms of 'language,' 'culture,' 'place' and 'identity.' As we will see shortly, language education is inscribed with the same tension.

Language Education

Critically oriented scholarship attending to the complexity of negotiated identity and interaction in language education, is engaged with accounting for and valuing diverse ways of being and belonging. Scholarship has been concerned with problematizing monolingual, decontextualized, one-size-fits-all approaches to language ownership, learning, use and instruction predicated upon essentialized and idealized nativeness. The special journal issue edited by Claire Kramsch (2014), for example, looks at how foreign language education is prompted to grapple with and reconsider conceptualizations of and approaches to classroom practice, in light of sociohistorical movement, change and diversity (see also Block & Cameron, 2002). Macedo (2019) seeks to address the colonial underpinnings of foreign language education, yet undismantled. A special journal issue edited by Kubota and Austin (2007) focuses on critical approaches to world language education in the United States, that challenge ideologies of ethnocentrism and monoculturalism, the perpetuation of a belief in monolingualism in English as normative, both socially and in education. Creese and Blackledge (2010), Lewis *et al.* (2012) and Martínez, *et al.* (2015), explore the ideological underpinnings and practice of translanguaging in the classroom, which counter dominant notions of 'purity' and 'correctness,' as well as the *monolingual principle* (Howatt, 1984), or notion that languages are best taught in that tongue. Manan and David (2014) and Stranger-Johannessen and Norton (2019) examine language teaching and literacy, and the prioritization of dominant languages (e.g. English and Urdu) at the expense of local language and ways of being. The volume by Selvi and Rudolph (2018) explores the theme of teaching attending to contextualized, local–global interaction and identity negotiation, and the problematization of ideologies of nativeness. A large body of scholarship examining 'English' language teaching through differing lenses, has touched upon the incorporation of global Englishes into the classroom (e.g. Galloway, 2017), as well as English as a (multi) lingua franca (e.g. Dewey, 2014), and English as an international language (e.g. Matsuda, 2017; Sharifian, 2009). The guest edited issues by Lämmerer and Mercer (2019) and Yazan *et al.* (2019), as well as the edited volume by Kostoulas (2019), examine the construction, maintenance and challenging of borders drawn within language education, and highlight the need to attend to individuals' border crossing and borderland negotiations of identity and interaction.

Language learner, user and teacher identity has been a popular area of recent critical focus, with countless publications examining identity negotiation in and beyond the classroom (e.g. Barkhuizen, 2016; De Costa & Norton, 2017; Higgins, 2011; Varghese *et al.*, 2005; Yazan & Rudolph, 2018). Increasing attention has been paid to the lived experiences of language learners, teachers and users, whose identities do not correspond with dominant notions of idealized nativeness and community membership, linguistically, culturally, ethnically and otherwise.

The body of scholarship examining the ownership, learning, use and instruction of English is a robust one, which we present here as exemplary of conceptualizations of and approaches to criticality. One prominent theoretical approach to apprehending the perpetuation and effects of 'nativeness,' is Holliday's (2005, 2006) concept of *native speakerism*. This lens, applied to the field of English language teaching (ELT), imagines native speakerism as a globalized discourse, flowing from the West. This discourse privileges the idealized knowledge, skills, behavior, thinking, speech and experiences of a monolingual, white, western, male 'native speaker' of English, affording privilege to those whose identities align with the construct. Holliday (2009) notes that 'NNESTs' (non-native English-speaking/er teacher) and those 'native-speaking' individuals from former colonies, who are nevertheless positioned as 'non/not-natives,' find their localized linguistic, cultural, ethnic, political and religious ways of being and knowing marginalized. Native speakers are afforded the 'ownership' of English (Widdowson, 1994), and are considered the de facto 'best' teachers, a notion referred to by Phillipson (1992) as the *native speaker fallacy*. The concept of native speakerism has been utilized to conceptualize privilege-marginalization in other domains of language teaching, including Japanese (e.g. Hashimoto, 2018; Nomura & Mochizuki, 2018). Scholarship focused on English and ELT that predates Holliday's formulation 'native speakerism,' indeed addressed the need to challenge, and move beyond, idealized nativeness in the interest of attending to inequity and shaping classroom practice to better reflect the complexities of interaction. As mentioned above, this work has been engaged with documenting the diverse array of contexts, varieties, functions and users of 'English' emergent from colonialism, imperialism, neoliberalism and overall movement (for a full summary see Yazan & Rudolph, 2018).

Within ELT and applied linguistics in general, scholars have, critically and otherwise, often drawn upon the terms 'native' and 'non-native' to discuss ability, experience and value (see Aneja, 2016). Though questioned for their historically ideological implications (e.g. Jain, 2018), these categories have served, for many scholars, as a means of organization, empowerment and emancipation. Work by Medgyes (2001), for instance, does not problematize idealized nativeness, nor the idea that learners are to become like the 'native speaker,' though it does challenge the monolingual principle. Rather, it is a lens of 'juxtaposed nativeness' (Yazan & Rudolph, 2018). The 'non-native' English teacher, native speaker of a local language, is owner of that language, and can best empathize and connect with their students. This symbiotically complements the 'nativeness' of the native English speaker in language education. Challenging this 'deficiency' model, and seeking to move beyond idealized nativeness, Mahboob (2010) alternately proposes the 'NNEST lens,' which he calls the lens of 'multilingualism, multiculturalism, and multinationalism' (Mahboob, 2010: 15). The NNEST lens, while highlighting, valuing and seeking to attend to the complexity of negotiated identity and interaction in ELT, nevertheless relies on categories to apprehend identity, knowledge, skills, experience and (in)equity. Drawing on the concept of 'native speakerism,' the lens presupposes that (white, western) 'native speakers' are universally privileged in societies and educational settings therein, and that 'non-native speakers' are marginalized in a corresponding fashion. Idealized nativeness pertaining to English, shaping theory, research, professional activities, materials design and creation, assessment, teacher education, language and education policymaking, assessment, classroom practice and hiring practices, is the target to be addressed in the interest of addressing equity and fostering diversity and inclusivity.

Though differing in what they seek to problematize, the lens of juxtaposed nativeness and the NNEST lens share a few key elements in common: (a) the categorical apprehension of being and belonging; (b) the assignment of ownership of local language to 'local' NNESTs (e.g. Medgyes, 2001; Mahboob & Lin, 2018), creating an additional binary: local 'NNEST' vs non-local 'NNEST'; (c) the challenging of the monolingual principle. Rudolph and Rudolph (2018), Rivers (2016) Sewell (2019), Yazan and Rudolph (2018) and the special journal issue edited by Rudolph *et al.* (2019) details how the categorical apprehension of identity, experience and inequity underpins dominant approaches to privilege-marginalization embedded in applied linguistics scholarship and approaches to English language teaching, and serves as the foundation for apprehensions of inequity within World Englishes (e.g. Braine, 2010), ELF (e.g. Dewey, 2014), Global Englishes (e.g. Galloway, 2017) and English as an International Language (e.g. Sharifian, 2009) scholarship attending to (English) language education.

Scholars, drawing upon social constructivist, critical realist, postcolonial, postmodern and poststructural theory, and apprehending identity as dynamically, sociohistorically and contextually negotiated in interaction (Yazan & Rudolph, 2018), have problematized the 'assumptions' (Rudolph *et al.*, 2019) inscribed in categorical approaches to identity, experience, knowledge, skills and (in)equity. Erling (2017), Rivers (2019) and Rudolph (2018, 2019a), for instance, note that teachers positioned as 'native speakers' may find their diverse identities, lived experiences, knowledge and skills stripped away, along with their voice, by the use of categories. Rivers and Ross (2013) Charles (2017, 2019) and Weekly (2018) note the concomitant privilege-marginalization teachers positioned as '(inauthentic) native speakers' experience, due to their identities not corresponding with idealized nativeness linguistically, culturally, ethnically and religiously. Manara (2018), Park (2017), Rudolph (2012) and Rudolph *et al.* (2018) highlight the lived experiences of teachers positioned as 'NNESTs,' who experience fluid privilege-marginalization in and beyond the classroom.

Additional work, drawing upon transdisciplinary scholarship, has expanded conceptualizations of privilege-marginalization focused on idealized nativeness in English, to account for individuals' negotiation of identity in the communities wherein they live, work and study. This scholarship seeks to situate explorations of 'nativeness/non-nativeness' and 'nativeness/not nativeness' within larger societal negotiations of 'Self-Otherness' pertaining to a given community, and the 'world beyond.' With a focus on university-level language education in Japan, for instance, scholars including Houghton and Rivers (2013), Houghton *et al.* (2018), Rudolph (2016, 2018, 2019a) Rivers (2016) and Toh (2016, 2019) have documented how essentialized and idealized discourses of personal-professional being and belonging relating to nativeness in English and Japanese, have served to fluidly privilege-marginalize teachers positioned as 'native English-speaking/non-native Japanese speakers' and 'non-native English-speaking/native speakers of Japanese.' This shapes things including the roles they are given, the opportunities they are provided with to draw upon their translinguistic and transcultural identities in and beyond the classroom, the value they are assigned as faculty members by stakeholders in ELT and the job opportunities and security they are afforded (see Rudolph, 2019a). Teachers whose identities do not align with constructions of idealized nativeness (e.g. South Korean, Filipino and Singaporean professionals), most often find job opportunities limited or non-existent (Rudolph, 2019b). Faculties are thus generally composed of a majority of 'Japanese' teachers, and a small handful of western 'native speaker' teachers, with job advertisements divided implicitly and explicitly between '(native) Japanese speakers' and 'native English speakers' (e.g. Rivers, 2016). Rudolph (2019a) notes, however, that privilege-marginalization is not experienced uniformly across university-level education, and that hiring practices and issues of equity manifest in diverse ways within other forms of English language education (e.g. English conversation schools for all ages; cram schools; dispatch companies providing teachers to primary, secondary and tertiary institutions).

Work in this vein prompts scholars and other stakeholders in language education to consider a few key concerns, including the following: To what degree does our scholarship link with the dialogue found within transdisciplinary scholarship and social movements, which have observed and documented the ongoing negotiation of being and belonging, and individuals' contextualized, sociohistorical lived experiences negotiating privilege-marginalization? If our work is detached from such scholarship, we may render individuals marginalized or invisible, and the nature and origin of manifested privilege-marginalization partially or wholly unaddressed. Second, are we paying attention to the potential for conceptual inconsistencies within our work and that of others? If we are seeking to account for the rich complexity of the world in which we live and interact, why are we not attending to identity, experience and (in)equity in a similar fashion? Kubota (2019) reminds us that categories can afford individuals and groups a means to organize and address inequity. Yet, they may also be employed to Other (Rivers, 2018).

Scope and Contents of the Volume

In this volume, we seek to address two specific issues: (a) the ongoing call for transdisciplinary attention to the complexity of negotiated identity and interaction characterizing classrooms and the communities in which they are located, and resistance stakeholders face; and (b) the call to situate critical conceptualizations of and approaches to (in)equity in sociohistorical context. Our first concern is captured in the words of Lämmerer and Mercer (2019), who write:

> 'In the age of translanguaging, multilingualism, multiculturalism, globalization, international migration, transnationalism, and the blending of content and language education, there is an ever greater need in language education to reflect on the interconnections and overlap between languages, disciplines, constructs, and contexts that have traditionally been conceptualized in bounded ways'. (2019: 447)

Attending to the second, drawing on scholarship problematizing the categorical apprehension of identity, experience, knowledge, skills and (in) equity, we desire to heed the call for criticality in language education that is,

> 'academically transdisciplinary, decentralized, sociohistorically contextualized and connected to the community in which it is situated, and for one that prompts individuals toward self-reflexive attention to positionality; to what frames our seeing (Lather, 1993).' (Rudolph, 2019a: 105)

We are prompted, as well, by Pennycook (2018), who challenges the notion of applied linguistics (or, for example, language education) as a distinct academic 'field,' alternately proposing the notion of 'epistemic assemblages,' or domains wherein scholars are engaged with questions that transcend areas of study. These concerns underpinned our approach to crafting our call for chapter proposals, and to providing feedback to authors, as did our desire for authors to attend to conceptual congruity, in approaching the negotiated complexity of identity and interaction. Readers will note, however, that we did not specifically ask our authors to reflect upon the ontological and epistemological commitments underpinning their use of terminology such as 'translanguaging,' or naming and boundary drawing relating to languages (e.g. 'French'), thus rendering the volume haunted by the ongoing debate over how to apprehend language practices.

The first section of the volume, *Learners, Teachers, and the 'Ares,' 'Cans' and 'Shoulds' of Being and Becoming,* attends in detail to the ideologies learners and teachers encounter and wrestle with in their negotiations of identity in (and beyond) the classroom. These include the promotion of monolingual approaches to education, and the perpetuation and maintenance of idealized nativeness and community membership. Syed Abdul Manan, Maya Khemlani David, Liaquat Ali Channa and Francisco Perlas Dumanig (Chapter 1) examine English-only language policies and practices in schools in Pakistan, which purposefully neglect the pluri- and translingual complexity of society, and marginalize the identities of teachers and students alike. In Chapter 2, Meike Wernicke explores how 'non-francophone' teachers of French in Canada negotiate positionality when wrestling with essentialized and idealized notions of nativeness saturating their professional spaces. In Chapter 3, Lobat Asadi, Stephanie Moody and Yolanda Padrón discuss their participants' lived experiences negotiating translingual identities and implementing translingual practice in the United States. Asadi, Moody and Padrón contend that space for translanguaging in the classroom is contingent on destabilization of the colonial epistemes underpinning language education. Véronique Lemoine-Bresson, in Chapter 4, explores how teachers in France and Germany problematize and reify essentialized and idealized constructions of Self and Otherness in their negotiations of personal-professional identity, while grappling with local and national policies, legislated and implicit. In Chapter 5, Jeremy Gombin-Sperling and Melanie Baker Robbins present a chapter unpacking their reflection upon the research biases embedded within the lens through which they approached inquiry pertaining to criticality, Cubanness and English language education in Cuba. Uniquely, in the chapter by Gombin-Sperling and Baker Robbins, we see the authors' imposition of, and subsequent reflection upon, a critical lens, which they employed to imagine the concerns Cuban teachers of English language education in Cuba might have in terms of empowerment and social transformation.

In Part 2, *Teacher Identity as/in/Beyond Practice*, authors explore the lived experiences of teachers, novice and veteran, negotiating and transcending linguistic, cultural, ethnic, geographical and professional borders of identity in and beyond the classroom, and how they draw upon their identities and experiences in their classroom practice. Additionally, the chapters highlight dialogue the teachers engaged in internally, and with fellow professionals, through which they reflected on their negotiation of personal-professional identity and value. Şeyma Toker (Chapter 6) undertakes narrative inquiry to examine one individual's linguistic, cultural and transnational journey of academic socialization, from language teaching to graduate student-teaching. In Chapter 7, Naashia Mohamed presents an account of a Maldivian teacher's lived experiences negotiating positionality in the Maldives, during her transition from being a novice English teacher to a university instructor of Dhivehi, the national language. Mohamed discusses how her participant, Hawwa, initially feels relegated to a second-class occupation, experiences a shift in how she perceives the role and value of Dhivehi, rebuilds her sense of professional identity and authority and moves forward to advocate for the value of her profession and the language itself. Chapter 8, by April Salerno and Elena Andrei, follows by unpacking a dialoguing method for teachers and language teacher educators to self-explore their language identities and how those identities shape their language-teaching practices, with an exemplary focus on their reflection upon their own self-described identification as bilingual (Romanian and English) teacher educators. In Chapter 9, Alfredo Urzúa highlights the benefits afforded to novice Spanish teachers in his study through engaging in reflective dialogue in interaction with others. This, Urzúa contends, prompts them towards examination and evaluation of their practices, positions, roles and beliefs, and aid them in the construction of an emergent professional identity. Next, in Chapter 10, Sedat Akayoğlu, Babürhan Üzüm and Bedrettin Yazan argue for the value of telecollaboration in teacher education, to afford individuals the space to reflect upon their personal-professional positionality and identity negotiation with teachers in settings beyond their own, and potentially problematize essentialized and idealized notions of self and otherness in the process. Their study takes place in classrooms located in Turkey and the United States.

In Part 3, *Learner Negotiations of Identity in and Beyond the Classroom*, the first two chapters explore learners' negotiation of identity and meaning-making in interaction with their classmates, teachers and classroom materials. Chapters 13 and 14 expand their focus to highlight the great degree to which societal and transnational negotiations of being and belonging give shape to students' negotiations of identity within the classroom, and that classroom experiences, in turn, play a pivotal role in giving shape to how students view and value themselves and others. Shinji Kawamitsu (Chapter 11) explores one Japanese language learner's lived experiences negotiating identity and meaning-making through her writing assignments. Adolfo Arrieta and Nayibe Rosado, in Chapter 12, share an account of students and their teacher negotiating positionality, agency and meaning-making in a university classroom in Colombia. In Chapter 13, Sarah Hopkyns next sheds light upon the complexity of Emirati university students' negotiation of hybridized, linguistic and cultural identities as they shift between spaces populated, on the one hand, by friends and family, and on the other, by other members of the community/ies in which they participate. In Chapter 14, Eliana Hirano and Caroline Payant explore the lived experiences of one individual, Tabasum, who leaves Afghanistan as a refugee and eventually enrolls in university in the United States. Though confident in secondary school, Tabasum grapples with her positionality as a language learner and refugee at the university level, due to the divergent feedback she receives from professors regarding her background and performance.

References

Anderson, M. and Heinrich, P. (eds) (2014) *Language Crisis in the Ryukyus*. Newcastle: Cambridge Scholars Publishing.

Aneja, G.A. (2016) (Non) native speakered: Rethinking (non) nativeness and teacher identity in TESOL teacher education. *TESOL Quarterly* 50 (3), 572–596.

Appadurai, A. (1996) *Modernity al Large: Cultural Dimensions of Globalization* (Vol. 1). Minneapolis, MN: University of Minnesota Press.

Arnaut, K., Blommaert, J., Rampton, B. and Spotti, M. (eds) (2015) *Language and Superdiversity*. London: Routledge.

Avalos, M.A. and Augustin, J. (2018) Haiti's language-in-education policy: Conflicting discourses at the local level. In A.F. Selvi and N. Rudolph (eds) *Conceptual Shifts and Contextualized Practices in Education for Glocal Interaction* (pp. 37–54). Singapore: Springer.

Barkhuizen, G. (ed.) (2016) *Reflections on Language Teacher Identity Research*. London: Taylor and Francis.

Benedikter, T. (2009) *Language Policy and Linguistic Minorities in India: An Appraisal of the Linguistic Rights of Minorities in India* (Vol. 3). Münster: LIT Verlag.

Block, D. and Cameron, D. (eds) (2002) *Globalization and Language Teaching*. Routledge.

Blommaert, J. (2010) *The Sociolinguistics of Globalization*. Cambridge: Cambridge University Press.

Blommaert, J. (2015) Commentary: Superdiversity old and new. *Language and Communication* 44, 82–88.

Boix-Fuster, E. (ed.) (2015) *Urban Diversities and Language Policies in Medium-Sized Linguistic Communities*. Bristol: Multilingual Matters.

Braine, G. (ed) (2010) *Nonnative Speaker English Teachers: Research, Pedagogy, and Professional Growth*. New York, NY: Routledge.

Canagarajah, S. (2012) *Translingual Practice: Global Englishes and Cosmopolitan Relations*. London: Routledge.

Canagarajah, A.S. (ed.) (2013) *Literacy as Translingual Practice: Between Communities and Classrooms*. London: Routledge.

Canagarajah, S. (ed.) (2017) *The Routledge Handbook of Migration and Language*. London: Taylor and Francis.

Cenoz, J. (2019) Translanguaging pedagogies and English as a lingua franca. *Language Teaching* 52 (1), 71–85.

Charalambous, P., Charalambous, C. and Zembylas, M. (2016) Troubling translanguaging: language ideologies, superdiversity and interethnic conflict. *Applied Linguistics Review* 7 (3), 327–352.

Charles, Q.D. (2017) Black Teachers of English in South Korea. Unpublished doctoral dissertation. Indiana University of Pennsylvania.

Charles, Q.D. (2019) Black teachers of English in South Korea: Constructing identities as a native English speaker and English language teaching professional. *TESOL Journal* 10 (4). Online at: https://onlinelibrary.wiley.com/doi/full/10.1002/tesj.478

Creese, A. and Blackledge, A. (2010) Translanguaging in the bilingual classroom: A pedagogy for learning and teaching? *The Modern Language Journal* 94 (1), 103–115.

Davies, B. and Harré, R. (1990) Positioning: The discursive production of selves. *Journal for the Theory of Social Behaviour* 20 (1), 43–63.

De Costa, P. (2019) Elite multilingualism, affect and neoliberalism. *Journal of Multilingual and Multicultural Development* 40 (5), 453–460.

De Costa, P.I. and Norton, B. (2017) Introduction: Identity, transdisciplinarity, and the good language teacher. *The Modern Language Journal* 101 (1), 3–14.

De Costa, P., Park, J. and Wee, L. (2016) Language learning as linguistic entrepreneurship: Implications for language education. *The Asia-Pacific Education Researcher* 25 (5–6), 695–702.

Dewey, M. (2014) Pedagogic criticality and English as a lingua franca. *ATLANTIS Journal of the Spanish Association of Anglo-American Studies* 36 (2), 11–30.

Doerr, N.M. (ed.) (2009) *The Native Speaker Concept: Ethnographic Investigations of Native Speaker Effects* (Vol. 26). Berlin: Walter de Gruyter.

Erling, E.J. (2017) Being 'the villain': Globalization and the 'native speaker' English language teacher. In M. Borjian (ed.) *Language and Globalization: An Autoethnographic Approach* (pp. 90–102). London: Routledge.

Extra, G. and Gorter, D. (eds) (2001) *The Other Languages of Europe: Demographic, Sociolinguistic, and Educational Perspectives*. Clevedon: Multilingual Matters.

Extra, G. and Yağmur, K. (eds) (2004) *Urban Multilingualism in Europe: Immigrant Minority Languages at Home and School*. Clevedon: Multilingual Matters.

Flores, N. (2013) The unexamined relationship between neoliberalism and plurilingualism: A cautionary tale. *TESOL Quarterly* 47 (3), 500–520.

Galloway, N. (2017) *Global Englishes and Change in English Language Teaching: Attitudes and Impact*. London: Routledge.

Galloway, N. and Rose, H. (2015) *Introducing Global Englishes*. London: Routledge.

García, O., Lin, A. and May, S. (eds) (2017) *Bilingual and Multilingual Education*. Cham, Switzerland: Springer.

Guerrero, C.H. (2008) Bilingual Colombia: What does it mean to be bilingual within the framework of the National Plan of Bilingualism? *Profile Issues in Teachers Professional Development* 10, 27–46.

Guerrero, C.H. and Quintero, A.H. (2009) English as a neutral language in the Colombian national standards: A constituent of dominance in English language education. *Profile Issues in Teachers' Professional Development* 11 (2), 135–150.

Hall, S. (2002) When was 'the post-colonial'? Thinking at the limit. In I. Chambers and L. Curti (eds) *The Postcolonial Question* (pp. 248–266). London: Routledge.

Hashimoto, K. (2018) 'Mother tongue speakers' or 'native speakers'?: Assumptions surrounding the teaching of Japanese as a foreign language in Japan. In S. Houghton and K. Hashimoto (eds) *Towards Post-Native-Speakerism* (pp. 61–77). Singapore: Springer.

Heinrich, P. (2012) *The Making of Monolingual Japan: Language Ideology and Japanese Modernity*. Bristol: Multilingual Matters.

Heinrich, P., Miyara, S. and Shimoji, M. (eds) (2015) *Handbook of the Ryukyuan Languages: History, Structure, and Use* (Vol. 11). Berlin: Walter de Gruyter.

Higgins, C. (ed.) (2011) *Identity Formation in Globalizing Contexts: Language Learning in the New Millennium* (Vol. 1). Berlin: Walter de Gruyter.

Holliday, A. (2005) *The Struggle to Teach English as an International Language*. Oxford: Oxford University Press.

Holliday, A. (2006) Native-speakerism. *ELT Journal* 60 (4), 385–387.

Holliday, A. (2009) English as a lingua franca, non-native speakers and cosmopolitan realities. In F. Sharifian (ed.) *English as an International Language: Perspectives and Pedagogical Issues* (pp. 21–33). Bristol: Multilingual Matters.

Horner, K. (2007). Language and Luxembourgish national identity: Ideologies of hybridity and purity in the past and present. In S. Elspaß, N. Langer, J. Scharloth and W. Vandenbussche (eds) *Germanic Language Histories from Below (1700–2000)* (pp. 363–378). Berlin: Walter de Gruyter.

Houghton, S.A. and Rivers, D.J. (eds) (2013) *Native-speakerism in Japan: Intergroup Dynamics in Foreign Language Education*. Bristol: Multilingual Matters.

Houghton, S.A., Rivers, D.J. and Hashimoto, K. (2018) *Beyond Native-Speakerism: Current Explorations and Future Visions*. London: Routledge.

Howatt, A.P.R. (1984) *A History of English Language Teaching*. Oxford: Oxford University Press.

Hua, Z. and Wei, L. (2014) Geopolitics and the changing hierarchies of the Chinese language: Implications for policy and practice of Chinese language teaching in Britain. *The Modern Language Journal* 98 (1), 326–339.

Jain, R. (2018) Alternative terms for NNESTs. In J.I. Liontas (ed.) *The TESOL Encyclopedia of English Language Teaching*, 1–5.

Jenkins, J. (2014) *Global Englishes: A Resource Book for Students*. London: Routledge.

Jenkins, J. (2015) Repositioning English and multilingualism in English as a Lingua Franca. *Englishes in Practice* 2 (3), 49–85.

Jenkins, J., Baker, W. and Dewey, M. (eds) (2017) *The Routledge Handbook of English as a Lingua Franca*. London: Routledge.

Kachru, B.B. (1986) *The Alchemy of English: The Spread, Functions, and Models of Non-native Englishes*. University of Illinois Press.

Kachru, B.B. (1991) Liberation linguistics and the Quirk concern. *English Today* 7 (1), 3–13.

Kachru, B.B. (ed.) (1992) *The Other Tongue: English Across Cultures*. Champaign-Urbana: University of Illinois Press.

Kallen, J.L. (2012) The English language in Ireland: An introduction. *International Journal of Language, Translation and Intercultural Communication* 1, 25–41.

Kirkpatrick, A. (ed.) (2010) *The Routledge Handbook of World Englishes*. London: Routledge.

Kostoulas, A. (ed.) (2019) *Challenging Boundaries in Language Education*. Cham, Switzerland: Springer.

Kramsch, C. (2014) Teaching foreign languages in an era of globalization: Introduction. *The Modern Language Journal* 98 (1), 296–311.

Kubota, R. (1998) Ideologies of English in Japan. *World Englishes* 17 (3), 295–306.

Kubota, R. (2002) The impact of globalization on language teaching in Japan. In D. Block and D. Cameron (eds) *Globalization and Language Teaching* (pp. 13–28). London: Routledge.

Kubota, R. (2013) 'Language is only a tool': Japanese expatriates working in China and implications for language teaching. *Multilingual Education,* 3, 1–20.

Kubota, R. (2019) Confronting epistemological racism, decolonizing scholarly knowledge: Race and gender in Applied Linguistics. *Applied Linguistics*. Online at: https://doi.org/10.1093/applin/amz033

Kubota, R. and Austin, T. (2007) Critical approaches to world language education in the United States: An introduction. *Critical Inquiry in Language Studies* 4 (2–3), 73–83.

Lämmerer, A. and Mercer, S. (2019) Editorial: Border crossing in language education. *Studies in Second Language Learning and Teaching* 9 (3), 447–449. http://dx.doi.org/10.14746/ssllt.2019.9.3.1

Lather, P. (1993) Fertile obsession: Validity after poststructuralism. *The Sociological Quarterly* 34 (4), 673–693.

Lewis, G., Jones, B. and Baker, C. (2012) Translanguaging: Developing its conceptualisation and contextualisation. *Educational Research and Evaluation* 18 (7), 655–670.

Macedo, D. (ed.) (2019) *Decolonizing Foreign Language Education: The Misteaching of English and Other Colonial Languages*. London: Routledge.

Mahboob, A. (ed.) (2010) *The NNEST Lens: Non native English Speakers in TESOL*. Cambridge: Cambridge Scholars Publishing.

Mahboob, A. and Lin, A.M. (2018) Local languages as a resource in (language) education. In A.F. Selvi and N. Rudolph (eds) *Conceptual Shifts and Contextualized Practices in Education for Glocal Interaction* (pp. 197–217). Singapore: Springer.

Makoni, S. and Pennycook, A. (2012) Disinventing multilingualism: From monological multilingualism to multilingual francas. In M. Jones, A. Blackledge and A. Creese (eds) *The Routledge Handbook of Multilingualism* (pp. 439–454). London: Routledge.

Makoni, S. (2012) A critique of language, languaging and supervernacular. Uma crítica à noção de língua, linguagem e supervernáculo. *Muitas Vozes, Ponta Grossa* 1 (2), 189–199.

Manan, S.A. and David, M.K. (2014) Mapping ecology of literacies in educational setting: The case of local mother tongues vis-à-vis Urdu and English languages in Pakistan. *Language and Education* 28 (3), 203–222.

Manara, C. (2018) 'What should I call myself? Does it matter?' Questioning the 'labeling' practice in ELT profession. In B. Yazan and N. Rudolph (eds) *Criticality, Teacher Identity, and (In)equity in English Language Teaching: Issues and Implications* (pp. 125–140). Cham, Switzerland: Springer.

Mar-Molinero, C. (2010) The spread of global Spanish: From Cervantes to reggaetón. In N. Coupland (ed.) *The Handbook of Language and Globalization* (pp. 162–181). Oxford: Wiley-Blackwell.

Mar-Molinero, C. and Paffey, D. (2011) Linguistic imperialism: Who owns global Spanish? In M. Diaz-Campos (ed.) *The Handbook of Hispanic Sociolinguistics* (pp. 747–764). New York: Wiley-Blackwell.

Martin-Jones, M., Blackledge, A. and Creese, A. (eds) (2012) *The Routledge Handbook of Multilingualism*. London: Routledge.

Martínez, R.A., Hikida, M. and Durán, L. (2015) Unpacking ideologies of linguistic purism: How dual language teachers make sense of everyday translanguaging. *International Multilingual Research Journal* 9 (1), 26–42.

Matsuda, A. (ed.) (2017) *Preparing Teachers to Teach English as an International Language*. Bristol: Multilingual Matters.

May, S. (ed.) (2013) *The Multilingual Turn: Implications For SLA, TESOL, and Bilingual Education*. London: Routledge.

McCarty, T.L. (ed.) (2014) *Ethnography and Language Policy* (2nd edn). London: Routledge.

McCarty, T.L. and May, S. (eds) (2017) *Language Policy and Political Issues in Education*. Cham, Switzerland: Springer International Publishing.

McCarty, T., Romero, M. and Zepeda, O. (2006) Reclaiming the gift: Indigenous youth counter-narratives on native language loss and revitalization. *American Indian Quarterly* 30 (1/2), 28–48.

McCarty, T., Romero, M. and Zepeda, O., McCarty, T.L., Nicholas, S.E. and Wyman, L.T. (2015) 50 (0) years out and counting: Native American language education and the four Rs. *International Multilingual Research Journal* 9 (4), 227–252.

McNamara, T. (2014) The promise and threat of the shibboleth: Linguistic representations of asylum seekers. In D.H. Rellstab and C. Schlote (eds) *Representations of War, Migration, and Refugeehood* (pp. 107–122). London: Routledge.

Medgyes, P. (2001) When the teacher is a non-native speaker. *Teaching English as a Second or Foreign Language* 3, 429–442.

Meierkord, C. (2008) Lingua franca communication in multiethnic contexts. In H. Kotthoff and H. Spencer-Oatey (eds) *Handbook of Intercultural Communication* (pp. 199–218). Berlin: Mouton de Gruyter.

Mirhosseini, S.A. (2018) Issues of ideology in English language education worldwide: An overview. *Pedagogy, Culture and Society* 26 (1), 19–33.

Morris-Suzuki, T. (1997) *Re-Inventing Japan: Time, Space, Nation*. Armonk, NY: ME Sharpe.

Niño-Murcia, M., Godenzzi, J.C. and Rothman, J. (2008) Spanish as a world language: The interplay of globalized localization and localized globalization. *International Multilingual Research Journal* 2 (1–2), 48–66.

Nomura, K. and Mochizuki, T. (2018) Native-Speakerism perceived by 'non-native-speaking' teachers of Japanese in Hong Kong. In S. Houghton and K. Hashimoto (eds) *Towards Post-Native-Speakerism* (pp. 79–95). Singapore: Springer.

O'Regan, J.P. (2014) English as a lingua franca: An immanent critique. *Applied Linguistics* 35 (5), 533–552.

O'Regan, J.P. (2015) On anti-intellectualism, cultism, and one-sided thinking. O'Regan replies. *Applied Linguistics* 36 (1), 128–132.

O'Rourke, B. and Pujolar, J. (2013) From native speakers to 'new speakers'–problematizing nativeness in language revitalization contexts. *Histoire Épistémologie Langage* 35 (2), 47–67.

Otheguy, R., García, O. and Reid, W. (2015) Clarifying translanguaging and deconstructing named languages: A perspective from linguistics. *Applied Linguistics Review* 6, 281–307

Otsuji, E. (2011) Metrolingualism and Japanese language education: Linguistic competence across borders. *Literacies* 9, 21–30.

Otsuji, E. and Pennycook, A. (2010) Metrolingualism: Fixity, fluidity and language in flux. *International Journal of Multilingualism* 7 (3), 240–254.

Paffey, D. (2012) *Language Ideologies and the Globalization of 'Standard' Spanish*. London: Bloomsbury.

Park, G. (2017) *Narratives of East Asian Women Teachers of English: Where Privilege Meets Marginalization*. Bristol: Multilingual Matters.

Pavlenko, A. (2018) Superdiversity and why it isn't: Reflections on terminological innovation and academic branding. In S. Breidbach, L. Küster and B. Schmenk (eds) *Sloganization in Language Education Discourse* (pp. 142–168). Bristol: Multilingual Matters.

Pennycook A. (2012) Lingua francas as language ideologies. In A. Kirkpatrick and R. Sussex (eds) *English as an International Language in Asia: Implications for Language Education* (pp. 137–154). Dordrecht, Netherlands: Springer.

Pennycook, A. (2017) Translanguaging and semiotic assemblages. *International Journal of Multilingualism* 14 (3), 269–282.

Pennycook, A. (2018) Applied linguistics as epistemic assemblage. *AILA Review* 31 (1), 113–134.

Pennycook, A. and Otsuji, E. (2015) *Metrolingualism: Language in the City*. London: Routledge.

Pennycook, A. and Otsuji, E. (2019) Mundane metrolingualism. *International Journal of Multilingualism* 16 (2), 175–186.

Phillipson, R. (1992) *Linguistic Imperialism*. London: Routledge.

Quirk, R. (1990) Language varieties and standard language. *English Today* 6 (1), 3–10.

Rivers, D.J. (2016) Employment advertisements and native-speakerism in Japanese higher education. In F. Copland, S. Garton and S. Mann (eds) *LETs and NESTs: Voices, Views and Vignettes* (pp. 79–100). London: British Council.

Rivers, D.J. (2018) Speakerhood as segregation: The construction and consequence of divisive discourse in TESOL. In B. Yazan and N. Rudolph (eds) *Criticality, Teacher Identity, and (In) equity in English Language Teaching* (pp. 179–197). Cham, Switzerland: Springer.

Rivers, D.J. (2019) Walking on glass: Reconciling experience and expectation within Japan. *Journal of Language, Identity and Education* 18 (6), 377–388, DOI: 10.1080/15348458.2019.1674149

Rivers, D.J. and Ross, A.S. (2013) Idealized English teachers: The implicit influence of race in Japan. *Journal of Language, Identity and Education* 12 (5), 321–339.

Rivers, D.J. and Zotzmann, K. (eds) (2017) *Isms in Language Education: Oppression, Intersectionality and Emancipation* (Vol. 11). Berlin: Walter de Gruyter.

Rubdy, R. and Alsagoff, L. (eds) (2013) *The Global-Local Interface and Hybridity: Exploring Language and Identity*. Bristol: Multilingual Matters.

Rudolph, N.J. (2012) Borderlands and Border Crossing: Japanese Professors of English and the Negotiation of Translinguistic and Transcultural Identity (unpublished doctoral dissertation) College Park, MD: University of Maryland, College Park.

Rudolph, N. (2016) Negotiating borders of being and becoming in and beyond the English language teaching classroom: Two university student narratives from Japan. *Asian Englishes* 18 (1), 2–18.

Rudolph, N. (2018) Essentialization, idealization, and apprehensions of local language practice in the classroom. In B. Yazan and N. Rudolph (eds) *Criticality, Teacher Identity, and (In) equity in English Language Teaching* (pp. 275–302). Cham, Switzerland: Springer.

Rudolph, N. (2019a) Native Speakerism (?!): (Re) considering critical lenses and corresponding implications in the field of English language teaching. *Indonesian Journal of English Language Teaching* 14 (2), 89–113.

Rudolph, N. (2019b) Identity as/in language policy: Negotiating the bounds of 'education for participation in the global community' in Japanese university-level language education. In A.S.M. Al-Issa and S.A. Mirhosseini (eds) *Worldwide English Language Education Today: Ideologies, Policies, and Practices* (pp. 85–101). London: Routledge.

Rudolph, N. and Rudolph, J. (2018) ELF, 'English' Language Teaching and criticality: Assumptions, tensions and implications. *JACET ELFSIG Journal* 2 (2), 18–31.

Rudolph, N., Selvi, A.F. and Yazan, B. (2019) Destabilizing critical 'assumptions' in (English) language teaching: An introduction. *Journal of Language, Identity and Education* 18 (6), 349–351.

Rudolph, N., Yazan, B. and Rudolph, J. (2018) Negotiating 'ares,' 'cans,' and 'shoulds' of being and becoming in English language teaching: Two teacher accounts from one Japanese university. *Asian Englishes* 21 (1), 22–37.

Schneider, E.W. (2014) New reflections on the evolutionary dynamics of world Englishes. *World Englishes* 33 (1), 9–32.

Selvi, A.F. and Rudolph, N. (2018) *Conceptual Shifts and Contextualized Practices in Education for Glocal Interaction*. Cham, Switzerland: Springer.

Sewell, A. (2019) Whose English (es)?: Naming and boundary-drawing as language-ideological practices in the global English debate. In A. Al-Issa and S. Mirhosseini (eds) *Worldwide English Language Education Today: Ideologies, Policies and Practices* (pp. 1–17). London: Routledge.

Sharifian, F. (ed.) (2009) *English as an International Language: Perspectives and Pedagogical Issues*. Bristol: Multilingual Matters.

Shimoji, M. and Pellard, T. (2010) *An Introduction to Ryukyuan Languages*. Tokyo University of Foreign Studies: Research Institute for Languages and Cultures of Asia and Africa.

Shin, H. and Park, J.S.Y. (2016) Researching language and neoliberalism. *Journal of Multilingual and Multicultural Development* 37 (5), 443–452.

Soler-Carbonell, J. (2011) Speakers' evaluations of the Estonian and the Russian languages in Tallinn. Between linguistic stability and inter-ethnic tension. *Journal of Estonian and Finno-Ugric Linguistics* 2 (1), 315–333.

Soler-Carbonell, J. (2014) Emerging ELF as an intercultural resource: Language attitudes and ideologies. *Journal of English as a Lingua Franca* 3 (2), 243–268.

Springer, S., Birch, K. and MacLeavy, J. (eds) (2016) *Handbook of Neoliberalism*. London: Routledge.

Sridhar, K.K. (1996) Language in education: Minorities and multilingualism in India. *International Review of Education* 42 (4), 327–347.

Steckbauer, S.M. (1997) El español como lingua franca de los inmigrantes indígenas en Lima. In *Lenguaje y comunicación intercultural en el mundo hispánico: [ponencias presentadas en la sección 'Lenguaje y comunicación intercultural' del Congreso de Hispanistas Alemanes en Bonn, 2–4 de marzo de 1995]* (pp. 147–167).

Stranger-Johannessen, E. and Norton, B. (2019) Promoting early literacy and student investment in the African Storybook. *Journal of Language, Identity & Education* 18 (6), 400–411.

Toh, G. (2016) *English as Medium of Instruction in Japanese Higher Education: Presumption, Mirage or Bluff?* London: Palgrave Macmillan.

Toh, G. (2019) *Effecting Change in English Language Teaching: Exposing Collaborators and Culprits in Japan.* Springer International Publishing.

Train, R. (2007) 'Real Spanish:' Historical perspectives on the ideological construction of a (foreign) language. *Critical Inquiry in Language Studies* 4 (2/3), 207–235.

Valdés, G. (1997) The teaching of Spanish to bilingual Spanish-speaking students: Outstanding issues and unanswered questions. In M.C. Colombi and F.X. Alarcon (eds) *La Enseñanza Del Español a Hispanohablantes: Praxis y Teoría* (pp.8–44). Boston, MA: Houghton Mifflin.

Varghese, M., Morgan, B., Johnston, B. and Johnson, K.A. (2005) Theorizing language teacher identity: Three perspectives and beyond. *Journal of Language, Identity, and Education* 4 (1), 21–44.

Vertovec, S. (2007) Super-diversity and its implications. *Ethnic and Racial Studies* 30 (6), 1024–1054.

Warriner, D.S. (2007) Language learning and the politics of belonging: Sudanese women refugees becoming and being 'American.' *Anthropology and Education Quarterly* 38 (4), 343–359.

Wernicke-Heinrichs, M. (2013) Authenticating 'Non-native Speaker Teacher' Professional Identity in French as a Second Language (FSL) Education. Unpublished doctoral dissertation. Vancouver, CA: University of British Columbia.

Wernicke, M. (2017) Navigating native-speaker ideologies as FSL teacher. *Canadian Modern Language Review* 73 (2), 208–236.

Weekly, R. (2018) Accepting and circumventing native speaker essentialism. In B. Yazan and N. Rudolph (eds) *Criticality, Teacher Identity, and (In) equity in English Language Teaching* (pp. 141–162). Cham, Switzerland: Springer.

Widdowson, H.G. (1994) The ownership of English. *TESOL Quarterly* 28 (2), 377–389.

Wiley, T.G., Peyton, J.K., Christian, D., Moore, S.C.K. and Liu, N. (eds) (2014) *Handbook of Heritage, Community, and Native American Languages in the United States: Research, Policy, and Educational Practice.* London: Routledge.

Woolard, K.A. (1998) Introduction: Language ideology as a field of inquiry. In B.B. Schieffelin, K.A. Woolard and P.V. Kroskrity (eds) *Language Ideologies: Practice and Theory* (pp. 3–51). New York, NY: Oxford University Press.

Yazan, B. and Rudolph, N. (eds) (2018) *Criticality, Teacher Identity, and (In)equity in English Language Teaching: Issues and Implications* (Vol. 35). Cham, Switzerland: Springer.

Yazan, B., Rudolph, N. and Selvi, A.F. (2019) Borderland negotiations of identity in language education: Introducing the special issue. *International Multilingual Research Journal* 13 (3), 133–136. DOI: 10.1080/19313152.2019.1633095

Part 1

Learners, Teachers, and the 'Ares,' 'Cans' and 'Shoulds' of Being and Becoming

1 The Monolingual Bias: A Critique of Idealization and Essentialization in ELT in Pakistan

Syed Abdul Manan, Maya Khemlani David, Liaquat Ali Channa and Francisco Perlas Dumanig

Introduction

Recent research problematizes the use of English medium policy in Pakistan, particularly in the under-resourced settings such as low-cost private schools and government schools (Coleman, 2010; Manan, 2018a; Manan *et al.*, 2015a; Mustafa, 2011, 2016; Rahman, 2004). The aspects that make English medium policy in these settings problematic mainly include the under-resourced infrastructure, incompetent teachers and disjunction between students' home and school languages. These studies also indicate that the use of English medium policy could only succeed in, and best suit, upscale elite schools for reasons including their highly resourced infrastructure, competent and qualified English teachers and students' strong home-based English support system. So far, there is no evidence of a research study on the upscale elite schools in Pakistan, particularly a study that could bring forth the lived experiences and narratives of teachers to share their first-hand experiences and impressions as to how successfully and effectively English medium policy functions in such schools. Therefore, this study draws on interviews of teachers from the above category of schools in part of Pakistan to fill this apparent research gap. The study aims to explore and take a critical look at the way these apparently well-resourced schools manage and maintain their language policies and practices. The study particularly seeks to analyze how administrators' theorization of an essentialized use of English-only policy in a diverse multilingual setting, and their idealization of a monolingual perspective suppresses the less proficient students from participating meaningfully, and from voicing their identities. In addition, the study also indicates how administrators' exclusive emphasis on an English-only policy, their insensitivity towards the linguistic resources of students and their monolingual bias result in compromising students' learning of the course contents, concept development, critical thinking and creative engagement in the educational processes. Towards the end, the study concludes that given the orthodox approaches of the administrators, and their obliviousness towards the local multilingual realities within the classrooms, the administrators need to be sensitized, informed and inspired towards the 'Multilingual Turn' (May, 2014), an academic enterprise, which promotes a critical perspective on monolingual biases and monolingual ideologies in the educational domains, particularly in the postcolonial multilingual contexts. The following research questions precisely anchor this study:

- What are policies, prescriptions and practices regarding the use of language (s) in the upscale English-medium schools?
- How do policies and perceptions impact teaching and learning practices in the concerned schools?

Theoretical/Conceptual Underpinnings

Theoretically, the study analyzes data, and discusses the emergent themes through the lens of a growing amount of scholarship that challenges the monolingual bias, and represents a 'Multilingual Turn' in Teaching English to the Speakers of Other Languages (TESOL)/English as a Foreign Language (EFL) contexts. Additionally, the study also critiques the methodological and instructional practices in these schools through the prism of the 'Postmethod era' or 'Postmethod conditions' (Kumaravadivelu, 2006), and envisions the possibilities of founding pedagogies on 'glocal approaches towards English teaching' (Kubota, 2011). May (2014) contends that despite the burgeoning of the 'Multilingual Turn' globally, the 'mainstream applied linguistics' in Second Language Acquisition (SLA) and TESOL tends to stay indifferent, and continues to treat the acquisition of an additional language (most often, English) as an ideally hermetic process uncontaminated by the knowledge and use of one's other languages. Scholars have variously described such an approach as monolingual bias (May, 2014), monolingual language ideology (Wiley, 2014), two-solitude assumption (Cummins, 2007) and Monoglossic beliefs (García & Baetens Beardsmore, 2009). Several other scholars describe the same kind of rigidly compartmentalized language policy orientations and practices as monolingual habitus (Benson, 2013), the English-vernacular divide (Ramanathan, 2005), the double divide (Mohanty, 2017) or 'the nexus of idealization and essentialization' (Selvi, 2018). Alternatively, scholars who draw on 'Multilingual Turn', raise their concerns against the rigid separation of languages, and expose the theoretical fallacies of those schools that continue to operate on the traditionalist monolingual and monoglossic lines. These scholars advocate fluid and dynamic pedagogies proposing a productive utilization of the multilingual repertoires of the learners by deploying the constructs of translanguaging or multilinguality (Agnihotri, 2010; Canagarajah, 2013; Creese & Blackledge, 2010; Cummins, 2016; García & Leiva, 2014; García & Wei, 2014; Hornberger & Link, 2012; Mahboob & Lin, 2018; Manan, 2016).

Background Sociolinguistic and Policy Setting

Pakistan is a multilingual and multiethnic country. According to Ethnologue (2019), there are 77 languages in Pakistan. Urdu is the national language, while English is the official language. English is used in the domains of power such as government, education, law, corporate sector, research and media. Language hierarchy is based on power in which English stands as the most powerful; Urdu occupies the second position, while the rest of the minor and major indigenous languages stand at the lowest rung in the language hierarchy ladder (Channa, 2017; Mustafa, 2011; Rahman, 2002). Urdu and English receive substantial institutional support in the domains of power, especially in education; however, the indigenous languages with the exception of the Sindhi and to negligible degree Pashto language remain excluded from all domains of power including education (Channa, 2014; Mustafa, 2011; Rahman, 1996, 2002; Rassool & Mansoor, 2007). The constitutional provision of the 1973 regarding language policy proclaims the official language policy in the following statements:

> The National language of Pakistan is Urdu, and arrangements shall be made for it being used for official and other purposes within fifteen years from the commencing day (1973).
>
> Subject to clause (1), the English language may be used for official purposes until arrangements are made for its replacement by Urdu.
>
> Without prejudice to the status of the National language, a Provincial Assembly may by law prescribe measures for the teaching, promotion, and use of a provincial language in addition to the national language.

Scholars argue that the constitutional caveat ('without prejudice') denotes that no such effort should be attempted for the promotion of regional languages at the cost of the national language Urdu (Rahman, 1999). Urdu receives considerably greater state support *vis-à-vis* the rest of the local mother tongues. Government policies about the medium of instruction suffer from several limitations of which, the most important is 'the great disconnect between policy and implementation' (Mustafa, 2011: 120). Historically, language policy and planning in Pakistan is marked by consistent twists and turns. According to Mustafa (2011), 'education authorities are shirking their responsibility of taking a categorical decision on this issue,' and she proposes that the language policy needs to be 'formulated clearly and pragmatically' (Mustafa, 2011: 47). Although the policy statements, the real policy with regard to teaching mother tongues or one regional language has not been implemented nor has a uniform policy across provinces and urban and rural areas occurred yet. The English-medium education policy in most private schools is also outwardly different from broad policy outlines in the National policy (Manan *et al.*, 2015b). There are still 'tensions between policy and practice'(Canagarajah & Ashraf, 2013: 263).

The Study

Context and approach

The context of this research is upscale elite English medium private schools. These schools are small in number; however, they are very expensive, charging exorbitantly high tuition fees. Coleman (2010) writes that 'The number of private elite English medium schools is very small. They are extremely expensive and provide education for the children of a small and powerful elite section of the population' (2010: 10). Earlier, those elite English medium schools were patronized by the Christian missionaries, the convent schools established in all the major cities of Pakistan. The trends from convent schools gradually changed to other streams of elite private schools such as Beaconhouse, the City School systems and two other highly expensive English medium schools. These schools have affiliations with the Cambridge system of schooling in England and follow their examination system, curricula and O (now GCSE)/A levels. The exorbitantly high tuition fee, admission fee and the allied expenditure plainly shut the doors to children from the middle, lower-middle or working classes. Since the overarching purpose of this study was to make sense of the dynamics of policies, prescriptions and practices; therefore, we drew upon the qualitative paradigm of research to understand the administrators' perspectives and explore their practices in the upscale elite English-medium private schools. In particular, we employed semi-structured interviews to collect our data. Likewise, we had an interview schedule for the interviews that we had developed after a couple of deliberations among us. We piloted and refined the interview guide before we finally used it for data collection purposes. We used convenient sampling strategy and recruited seven teachers who either taught or have been teaching in the elite English medium private schools. Table 1.1 presents their background information.

Six of the participants were female and one was male. All the participants held Master's degrees, except one who held a Bachelor's degree. Their areas of specialization were applied linguistics and English literature. Their teaching experience in the elite English medium schools ranged from one to three years. The interviewees spoke various native languages such as Pashto, Punjabi, Sindhi, Balochi and Burahvi. We tried to ensure that there was maximum variation in convenience sampling so that we could fully understand their perspectives and practices.

Table 1.1 Participants' information

Name/label	Gender	Teaching experience	Academic qualification	First language
Respondent 1	Female	One year	Masters	Siraiki
Respondent 2	Female	Three years	Masters	Punjabi
Respondent 3	Female	Two years	Masters	Punjabi
Respondent 4	Female	One year	Masters	Burahvi
Respondent 5	Female	Two years	Masters	Pashto
Respondent 6	Female	One year	Bachelor	Pashto
Respondent 7	Male	Three years	Masters	Punjabi

The interviews lasted from around 19 to 35 minutes on average. We first obtained the interviewees' consent and then conducted the interviews. The interviews were audio-recorded. Depending upon the flow and the nature of the conversation, we translanguaged in English, Urdu and native languages. Subsequently, we transcribed-cum-translated the interview recordings. We maintained the participants and their schools' anonymity while we transcribed-cum-translated the interview recordings. Then, we thematically analyzed the transcriptions by following the six steps suggested by Braun and Clarke (2006). During analysis, the direct quotations were labeled after RESPONDENT 1 and so on.

Results: Teachers' Insights on School Contexts, Teaching and Learning Policies and Practices

The monolingual bias – imposition of rigid English-only monolingual policy

Monolingual bias in the present context refers to the school administrators' uncompromisingly strong emphasis on English as the only medium of classroom transaction, and preventing teachers from code-switching or using other languages such as Urdu and native languages as pedagogical resources in the classrooms. In addition, this monolingual bias also extends beyond classrooms as English also stands as the idealized medium of interaction within the school premises. This applies to both teachers as well as students. The administrators do their best to not only bring an English-only monolingual policy rigidly into practice, but they also spread and display messages about the use of English to make students and teachers realize the symbolic, economic and social value of the language. Thus, the schools overtly inculcate the idea of spreading an 'English-speaking culture.' They also instruct students that 'Your conversation with your friends and teachers must be in English,' and that 'Speak English! It is the need of the hour'. Figure 1.1, an image from one of the schools, illustrates this strategy.

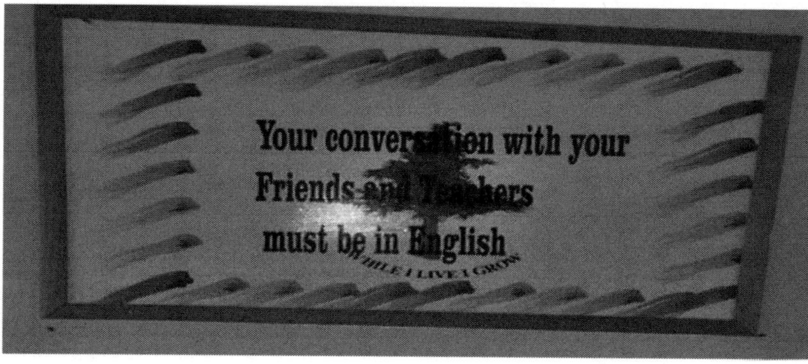

Figure 1.1

According to a teacher, the schools hand over a brochure to the newly appointed teachers in which '*they have written their policy about the use of medium in the class. It says that you have to use English*' (RESPONDENT 1).

Another respondent observed that fluency in English is the fundamental benchmark during the interview and initial demonstration during recruitment. The hiring team carefully checks whether the newly appointed teachers can use English fluently in the class. The respondent also added that the schools '*promote English. Even when they observe the first demonstration, if you are fluent, you get the job. Otherwise not. They also tell you to use only English* (RESPONDENT 4). Similarly, another respondent reveals the experience of her first demonstration in the school:

> ...the one who was monitoring me, she told me that I'm supposed to use only English. When I was giving my presentation, I sometimes used code-switching, so then she warned me that I must be using only English (RESPONDENT 3).

Other respondents also confirmed that their employers strictly instructed them to use only English in the classrooms. They reported that using native languages was considered a taboo within the classrooms and on school premises. Sports teachers are also instructed to use English during sports sessions within the playground. According to a respondent, '*Mother tongues were strictly prohibited. Sometimes, even if I mistakenly or unintentionally used a Pashto word, the reaction of the students would be strange.*' (RESPONDENT 5).

In addition, teachers are also expected to use English among themselves in the staffrooms. To implement this policy, the administrators watch over classrooms through their coordinators to inspect that teachers fully comply with the prescribed English-medium policy. Violation of the recommended policy could result in punitive actions and penalties that could involve show–cause notices, warnings, rebukes or sometimes deduction of some amount from the teachers' salaries. A respondent reported that the schools,

> *...issue warnings and show cause notices. If you violate, their behavior with those teachers was quite insulting, and that too in front of the students*' (RESPONDENT 1).

One of the respondents said that two teachers were once fired from their jobs when the school principal saw them code-switching from English to Urdu during their teaching. Such threats of losing jobs make teachers rather cautious about enacting schools' mandated policy compliantly, regardless of whether the given policy is in the students' favor or not.

> They have this opinion that if those kids are allowed to speak their mother tongues, then how they would learn the English language. So they have this view that if we keep on forcing children to speak English, and to study English, there might be a day that they would understand equally well like other children (RESPONDENT 1).

One basic rationale these schools provide for the justification of the exclusive use of the English language is their assumption that those schools are fundamentally meant for the dissemination of the English language rather than other languages. In addition, they also tend to theorize that children already know Urdu and their native languages from their homes; therefore, there is no point in considering those languages as teaching–learning resources. They put forward a rather commonplace argument that the more the English language in the school landscapes, the greater the chances for learning the language (Manan & Khadija-Tul-Kubra, 2017). A respondent said that the schools impose a strict English policy because it is how they understand language learning. She observed that '*I guess they have just heard this that if students keep listening to English, they would finally learn it.*' (RESPONDENT 2). According to another respondent,

> if those kids are allowed to speak their mother tongues, then how would they learn the English language. So if we keep forcing children to speak English, and studying English, there might be a day that they would understand English well like other children do (RESPONDENT 1).

The respondents suggested that the administrators are apprehensive that linguistic conflict and ethnic divide might develop among students who bring different languages and ethnic affiliations to the classrooms. Such liberty might also embolden them to assert their linguistic and ethnic identities in the schools. Another reason the administrators do not entertain and encourage the native languages is that they feel that parents would react to it negatively because they basically pay a hefty amount to those schools and in return they want the schools to build and develop their children's English language proficiency. A respondent narrated the story of one parent who was angry over the higher grades of his son in the Urdu language. The respondent recounted that the parent even used abusive language about Urdu language, saying, '*I want my son to speak English. What will I do with Urdu language? We don't want this at all. We pay that much money only for English!*' (RESPONDENT 6). Importantly, English also serves the commercial and profit-making agenda of the schools to keep their clientele satisfied. According to a respondent, '*They basically thought that if they allow Urdu or mother tongues, parents might think that the school doesn't teach the English language, it teaches other languages.*' (RESPONDENT 4).

The respondents criticized the way schools narrowly approach the policy as they '*don't understand that there is no limitation to learning language. They can always learn that. And they can learn English simultaneously too. But no, they won't understand this*' (RESPONDENT 1). In the respondents' view, schools are also indifferent towards local and contextual dynamics. The linguistic and academic conditions in Balochistan are markedly different than other provinces and other big cities than Quetta. Classes in this part of the country are highly diverse linguistically and ethnically. Moreover, compared with the other provinces, Balochistan is comparatively underdeveloped economically. Most parents are not educated in English, and students usually receive very limited exposure to English in their sociocultural ecology. Researchers suggest that parental support and sociocultural contact and exposure to English is rather crucial for children in these contexts to manage their academic activities well (Manan *et al.*, 2015c; Mohanty, 2017). A respondent aptly comments that,

> When the education system is not educated, how would it understand the issue? They aren't themselves aware of the value of cultural diversity or linguistic diversity. They have a limited understanding. I'm sure they are not informed (RESPONDENT 1).

Some of the respondents complained that the administrators do not pay any attention to teachers' concerns and proposals regarding the use of languages. They mostly feel disempowered before the insensitivity and indifference of the school authorities as they want pedagogies to be contextualized, and synchronized to the local social, linguistic and cultural conditions; this is a theoretical and methodological slant which we generally see in the agenda of postmethod conditions (Kumaravadivelu, 2006). Another respondent made the same argument, pointing out the contextual mismatches:

> ...all the time, I feel I'm disempowered. We are given strict guidelines. These policies I feel are not matched with the context of Quetta. People sitting and planning language policies in other cities like Karachi can't design good policies.

According to another respondent,

> We have kids whose parents are not educated, they don't have exposure, although they may have money, but they didn't have support from their homes.

As a consequence of idealizing, essentializing and glorifying English in schools, many teachers of other subjects whose own proficiency is lower or weaker than the English teachers, tend to feel inferiority complexes before English teachers. A respondent said that in fact, 'We the English teachers don't think so about them, but they tend to think they are weak in English' (RESPONDENT 3). Thus, English language proficiency, or lack thereof, creates a divide and identity crisis among teachers. Schools also treat English and non-English teachers differently. Non-English teachers refer to those who hold specialization in subjects other than English such as social studies, sciences, mathematics or Urdu. A respondent recounted that schools offer more privileges, rewards and appreciation to English teachers than other teachers.

> English teachers are treated leniently. I'm a teacher trainer. I train teachers how to teach English. I'm have been coming late for the last three years. But authorities are lenient toward me, but they are strict to others (RESPONDENT 7).

The respondents were asked how effective their policies were in implementational terms. The respondents revealed that although they did not approve of most of the stringent prescriptions of the monolingual bias, they could not assert their genuine positions as they wanted to keep their employment secure. However, the respondents explained that students were mostly violating those policy prescriptions as they often talked to each other either in Urdu or in their native languages, depending on who their interlocutors were. For example, Pashto-speaking children used Pashto with other Pashto-speaking children, while Balochi-speaking children often used Balochi with their Baloch acquaintances; however, Urdu was the medium of interaction in interethnic contacts. The respondents also explained that the administrators' policy with regard to the Urdu language was relatively relaxed and lenient as compared to the native languages.

What would have been the causes of a relaxed and tolerant stance of the administrators towards Urdu as compared to the native languages? The respondents suggest that since Urdu is the national language of Pakistan, it naturally wields more power, symbolic significance and social prestige than the native languages. Moreover, Urdu is seen as a neutral language, which those schools think would neutralize the potential for ethnic language-based sub-nationalism. Urdu also has the advantage of being the language of wider communication and as a local lingua franca. Most ironically, there are also students who take pride in not using and not knowing good Urdu.

The respondents reported that those administrators are neither aware of sensitivity towards cultural and linguistic diversity, nor are they bothered about it. In fact, they do their jobs as per the prescriptions and dictations of the headquarters. The primary job is thus to sell and project the English language as their chief selling commodity and make their clients realize that they actually sell the best form of English in their schools. Respondents also revealed that since business and profit-making are basically their topmost motives, English with its accompanying economic and social capital serves as the most feverishly sought-after commodity in the current market (Manan *et al.*, 2015, 2015c).

Students' power of self-expression silenced – the exclusionary impact of English-only monolingual policy

In this section, we delineate the impacts, which the above policies, prescriptions and practices exert on teaching and learning. We find that the respondents identify an array of negative effects that the stringent English-only policy and the monolingual bias leave on teaching and learning processes. The negative effects are multifaceted and range from students' silencing and marginalization to teachers' limitations of finding the adequate level of expression, students' devaluing of their native languages, suppression of linguistic/cultural diversity and most critically compromise on meaningful and deeper learning of the content/subject material.

The mandated English-only policy and idealized use forces most of the disadvantaged students to silence. This particularly affects those students who hold either no proficiency or hold less proficiency in the English language. The small number of children who are advantaged are those who face no serious issues with English-only policy, and consequently participate actively and productively in the teaching and learning processes. These children basically receive a substantial amount of cultural and linguistic support from their families and their parents. On the other hand, the less proficient students who form a significant portion of classes, find it difficult and challenging to cope with their academic activities that are transacted with exclusive use of the English language. The respondents said that these students tend to find lectures and other classroom activities, boring and burdensome. It also results in limiting their abilities to creative and critical thinking. In order to survive and stay in the system, such students are forced to resort to rote learning and cramming.

To address this challenge, the respondents suggested that there is a need to plan medium of instruction to the needs of most students rather than to stick inflexibly to an English-only policy. This signifies these teachers' dissatisfaction with the current policies and practices, and they basically want to propose a dynamic, fluid and flexible approach in which teachers could strategically tune their pedagogies to the existing linguistic and cultural repertoires of the students for better and smooth understanding of the course contents/subject material. They observed that utilizing and recognizing the existing linguistic resources of the students led to more engaged learning and deeper understanding of the contents, and allowed classroom activities to become more alive, dynamic and moving (Baker, 2011; Creese & Blackledge, 2010; Hornberger, 2003). One of the respondents described her experience of how her pedagogy of trans-languaging transformed the dynamics of the class as it helped break students' silence, and cultivate meaningful class participation and deeper understanding of the course contents:

> There were so many brilliant students. For instance, when I would allow them to explain the concepts to each other in the Pashto language. Those students would come up with a much deeper understanding of the contents, in presentations, and various activities. When I asked them what they were doing. They said that they were discussing stylistics in Pashto. And when I took presentations, their performances were marvelous. (RESPONDENT 1).

One of the respondents narrated the story of a child who was facing problems in English and was consequently excluded. When she sympathized with him by using Urdu with him, the school authorities stopped her from doing this. Therefore, she had to quit that job. According to that respondent,

> There was a child. He used to sit in the corner and used to cry all the time. When I paid attention to him, he approached me saying I must use Urdu during the lecture because he did not understand English. When I did this, this opened my eyes. The child was brilliant. I observed that when I spoke only English during class, students were not listening to me. But when I used Urdu, they paid attention; they took an interest. (RESPONDENT 4).

In the same vein, other respondents also endorsed the advantages of a multilingual pedagogy, and criticized the lack of understanding and insensitivity that those schools showed to the disadvantaged students,

> In the beginning, I used only English. They were lost. But now, when I do code-switching and explain concepts in Urdu, they have become more active. The participation level has increased a lot than during English-only lectures' (RESPONDENT 3).

A respondent also observed that she found course contents way beyond students' age. In other words, course contents were not age-appropriate.

> I taught 8th grade, and they were studying Shakespeare and Charles Dickens that we teach mostly in colleges. It means when your course contents are not age-appropriate, that are not language-appropriate either because of that use such a tough language for kids to understand. Isn't it unjust that you are teaching 8th grade Shakespeare when they don't know what prepositions are when they don't know how to use basic punctuations like full stop and question mark?

These disadvantages as a whole seem to hold the learning process back and minimize the potential for quality and meaningful education. The respondents observed that the unnecessary emphasis on the exclusive use of English results in the educational failure of a significant number of students. We may argue that exclusive emphasis on English, discouragement of translation and translanguaging apparently curtail the capabilities of those disadvantaged students, and restrain them from meaningful engagement in the educational processes. Instead, we believe that allowing translanguaging could have served as an 'enabling factor' (Mohanty, 2017) in their education, and worked against the 'voicelessness' and 'unfreedom' (Dreze & Sen, 2002) of students, optimizing conditions for 'creating capabilities' (Nussbaum, 2011). The concerned stakeholders should also be informed that language discrimination and marginalization could promote what Dreze and Sen (2002) describe as 'discouragement effects' that are responsible for the educational backwardness of the disadvantaged communities. According to Mohanty (2009),

> The exclusion and nonaccommodation of languages in education denies equality of opportunity to learn, violates linguistic human rights, leads to the loss of linguistic diversity, and triggers a vicious cycle of disadvantage perpetuating inequality, capacity deprivation, and poverty. (Mohanty, 2009: 121)

Secondly, the same policy also restricts the less proficient English teachers of other subjects from giving their 100% performance as they find their expressiveness stifled during their lecture delivery and other classroom transactions. This happens despite their strong command and sufficient knowledge of their respective subjects. Thirdly, this causes divide among the more and less proficient English students, which further exacerbates the situation for less proficient students as they suffer from inferiority complexes, decreased level of confidence, anxiety and fear of negative evaluation, identity crisis and a sense of educational failure. Finally, and most critically, such an uncompromisingly rigid stance on English-only instruction forces teachers to compromise on content learning and concept development of the students.

Pedagogical orthodoxy and the missing link – mapping the complexity of mandated policy, on-ground practices and future possibilities

In this section, we discuss the emerging issues in light of the data. The policies and practices appear to suffer from a lack of proper planning and coordination as different stakeholders seem to hold divergent views and positions on the core issues both in theory as well as in practice. Such an 'unplanned policy' and divergent positions keep the policy from yielding productive outcomes. On the one hand, school administrators and parents tend to ambitiously idealize English-only policy regardless of the on-ground conditions, while on the other hand experiencing limitations of the essentialized English-only policy, and its incompatibility with the local sociolinguistic and sociocultural milieu, teachers carry strong reservations within themselves but they cannot express their reservations to the schools. Similarly, the situation about students also presents a rather complex picture. Therefore, this whole issue of deciding about, and applying, an appropriate language teaching plan is fraught with numerous challenges and constraints. Critically, teachers who are more informed, and well aware of the actual problems of students facing language disadvantage, have been strictly restricted and regularly guarded not to exercise any pedagogical act that might go against the mandated English-only policy of the schools. Thus, the dependent and subordinate nature of their private jobs also force most teachers to become silent, and secure their jobs rather than assert their genuine positions on the current misinformed policy and misdirected practices.

The data show that the policies and prescriptions which the administrators accentuate are predicated on what scholars describe as 'monolingual instructional assumptions' (Cummins, 2016), 'two solitudes assumptions' (Cummins, 2007) or 'monoglossic beliefs' (García & Baetens Beardsmore, 2009). We can clearly see that the language of school (English), the language of home (native languages) and the lingua franca or link language (Urdu) are rigidly kept separate, a policy which Cummins (2007) aptly describes as 'two solitudes assumption.' However, such monolingual assumptions have been recently called into question by scholars on both theoretical and empirical grounds. In contrast to the monolingual assumptions pervasive largely in the traditionalist quarters of the mainstream applied linguistics, a host of scholars and educators working on the use of languages in diverse bi/multilingual contexts, emphasize an exploration of alternative approaches where the home and school languages could be productively and judiciously brought together to develop and affirm both (Canagarajah, 2011; Creese & Blackledge, 2010; Cummins, 2007, 2009; García & Wei, 2014; Helot & Laoire, 2011; Mahboob & Lin, 2018; Manan, 2018b; May, 2014, 2017; Romaine, 2015).

Mahboob and Lin (2018) identify reasons why stakeholders, particularly administrators and teachers, tend to show negative attitudes towards the use of the local languages in English language teaching. They argue that one possible reason for their negative attitudes is that much of the dominant theory building in TESOL and Teaching English as a Foreign Language (TEFL) over the last century was dominated by native speakers of English in the Inner Circle countries (for the teaching of English in inner circle countries); therefore, this work did not need to consider a role for local languages. Thus, the teaching and learning dynamics were entirely different in the largely monolingual Inner Circle countries from that of teaching English in the highly diverse multilingual/multiethnic countries of the Outer Circle or postcolonial contexts. These scholars further argue that non-recognition of the native languages not only restricts the role of the native languages, but such attitudes also promote hegemonic practices.

Another potential reason behind the monolingual bias and that of the idealized exclusive imposition of the English language has its roots in the macro-level status policy and planning in the country. The monolingual ideology, which characterizes the macro-level top-down policymaking in Pakistan, seems to have influenced and shaped the attitudes of the school administrators at the bottom level. Their dispositions could be the result of a 'monolingual habitus' (Benson, 2013) that actually prevails in the country. The hierarchical linguistic structure in Pakistan sets English right at the top of other languages, whereas Urdu stands the second most sought after language. The rest of the native languages stand at the bottom of the hierarchy. Historically, one sees that neither linguistic diversity nor the native languages have received a positive response from the governments. Ideological monolingualism and language-as-a-problem orientation mark status policy and planning in Pakistan. Scholars contend that there is apprehension that the official recognition of the native languages might pose a threat to national unity or cause disintegration of the federation (Ayres, 2009). Evidently, the official stance looks upon linguistic diversity as a problem, envisaging a uni-national thesis for national unity (Rahman, 1997).

Other relevant questions are: why do administrators show insensitivity and indifference towards the native languages, and why do they fail to understand the real worth these languages hold as useful educational as well as communicative resources? One explanation could indeed be the prestige and economic benefits associated with English, but another major reason fundamentally lies in their lack of critical awareness and knowledge about theory and research in applied linguistics, and bi/multilingual education (Manan & Channa, 2015; Manan & David, 2019) and the empirically proven positive effect of L1s on the learning of a second/foreign language(Cummins, 2005, 2009). The policy implementers are yet to break from the traditionalist spell of TESOL, English as a Second Language (ESL) and TEFL orthodoxy, and their conservatism of methods and methodologies. Similarly, these schools and their administrators are yet to become knowledgeable and educated to envision language pedagogies beyond methods, and realize the urgency of 'postmethod conditions' (Kumaravadivelu, 2006, 2008).

Conclusion

In this study, we demonstrate that misinformed beliefs and 'unplanned' language policies cause students' educational failure and academic setbacks not only in the under-resourced low-cost English medium schools and government schools, but many students in the upscale elite English medium schools also suffer from the unplanned policies. We find that the monolingual bias, the English-medium-fever and misinformation about theory and latest research trends in the academia about English education in Pakistan-like sociolinguistic contexts, still hold these schools back from making a judicious departure from the old-fashioned colonized, and traditionalist TESOL/TEFL/ESL orthodoxy. The missing link in the aspirational mandated policy, conflicting on-ground practices, and the resultant linguistic, educational and psychological disadvantages to the students typify what Romaine (2015) calls the 'pushmi–pullyu of language policy.' In these circumstances, there is an urgent need not only for a departure from the current narrow monolingual bias, and idealism of a monolingual English-only model, but there is also a dire need for a paradigmatic shift and alternative pedagogic models and approaches, which take into account the social, cultural and linguistic sensitivities of the particular local contexts. The stakeholders also need to be sensitized and informed about the potential educational, linguistic, sociocultural and socioeconomic advantages of a dynamic and engaging language pedagogy that values, embraces and capitalizes on the existing linguistic and cultural resources.

We propose that translanguaging could be the most appropriate pedagogical approach for English education in the diverse, multilingual setting of Pakistan. Translanguaging pedagogy engages bi-/multilingual learners to gain knowledge, to make sense, to articulate their thoughts and to communicate about using language (Wei, 2011). This pedagogy involves systematic and strategic use of students' total linguistic repertoire, which includes their prior linguistic knowledge to facilitate learning and to mediate mental processes in understanding the content of teaching and participate in classroom activities (Creese & Blackledge, 2010). A number of studies have recently found that a monolingual approach to language education is both inappropriate for all bi-/multilingual students and discriminatory (García & Baetens Beardsmore, 2009; May, 2014).

References

Agnihotri, R.K. (2010) Multilinguality and the teaching of English in India. *EFL Journal* 1 (1), 1–13.

Ayres, A. (2009) *Speaking Like a State: Language and Nationalism in Pakistan*. Cambridge: Cambridge University Press.

Baker, C. (2011) *Foundations of Bilingual Education and Bilingualism* (5th edn). Bristol: Multilingual Matters.

Benson, C.J. (2013) Towards adopting a multilingual habitus in educational development In C. Benson and K. Kosonen (eds) *Language Issues in Comparative Education: Inclusive Teaching and Learning in Non-Dominant Languages and Cultures* (pp. 283–303). Rotterdam: Sense Publishers.

Braun, V. and Clarke, V. (2006) Using thematic analysis in psychology. *Qualitative Research in Psychology* 3, 77–101.

Canagarajah, S. (2011) Translanguaging in the classroom: Emerging issues for research and pedagogy. *Applied Linguistics Review*, 2, 1–28. DOI: 10.1515/9783110239331.1

Canagarajah, S. (2013) *Literacy as Translingual Practice: Between Communities and Classrooms*. London: Routledge.

Canagarajah, S. and Ashraf, H. (2013) Multilingualism and education in South Asia: Resolving policy/practice dilemmas. *Annual Review of Applied Linguistics* 33, 258–285. doi: 10.1017/S0267190513000068

Channa, L.A. (2014) English medium for the government primary schools of Sindh, Pakistan: An exploration of government primary school teachers' attitudes. Unpublished PhD thesis, The University of Georgia.

Channa, L.A. (2017) English in Pakistani public education: Past, present, and future. *Language Problems and Language Planning* 41 (1), 1–25. doi:https://doi.org/10.1075/lplp.41.1.01cha

Coleman, H. (2010) Teaching and learning in Pakistan: The role of language in education. In H. Colewell (ed.) *Islamabad: The British Council* (pp. 148–157). London: British Council.

Creese, A. and Blackledge, A. (2010) Translanguaging in the Bilingual classroom: A pedagogy for learning and teaching? *The Modern Language Journal* 94 (1), 103–115. DOI:10.1111/j.1540-4781.2009.00986.x

Cummins, J. (2005) Teaching for Cross-Language Transfer in Dual Language Education: Possibilities and Pitfalls. Paper presented at the TESOL Symposium on dual language education: Teaching and learning two languages in the EFL setting.

Cummins, J. (2007) Rethinking monolingual instructional strategies in multilingual classrooms. *Canadian Journal of Applied Linguistics* 10, 221–240.

Cummins, J. (2009) Pedagogies of choice: Challenging coercive relations of power in classrooms and communities. *International Journal of Bilingual Education and Bilingualism* 12 (3), 261–271.

Cummins, J. (2016) Teaching for transfer in multilingual school contexts. In O. García, A. Lin and S. May (eds) *Bilingual and Multilingual Education* (pp. 1–13). Cham: Springer International Publishing.

Dreze, J. and Sen, A. (2002) *India: Development and Participation*. New Delhi: Oxford University Press.

Ethnologue (2019) *Languages of the World*. Retrieved from https://www.ethnologue.com/statistics/country

García, O. and Baetens Beardsmore, H. (2009) *Bilingual Education in the 21st Century: A Global Perspective*. Malden, MA; Oxford: Wiley-Blackwell Pub.

García, O. and Leiva, C. (2014) Theorizing and enacting translanguaging for social justice. In A. Blackledge and A. Creese (eds) *Heteroglossia as Practice and Pedagogy* (Vol. 20, pp. 199–216): Springer Netherlands.

García, O. and Wei, L. (2014) *Translanguaging: Language, Bilingualism and Education*. Basingstoke: Palgrave Macmillan.

Hélot, C. and Laoire, M. (2011) *Language Policy for the Multilingual Classroom: Pedagogy of the Possible*. Bristol: Multilingual Matters.

Hornberger, N.H. (2003) *Continua of Biliteracy: An Ecological Framework for Educational Policy, Research, and Practice in Multilingual Settings*. Clevedon: Multilingual Matters.

Hornberger, N.H. and Link, H. (2012) Translanguaging and transnational literacies in multilingual classrooms: A biliteracy lens. *International Journal of Bilingual Education and Bilingualism* 15 (3), 261–278. DOI:10.1080/13670050.2012.658016

Kubota, R. (2011) Immigration, diversity and language education in Japan: Toward a glocal approach to teaching English. In P. Seargeant (ed.) *English in Japan in the Era of Globalization* (pp. 101–122). London: Palgrave Macmillan UK.

Kumaravadivelu, B. (2006) *Understanding Language Teaching: From Method to Postmethod*. Mahwah, NJ: Lawrence Erlbaum Associates, Inc.

Kumaravadivelu, B. (2008) *Beyond Methods: Macrostrategies for Language Teaching*: Yale University Press.

Mahboob, A. and Lin, A.M.Y. (2018) Local languages as a resource in (language) education. In A.F. Selvi and N. Rudolph (eds) *Conceptual Shifts and Contextualized Practices in Education for Glocal Interaction: Issues and Implications* (pp. 197–217). Singapore: Springer Singapore.

Manan, S.A. (2016) Building on children's linguistic resources: A socio-culturally responsive pedagogy for English language teaching in Pakistan. *Philippines ESL Journal* 17 (July), 67–85.

Manan, S.A. (2018a) Myth of English teaching and learning: A study of practices in the low-cost schools in Pakistan. *Asian Englishes* 21 (2), 1–18. DOI:10.1080/13488678.2018.1503041

Manan, S.A. (2018b) Silencing children's power of self-expression: An examination of coercive relations of power in English-medium schools in Pakistan *L1–Educational Studies in Languages and Literature* 18, 1–25.

Manan, S.A. and Channa, L.A. (2015) Significance of critical applied linguistics for applied linguists and English teaching professionals in Pakistan. *BUITEMS Journal of Social Sciences* 1 (2), 70–89.

Manan, S.A. and David, M.K. (2019) Deprescriptivizing folk theories: Critical multilingual language awareness for educators in Pakistan. *The Language Learning Journal*. DOI:10.1080/09571736.2019.1657487

Manan, S.A. and Khadija-Tul-Kubra, K. (2017) The younger, the better: A critical analysis of educators' beliefs about age and instruction of English as a second/foreign language in Pakistan. *Language Sciences*. DOI: http:// dx.doi.org/10.1016/j.langsci.2017.07.002

Manan, S.A., Dumanig, F.P. and David, M.K. (2015) The English-medium fever in Pakistan: analyzing policy, perceptions and practices through additive bi/multilingual education lens. *International Journal of Bilingual Education and Bilingualism*, 1–17. doi:10.1080/13670050.2015.1080659

Manan, S.A., David, M.K. and Dumanig, F.P. (2015a) Disjunction between language policy and children's sociocultural ecology – an analysis of English-medium education policy in Pakistan. *Language and Education*, 1–21.

Manan, S.A., David, M.K. and Dumanig, F.P. (2015b) English Language Teaching in Pakistan: Language Policies, Delusions and Solutions. In R. Kirkpatrick (ed.) *English Education Policy in Asia and the Middle East*. Dordrecht, The Netherlands: Springer.

May, S. (2014) *The Multilingual Turn: Implications for SLA, TESOL, and Bilingual Education*. New York: Taylor and Francis.

May, S. (2017) Bilingual education: What the research tells us. In O. García, A.M.Y. Lin and S. May (eds) *Bilingual and Multilingual Education* (pp. 81–100). Cham, Switzerland: Springer.

Mohanty, A.K. (2009) Perpetuating inequality: Language disadvantage and capability deprivation of tribal mother tongue speakers in India. In W. Harbert, S. McConnell-Ginet, A. Miller and J. Whitman (eds) *Language and Poverty* (pp. 102–126). Bristol: Multilingual Matters.

Mohanty, A.K. (2017) Multilingualism, education, English and development: Whose development? In H. Coleman (ed.) *Multilingualism and Development* (pp. 261–281). London: British Council.

Mustafa, Z. (2011) *Tyranny of Language in Education, the Problems and Its Solutions*. Karachi: Ushba Publishing International.

Mustafa, Z. (2016) The destruction of Nadia's dream: The English language tyrant in Pakistan's education system. In P. Bunce, R. Phillipson, V. Rapatahana and R. Tupas (eds) *Why English?: Confronting the Hydra* (pp. 185–196). Bristol: Multilingual Matters.

Nussbaum, M.C. (2011) *Creating Capabilities: The Human Development Approach.* Cambridge, MA: Harvard University Press.

Rahman, T. (1996) *Language and Politics in Pakistan.* Oxford: Oxford University Press.

Rahman, T. (1997) The medium of instruction controversy in Pakistan. *Journal of Multilingual and Multicultural Development* 18 (2), 145–154. doi:10.1080/01434639708666310

Rahman, T. (1999) *Language, Education, and Culture.* Karachi, Pakistan: Oxford University Press.

Rahman, T. (2002) *Language, Ideology and Power: Language Learning Among the Muslims of Pakistan and North India.* Karachi: Oxford University Press.

Rahman, T. (2004) *Denizens of Alien Worlds: A Study of Education, Inequality and Polarization in Pakistan.* Oxford: Oxford University Press.

Ramanathan, V. (2005) *The English-Vernacular Divide: Postcolonial Language Politics and Practice.* Clevedon: Multilingual Matters.

Rassool, N. and Mansoor, S. (2007) Contemporary issues in language, education and development in Pakistan. In N. Rassool (ed.) *Global Issues in Language, Education and Development: Perspectives from Postcolonial Countries* (pp. 218–244). Clevedon: Multilingual Matters.

Romaine, S. (2015) Linguistic diversity and global English: the pushmi–pullyu of language policy and political economy. In T. Ricento (ed.) *Language Policy and Political Economy–English in a Global Context* (pp. 252–276). New York: Oxford University Press.

Selvi, A.F. (2018) Foreword – Conceptualizing and approaching identity and inequity: An account of a shifting paradigm. In B. Yazan and N. Rudolph (eds) *Criticality, Teacher Identity, and (In)equity in English Language Teaching: Issues and Implications* (pp. v–vii). Cham: Springer International Publishing.

Wei, L. (2011) Moment analysis and translanguaging space: Discursive construction of identities by multilingual Chinese youth in Britain. *Journal of Pragmatics* 43 (5), 1222–1235.

Wiley, T.G. (2014) Diversity, super-diversity, and monolingual language ideology in the United States: Tolerance or intolerance? *Review of Research in Education* 38 (1), 1–32.

2 Constructing 'Other' Identities as a French Second Language Teacher

Meike Wernicke

Introduction

The native-speaker standard – the view that only native speakers can be expert language teachers – continues to shape teachers' identity construction, despite long-standing critiques of this construct as the standard ideal of language competency. The decades-long debate has been articulated largely in English language education, with some scholars attributing the debate directly to English language teaching (ELT) researchers and practitioners (Kramsch & Zhang, 2018). While nativist notions of 'authentic' language and culture can be traced back to antiquity (Train, 2009), modern understandings of 'native-speakerism' (Holliday, 2005) associate the construct with national belonging and the privileging of a Eurocentric or Western standard of language use and teaching (Hackert, 2012; Rivers, 2018) with implicit assumptions about race (Amin, 1997; Park, 2009) and social class (Kramsch, 1997). In language teaching, the native speaker is perpetuated through monoglossic approaches based on a 'container' view of language (Martin-Jones, 2007) that insists on purist or a balanced notion of bi- or multilingualism. As a colonial project of the 19th century, these conceptions of the native speaker emerged out of German Romanticism and the veneration of the oral vernacular to be cultivated into an ideal stabilized form within Saussurean structuralism (Dasgupta, 1998). While the 'native speaker fallacy' (Phillipson, 1992) remains socially relevant, not only in ELT but in a growing number of other language contexts, it is also increasingly contested. In recent critical scholarship, the decades-long preoccupation with the native speaker, specifically the native/non-native speaker dichotomy, is being interrogated in terms of how these approaches have tended to reproduce essentializing and idealizing categorizations of language users and teachers (Yazan & Rudolph, 2018). The variously constructed, sociohistorically situated nature of the native speaker also points to its complexity in other language domains.

In French, the inferred orientation to authentic or 'real' language (Train, 2007) and unquestioned insistence on correct or '*bon usage*' manifests itself, for example, in *l'insécurité linguistique* among francophone (L1) speakers of French in minority contexts (e.g. Bergeron, 2019). The renewed critical interest in native-speaker ideologies in conjunction with L2 teacher identity points to the need for alternative ways of conceptualizing and analyzing second language teacher identity that moves beyond dichotomous approaches by problematizing reductionist categorizations of teacher identity (e.g. Rudolph, 2018).

This chapter contributes to this area of research with a study that investigated the salience of native-speaker ideologies in the identity construction of French second language (FSL) teachers in Canada, highlighting teachers' own understandings of who owns, uses and can teach French. Attending to the complexity of teacher identity means taking into account participants' identity construction as situated within a particular geographical, socio-political and historical space that has shaped specific understandings of linguistic and cultural authenticity in the form of the native-speaker construct (Yazan & Rudolph, 2018). In the Canadian context, the native-speaker construct is embedded in ideologies of official bilingualism, the Eurocentric hierarchization of French language varieties, and the politicization of language in terms of national identity (Wernicke, 2017). The study showed non-francophone FSL teachers constructing alternative teacher identities by way of a 'process of authentication' (Bucholtz & Hall, 2005), that is, as a means of negotiating or challenging the native-speaker standard. The discussion below offers a consideration of the complexities of constructing an identity as language professional beyond the simplistic native/non-native binary by analyzing teacher identity from a discursive-constructionist perspective within a discursive psychological tradition (Potter & Hepburn, 2008) that foregrounds the interactionally co-constructed nature of teacher identity as emerging within the research process. Deconstructing traditional binaries is accomplished here by conceptually and analytically focusing on the process of identification itself and the use of binary categories as a means of highlighting the complexity of this process.

Beyond the So-called Native Speaker Teacher

Increasingly, both in ELT and beyond, researchers are challenging static, essentializing labels to take into account the complex and dynamic nature of L2 teacher identity and acknowledge the lived experiences of L2 teachers navigating inequity within their professional contexts (Rudolph *et al.*, 2015). English language teacher interactions in Japan, for example, point to the ideological underpinnings of native-speakerism and the commodification and 'deskilling' (De Costa, 2019) of Inner-Circle English teachers by local Japanese teachers of English (Appleby, 2016; Houghton *et al.*, 2018), which pits idealized nativeness in Japanese against idealized nativeness in English (Rudolph, 2018). A similar orientation is evident in Outer-Circle ELT settings, where local English teachers are determining what gets valued in terms of their teaching expertise (Swan, 2015). Moreover, Teaching English to the Speakers of Other Languages (TESOL) teachers' intercultural identities and transnational professional trajectories have provided evidence for the inadequacy of the 'NNST' (non-native speaker teacher) label (Menard-Warwick, 2008) with more recent research explicitly deconstructing the myths associated with this term (Selvi, 2014) and exemplifying new ways of theorizing language teacher identity (Varghese *et al.*, 2016).

While the native-speaker construct has received little attention beyond ELT (Muni Toke, 2013), current conceptual and analytical approaches in English language education inform research undertaken in other language teaching domains. For example, a collection of research with teachers of other languages examines the different ways teacher legitimacy intersects with a native-speaker standard across geographical contexts such as Malaysia, Vietnam and Greece, as well as by teachers of sign language (Dervin & Badrinathan, 2011). Despite important geographical distinctions, ELT research offers relevant insights for minority language education in English-dominant settings. In Canada, nativist ideologies constitute an evident preoccupation for French language teachers (Salvatori, 2007; Weinberg *et al.*, 2017), especially among non-francophone FSL teachers who have to navigate the conflictual dual identity of both learner *and* teacher of French (Wernicke, 2017). The native/non-native binary is commonly articulated in terms of 'Francophone' versus 'Francophile' (Dallaire & Denis, 2000), the latter label indexing mere aspirations to authentic Frenchness as opposed to birthright, preferably one that is still hearably representative of European French as opposed to 'bastardized' French Canadian ancestry (Bouchard, 2002). Among FSL teachers, the label '*locuteur non-natif*' is thus tacitly attached to those not able to claim the idealized 'Francophone' label, indexing a lesser legitimacy as French language speaker and thus teacher (Wernicke, 2017). Examining how native-speakerism is constructed and operates in processes of identification for French language teachers contributes to a better understanding of how language teacher identity can be productively rearticulated in more equitable, non-essentialist terms. As will be discussed below, this research also aligns with increasing calls for pluri-/multilingual perspectives in language education to counter persisting monolingual approaches grounded in native-speaker ideologies (e.g. Bento, 2011; Canagarajah, 2013; Castellotti, 2011; Derivry-Plard, 2018) by providing empirical evidence that plurilingualism can offer language teachers a conceptual tool to construct a legitimate L2 teacher identity (Wernicke, 2018; see also Ellis, 2016).

Theorizing and Analyzing L2 Teacher Identity

Present-day theoretical understandings view identity as multiple, dynamic and conflictual, as 'crucially related to social, cultural, and political context' and as discursively negotiated and maintained (Varghese *et al.*, 2005: 23). Extended to language teachers, it means that linguistic birthright or cultural heritage does not define the knowledge, experiences, and competency of language educators. Highlighting teachers' varied professional practices and experiences help to deconstruct binary conceptions of L2 teacher identity and focus on 'the fluid complexity of privilege and marginalization' that informs many teachers' professional lives (Rudolph *et al.*, 2015: 40). The discursive-constructionist theorization of identity adopted here views identity as taking shape and operating 'in local discourse contexts of interaction' (Bucholtz & Hall, 2010), contexts which are conceived as locally emergent but infused with globally available resources and knowledge (Blommaert & Rampton, 2011: 9). In the analysis below, identities are taken to be attributes of situations rather than of individuals or groups (Bucholtz & Hall, 2004: 376), which shifts the analytic focus from a particular identity to the process of identification – the interactional work that is being done in the research interaction, with a view to how this local action is linked to larger social structures 'through the socially distributed knowledge participants have about them' (Zimmerman, 1998: 94).

The present chapter joins studies that have shown teacher-participants accessing alternative understandings of professional legitimacy. Among these are studies that have adopted a social theoretical perspective to examine teacher identity within communities of practice, commonly through narrative inquiry. Analysis in these studies has employed coded themes (Reis, 2011) or comparative categories (Golombek & Jordan, 2005) or has focused on the discursive positioning of participants (Pavlenko, 2003). Other investigations have centered on professional identity in conjunction with teacher agency, using narrative analyses of participants' accounts that detail experiences and reflections about teaching (e.g. Tao & Gao, 2017) in terms of self-efficacy (e.g. Ruohotie-Lyhty, 2011) or agentic positionings (e.g. Kayi-Aydar, 2015; Søreide, 2006). Aneja's study on teacher identity adopts a post-structuralist perspective in conceiving of L2 teacher identity negotiation as '(non)-native speakering' to shift the research focus 'toward developing identity-driven approaches' (2016: 573) that avoid reductionist, *a priori* categorization of participants. The present study most resembles this type of research as well as studies highlighting L2 teachers' plurilingual or composite identities (e.g. Ellis, 2016; Huang & Varghese, 2015). Specifically, the analysis below attends to the discursive tactics co-constructed in participants' emerging identity displays during the course of the research interaction. As predetermined researcher-imposed labels, identity categories such as 'native/non-native speaker' may seem 'hopelessly inadequate for their investigative purposes' (Kumaravadivelu, 2015: x). However, examining how these discourse-embedded categories are drawn on and utilized by participants as part of a process of identity-making can provide significant insights into how teachers make meaning of who they are as legitimate language educators.

Methodology

Research context and data generation

The analysis and findings presented below are part of a multiple case study conducted with over 80 FSL teachers from Western Canada. The teachers participated in a two-week professional development sojourn in France to learn about the Common European Framework of Reference (CEFR) and be trained as examiners for the *Diplôme d'études en langue française* (DELF). Participants were recruited upon arrival in France, with data generated through pre- and post-questionnaires, travel journals, classroom observations and field notes. The majority of participants included experienced teachers with relatively high levels of language expertise. Two-thirds of teachers self-identified as L2 speakers and the remainder as L1 speakers of French, which is more or less typical across Canada (Lapkin *et al.*, 2006). Significant here is that the analysis of questionnaire data showed consistent references to idealized nativeness in French as these teacher-participants accounted for increased confidence and competency as 'French language teachers' in their responses (Wernicke & Talmy, 2018). More importantly, it pointed to a tension that arose for those who are negotiating their professional legitimacy across conflicting identities as both language learner *and* language teacher, which poses a dilemma given that 'native speakerness' ideologically precludes any ongoing language development.

The negotiation of this dual identity became a focus of analysis during the second phase of the study in Canada. Data from focal participants (all of whom identified as L2 speakers of French) were produced through interviews, classroom visits and email correspondence, with a focus on participants' language learning and professional backgrounds, sojourn experiences, instructional practices and relationships with colleagues, students and parents.

Research questions and analytic focus

The study's research questions focused specifically on (a) how participants discursively represented their professional experiences in relation to authentic language and culture, (b) how the notion of authenticity was used to construct an identity as FSL teacher and (c) the larger discourses in play constructing ideological understandings of language learning and teaching in FSL education. The notion of authenticity was conceptualized as both an inherent quality of language or culture and as a process of authentication 'by which speakers make claims to realness' (Bucholtz & Hall, 2005: 601; see also Lowe & Pinner, 2016). Important here is that authenticity as a process is not seen to exist 'prior to the authenticating practices that create it,' thereby distinguishing 'authenticity as an ideology from authentication as a social practice' (Bucholtz, 2003: 410). Identity was theorized as relational and emergent, meaning that participants' identity construction attended to how identity was discursively invoked through a set of relations called 'tactics of intersubjectivity,' specifically the 'tactic of authentication' which produces authenticity as its effect (2003: 408). While teacher-participants mobilized a range of discursive resources across various research interactions – story roles, places, travel accounts, recitations, iconic French symbols, cultural artifacts, and educational resources (Wernicke, 2017) – the analysis and findings presented below will focus solely on the identities or social categories participants recruited as part of a process of authentication.

Analytic approach

The discursive-constructionist approach I have taken here draws on several conceptual orientations. It theorizes participants' accounts as interactionally co-produced narratives while foregrounding a participant-based perspective. A participant-relevant perspective requires attending to how participants themselves orient to and make relevant different interpretations of the emerging discursive actions, instead of relying on researcher-identified meanings attributed to the text (Wiggins, 2017). With the focus on storied accounts, narrative is conceptualized as interactional work (Pavlenko, 2007), thereby foregrounding the narrative resources teachers have access to and the institutional structures in which these resources are embedded (Søreide, 2006).

Hand-written and audio-recorded data were re-contextualized into a digital text format and organized using a qualitative analysis software to gain an overview of pertinent discourse themes and interactions for subsequent in-depth analysis. Interview extracts of particular interest were re-transcribed using Jeffersonian conventions (Hepburn & Bolden, 2013) to take into account 'the sequential and locally-built nature of social actions ... [and] make visible interactants' various communicative resources' (Prior & Talmy, 2020, unpaginated). Understanding data as collaboratively produced by both interviewee and interviewer aligns with a social practice approach which views meaning as 'not merely directly elicited by skilful questioning, nor ... simply transported through truthful replies [but as] strategically assembled in the interview process' (Holstein & Gubrium, 2016: 69).

To make sense of participants' narrated processes of authentication, the analytic focus is on what Zimmerman (1998) describes as 'identities-in-context,' as a way of connecting the emerging actions with the extra-situational agendas and relevant knowledge participants draw on during the research interaction. The three types of contextual identities include *discourse identities*, which highlight the moment-by-moment, sequential organization of the interaction (e.g. questioner, storyteller), *situational identities*, which bring into play pertinent skills, knowledge, and concerns associated with particular situations and institutional contexts (e.g. French teacher, research participant), and *transportable identities*, which are latent, extra-situational identities that function as brought-along-resources across situations but are only oriented to when relevant to a particular interaction. As the analysis below exemplifies, each research interaction has teacher-participants narrating their experiences by drawing on their personal-professional histories and, in the process, recruiting these identities in different ways.

Given the situatedness of each identity display, these identities are not to be taken as generalizable or as existing beyond the research process in an a priori manner. That being said, various identities were made relevant by the participant across different research encounters with 'relative coherence and continuity' (Georgakopoulou, 2007: 60); in other words, they were 're-constituted in discourse' (Menard-Warwick, 2005). Thus, individual instances of identity displays can be understood both in terms of their immediate local context and also as connected to previous or future performances (Butler, 1999), precisely because they are tied to social practices as the product of larger discourses which provide a sense of constancy while making them analyzable as 'identities-in-context.' Understanding participants' accounts as interconnected instances of meaning-making take into account the continuity of identity construction as a process while avoiding the idea that identity itself is a consistent phenomenon.

The analysis

Due to limited space, this section exemplifies a discourse analysis of one data excerpt to support the discussion findings presented in the next section. The analysis thus serves as an example of how participants' narratives brought into play particular identities during a given research interaction and illustrate the discursive resources and authenticating tactics used to construct a legitimate identity as an FSL teacher. The overview of identities produced by the other participants is thus, to some extent, grounded in this exemplary analysis. The interview excerpt (Figure 2.1) is taken from my interaction with a focal participant named Christa,[1] who recounts a dinner conversation with Mme M, her host in

C: Madame M had um- she's had a very difficult life [and
M: [uhuh
C: and her daughter had committed sui[cide an'
M: [oh gawd
C: so this is a granddaughter that she has been [raising] and [the
M: [o:::::h] [I see
C: granddaughter- I think is about eighteen now
M: okay=
C: =and had just moved out with her boyfriend
M: okay
C: so grandma was not- she's not delighted with this
M: no heh heh I g-heh [heh]
C: [and-] she's not, but she's trying hard to- she doesn't want to lose her? doesn't want to alienate her
M: yeah
C: um- and the boyfriend was a bit of a bump on a log at this particular-
M: hehehe
C: particular dinner, and they- the granddaughter was just very young and she's- *elle taquinait t'sais*
she was teasing y'know
M: mhm mhm
C: so it was <u>very</u> funny but it was-
M: a:h okay
C: you know [she was-]
M: [bu- but] Madame M was there as well? it was the four of you then, okay
C: and so Madame M was trying- I can't remember what it was particularly that she was trying to get this granddaughter to do she's tryin' to keep her in school she's tryin'-
M: okay
C: to keep her moving and .hh she's trying very gently an- an' this kid just kept making these- they were funny but they were real putdown-grandma putdowns
((cell phone starts ringing))
M: oh
((cell phone stops ringing))
C: so, it was <u>very</u> interesting because- this girl's a little bit younger than my daughter
M: so she- she likes to sort of- the people that she has um residing with her- uh was it at her place?
C: mhm
M: oh okay and then the granddaughter=
C: =and the granddaughter had been living there up until very recently so-
M: oh okay
(1.0)
C: a- and obviously played a big role in the dynamics of having the students because often she was very close to the same age as the students
M: right of course [yes]
C: [but] I was- (.) so much older than her that Madame M and I had a-
M: (smiling) [a l-
C: [a really nice relationship
M: yeah exactly=
C: plus I spoke- because of my level of French- I don't think she got very many students that stayed with her who she could actually converse with
M: oh I see, yeah okay [okay
C: [so we- yeah we had lovely conversations about the state of the medical system in France and the- you know all the various things it was v- I really enjoyed her
M: yeah...

Figure 2.1 Extract: Authenticating French language teacher identity (interview/41:47–42:15)

France. Christa had briefly referred to this conversation in her journal and during our interview, I asked her to elaborate on it. The excerpt begins with her response to my request.

The main action of this narrative is the 'really nice relationship' (line 55) Christa had with her host, which she accomplished by recruiting a number of identities that work up a claim to an identity as a competent French speaker. The story's focal point is a dinner interaction in which Christa participated with the host, the host's granddaughter and the granddaughter's new boyfriend. Prior to turning to the particulars of the dinner, Christa provides some background about her host's family history – the suicide of Mme M's daughter and Mme M's challenges in having to raise a teenage granddaughter (lines 1–10), all of which allows her to demonstrate knowledge Christa has acquired through presumably prior (and similarly intimate) conversations with her host. However, it is not only the content but Christa's role in the story itself that positions her as an equal conversation partner to her French-speaking host. In relating this story, we see Christa emerging as a trustworthy and sympathetic confidante to Mme M, as someone who is privy to sensitive details about her host's personal life – a sanctioned listener (Zimmerman, 1998). This display of empathy is achieved as Christa recounts the concerns expressed by Mme M about the granddaughter's new relationship with the boyfriend (line 8) and her fear of 'losing' or 'alienating' her granddaughter (lines 11–14), showing delicate awareness on Christa's part of the nuanced dynamic between granddaughter and grandmother. This is reinforced with mention of Christa's own daughter (line 39), which mobilizes the affiliative transportable identity category of a parent, thereby underscoring her alignment with Mme M as someone who is able to understand the difficulties of raising an adolescent. Similarly, the explicit reference to her 'level of French' justifies her claim to an identity as a competent conversationalist, i.e. as someone her host 'could actually converse with' (lines 57–59). This is further reinforced with her mention of particular conversation topics that require a certain level of abstract and technical language, such as 'the state of the French medical system' (line 62), for example. Likewise, Christa's recounting of the nuanced instances of humour displayed during the dinner conversation by the other people at the table, the granddaughter's teasing and the boyfriend's 'grandma putdowns' (lines 33–34), can all be seen to demonstrate her ability to grasp the subtle elements of this intergenerational family interaction, in French. Thus both the topic of discussion and the detailed retelling of intimate and complex family relations during our interview constitute actions which index a considerable level of expertise in French.

On an interactional level, the extract makes evident my role as affiliative listener/interviewer in co-constructing the narrative with instances of overlap (e.g. lines 1–6) and latched turns (e.g. lines 8–9), requests for clarification (lines 26 and 40–41), an almost complete absence of gaps between turns, and frequent backchannel-responses ('mhm, okay, oh right, I see'). Christa's code-switch to French, *'elle taquinait t'sais'* (line 20) is uttered in an informal register with the vowel elision of the tagged-on discourse marker signaling a common French nativist, in this case, Québécois, usage. Not only does this phrase function as a key authenticating device in performing 'expert French speaker,' my backchanneling-response directly addresses the interviewer and thus ratifies my participation status as story recipient in this interaction (Goffman, 1981). All of these discursive moves serve to underline the discourse identities of an engaged storyteller on Christa's part and sanctioned listener on my part during the interview, emulating to some extent the discourse identities of Mme M and Christa in the story. Connecting the identities produced in the story to those of the interview interaction can thus be seen as another authenticating tactic, with the effect of extending Christa's demonstrated authority as competent speaker to the local context of the research interaction for my benefit, the interviewer and researcher of FSL teachers.

Findings

This section offers an overview of the different identities-in-context made relevant during the course of the research interactions as well as the discursive resources or authenticating tactics focal participants used to enact these identities (see Table 2.1). While selective and cursory, the following discussion summarizes how these identities functioned as part of the authentication process, both in response to and as alternative ways of doing 'FSL teacher,' for the most part within the implicit constraints imposed by a nativist orientation to French. That is, it offers insight into how these identity displays served to negotiate an identity as French language teacher by orienting away from, accounting for, or rearticulating a sense of legitimacy as 'authentic' language professionals.

In Christa's case, the transportable identities recruited in her narratives tend not to be directly related to identity as an FSL teacher. Projecting a sense of legitimacy involved two distinct but, at times, overlapping identities produced primarily in interview and journal narratives: a foregrounding of her administrator position and her experiences as an expert speaker in the context of her travels abroad. The administrator identity was accomplished with narratives that framed her professional experiences in association with institutional units beyond the classroom – the school, the district, the ministry. Furthermore, consistent use of 'we' and 'our' in her accounts indexed a more distant interactional relationship with colleagues in keeping with an administrative position, that is, as someone who speaks *for* others (Goffman, 1981). This process of upscaling from a personal to an impersonal context (Blommaert, 2010) accomplished a re-positioning of her identity in terms of authority and responsibility as an administrator rather than as a teacher. The other

Table 2.1 Oriented to identities by focal participants during the research interactions

Participant*	Identities*	Discursive resources
Christa	Administrator (T)	Explicit mention of position as Vice Principal; authoritative/supervisory positioning vis-à-vis her colleagues on study abroad through references to larger institutional units; use of plural participant deictics 'we' and 'our' index a more distal, supervisory position
	Expert traveler (T)	Detailed accounts of touristic visits and interactions with local experts (archivists, museum curators)
	Confidante (S/D)	In her story she recounts her position as confidante to her host in Vichy – demonstration of expert French speaker
Janet	Advocate for correct, standard French (S)	Emphasis on grammatical accuracy in teaching; explicit request for more standardization of grammatical concepts and structures across grades; frequent references to and use of dictionaries and verb conjugation guides
Karin	Mother (T)	Characterization of students as 'my little ones' and self-identification as students '*presque-maman* (almost-mom)'; comparisons to 'mother-role' as L1 speaker
	Monolingual speaker of French (S)	Classroom décor; French-only language policy; language preference for French for entirety of research interactions
Helen	Speaker of European French (S)	Use of and talk about accent; explicit mention of having acquired French in France
Carolyn	Model and ongoing learner of French (T)	Sojourn/touristic experiences framed as teachable knowledge; collecting artifacts as useful teaching resources; repeated references to own language development and ongoing learning strategies
Tamara	Music teacher/ musician (T)' old-fashioned' European (T)	Reference to music teaching, types of songs used in class, stories about piano lessons; breaking into song mention of literary works, people, iconic places evoke European cultural tradition and history
Sara	Teacher of French (S) and Spanish (T) plurilingual teacher (S) global citizen (S)	Drawing on the CEFR's conception of plurilingualism and interculturality; narratives of plurilingual and intercultural interactions abroad; orientation to international/world French, language as constituted by mobile linguistic resources

* (D) = discourse identity, (S) = situated identity, (T) = transportable identity

prominent extra-situational identity was made relevant through numerous and detailed travel stories about touristic visits, casting Christa as an engaged tourist who is able to extensively interact (in French) with local experts on French history, architecture, geography, and so on. Similar to the interaction analyzed in the previous section, this identity ultimately worked to construct her as an expert speaker of French, this time by way of her expertise as a traveler in a French-speaking environment.

The transportable identity of 'mother' was repeatedly made relevant by Karin with references to her students as *'mes petits'* (questionnaire and journal accounts) and to herself as their caregiver – *'je suis leur presque-maman'* (interview#1/8:59). This identity category, which is implicit with assumptions of authenticity associated with the 'mother tongue' and a 'natural' learning environment,' works to equate Karin's French immersion classroom with a first language socialization setting (Schieffelin & Ochs, 1986). In both journal and interview accounts, this transportable identity was reinforced by a situated identity of 'monolingual speaker of French,' the latter oriented to in various ways through the physical décor of Karin's classroom and her expressed language preference. The monolingual 'linguistic landscape' of her classroom was evident in posters, signs, books, games, even storage box labels, which all clearly demonstrated a 'French–only' language policy. This policy extended to her own preferred use of French in questionnaire responses, journal entries, and email exchanges, as well as in her explicit request that our interviews be conducted in French. As an authentication device, her use and insistence on French only offered a concrete display of her language expertise, allowing her to demonstrate 'competent speaker' as a research participant in a study investigating French teachers.

During my interview with Tamara, self-ascribed identities included 'music teacher/musician' (as opposed to FSL teacher) and 'old-fashioned European.' These identities were made relevant in accounts about her music education and knowledge of French literature, foregrounding her European background and her explicit concern for cultural traditions. In her narratives about the time she had spent in Europe (and France), the two identities – musician and European – functioned interrelatedly to articulate a conception of authenticity through a process of historicization. This notion of authenticity was, in part, produced through discussions of cultural artifacts such as state diplomas, musical compositions, and French schoolbook anthologies and even included a poetry recitation. This focus on historicity allowed her to re-contextualize her position as teacher within the local Canadian context by connecting it to a larger context, a process described by Bauman (1992) as an 'act of authentication akin to the art or antique dealer's authentication of an object by tracing its provenience' (1992: 137), at the same time highlighting 'the temporal dimension of authentication, which often relies on a claimed historical tie to a venerated past' (Bucholtz & Hall, 2005: 602).

Across these different cases, the transportable identities are seen to function as authenticating devices in that they convey an authority that indexes a high level of expertise (as administrator, traveler, caregiver, artist, etc.), and thereby provides these teachers with a sense of legitimacy that a claim to a 'non-native speaker' identity does not. Conversely, the situated identities oriented to by focal participants demonstrate most clearly the tension that a dual identity of learner/teacher produces, manifested here by the extent to which participants avoided an identity as 'French language teacher' – even though this was the identity under which they had been recruited to the study. For the most part, the situated identities in Table 1 appear to represent a particular type of French *speaker* – of standardized or European French, a monolingual speaker, or an expert (i.e. 'native-like') speaker – again pointing to language competency as the defining criterion of L2 teacher identity. One exception is Carolyn, who constructed an identity as 'model language learner' (see also Derivry-Plard, 2018) as a way of rearticulating her sense of legitimacy as a non-francophone teacher of French.

Among the seven focal participants, only one teacher moved beyond the constraints of a native-speaker ideology in her construction of an L2 teacher identity. This was accomplished by foregoing a strict association with only French as a language teacher and making relevant her identity as also a teacher of Spanish. Similar to the focal participant in Aboshiha's (2015) study, Sara redefined her authority as an L2 teacher by conceptually shifting her understanding of what it means to be a legitimate speaker and teacher of French (and of other languages), mainly in overtly mobilizing a situated identity as plurilingual. Attributed partly to her graduate studies and her involvement in CEFR-oriented curricula revisions, Sara reconceptualized French as an international language with an emphasis on multilingual speakers and a focus on language use as opposed to an ideal standard (House, 2003). We might say that it was her 'access to alternative discursive practices and the means to mobilise them' (Davies, 1990: 344) that allowed her to rearticulate a position as FSL teacher outside the constraints of a native-speaker orientation (Wernicke, 2018).

Discussion

In comparing the different identity orientations of the focal participants, it is worthwhile noting *what* each participant chose to talk about and *how* these topics were developed in the course of the interaction. Although a standard interview protocol was followed, interview interactions unfolded with considerable flexibility to allow for participant-identified themes as the focus of the talk. As pointed out in the discussion of findings, participants often showed an overlapping orientation to two identities simultaneously. In Tamara's case, for example, an identity as a music teacher/musician was constructed through narratives that referenced a European tradition, demonstrating how both her European identity and her identity as a musician intertwined to produce the desired authenticity effect. In Karin's case, the recruited identity as 'mother' was grounded in the desired ideal of a 'monolingual French speaker.'

With regard to insights into the discursive processes of L2 teacher identity construction, the findings from this study point, on the one hand, to the distinctly complex nature of participants' identity displays, which, on the other hand, draw on common discourses that articulate widely accepted language ideologies. In other words, participants were seen to construct distinct identities through a wide range of authenticity tactics that are nevertheless grounded in prevalent conceptualizations of authenticity, language learning and teaching, French language and culture, and notions of national, ethnic, linguistic and cultural affiliation. At the same time, these identities served different purposes for different participants. For example, although both Tamara and Karin made relevant transportable identities as musicians, they did so in different ways – Karin merely as part of her educational and professional trajectory while for Tamara, this identity served as an important resource in 'performing' her European heritage. Similarly, whereas Tamara described the DELF as a stabilizing force representative of European tradition, Sara drew on the DELF training to foreground a plurilingual identity by drawing on the CEFR's fundamental concept of plurilingualism as a means of circumnavigating an idealized nativist conception of French altogether. In other words, participants' orientation to various resources or tactics in constructing a legitimate identity cannot be taken for granted in terms of their meanings and functions from one case to the next. This illustration of similar identity categories, utilized and recruited by more than one participant in different ways and for different purposes, attests to the very complex, individualistic, and agentive nature of this identity work for each of the participants in this study.

Conclusion

This chapter reports on a study that investigated the salience of the so-called 'native speaker' among FSL teachers in Western Canada with a focus on the construction of teacher identity from an interactional, participant-relevant perspective that foregrounds teachers' own understandings of professional legitimacy. The discussion focused on teachers' narratives about their learning experiences during a short-term study abroad in France and the ways in which these identity displays were produced and mobilized in constructing a legitimate identity as a French language educator. A crucial issue for these teachers is that they are language learners themselves, an identity that can conflict with normative assumptions of language teacher as a 'natural' expert (Johnson, 2009). One way participants in the study sought to resolve this tension was through authenticity tactics – touristic knowledge, French literary works, reference materials, local interactions, and plurilingual competences – to make a claim to a 'real' French self or to an alternative identity that eschews reliance on a native speaker ideal. During the research interaction, teacher-participants could be seen to draw on their personal-professional histories in recruiting relevant, transportable, situated and discourse identities (Zimmerman, 1998), moving the analysis beyond traditional relational categories of 'native' versus 'non-native speaker' teacher to context-dependent member-oriented conceptions of language learning and teaching.

The table summary of participants 'identities-in-context' presented above is not to be taken as a typology of possible alternative identities to 'non-native speaker' teacher, but rather, as a range of discursively constructed interactional resources that provided these teacher-participants with a means of establishing a legitimate professional identity as language educators. More importantly, the various identity displays make evident the ideological grounding of native-speakerism in discourses of language teaching that privilege a Eurocentric, monoglossic, standardized, or expert conception of language, learning, and hence language teaching. In sum, the various types of identities can be seen as connecting to and making relevant larger discourses about French language learning and teaching, with authenticity implicit in pervasive native-speaker ideologies. The analysis thus effectively demonstrates that teachers' 'orientations to this or that identity – their own and others – is a crucial link between interaction on concrete occasions and encompassing social order' (Zimmerman, 1998: 88).

The analysis above extends critical work in English language education to the complexities of French language teaching within a minority language context by highlighting the complex interaction of power, language ideology, and interactionally mediated agency (Wernicke, 2018) on FSL teachers' instructional practices and professional learning. While still showing evidence of a prevailing native-speaker orientation, participants' identity displays nevertheless also attest to a wide range of personal, educational, and professional experiences and expertise that amount to much more than a simplistic linguistic category. The challenge is to foreground this complexity as a valuable resource in teacher education and professional development programs to allow all teachers to move beyond the limited constraints of a position as a merely proficient speaker.

Note

(1) Focal participant names are pseudonyms.

References

Amin, N. (1997) Race and the identity of the nonnative ESL teacher. *TESOL Quarterly* 31, 580–583.

Aneja, G.A. (2016) (Non) native speakered: Rethinking (non) nativeness and teacher identity in TESOL teacher education. *TESOL Quarterly* 50 (3), 572–596.

Appleby, R. (2016) Researching privilege in language teacher identity. *TESOL Quarterly* 50 (3), 755–768.

Bauman, R. (1992) Contextualization, tradition, and the dialogue of genres: Icelandic legends of the Kraftaskáld. In A. Duranti and C. Goodwin (eds) *Rethinking Context: Language as an Interactive Phenomenon* (pp. 125–145). Cambridge: Cambridge University Press.

Bento, M. (2011) Les enseignants natifs dans les approches plurilingues: Un atout? In F. Dervin and V. Badrinathan (eds) *L'enseignant Non Natif: Identités et Légitimité dans L'enseignement-apprentissage des Langues Etrangères: Ouvrage de Référence sur L'éducation* (pp. 103–115). Bruxelles-Fernelmont: EME éditions.

Bergeron, C. (2019) L'importance de préserver la diversité des accents pour contrer l'insécurité linguistique en Ontario français. *Alternative Francophone* 2 (4), 92–107.

Blommaert, J. (2010) *The Sociolinguistics of Globalization*. Cambridge: Cambridge University Press.

Bouchard, C. (2002) *La Langue et le Nombril: Une Histoire Sociolinguistique du Québec*. Montréal, Canada: Éds. Fides.

Blommaert, J. and Rampton, B. (2011) Language and superdiversity. *Diversities* 13, UNESCO.

Bucholtz, M. and Hall, K. (2004) Language and identity. In A. Duranti (ed.) *A Companion to Linguistic Anthropology* (pp. 369–394). Malden, MA: Blackwell.

Bucholtz, M. and Hall, K. (2005) Identity and interaction: A sociocultural linguistic approach. *Discourse Studies* 7, 585–614.

Bucholtz, M. and Hall, K. (2010) Locating identity in language. In C. Llamas and D. Watt (eds) *Language and Identities* (pp. 18–28). Edinburgh: Edinburgh University Press.

Butler, J. (1999) *Gender Trouble: Feminism and the Subversion of Identity*. New York, NY: Routledge.

Canagarajah, S. (2013) Theorizing a competence for translingual practice at the contact zone. In S. May (ed.) *The Multilingual Turn: Implications for SLA, TESOL, and Bilingual Education* (pp. 88–112). New York, NY: Routledge.

Castellotti, V. (2011) Natif, non natif, ou plurilingue: Dénativiser l'enseignement des langues? In F. Dervin and V. Badrinathan (eds) *L'enseignant Non Natif: Identités et Légitimité dans L'enseignement-apprentissage des Langues Etrangères: Ouvrage de Référence sur L'éducation* (pp. 29–50). Bruxelles-Fernelmont: EME éditions.

Dallaire, C. and Denis, C. (2000) 'If you don't speak French, you're out': Don Cherry, the Alberta Francophone Games, and the discursive construction of Canada's francophones. *The Canadian Journal of Sociology* 25, 415–440.

Dasgupta, P. (1998) The native speaker: A short history. In R. Singh (ed.) *The Native Speaker: Multilingual Perspectives* (pp. 183–192). New Delhi: Sage Publications.

Davies, B. (1990) Agency as a form of discursive practice. A classroom scene observed. *British Journal of Sociology of Education* 11 (3), 341–361.

Derivry-Plard, M. (2018) A multilingual paradigm in language education: What it means for language teachers. In S.A. Houghton and K. Hashimoto (eds) *Towards Post-Native-Speakerism: Dynamics and Shifts* (pp. 131–148). Singapore: Springer Singapore.

Dervin, F. and Badrinathan, V. (2011) *L'enseignant Non Natif: Identités et Légitimité dans L'enseignement-apprentissage des Langues Etrangères: Ouvrage de Référence sur L'éducation*. Bruxelles-Fernelmont: EME éditions.

Ellis, E.M. (2016) 'I may be a native speaker but I'm not monolingual': Reimagining all teachers' linguistic identities in TESOL. *TESOL Quarterly* 50 (3), 597–630.

Georgakopoulou, A. (2007) *Small Stories, Interaction and Identities*. Philadelphia, PA: John Benjamins Publishing Company.

Goffman, E. (1981) *Forms of Talk*. Philadelphia, PA: University of Pennsylvania Press.

Golombek, P.R. and Jordan, S.R. (2005) Becoming 'black lambs' not 'parrots': A poststructuralist orientation to intelligibility and identity. *TESOL Quarterly* 39, 513–533.

Hackert, S. (2012) *The Emergence of the English Native Speaker: A Chapter in Nineteenth-Century Linguistic Thought*. Berlin: Walter de Gruyter.

Hepburn, A. and Bolden, G.B. (2013) The conversation analytic approach to transcription. In J. Sidnell and T. Stivers (eds) *The Handbook of Conversation Analysis* (pp. 57–76). Chichester: Wiley Blackwell.

Holliday, A. (2005) *The Struggle to Teach English as an International Language*. Oxford: Oxford University Press.

Holstein, J.A. and Gubrium, J.F. (2016) Narrative practice and the active interview. In D. Silverman (ed.) *Qualitative Research* (pp. 67–82). London: SAGE Publications.

Houghton, S.A., Rivers, D.J. and Hashimoto, K. (2018) *Beyond Native-Speakerism: Current Explorations and Future Visions*. New York: Routledge.

House, J. (2003) English as a lingua franca: A threat to multilingualism? *Journal of Sociolinguistics* 7, 556–578.

Huang, I.-C. and Varghese, M.M. (2015) Toward a composite, personalized, and institutionalized teacher identity for non-native English speakers in US secondary ESL programs. *Critical Inquiry in Language Studies* 12 (1), 51–76.

Johnson, K.E. (2009) *Second Language Teacher Education: A Sociocultural Perspective*. New York: Routledge.

Kayi-Aydar, H. (2015) Teacher agency, positioning, and English language learners: Voices of pre-service classroom teachers. *Teaching and Teacher Education* 45, 94–103.

Kramsch, C. (1997) The privilege of the non-native speaker. *PMLA* 112, 359–369.

Kramsch, C. and Zhang, L. (2018) *The Multilingual Instructor*. Oxford: Oxford University Press.

Kumaravadivelu, B. (2015) Foreword. In A. Holliday, P. Aboshiha and A. Swan (eds) *(En) Countering Native-speakerism: Global Perspectives* (pp. viii–xi). London: Palgrave Macmillan UK.

Lapkin, S., MacFarlane, A. and Vandergrift, L. (2006) *Teaching French as a Second Language in Canada: Teachers' Perspectives Research Report*. Ottawa: CASLT.

Lowe, R.J. and Pinner, R. (2016) Finding the connections between native-speakerism and authenticity. *Applied Linguistics Review* 7 (1), 27–52.

Martin-Jones, M. (2007) Bilingualism, education and the regulation of access to language resources. In M. Heller (ed.) *Bilingualism: A Social Approach* (pp. 161–182). New York: Palgrave Macmillan.

Menard-Warwick, J. (2005) Both a fiction and an existential fact: Theorizing identity in second language acquisition and literacy studies. *Linguistics and Education* 16, 253–274.

Menard-Warwick, J. (2008) The cultural and intercultural identities of transnational English teachers: Two case studies from the Americas. *TESOL Quarterly* 42 (4), 617–640.

Muni Toke, V. (2013) Le locuteur natif et son idéalisation: Un demi-siècle de critiques. *Histoire Epistémologie Langage* 35 (2), 5–15.

Park, G. (2009) 'I listened to Korean society. I always heard that women should be this way…': The negotiation and construction of gendered identities in claiming a dominant language and race in the United States. *Journal of Language, Identity, and Education* 8 (2–3), 174–190.

Pavlenko, A. (2003) 'I never knew I was bilingual': Reimagining teacher identities in TESOL. *Journal of Language, Identity, and Education* 2, 251–268.

Phillipson, R. (1992) *Linguistic Imperialism*. Oxford: Oxford University Press.

Potter, J. and Hepburn, A. (2008) Discursive constructionism. In J.A. Holstein and J.F. Gubrium (eds) *Handbook of Constructionist Research* (pp. 275–293). New York: Guilford Press.

Prior, M.T. and Talmy, S. (2020) A discursive psychological approach to the analysis of talk and text in applied linguistics. In J. McKinley and H. Rose (eds) *The Routledge*

Handbook of Research Methods in Applied Linguistics (unpaginated). London: Routledge.

Reis, D.S. (2011) Non-native English-speaking teachers (NNESTs) and professional legitimacy: A sociocultural theoretical perspective on identity transformation. *International Journal of the Sociology of Language* 208, 139–160.

Rivers, D.J. (2018) The idea of the native speaker. In S.A. Houghton and K. Hashimoto (eds) *Beyond Native-Speakerism: Current Explorations and Future Visions* (pp. 15–35). New York: Routledge.

Rudolph, N. (2018) Essentialization, idealization, and apprehensions of local language practice in the classroom. In B. Yazan and N. Rudolph (eds) *Criticality, Teacher Identity, and (In)equity in English Language Teaching: Issues and Implications* (pp. 275–302). Cham, Switzerland: Springer.

Rudolph, N., Selvi, A.F. and Yazan, B. (2015) Conceptualizing and confronting inequity: Approaches within and new directions for the 'NNEST movement.' *Critical Inquiry in Language Studies* 12 (1), 27–50.

Ruohotie-Lyhty, M. (2011) Constructing practical knowledge of teaching: Eleven newly qualified language teachers' discursive agency. *The Language Learning Journal* 39 (3), 365–379.

Søreide, G.E. (2006) Narrative construction of teacher identity: Positioning and negotiation. *Teachers and Teaching: Theory and Practice* 12 (5), 527–547.

Salvatori, M. (2007) Learning, Discerning and Yearning: The Development of Language Proficiency of Non-Native Speaker French as a Second Language Teachers in Ontario (Unpublished doctoral dissertation). Toronto, ON: University of Toronto.

Schieffelin, B.B. and Ochs, E. (1986) Language socialization. *Annual Review of Anthropology* 15, 163–191.

Selvi, A.F. (2014) Myths and misconceptions about nonnative English speakers in the TESOL (NNEST) movement. *TESOL Journal* 5 (3), 573–611.

Swan, A. (2015) Redefining English language teacher identity. In A. Swan, P. Aboshiha and A. Holliday (eds) *(En)Countering Native-Speakerism: Global Perspectives* (pp. 59–74). London: Palgrave Macmillan UK.

Tao, J. and Gao, X. (2017) Teacher agency and identity commitment in curricular reform. *Teaching and Teacher Education* 63, 346–355.

Train, R.W. (2007) Language ideology and foreign language pedagogy. In D. Ayoun (ed.) *French Applied Linguistics* (pp. 238–269). Amsterdam: John Benjamins.

Train, R.W. (2009) Toward a 'natural' history of the native (standard) speaker. In N.M. Doerr (ed.) *The Native Speaker Concept: Ethnographic Investigations of Native Speaker Effects* (pp. 47–80). Berlin: Walter de Gruyter.

Varghese, M., Morgan, B., Johnston, B. and Johnson, K.A. (2005) Theorizing language teacher identity: Three perspectives and beyond. *Journal of Language, Identity and Education* 4, 21–44.

Varghese, M., Motha, S., Park, G., Reeves, J. and Trent, J. (2016) Language teacher identity in multilingual settings. *TESOL Quarterly* 50 (3), 545–571.

Weinberg, A., Seror, J. and Simonet, T. (2017) Sur la piste des facteurs d'attrition et de rétention au sein du régime d'immersion en français à l'Université d'Ottawa. *La Revue Canadienne Des Langues Vivantes*.

Wernicke, M. (2017) Navigating native-speaker ideologies as FSL teacher. *Canadian Modern Language Review* 73 (2), 1–29. https://doi.org/10.3138/cmlr.2951

Wernicke, M. (2018) Plurilingualism as agentive resource in L2 teacher identity. *System* 79, 91–102. https://doi.org/10.1016/j.system.2018.07.005

Wernicke, M. and Talmy, S. (2018) Interaction in qualitative questionnaires: From self-report to intersubjective achievement. *Applied Linguistics Review* 9 (4). https://doi.org/.org/10.1515/applirev-2017–0030

Wiggins, S. (2017) *Discursive Psychology: Theory, Method and Applications.* Los Angeles: SAGE Publications.

Yazan, B. and Rudolph, N. (2018) *Criticality, Teacher Identity, and (In)equity in English Language Teaching: Issues and Implications.* Cham, Switzerland: Springer.

Zimmerman, D.H. (1998) Identity, context and interaction. In C. Antaki and S. Widdicombe (eds) *Identities in Talk* (pp. 87–106). Thousand Oaks, CA: Sage

3 'English is the Commercial Language Whereas Spanish is the Language of my Emotions': An Exploration of TESOL and Bilingual Teacher Identity and Translanguaging Ideologies

Lobat Asadi, Stephanie Moody and Yolanda Padrón

Introduction

The performativity of discourse (Butler, 1999) is embodied in language learning. The performance of a language introduces the concept of the phenomenon *in situ* – often observed in translanguaging practices. Spence (2017) explains that truth may be rhetorical, given that the memory of the mind's eye may only hold fragments of it, yet 'they are taken as reliable clues to one or more actual events' (2017: 882). Thus, when perception is based on memory and performed linguistically according to one's context, language pedagogy can only be a dialogic process among participants, not a means to an end-result. Pennycook (2018) explains that the organic nature of discourse is historically sedimented, yet generative as it is ever-changing. Past language use, present context and a projected linguistic future are enfolded into one's linguistic repertoire. *Translanguaging* is a type of such organic discourse that emphasizes how people use their knowledge of multiple languages to socially engage with the world (García, 2017). Many scholars believe that it is an effective learning strategy for multilinguals because it allows learners to make connections between past experiences and the classroom in ways that teachers may not be able to (Conteh, 2018; Gort & Sembiante, 2015; Henderson & Palmer, 2015). Despite this, translanguaging has been met with resistance in the field, and thus has not been incorporated into the mainstream curriculum (Bilgin, 2015; Cheng, 2013). Instead, language pedagogies such as bilingual and English-only language education have been utilized to position 'standard English' as the language of power (Crystal, 2003; García *et al.*, 2017).

In order to explore the lived experiences and resultant ideologies of multilingual language teachers, we need to better understand the complexities between language and power in relation to teachers' intersectional identities. For the present study, bilingual and Teaching English to the Speakers of Other Languages (TESOL) in-service teachers at a large public university in Texas were interviewed about their identity and any relationship to translanguaging. Semi-structured interviews and researcher observations were deconstructed through narrative inquiry (Clandinin & Connelly, 2000) to determine ideologies about monolingualism versus translanguaging. Based on our findings, we provide a rationale for making translanguaging a mainstream educational practice that counteracts traditional hegemonic language instruction (Darder & Uriarte, 2012; Gramsci, 1999; Phillipson, 2009). We warn that translanguaging will never become a mainstream educational practice unless language instructors reflect upon the settler origins of the current language pedagogy in the United States, and consider the global neo-colonial manifestations.

Literature Review

Since meaning within all languages is enforced by dominant ideologies and institutions, there arises a need to understand the multiple values. Bakhtin (1983) examines the historical merge of past and present as an internal drive that produces states of language. Thus, conflicting forces and genre conventions may demonstrate various ideological associations from language use. Thus, language acquisition is, in part, based on the historical, socially constructed environment, which minimizes conflicting voices, causing monologic discourse, or enables conflicting voices, causing dialogic discourse.

The relationship between history and discourse indicates the need for deconstruction and re-examination of language instruction. In fact, the cognition of one's surroundings varies based on the privilege one has in the given environment and space (Allen, 1999). These spaces are projects embedded in spatial memory that have specific roles within historical contexts. Even though imaginary spaces may only remain in memory, they can be witnessed through symbolic realms such as language. Thus, they can provide guidelines on how thought may become action in curriculum and pedagogy. Therefore, we envision that current mainstream pedagogies in language instruction should be determined by the geo-political and geo-spatial histories that have formed the conditions in which they are instructed, such as present or former English-speaking colonies of dominant western nations.

Englishness

Before we can understand current language policies, we need to familiarize ourselves with the global spread of 'Englishness' (Ezroura, 2018) to recognize how it has always been constructed to fit the agendas of English-speaking globally dominant nations. Ezroura (2018) states, 'such an astounding success of English (as language, culture, episteme, and economy, hence the term "Englishness") is directly indebted to the great achievements of the British Empire since the 17th Century' (2018: 3). Today, scholars agree that the global linguistic spread of English is more powerful than any other past attempts at linguistic dominance (Pennycook, 1998; Phillipson, 1992; Sekhar, 2012). English is now the dominant or official language in 60 countries, and in countries that lack formal ties to English, it is still widely represented and influential in media. Clearly, the English language influences culture, epistemology, and economy across the globe (Sekhar, 2012).

Thus, the umbrella term *Englishness* is utilized to address our argument that English-language instruction has manifested sociohistorically. Understanding these roots, aids in analyzing who and what ELT does. The term *decolonial* is used when deconstructing the remains of colonial practices in places often viewed as presently colonized such as North America (Quijano, 2000; Tuck & Yang, 2012). Participants' educational experiences are presented using narrative discourses about language, culture, and identity, so two areas of debate are examined regarding the expansion of English: (a) how the historic colonial spread of the British Empire is reflected in English language instruction, and (b) the global domination of English and how that impacts English language learning and instruction in the United States.

Colonial education in the United States

While a thorough analysis of linguistic imperialism is outside the scope of this study, such aims are tangible in the historical view of systems that developed out of the pedagogies of Anglo-Saxon settlers in North America. To demonstrate, in 1823, the Monroe Doctrine, laid out the blueprints and the systems to maintain the western Empires, including linguistic aims as colonizers in North America forced Native Americans and enslaved Africans to learn English (Passe & Willox, 2009; Phillipson, 2009). In the 19th century, a desire for homogenized North American culture emerged; thus English language and literature were also studied to 'foster a sympathetic identification' with 'America' and show 'patriotic devotion' (Brass, 2011: 344). Prime Minister Winston Churchill, whose mother was American, outlined it in *A History of English-Speaking Peoples* (Phillipson, 2009). During the 20th century, immigration to America increased and English instruction became one way to indoctrinate newcomers into American culture and form solidarity (Brass, 2011). This process of replacing knowledge constituted a 'coloniality of knowledge' (Quijano, 2000). As a result, the Anglo-Saxon English-speaking people(s), and others who assimilated linguistically were privileged in North America (Ramsey, 2010; Rury, 2012).

However, in 1968 Congress passed the Bilingual Education Act, which granted second language use in education but did not require schools to do so (Kim *et al.*, 2015). However, the legislation was accompanied by laws in several states that prohibited BE, which again placed language minority students under linguistic disadvantage.

The entire English-only movement is supported by the concept of the 'achievement gap.' Yet, the entire concept of the 'achievement gap' is skewed because high-stakes tests, always in English, make it impossible to separate linguistic proficiency from content knowledge (Menken, 2010). The resulting scores of language minority students are less indicative of a lack of content knowledge, and more an affirmation of the language learner disadvantage. With this achievement gap fallacy, monolingual ideologies and interests of globally dominant western nations are reinforced and promoted.

Theoretical Framework

Translanguaging

The language use of bilinguals has been given many different names, each of which reflects a specific ideological stance based on the roots through which the term was created. We focus specifically on 'translanguaging,' in which individuals utilize their entire linguistic repertoire to communicate (García, 2017), and 'translingualism,' used to discuss the contact between languages that occurs through writing and meaning-making (Canagarajah, 2013). Both concepts challenge the settler colonial pedagogy sociopolitics of language (Guerra & Shivers-McNair, 2017). Translanguaging pedagogy advocates for language development to be viewed as closely related to the contextual, historical, and sociolinguistic circumstances of the language teacher and learner. Thus, it may be used as a means of decolonization in formerly colonized lands (Horner & Tetreault, 2017).

Yet, translanguaging has been met with resistance by policymakers and administrators. Much of this stems from deeply entrenched beliefs about social and political forces used to categorize and rank languages. Translanguaging may remove such hierarchies and allow for linguistic acceptance. In Botswana, for example, languages are assigned to categories of 'school' and 'home' to indicate when they should be used, and their level of prestige (Bagwasi, 2017). Translanguaging pedagogy threatens categorization by asking governments around the world to recognize the legitimacy of 'lower-class' languages for academic and professional purposes. At the same time, fear stems from governments' preoccupation with native language loss, making many hesitant to accept translanguaging as a tool (Conteh, 2018). Schools are equally resistant because they contend that language is a neutral tool for acquiring academic concepts and ignore that language choices may reinforce colonial beliefs and power (García, 2017).

Likewise, schools with bilingual and multilingual education programs remain resistant to translanguaging. Ironically, these language pedagogies may have emerged as sociolinguistic matching methods from the same colonial pedagogies that they purport to resist (Guerra & Shivers-McNair, 2017). Dual-language and two-way immersion programs are widely touted as additive approaches to bilingual education, even though they maintain and perpetuate monolingual ideologies of 'two solitudes' (Cummins, 2008). In these schools, students may only use Standard English, and translanguaging as well as translingual writing practices are shunned. In this way, monolingualism continues to be positioned as the norm, and bilingualism is judged through a monolingual framework (Flores & Rosa, 2015).

Translanguaging as decolonizing pedagogy

In order to deconstruct settler pedagogies, we have to reimage what decolonizing pedagogies might look like (Pérez, 1999). In North America, colonialism began in 1519 with Castilian settlers after the Spanish conquest of the Aztec people in Mesoamerica. Yet today, after the second wave of Anglo-Saxon colonialism, there are ongoing pedagogic and policy efforts to include Latinx peoples' history and the Spanish language in education (Cabrera *et al.*, 2014). Linguistically, Flores and Rosa (2015) push for a critical heteroglossic perspective where the listener is challenged about their preconceived ideas of native speakers, accents, and interpretations. On the other hand, translanguaging pedagogy (García *et al.*, 2017) acknowledges diverse linguistic practices for problem-solving (Kabuto, 2010), making connections to prior knowledge (Garrity *et al.*, 2015), and the negotiation of meaning (Worthy *et al.*, 2013). Combining these two approaches, Cummins (2017) suggests changing the standard additive bilingual approach to an *active* approach. Thus, translanguaging pedagogy proposed by García (2009, 2017) would be legitimized, and the two-way transfer of language would be promoted. Likewise, the heteroglossic perspective would be privileged, 'highlighting the impact of societal power relations and their reflection in patterns of teacher-student identity negotiation as determinants of the achievement gap between social groups,' (Cummins, 2017: 420). For decolonization of language education, educators must examine the relationship to power and the positions of all stakeholders.

Identity, power and discourse

By considering translanguaging a decolonial method, and through discussions about global Englishness, linguistic imperialism, and heteroglossia, it becomes evident that our current English language instruction is derived from the colonial spread of the British Empire and is centered around privilege and power. As Bakhtin (1981) asserts, 'language is not a neutral medium that passes easily and freely into the private property of the speakers' intentions; it is populated – overpopulated with the intentions of others' (1981: 294). Therefore, language teachers from different backgrounds may differ in how historical circumstances and geopolitical social constructs have linguistically shaped them. Likewise, they may manipulate, ignore, and support learning depending on how their own identities and linguistic repertoires have developed in relationship with power.

Intersectionality

Cho *et al.* (2013), explain that intersectionality is a theoretical and methodological paradigm that examines the interplay of difference and sameness when considering 'gender, race, and other axes of power in a wide range of political discussions and academic disciplines' (2013: 787). These crossroads of experience that vary among people based on their lifestyles, ethnicity, and other factors, shape the identity of individuals living with multiple realities. By including intersectionality of teachers' linguistic positioning, ethnicity, sociocultural, and political experiences, the examination of how lived experiences influence their respective views on translanguaging emerge. Guided by intersectionality, we prioritized exploring ways in which the dimensions of identity inform our analysis of teacher's perspectives on language instruction.

Idealized nativeness

Bakhtin (1981) explains that language education has been modelled on the idealized nativeness of a language speaker. Yet, no universal linguistic code that acts as one voice for all speakers exists. In fact, scholarship recognizes that the entire concept of a native speaker is a fallacy (Phillipson & Skutnabb-Kangas, 1996). In the case of standard English, the idea of the native speaker was built on the belief that imperialist European nations are intellectually and culturally superior, which led to a fixed system of languages that marginalizes the 'other' (Pennycook, 2004). Thus, in order to survive, immigrants have had to socially and linguistically assimilate (Ong *et al.*, 1996) to gain linguistic capital (Bourdieu, 1986).

Thus, eschewing the entire concept of a native or non-native speaker, asserting that 'individuals are not native or nonnative speakers per se, but rather are *(non) native speakered* with respect to different characteristics, through different institutional mechanisms, individual performances, and social negotiations' (Aneja, 2016: 576). With the *(non) native speakered* approach, we are able to move beyond the categorization of individuals and consider how language identity is negotiated and developed.

Teacher identity

The identity of teachers is developed largely around their perceptions, and their students' perceptions, of them as native or non-native speakers. For the most part, native English-speaking teachers are assumed monolingual, and non-native speakers are defined 'less by their plurilingualism than by their perceived deficiencies in English,' (Ellis, 2016: 597). Rich language learning experiences of teachers and their pedagogical resources are ignored – not used as a strength (Ellis, 2016). By ignoring or inaccurately perceiving the linguistic identities of educators, teachers are not able to use their own experiences pedagogically. When translanguaging, teachers are expected to exhibit a monolingual English stance. The natural practice of translanguaging is both shamed and stifled, prohibiting teachers from using it with their own students.

Methods

Research design

While most empirical research indicates that effective educational reforms rely on long-term inquiry as well as critical thinking, most studies have not looked at the identity-related dispositions of teachers. Thus, the specific stories behind the teachers' ideologies are often omitted or reduced to the overall findings. In this study, narrative inquiry, the 'experiential study of experience' (Xu & Connelly, 2010), is used to examine the identity development of six bilingual and TESOL teachers. It is research about people, understanding that they exist in relationship to other people, places, and things (Clandinin & Connelly, 2000).

Traditional axioms of truth look for ontological claims of generalizability (Dewey & Bentley, 1949). However, this study seeks narrative truth as opposed to paradigmatic truth (Bruner, 1962/1979). Narrative inquiry is not a method for answering specific questions, but instead a pathway towards understanding the actions and events that become stories (Xu & Connelly, 2010). Thus, in contrast to generalizable systemic research, narrative inquiry is contextual and deliberately specific to the person(s), context and being studied (Craig, 2003; Craig *et al.*, 2017). 'Narrative inquiry is experiential because it is fundamentally concerned with human activity and how humans make meaning as individuals and in community with one another' (Craig, 2003: 7). This fluid representation and analysis of teacher identity allow for intersectional identities of the teachers to emerge and be explored by the researchers.

Participants

Inspired by a narrative inquiry study into ethnic identity by Chan (2010), participants were sought, who would vary greatly from both their parents and their children, due to sociolinguistic and political influences in their lives. Thus, participants were not randomly selected, but chosen for their intersectional identities as transnational or married to one or international student. It was assumed that participants may have views on what language they should use pedagogically, versus with their families. Combined, six BE and TESOL teachers, all of whom are pursuing a doctorate in their respective fields, were interviewed. All participants either speak two or more languages, and have extensive experience with language education in Teaching English as a Foreign or Second Language, or as a bilingual educator (Table 3.1).

Study instruments

For this study, we conducted six open-ended interviews, each of which lasted approximately one hour. These interviews were conducted individually with the researchers and participants. We allowed the participants to dictate the direction of the interview, as we hoped that individual stories would guide our understanding of our participants' beliefs about their identities as language teachers and their perceptions of translanguaging pedagogy.

Analysis

As researchers, we enter this study as both experienced language educators and peers to the educators we interviewed. We acknowledge that our beliefs about language learning pedagogy and our experiences as English speakers and speakers of other languages exert influence over our interactions with our participants as well as in our interpretation of the data.

First, we conducted a content analysis (Lincoln & Guba, 1985) that looked for teacher quotes allowed for emergent key concepts; native speaker, colonialism, sociopolitical, language learning and language teaching. The results were cross-checked by all three researchers for reliability. At this stage, the most relevant concepts to the teachers' identities were: (a) past personal lived English language-related experiences, (b) present teaching/use of heritage language and English both in their personal lives and in classroom language and finally (c) sociopolitical associations with English and translanguaging in their personal/familial use and their instructional methods.

After conducting the content analysis, it was noted that the transnational or international participants often referred to sociopolitical issues that formed their language beliefs. This indicated that certain

Table 3.1 Teacher identity

TESOL Teacher	**Identity Power & Discourse Analysis**	**Historical Identity Analysis**	**Translanguaging Identity Analysis**
Fariba; *female, Kurdish-Iranian international student, married to Kurdish-Iranian, fluent in three languages. Wishes to immigrate to US. Taught EFL in Iran adult education & US higher education preservice teacher ed.*	Idealized nativeness felt as EFL teacher in US. Also felt this as Kurdish speaker in Iran (Farsi prestige language).	Sociocultural associations with her own heritage languages. Does not prestige English or idealized nativism.	Uses and agrees with translanguaging.
Emma; *single female, Chinese, no kids, fluent in two languages. International student, does not wish to immigrate to US. Taught in US in higher education preservice teacher ed.*	English was a prestige language even though China was cloistered. Grew up trying to sound native and imitating sitcoms like *Friends.*		Does not agree with translanguaging, even though she learned by watching sitcoms with subtitles in China.
Peter, *Married Anglo-Saxon male, Chinese spouse, mixed race kids, fluent in three languages, US-born national, lived in Taiwan as a math teacher. Taught K-12 math in US and TESOL preservice teacher ed in higher ed.*	Experienced privilege as native speaker, Anglo-American in Taiwan. Met spouse abroad, who is also Chinese.	Associations with French relatives. No connection with much with teaching in Taiwan.	Does not use translanguaging, not agree with it. Uses dual language instead at home with mixed marriage & children.
Bilingual Teacher	Identity Power & Discourse Analysis	Historical Identity Analysis	Translanguaging Identity Analysis
Clarita, *Puerto-Rican Hispanic-American, immigrated to US as 1st gen, married to Anglo-American, mixed race kids, fluent in three languages. Taught in K-12 US system.*	Had to learn heritage language on her own due to leaving Puerto Rico at early age.	Puerto Rico was colonized and this disrupted her life and that of her family. Second-class citizens abroad and in US.	Idealized nativeness issues experienced as US citizen.
Valentina; *Colombian Hispanic-American 1st gen, married to Anglo-American, mixed race kids. Taught in K-12 US system.*	Idealized nativeness indicated, not stated. Prestige language indicated. Native speaking privilege indicated.	No associations with being immigrant from Columbia.	Does not use translanguaging, not agree with it. Uses dual language instead at home with mixed marriage & children.
Leticia; *single female, Mexican-American, immigrated parents, 2nd generation. Taught in K-12 US system.*	English as prestige language indicated. Idealized nativeness privilege indicated.	Border and identity issues growing up in US with MX parents. MAS/language issues in CA & TX experienced personally and as a teacher.	Uses translanguaging for social justice and educational purposes as needed, regardless of curriculum. Must use Spanglish with parents and siblings. Prefers dual language education, not opposed to trans as needed.

sociocultural and sociopolitical contexts and mitigating factors were interconnected to their relationship(s) English. Therefore, the researchers conducted a second level of a priori coding to identify the themes within three emergent themes, specifically related to intersectional teacher identity. The aspects of the teachers' intersectional identities were expressed in relation to: (a) power and discourse, (b) historical and geopolitical backgrounds and (c) translanguaging (displayed in Table 3.1).

Findings

The pre-service teachers' past experience with language learning seemed to form their ideologies, beliefs and even impacted their relationships to language learning. The participants' attitudes towards teaching language versus using translanguaging at home vary. Most differentiated their speech save for Leticia, who seemed consistent in translanguaging use in both her personal and professional life.

Teachers' nationality, status and heritage language

Leticia explained that she prefers to be able to use the same methods of looking up words, mixing languages and explaining in the heritage language, as determined by the needs of individual students:

> The students mix languages naturally like you would at home. The academic goal is for them to be proficient in English reading, writing, speaking and listening, but in order to move them from only speaking Spanish to being bilingual, we are not just taking their language, we're taking them as an entire person, as an entire entity. And that comes with culture, their heritage, you know, whatever their passions are, their love, their background, their family.

Leticia considered nationality, sociopolitical status, and prior heritage language use as impacting translanguaging. Likewise, translanguaging seemed especially beneficial for most of the teachers who immigrated and/or naturalized citizens because it helped to stabilize their hybrid identities. Translanguaging appeared to encourage positive feelings of sociocultural memories and enhance the teachers' sense of social justice in the US, a primarily monolingual education nation.

Monolingualism never took off in Puerto Rico, Clarita explained; 'English is the commercial language whereas Spanish is the language of my emotions. Language is culture...you can learn without losing your identity.'

While Clarita described her resistance to English-only curriculum, she did not face the physical punishment for speaking Spanish school that her elders and many others described facing during the earlier days of US colonization:

> There's more allegiance to the Spanish language that feels like your culture. We had leaders, we had art, we had institutions, newspapers and things like that. So, when the United States came, it was even really hard for the Americans to assimilate the Puerto Ricans.

Today, Clarita uses translanguaging to teach, just like Leticia and Fariba. Ironically, all three hail from nations that were directly impacted by colonization and/or prestige languages be it in Mesoamerica/North America, Iran, or Puerto Rico. Leticia, Clarity and Fariba had entanglements with language, power, and identity, often related to the use of English. In the case of Fariba, a Kurdish mother-tongue speaker, she experienced this reduction of prestige associated with native-language abilities in both Farsi and English.

Furthermore, three teachers in this study married nationals from other nations. Clarita and Valentina married Anglo-Americans and became naturalized citizens, while Peter, a native-born US citizen, married an Asian woman, whom he met while teaching in Taiwan. While in Taiwan, Peter learned Chinese and continues to speak it with his wife and kids, hoping that his children will grow up bilingual. All three have mixed-race children and use translanguaging at home. Yet, their opinions about the use of translanguage varied. This may have been due to prestige languages and language policies in tandem with their ancestral lands having been colonized.

Teachers' identity reflected in privilege and prestige

Privilege associated with idealized nativeness and English as a prestige language was referenced several times by both TESOL and BE instructors. Due to the diverse languages, backgrounds and identities of the teachers in the study, it is interesting to note that the prestige of English native-language speech was the strongest influence over the pedagogical choices and professional stances the teachers expressed. Fariba, a Kurdish minority who hails from Iran, said she often feels like a second-class teacher because she is not a native speaker, despite the fact that she holds the same credentials as other instructors:

> I was once rejected in an interview for an English language institution in Iran. The reason that they rejected me is that I did not sound like a native speaker. You can only teach lower levels otherwise (in Iran). Here (US), I met a lot of professors in my department that are not native speakers. They have no problem. Some have accents, but they can communicate easily, and there's no problem interacting with those professors. I think whether you sound like a native speaker or not; you should have a good relationship with students and communicate as you need to in order to teach them.

Fariba uses translingual writing practices herself as a learner, with both Farsi and English in her academic life and believes one can learn by using multiple languages:

> It makes me feel so confident than I'm going back to my first language. I just translate. For example, I write a sentence and translate it have a better understanding. When I write notes in English, I lose some concepts that I want to take away, but if it (notes) is in Farsi, I can convey more information than in English.

Perhaps sociocultural memories embedded in Fariba's notes and associations with Farsi add confidence. 'It's really beautiful when we hear a lot of languages. It's like a garden full of different flowers.' Yet, Fariba explained that in familial situations, she uses translanguaging between Kurdish and Farsi:

> I was born as a simultaneous learner because I was speaking Kurdish with my parents until the age of four or five. At the same time, I was looking at the cartoons and movies in Farsi. Uh, so because I learned Kurdish first, that's the language I use when speaking with my parents and my brothers. When angry or become very emotional, I also automatically go back to Kurdish.

Opposite to the intentional use of these practices expressed by Fariba, Clarita and Leticia, Peter states that translanguaging is a spontaneous action, not a pedagogic tool. Both Peter and Emma, who is near-native in English and native in Chinese, reported using translanguaging spontaneously in personal conversations. Similarly, Valentina shares the belief that translanguaging occurs naturally but asserts that is it not the best language practice or pedagogic tool – opting for dual monolingualism in both language praxis and personal life.

In addition, non-native speakers gaining status with the spread of Englishness and English, (Crystal, 2003; Ezroura, 2018) Peter, as a native-speaking, Anglo-American male, could be more privileged than others in this study. Critical race theorists may argue that those more closely associated with Anglo-America, either through racial attributes or by marriage, hold whiteness as a form of property and possess more sociocultural and economic privileges than those with intersectional identities (Crenshaw, 1994; Harris, 1995). Ironically, Peter stated that he prefers teaching in Taiwan over the US because he could speak Chinese and access it personally and professionally as needed, whereas in the US, he feels confined to using English-only whenever he has taught math. 'I find it cognitively stimulating to be in a country and a culture and a situation where I'm able to use two languages however I feel throughout the day, and the fact that I'm able to be exposed to a foreign language and engage in conversations, I think for me is fulfilling, and I can't do that in the US.'

This may impact his identity and translanguaging ideologies, as he only uses it randomly with his Chinese-speaking family. Furthermore, under the perspectives of intersectionality and critical theories, learning Chinese would be perceived by dominant global perspectives as an accomplishment for Peter. Since speaking Chinese is not a requirement to the teaching profession, Peter may experience multiple levels of privilege both as a math teacher and currently as a TESOL teacher educator doctoral student. Regardless of native-speaking or Anglo-American status, Peter would like for translanguaging to become more mainstream as a pedagogic tool, indicating that he feels some constraints by monolingual curricula.

Ironically, Leticia, the only other native speaker besides Peter, admitted that English is a prestige language amongst Hispanic people, which disrupts her social justice stances. While she was ashamed of her Spanish-only speaking parents as a child growing up in California, she admits to now rebelling against this negative imagery by using both translanguaging personally and professionally. The two other teachers, Emma and Valentina, who both sound like a 'traditional' native-speaker, expressed privilege and may unknowingly possess even more. It is interesting to note that Emma speaks English and Chinese, often mixing the two spontaneously when in China. She acknowledged that it is prestigious to speak English in China, in personal and academic contexts. Yet, like Peter and Valentina, she was opposed to using translanguaging as a pedagogic tool. Valentina is also near-native in speech, and married to an Anglo-American, indicating that she may experience a higher level of status associated with idealized nativeness of English as the prestige language in North America. Valentina did not say she was aware of any privileges and asserted that it is important to stay monolingual when learning a language. 'I choose the language that I'm going to communicate with and stay with that language. I think it's important for language preservation purposes and at home just to use the language that I'm going to communicate with.'

Thus, due to ideological or curricular issues, most of the teachers, who have English native or near native-speaking status, only use translanguaging spontaneously in their private lives. Leticia is a native-speaking exception but also remains passionate about linguistic rights and equity. Fariba is not a native speaker, nor is she a US citizen, but she does use translanguaging personally and pedagogically. Given the sociocultural references and the fact that she is a student-visa resident, not a US citizen, she may be experiencing the joy of using Farsi as it connects her to her heritage and associated memories.

'Native speaking' abilities

In tandem with monolingual constructs that often advocate idealized nativeness, half of the teachers (Leticia, Fariba, Clarita) stated that they were somehow impacted by idealized nativeness, and all were in favor of translanguaging. While Peter and Valentina may have unknowingly benefited by sounding like a native English speaker, it is indicated in the cultural capital-related intersectional markers of more prestige associated with their race and/or nationality associated with native speaking abilities. Emma expressed awareness of native-speaking privilege, yet she remained uncertain about the use of translanguaging pedagogy. Overall, a higher level of teachers' native English language speaking ability may indicate uncertainty about translanguaging.

To illustrate, confidence and ideologies about language instruction seemed to vary based on how native the teacher sounded. Peter and Leticia are the only two natural-born US citizens with native-speaking teachers in the study, yet Leticia speaks Spanish as a Mexican-American, and Peter speaks Chinese that he learned, in part while working in Taiwan, and in his interracial marriage. Peter stated that he thinks translanguaging use is determined to the identity of the speaker, rather than being a pedagogic tool, and he only uses it in his personal life. Peter asserted that translanguaging was a random phenomenon, and it would not appear in speech until the learners had acquired advanced levels of proficiency in the second language. Leticia, however, is a Mexican-American, and passionately endorses translanguaging praxis.

Both Leticia and Peter stated that they had witnessed translanguaging happening spontaneously in their multi-lingual lived experiences, but Peter preferred the use of dual language practices in overall language learning, while Leticia used translanguaging regardless of the curricula. However, Leticia is also second-generation binational. Growing up, she was disturbed by the way her parents were treated as non-native and foreign-language speakers in the United States. Leticia remembers feeling rebellious when told to use English-only and continues to resist it actively. This is because she dislikes the perception in Mexico, and in North America, speaking English over Spanish elevates one's sociocultural status. She perceives translanguaging as an equity-oriented discourse, in tandem with its instructional benefits.

Implications

Teacher education

Acknowledging that this study cannot claim an ultimate truth, we have instead explored narrative storied by the participants that we have re-storied and explored using our perspectives. As we dissected the epistemological influences of settler pedagogy, we assessed the curricular responses, which varied somewhat between TESOL and BE teachers. Overall, teachers' preservice training of TESOL or BE may have impacted their use and opinions of translanguaging. Yet, it emerged as a pedagogy that supported many transnational teachers' restructuring of their own ideologies about language learning. Overall, translanguaging was perceived as equitable, culturally responsive, transformative, as a pedagogical tool – in accord with accessing the entire linguistic repertoire of the learner (Otsuji & Pennycook, 2011).

Overall, the TESOL teachers were in support of its use in non-academic contexts at home, with family and spontaneously. However, Fariba supported its use in academic contexts and passionately shared her translingual writing practices with the researchers. She was determined to demonstrate its usefulness but expressed feeling an enriched, happier sense of ethnic and national origins when she used both Farsi, her academic first language, and English in academia and instruction as TESOL teacher and preservice teacher educator.

Linguistic imperialism

The study raises many questions for further study such as: what do the attitudes language instructors have towards translanguaging at home, versus its use at an institution of learning, indicate (particularly when these instructors are multilinguals)? Should language-related pedagogy be different for learners who hail from nations that are sociopolitically challenged by Englishness or other Western-centric issues? Further study is also needed about the ways in which TESOL and BE teacher education vary and how the differences impact instructors' translanguaging ideologies.

Guerra and Shivers-McNair (2017) place the current language pedagogies into an accessible historical framework that enables our comprehension of language policy and praxis. Their connection of language instruction to coloniality, broaden, *yet also* further entangle, how linguistic imperialism has been constructed by globally dominant powers to maintain their hegemonic systems (Phillipson, 1992). Likewise, looking back into historical influences of teachers through their narratives juxtaposed with the intersections of their nationalities, race, and English-idealized nativeness, we can see how each teacher has been linguistically managed through prestige languages or otherwise impacted by colonization and resultant discourses of privilege.

Leticia, Fariba and Clarita explicitly stated colonial and sociopolitical issues that impacted their identity and linguistic use ideologies. In addition, it may be argued that Peter was privileged as an Anglo-American male, given ancestral colonization of North America from Europe. The issues of English language prestige, idealized nativeness, and any sociocultural or rebellious responses indicate that colonial factors have not been well mitigated, and current language pedagogies are immersed in sociolinguistic issues. These findings support Phillipson's assertions that monolingual curricula and native-speaking abilities are some of the underpinning fallacies of pedagogic expertise (Phillipson, 2009). The indications that neo-colonial pedagogies and ideologies exist among language teachers in this study indicate that some institutions are functioning in a neocolonial English language curriculum in the United States, and the spell of Englishness has been cast globally. Thus, translanguaging, with its nod to social justice and dialogic discourse, may not be fully actualized in the current pedagogic system.

However, in this study, monolingual pedagogies and concepts of idealized nativeness have shown that traditional (monolingual) methods are not effective for all teachers and learners. Concerned language educators may consider resisting methods, which are often rooted in linguistic imperialism. For example, Kumaravadivelu (2001) suggests a 'three pedagogic parameters of particularity, practicality, and possibility as organizing principles for L2 teaching and education' instead of a method of transmission (2001: 537). In response to ineffective traditional and colonial conceived forms of pedagogy, which due to identity and sociocultural issues raised in this study, have not been holistically effective methods, we look towards translanguaging, translingual practice, and *postmethod pedagogy* (Kumaravadivelu, 1994, 2001).

This study into TESOL and BE teacher ideologies about translanguaging demonstrates that translanguaging is better understood by historical deconstruction and inquiry about linguistic imperialism by those teachers who possess less linguistic privilege. For several teachers in the study, translanguaging indicated that they have a personal history with linguistic imperialism and/or transnationalism. Thus, their ideologies about social justice have likely emerged from these, and often conflict-ridden lived experiences. As teachers, their complex histories with linguistic rights has allowed the often more marginalized teachers of both TESOL and BE to feel empowered as educators and language minority speakers. This was evident as most of the teachers who shared stories of marginalization also expressed support of the students they determined as needing linguistic support.

Teachers with privileges associated with their linguistic repertoires and identities questioned or were averse to translanguaging pedagogies. Though well-intentioned, these potentially more privileged teachers and curriculum-makers alike may oust practices that would benefit language learners. Due to these results, we look towards decolonizing linguistic pedagogies and encourage a forthcoming educational era that is no longer entrenched in linguistic imperialism, coloniality and Englishness. Likewise, monolingualism appears as a settler-colonial, hegemonic construct given the resulting power of Englishness displayed in the globally dominant spread through colonization. Furthermore, 'global' education and EFL perpetuate imperialism through neoliberal multicultural tactics of local and global governing systems of economy and education (Melamed, 2011). Pedagogy should include a wider range of political, sociocultural experiences that influence TESOL instruction other than Western-centric means.

References

Allen, R.L. (1999) The socio-spatial making and marking of 'us': Toward a critical post-modern spatial theory of difference and community. *Social Identities* 5 (3), 249–277.

Aneja, G.A. (2016) (Non)native speakered: Rethinking (non)nativeness and teacher identity in TESOL teacher education. *TESOL Quarterly* 50, 527–596. DOI: 10.1002/tesq.315

Bagwasi, M.M. (2017) A critique of Botswana's language policy from a translanguaging perspective. *Current Issues in Language Planning* 18 (2), 199–214.

Bakhtin, M. (1981) *The Dialogic Imagination: Four Essays* (C. Emerson & M. Holquist, Trans). Austin: University of Texas Press.

Bakhtin, M. (1983) *The Dialogic Imagination: Four Essays*. Austin: University of Texas Press.

Bilgin, S.S. (2015) Code switching in ELT teaching practice in Turkey: Teacher practices, beliefs and identity (unpublished doctoral dissertation). University of Warwick, England.

Brass, J. (2011) Sunday schools and English teaching: Re-reading Ian Hunter and the emergence of 'English' in the United States. *Changing English* 18 (4), 337–349.

Bruner, J. (1962/1979) *On Knowing Essays for the Left Hand*. London: Belknap Press of Harvard University Press.

Bourdieu, P. (1986) The forms of capital. In J. Richardson (ed.) *Handbook of Theory and Research for the Sociology of Education* (pp. 241–258). Westport, CT: Greenwood.

Butler, J. (1999) *Gender Trouble: Feminism and the Subversion of Identity*. London: Routledge.

Cabrera, N.L., Milem, J.F., Jaquette, O. and Marx, R.W. (2014) Missing the (student achievement) forest for all the (political) trees: Empiricism and the Mexican American studies controversy in Tucson. *American Educational Research Journal* 51 (6), 1084–1118.

Canagarajah, S. (2013) *Translingual Practice: Global Englishes and Cosmopolitan Relations*. London: Routledge.

Chan, E. (2010) Living in the space between participant and researcher: Examining ethnic identity of Chinese-Canadian students as conflicting stories to live by. *The Journal of Educational Research* 103, 113–122.

Cheng, T.P. (2013) Code-switching and participant orientations in a Chinese as a foreign language classroom. *The Modern Language Journal* 97 (4), 869–886.

Cho, S., Crenshaw, K.W. and McCall, L. (2013) Toward a field of intersectionality studies: Theory, applications, and praxis. *Signs, Intersectionality: Theorizing Power, Empowering Theory* 38 (4), 785–810.

Clandinin, M. and Connelly, J. (2000) *Narrative Inquiry Experience and Story in Qualitative Research*. San Francisco: Wiley.

Craig, C.J. (2003) *Narrative Inquiries of School Reform: Storied Lives, Storied Landscapes, Storied Metaphors*. Greenwich, Conn.: Information Age Publishers.

Craig, C., You, J. and Oh, S. (2017) Pedagogy through the pearl metaphor: Teaching as a process of ongoing refinement. *Journal of Curriculum Studies* 49 (6), 757–781.

Crenshaw, K.W. (1994) Mapping the margins: Intersectionality, identity politics, and violence against women of color. In M.A. Fineman and R. Mykitiuk (eds) *The Public Nature of Private Violence* (pp. 93–118). New York: Routledge.

Crystal, D. (2003) *English as a Global Language*. Cambridge: Cambridge University Press.

Conteh, J. (2018) Translanguaging. *ELT Journal* 72 (4), 445–447.

Cummins, J. (2008) Teaching for transfer challenging the two solitudes assumption in bilingual education. In J. Cummins and N.H. Hornberger (eds) *Encyclopedia of Language and Education* (pp. 65–75). Tonawanda, NY: Springer.

Cummins, J. (2017) Teaching minoritized students: Are additive approaches legitimate? *Harvard Educational Review* 87 (3), 404–425.

Darder, A. and Uriarte, M. (2012) The politics of restrictive language policies: A postcolonial analysis of language and schooling. In J. Lavia and S. Mahlomaholo (eds) *Culture, Education and Community: Expressions of the Postcolonial Imagination* (pp. 69–102). New York: Palgrave Macmillan.

Dewey, J. and Bentley, A. (1949) *Knowing and the Known*. Boston, MA: Beacon Press.

Ellis, E.M. (2016) I may be a native speaker but I'm not monolingual: Reimagining all teachers' linguistic identities in TESOL. *TESOL Quarterly* 50, 597–630.

Ezroura, M. (2018) Englishness, postcoloniality, and epistemicide: The mission of English and the Moroccan University. Retrieved from: https://www.academia.edu/38022167/Englishness_Postcoloniality_and_Epistemicide_The_Mission_of_English_and_the_Moroccan_University

Flores, N. and Rosa, J. (2015) Undoing appropriateness: Raciolinguistic ideologies and language diversity in education. *Harvard Educational Review* 85 (2), 149–171.

García, O. (2009) Education, multilingualism and translanguaging in the 21st century. In T. Skutnabb-Kangas, R. Phillipson, A.K. Mohanty and M. Panda (eds) *Social Justice Through Multilingual Education* (pp. 128–145). Bristol: Multilingual Matters.

García, O. (2017) Translanguaging in schools: Subiendo y bajando, bajando y subiendo as afterword. *Journal of Language, Identity and Education* 16 (4), 256–263.

García, O., Johnson, J. and Seltzer, K. (2017) *The Translanguaging Classroom: Leveraging Student Bilingualism for Learning*. Philadelphia: Caslon.

Garrity, S., Aquino-Sterling, C.R. and Day, A. (2015) Translanguaging in an infant classroom: Using multiple languages to make meaning. *International Multilingual Research Journal* 9 (3), 177–196.

Gort, M. and Sembiante, S.F. (2015) Navigating hybridized language learning spaces through translanguaging pedagogy: Dual language preschool teachers' language practices in support of emergent bilingual children's performance of academic discourse. *International Multilingual Research Journal* 9 (1), 7–25.

Gramsci, A. (1999) *Selections from the Prison Notebooks*. London: The Electric Book.

Guerra, J.C. and Shivers-McNair, A. (2017) Toward a new vocabulary of motive. In B. Horner and L. Tetreault (eds) *Crossing Divides: Exploring Translingual Writing Pedagogies and Programs* (pp. 19–30). Logan, UT: Utah State University Press.

Harris, C.I. (1995) *Whiteness as Property*. In K. Crenshaw, N. Gotanda, G. Peller and K. Thomas (eds) *Critical Race Theory: The Key Writings That Formed the Movement* (pp. 357–383). New York: The New Press.

Henderson, K.I. and Palmer, D.K. (2015) Teacher and student language practices and ideologies in a third-grade two-way dual language program implementation. *International Multilingual Research Journal* 9 (2), 75–92.

Horner, B. and Tetreault, L. (2017) *Crossing Divides, Exploring Translingual Writing Pedagogies and Programs*. Logan: Utah State University Press.

Kabuto, B. (2010) Code-switching during parent-child reading interactions: Taking multiple theoretical perspectives. *Journal of Early Childhood Literacy* 10 (2), 131–157.

Kim, Y.K., Hutchinson, L.A. and Winsler, A. (2015) BE in the United States: A historical overview and examination of two-way immersion. *Educational Review* 67 (2), 236–252.

Kramsch, C. and Nolden, T. (1994) Redefining literacy in a foreign language. *Die Unterrichtspraxis/Teaching German*, 28–35.

Kumaravadivelu, B. (1994) The postmethod condition:(E) merging strategies for second/foreign language teaching. *TESOL Quarterly*, 28 (1), 27–48.

Kumaravadivelu, B. (2001) Toward a postmethod pedagogy. *TESOL Quarterly* 35 (4), 537–560.

Lincoln, Y.S. and Guba, E.G. (1985) Establishing trustworthiness. *Naturalistic Inquiry* 289, 331.

Menken, K. (2010) NCLB and English language learners: Challenges and consequences. *Theory Into Practice* 49, 121–128.

Melamed, J. (2011) *Represent and Destroy: Rationalizing Violence in the New Racial Capitalism*. St. Paul, Minnesota: University of Minnesota Press.
Ong, A., Dominguez, V.R., Friedman, J., Schiller, N.G., Stolcke, V., Wu, D.Y. and Ying, H. (1996) Cultural citizenship as subject-making: immigrants negotiate racial and cultural boundaries in the United States [and comments and reply]. *Current Anthropology* 37 (5), 737–762.
Otsuji, E. and Pennycook, A. (2011) Social inclusion and metrolingual practices, *International Journal of Bilingual Education and Bilingualism* 14 (4), 413–426.
Passe, J. and Willox, L. (2009) Teaching religion in America's public schools: A necessary disruption. *The Social Studies* 100 (3), 102–106.
Pérez, E. (1999) *The Decolonial Imaginary: Writing Chicanas into History*. Bloomington: Indiana University Press.
Phillipson, R. (1992) *Linguistic Imperialism*. Oxford: Oxford University Press.
Phillipson, R. (2009) *Linguistic Imperialism Continued*. Routledge.
Phillipson, R. and Skutnabb-Kangas, T. (1996) English only worldwide or language ecology? *TESOL Quarterly* 30 (3), 429–452.
Pennycook, A. (1998) The right to language: Towards a situated ethics of language possibilities. *Language Sciences* 20 (1), 73–87.
Pennycook, A. (2004) Performativity and language studies. *Critical Inquiry in Language Studies* 1 (1), 1–19.
Pennycook, A. (2018) Repertoires, registers and linguistic diversity. In A. Creese and A. Blackledge (eds) *The Routledge Handbook of Language and Superdiversity* (pp. 3–15). London: Routledge.
Quijano, A. (2000) Coloniality of power and eurocentrism in Latin America. *International Sociology* (15) 2, 215–232.
Ramsey, P. (2010) *Bilingual Public Schooling in the United States: A History of America's Polyglot Boardinghouse*. Cham, Switzerland: Springer.
Rury, J.L. (2012) *Education and Social Change: Contours in the History of American Schooling*. New York: Routledge.
Sekhar, G.R. (2012) Colonialism and imperialism and its impact on English language. *Asian Journal of Multidimensional Research* 1 (4), 111–120.
Spence, D. (2017) Rhetorical truth. *The Psychoanalytical Quarterly* 72 (4), 875–903.
Tuck, E. and Yang, K.W. (2012) Decolonization is not a metaphor. *Decolonization, Indigeneity Education and Society* 1 (1), 1–40.
Worthy, J., Duran, L., Hikida, M., Pruitt, A. and Peterson, K. (2013) Spaces for dynamic bilingualism in read-aloud discussions: Developing and strengthening bilingual and academic skills. *Bilingual Research Journal* 36 (3), 311–328.
Xu, S. and Connelly, M. (2010) Narrative inquiry for school-based research. *Narrative Inquiry* 20 (2), 349–370.

4 Identity Dynamics in the Speech of Language Teachers in French and German Primary Schools: How Do They Go About Constructing 'Interculturality'?

Véronique Lemoine-Bresson

Introduction

This chapter analyses four focus groups composed of primary school teachers from Germany (Nordrhein-Westfalen and Hessen, *Grundschule*[1]) and France (*école élémentaire*[2]) gathered in different places to exchange on (inter)cultural practices in the classroom, and how they go about constructing 'interculturality.' In a period when open-mindedness to other cultures, to Europe and the international is advocated in everyday discourse (Taylor & Manes-Bonnisseau, 2018), how do they behave when it comes to teaching 'cultural content' about the 'other' whose 'language' they are teaching? How can they (co)construct their identities in interaction and communication with their colleagues when confronted by the language and culture they are teaching? The German curriculum text for learning a foreign language depends on the *Land,* and the French curriculum text is national. The text in *Land* Hessen deals with the development of interdisciplinary competences such as personal competence and social competence (core curriculum primary level). Unlike the text in *Land* Hessen, the German text in *Land* Nordrhein-Westfalen additionally recommends developing an understanding of other culture-specific peculiarities (*Lehrplan* English: See Ministerium, 2015). It is similar to the French text, which recommends focusing on the discovery of culture specifically associated with the language studied. According to the authors of the French curriculum, language teaching aims to anchor learning in culture (Ministère, 2015).

In order to better understand how the teachers go about constructing 'interculturality,' I studied their discourse through focus groups in both countries. The method of analysis is based on dialogical and enunciative work. It highlights the elusive aspects of identity to be considered as a dynamic process involving the heterogeneity of the subjects' positions and the multiple voices present in the teachers' discourse. In employing this approach, I aimed for a better understanding of the process of identification in interaction and its effects on teachers' professional identity construction.

Theoretical Framework

The tension between identity in communication and professional identity

In this chapter, it is accepted that there is 'an inevitable and close interrelationship between teacher identity, teacher-learning and teaching practices' (Yazan, 2018: 25) and that the interactions in focus groups develop a floating compromise between an identity defined by oneself and one defined or acknowledged by others, present or absent.

The phenomenon – identity in interaction – a framework for focusing on influences in interactions between teachers, has become a focus of attention in recent years. I argue, following Bucholtz and Hall (2005), that 'identity is a discursive construct that emerges in interaction,' and it has to be analyzed 'as an intersubjective accomplishment' (2005: 587). Second, research on teachers' identity rarely considers the dynamics in discourses to reflect on how identities co-construct in interactions between teachers who have values, projects, beliefs, ideological point of view about education and knowledge. Some teachers develop an expert identity in the language they teach; for example, by marking a border with other teachers who are considered as non-expert, or as native/nonnative. Indeed, the question of the native speaker in language teaching continues to be a myth: 'true English' would be the most legitimate person to teach 'good and true' English to students. In the background, this delegitimizes 'nonnative' teachers who often define themselves as inferior in this hierarchical scale. Portine (2011: 64) explains that this dichotomy is part of a socio-economic pressure and social beliefs and expectations.

The phenomenon – teachers' professional identity – is a negotiated identity depending on the constraints of the professional environment and the interests of the person (De Fina, 2006; Gohier *et al.*, 2001) the teachers have to cope with. These principles can help the study to understand how the French and German teachers construct their professional identity through representations of 'self' and the 'other', the relationship to work, to responsibilities, to students and colleagues. According to Yazan (2018), teachers 'negotiate their identities as they position themselves and are positioned by others' (2018: 143). In dialogue, anyone who takes the risk of showing themself to be seen can become aware of their internal contradictions and of their lack of knowledge on a subject that affects their profession. This in itself is not a problem as 'the discourses are in constant flux and often contradictory' (Rudolph *et al.*, 2018: 2). But also, everyone can become aware of what is being said by referring to their practices, by summoning their values in education and by considering identities acted out in the classroom and expected by their colleagues. In these exchanges, language is not only used to give information but 'language is a tool for three things: saying, doing and being' (Gee, 2015: 1).

Critical interculturality: Tension between conventional knowledge and complex aims

The school is one discursive space where the intercultural term is popular. In school programs, it is understood in terms of living together, taking the diversity of students and social changes into account for a better way to live together. But programs operate by reducing oneself and others, locking a diverse group of individuals into a category, in a so-called culture: teachers impose an origin or impose a culture to another, compare and contrast supposedly distinct cultures of the students. They also explain the behavior of students by using a national argument: the Turks are (they), but the French are (we). This inevitably poses a central question of the intercultural communication concerning the effects of interactions on oneself and others: agreements, disagreements, negotiations are constitutive of the acts of communication and interaction between people. Critical approaches to interculturality put at a distance *a priori* categorizations which are not relevant to understand what happens in interaction between people. This conception emphasizes the idea that we should not seek truth about a national culture or identity (Dervin & Fracchiolla, 2012: 10).

The French language programs in primary schools frequently refer to the word *culture* and distinguish cultural knowledge in two distinct paragraphs (knowledge and attitudes). It is stipulated that the student develops a sense of the relative, of otherness, a critical sense to get past stereotypes which are nonetheless presented to him/her across a mosaic of static elements that homogenize all that is foreign and lead the student to generalize about foreign cultures. The German language programs emphasize the development of transversal skills in order to manage contact and encounters with 'the other'. Those skills include, on the one hand, for example, that the learners present criticism constructively or take criticism from others and reflect on it. On the other hand, the text of the curriculum proposes similarities with the French text; for example, that the learners have to learn the different behaviors of people from other countries and interpret them as typical cultural habits. This perspective leads to treating cultures as synonymous with distinct blocks and comparing and contrasting national groups as if 'no group can escape culture' (Hofstede *et al.*, 2010: 11) in a culturalist approach which works in an essentializing vision.

The Study

Context

As part of my professional situation from 2007 to 2015 as a teacher trainer in the Academy of Lille, France, I had access to the dates of teacher training courses taking place in the Academy. After having received permission from the authorities, from the teachers in training and the teacher trainer, I integrated a focus group component into existing training courses about languages teaching in French primary schools, dividing participants into two groups. The grouping of German teachers was a more delicate task because I had only a vague idea of the training sessions' organization in each *Land* of Germany. My professional background at the time enabled me to be supported by the *Deutsch-Französisches Jugendwerk* in Berlin, an international organization dedicated to Franco-German cooperation, and to contact German teachers.

Data collection: Focus groups

As a method of qualitative research, the focus group can generate a subjective debate around 'a common project by confronting members with a complex problem' (Van der Maren, 2010: 130). The instruction given by the researcher to the teachers as a stimulus was to exchange on the (inter) cultural content they teach or would teach in class to prepare primary school pupils to go abroad. Using the focus group as an interesting toolkit to produce oral data, we then access the teaching motivations of some and the fierce resistance of others (sometimes the same individuals who were motivated earlier), the projects and the absence of projects, the first ideas and the ideas transformed by the exchanges between the interlocutors. The use of focus groups as a data collection tool allows for a discussion about moving identities, avoiding the fixed categories and the facilities of generalization and labeling. It is interesting to examine the different positioning of the teachers to understand how identity works: who does/says what and how in interaction? And how can personal or professional identities intersect? How do the teachers develop an image of themselves in agreement, tension and contradiction, and how do they develop their teaching knowledge again in interaction with others?

Each of the four focus groups, two in Germany and two in France, lasted approximately one hour. The exchanges were recorded with an audio recorder, and the meetings were filmed with a family-type camera. All the discourses were transcribed and translated.

Participants

The first French group (Bailleul) is composed of eight teachers with the same length of service who have known each other for a long time. In this group, one out of the eight participants defines herself as 'a native.' Another participant has already lived in Germany and is experienced in school exchanges. The other six teachers had no long international experience. The second French group (Grande-Synthe) brought together 12 teachers. They have little experience in teaching a foreign language and have a great heterogeneity of length of service. They follow an English course and show some reluctance to get involved in language teaching. They explain that they have other things to do than to train in English. They demonstrate resistance and use a cultural argument to declare themselves incompetent in language teaching: 'We are French, so we are bad in English.' In Germany, one focus group of four teachers was held in Duisburg (Nordrhein-Westfalen) and one of five teachers in Frankfurt-am-Main (Hessen). They teach French as a compulsory subject and English in optional workshops called *Arbeitsgemeinschaften* (AG). Some of them have been language assistants in France. The teachers in Frankfurt are carrying out an exchange project with a French class. Like two participants of the French group from Bailleul, all the German teachers have a long international experience, and unlike the French group from *Grande-Synthe,* they teach languages with enthusiasm.

Phenomenological data analysis

The analysis method is based on inductive qualitative analysis. The challenge of the data analysis is to describe the explicit and to track down the implicit in interactions where teachers influence and oppose each other. This makes it possible to account for the dynamics of discourses and identity construction (identity in communication and professional identity). For this study, I opted for an analysis of discourse in light of the works of Fairclough and Wodak (1997) and Van Dijk (2015), which define discourse as a social practice. The aim is to study the real use of language in exchanges between teachers in real focus group situations. The first step in the process consists of performing a floating attention reading to make way for unexpected elements. The second step is to start to examine significant themes by identifying clues in relation to the research question that articulates identity and interculturality while focusing on pieces of data that express the participants' views and meaning they place on their experience. The emphasis is on how to adhere to the other's point of view, how to negotiate the point of view, how to advance truths, how to change one's mind. That's why the theories of enunciation (Kerbrat-Orecchioni, 1999) and dialogism (with clues taken from the discourse produced in focus groups) help to observe how participants refer to experiences, to people, especially absent people and how these voices enter the scene, contradictions and adopt or not new points of view. Through discourse analysis, it is possible to 'observe how differences are negotiated and how consensus can be built or not' (Jovchelovitch, 2004: 247). As such, the speakers alternate, using past statements and creating new ones. Sometimes they have personal objections to others' points of view; sometimes, they shift their position. There is a modification, transformation and a discourse construction between the participants. The third step is to keep the significant themes that can be used to organize manageable sections of the findings.

Findings

At this point, I split the findings of this study into three sections. The study reveals that the declarations of practical experience of French and German teachers help to bring to light multifaceted findings which help us to understand identity in communication and some aspects of professional identity of the French and German teachers.

(1) ***There cannot be an ego without an alter:*** their personal and professional identities take diverse and changing forms in the confrontation of self with 'the other'.
(2) ***Shared knowledge in a culturalist approach:*** there are teaching routines embedded in a culturalist and traditional conception of 'the other' whose language they teach.
(3) ***Breaking points:*** the questioning of the problem of labels can exist in teachers' discourses and especially when their teaching is part of a set of routines. 'Routines' as an element of the teaching practices and as things that have been validated by experience (Prairat, 2017: 55) help to install and maintain effective classroom management. In particular, these routines are found in the discourse of the German teachers who describe how it works with success in pupils' exchanges and what is the important role of reflexivity in language and cultural teaching.

There cannot be an ego without an alter

The French focus group in Bailleul shows how tension and dialectic are established within the identity between the same and the other, the one and the multiple, the similarity and the difference (Lipiansky, 1992: 8). On the one hand, Kate wants to show her particularism (native) just like Cécile (expertise in school exchanges), but on the other hand, Cécile ends up accepting to be a novice like her other colleagues about pedagogical practice with an *in-situ* questionnaire.

In this part, the first item I discuss is the native/nonnative dichotomy as a dominant paradigm (Aneja, 2016) as an element of the self-enacted by Kate, one of the teachers in Bailleul, when she explains to her colleagues what is Christmas 'in the real' in England. Indeed, putting forward one's 'native' identity provokes expectations in other participants who want to know the truth about the 'real English cultural aspects they have to teach' instead of trying to cooperate in the construction of which cultural contents they could teach as relevant for young pupils. For example, according to Rampton (2003: 107), since the 'native' has inherited the language they are asked to teach as a foreign language, they must speak it 'perfectly.' But also it is required of a native speaker that they have a total understanding of the language or that if they speaks English, they come from Great Britain. Teachers are often surprised to welcome an Indian as a native foreign assistant to teach English because of 'the traditional monolingual and monocultural native-speakerist approach' and because the individuals who are not white and western, may not fit people's expectations of 'nativeness' in English (Selvi, 2014). In contrast, the nonnative is suspected of making harmful mistakes, having a questionable accent and limited comprehension, and, therefore, in an essentializing logic, not being competent in teaching the foreign language. This could almost imply that expertise is innate and cannot be learned. At the very least, we can say that 'in any interaction, while all facets of an individual's social identity are potentially relevant resources, individuals tend to present or to focus on particular aspects of their social identity, sometimes emphasizing power, authority or professional status' (Holmes, 2006: 167). Selvi (2014) points out that the native/nonnative dichotomy can put individuals in a competitive race that has effects on the self. This race juxtaposes the native speaker teacher defined as a language teacher who can be trusted against the nonnative defined as a defective teacher.[3]

The second item I discuss is the positioning as expert highlighted by another participant of the French focus group in Bailleul. At the very beginning of the debate, Cécile responds to the first question on the organization of a school trip abroad, and she justifies her intervention by the experience of it:

> *Cécile (Bailleul): Moi, j'vais prendre la parole parce que moi j'en organise* (Cécile: well, I'm going to speak because I'll be the one who organizes some trips)

Cécile explains to the others – novices to organizing school trips – her experience. She is the one who holds the knowledge, and she is not interested in the needs of her colleagues on this issue of school exchanges. As a starting point, she explains in detail how to supervise students, how to overcome difficult situations: what is to do or not as fixed elements. It thus establishes a hierarchy between herself and other colleagues. She then arouses the interest of the other participants. Two other teachers take part in the discussion questioning Cécile, backing up what she says about organizing school trips until Martine speaks and directs the debate to another pedagogical issue. She questions Cécile's methods about using a pedagogical questionnaire as a tool for students to reach out to people when they are abroad in the city center:

> *Martine (Bailleul): est-ce que tu fais un genre de questionnaire où les enfants sont laissés seuls pendant deux heures dans une ville en Allemagne où on peut…*
>
> (Martine: do you make some sort of questionnaire where the children are left alone for two hours in a city in Germany where one can…)
>
> *Cécile (Bailleul): alors on les laisse pas seuls par contre on est trois adultes: donc le directeur de l'école et une personne qui est… surtout j'dirai qui est là pour tout ce qui est soins hospitaliers etc qui a des connaissances au niveau intervention d'urgence*
>
> (Cécile: well, we don't leave them alone, there are three adults: well, the director of the school and someone who is well, I'll say, that as far as medical care, etc someone who has some level of training for emergencies)

Why doesn't Cécile answer Martine's question, which was pedagogical in nature, but diverted the subject to the question of the difficulties that may arise? She backs herself up with information about the general care of the children in order to parry difficult situations, and she only deals with one part of Martine's question. Here, whether or not they leave the children alone doesn't respond to the pedagogical question about using a questionnaire in her teaching methods. This doesn't seem to satisfy Martine as she repeats her question including in it another voice:

> *Martine (Bailleul): parce que j'ai une amie justement elle enseigne l'anglais et elle est partie à Londres et à un moment donné ils ont laissé les enfants pendant une heure ou deux … les enfants étaient obligés de se débrouiller et ils avaient un questionnaire pédagogique, on dit questionnaire ?*
>
> (Martine: because I have a friend, she teaches English, and she went to London, and at a given moment, they left the students for an hour or two … the children had to be on their own, and they had a pedagogical questionnaire, do we call it a questionnaire?)
>
> *Cécile (Bailleul): ça moi j'ai pas encore mis en pratique* (Cécile: that, well, I haven't done that yet)

Cécile accepts the status change momentarily from experienced to novice, to respond precisely to whether or not to use a pedagogical questionnaire with the students abroad. She does not want to lose face (Adelswärd *et al.*, 2004: 258; Goffman, 1967), and after that interaction she starts her discussion with 'although' as if to take back her initial experienced status. This allows her to remain self-confident and to continue to relate her experience. For her part, Martine has a third party, 'her friend,' who is an anonymous voice that has an important place in the polyphonic approach to interact with Cécile and to requestion her. This voice helps Martine to ask the same question again as she had no answer first and to maintain self-control because she began to show that she wasn't satisfied with Cécile's no answer. This puts an emotional distance between the two participants and does not push the subject with which Martine wants to continue and with which she is having trouble getting a response. These extracts show that Cécile ends up taking the other into account and that she includes herself in the group as a novice for a specific subject and for a short time. As such, the focus group allows its participants to change status during confrontations with others. In effect, Kerbrat-Orecchioni (1999) explains that 'natural discourse is [...] where one can continuously construct a social identity and interpersonal relations' (1999: 59). The focus group allows us 'to analyze from very close up, based on authentic data, the functioning of language exchanges' (1999: 52) and to understand what is taking place. There is a coming and going in Cécile's positioning that at first excludes her from the group as an expert individual but then includes her as an individual of equal status, in other words, as a novice when she accepts to shift her position.

Shared knowledge in a culturalist approach

The four focus groups show 'questionable, fragile shared knowledge' (Delamotte-Legrand, 1997: 9), such as the relevance of teaching typical fixed cultural contents. These knowledge contents are an omnipresent dimension in each Franco-German group, whose teachers mention, for example, the importance of teaching what the *other* eats often posed as different from what *we* eat. The theme of food, street furniture and the monuments frequently appear in the speeches of both French and German professionals, representing the teaching of knowledge about the culture of the other as different and fixed. It seems that 'a certain number of misunderstandings around the notion of interculturality' (Dervin, 2010: 33) result from factors including a failure to get rid of the compartmentalization of cultures, and a reliance on educational content that reduces the complexity of humanity to objects (e.g. typical dishes, living spaces) instead of trying to understand subjects (people). The following excerpts of the four focus groups show that there exists a shared knowledge in the culturalist approach. The polyphonic nature of teachers' discourse is linguistically induced here (Perrin, 2010: 4): use of certain connectors, specific lexical use, use of certain modal verbs. The terms that mark a culturalist conception are in bold.

In the following example, the use of the conjunction '*donc*' in French summarizes a whole positioning of the participant Cécile. It introduces and expresses the consequence of what is said above; the use of '*donc*' gives a status of truth to her affirmation (CNRTL).

> *Cécile (Bailleul): les Allemands mangent debout* **donc** *les tables sont hautes. J'veux dire l'environnement ou la couleur des toits des maisons qui est* ***différente***
>
> (Cécile: Germans eat standing up **so** the tables are tall. I want to say that the environment, or the color of the rooftops that's **different**)
>
> *Alexandra (Grande-Synthe): les plus grands monuments de Londres parce que ben c'est comme la Tour Eiffel j'veux dire t'as des monuments sur Londres* ***qu'on peut pas manquer.*** *Ils (élèves) ont constaté eux-mêmes les* ***choses différentes*** *les cabines téléphoniques, les boîtes aux lettres, les taxis*
>
> (Alexandra: the biggest monuments in London, because, well, it's like the Eiffel Tower, I'd say you've got monuments in London **you can't miss them**. They (the students) themselves noticed the **different things**, the telephone booths, the mail boxes, the taxis)
>
> *Tom (Frankfurt): Manchmal kommen so Sachen mit dem Essen,* ***die essen anders****, das wissen die Kinder schon. Oder sie haben Sachen gesehen, also ich kann mich erinnern, manchmal bringen sie auch was mit. Unser Supermarkt Aldi hat alle halbe Jahr so eine französische Woche, dann gibt es dort so irgendwelche Sachen, die so* ***typisch französisch*** *sind. Das erzählen sie manchmal*
>
> *Daniela: Ja, so* **Crêpes** *oder so was dann*
>
> (Tom: Sometimes things come with the food, **they eat differently**, pupils already know that. Or they've seen things, so I remember, sometimes they bring something. Our supermarket Aldi has a French week every six months, then there are things that are so **typically French**. That's what they say sometimes.
>
> Daniela: Yes, *crêpes* or something like that)

The Duisburg teachers also specify the cultural elements necessary to teach to students in the form of questioning of differences (in the excerpt, the relevant questions are underlined). The use of specific verbs shows the teachers' fixed and rigid culturalist positioning in discourses. The elements become the things that a teacher has to do, leaving no room for doubt or negotiations of cultural and professional identity.

> *Katrin (Duisburg): Ah, ja. Das heißt* ***man muss*** *mit den Kindern wenn man die vorbereitet, solche Sachen auch vorbereiten*
>
> *Anna: Genau*
>
> *Katrin: <u>Wie lebt eine französische Familie…</u>*
>
> *Susan: <u>Wie ist das Essen…</u>*

Katrin: Ja, wie ist das Essen…was also in Frankreich wird dann eben Mittags und Abends gegessen oder? Und dann Morgens ja eigentlich gar nicht, ne? Was ist anders? Also die Kinder müssen das wissen

(Katrin: Ah, yes. That means **you have to** prepare such things with the children when you prepare them

Anna: Exact

Katrin: How does a French family or an English family live?

Susan: How's the food?

Katrin: How is the food? So what, in France, they eat lunch and dinner or, and then in the morning, not at all, what's different? So that the children know that)

The participants collaborate to support a shared discourse on similar practices around cultural objects. The discussions are supported with concrete examples of monuments, places, and differences between 'us' and 'them' through objects, without mentioning human diversity. Such positioning brings to the forefront views of the nature of the term 'culture', when speaking of interculturality. Müller (2008: 7) indicates that it is about '*Beziehung zwischen verschiedenen Kulturen*' (Relationship between different cultures); Byram (2000: 55) advocates that teaching unveils new things about others, about their cultures and their identities. The accent is, therefore, put on the difference between cultures. Can we, in these definitions, detect the camouflage of a culturalist approach? The teachers often reduce the foreign to fixed objects, and I realize that a certain number of hoaxes emerge from their discussions when they talk about interculturality (Dervin, 2009). They use expressions like 'it's an adventure' as well as 'it's the fear of the unknown.' This expatriation that allies exoticism and fear seems to be presented as essential to the training of a future citizen. It is sometimes posed as if it were a matter of radical separation between 'us' and 'them' that we would have to know in order to connect with 'others' better.

Breaking points: Specific points in specific groups

Some salient breaking points emerge in the discourses of the teachers of a German focus group in Frankfurt-am-Main, whereas those points do not in the discourses of the teachers of the other focus groups. The points testify to an organization that is well established in the exchange, and they show a strong link with parents and the French partner team. They do not express fear of strangers but a certain weariness in repeating the same visits and activities year after year in school exchanges: they wonder about the degree to which they are still motivated to continue or not. They question the notion of plural identity, in contrast, the other groups do not.

The French focus in the Bailleul group also presents a strong contrast with the other groups of teachers by defining the other as a subject to be wary of. Teachers construct essentialized categories that tend towards a dichotomous discourse where the other represents a threat. For example, in the following excerpt, the remark of the participant Michèle is based on a quasi-generalization when she says: '<u>They</u> tend to' about the conduct of shopkeepers in England when they meet French schoolchildren. She holds some reified and solid views of the other, and she includes in her remark a vigilance addressed to the students. Michèle says to her colleagues:

> *Michèle[4] (Bailleul): faites attention à ce qu'ils (les commerçants) vous rendent (la monnaie) parce que bon dans les magasins <u>ils ont tendance</u> à prendre dans les porte-monnaie des enfants pour payer[5]*
>
> Michèle (Michèle: pay attention to what they (shopkeepers) give you back (the change) because, well, in the stores, <u>they tend to</u> take themselves money in the children's wallets to pay)

Shortly before, the same participant explained that she was teaching currency to the children not only because they 'don't use the euro, but rather the Sterling' but also 'to prevent the children from being cheated.' Here she refers to the category 'dangerous strangers' while adding a value judgment. Vasseur (2000) explains that in this discourse with deep-rooted prejudices against the other, the reference is the personal experience, and the remarks made 'present themselves as pseudo-objective findings' (2000: 50). The participant's remarks are put forth without restraint as if acquired and familiar and tended to establish boundaries and distance as an otherization phenomenon, through the use of reductive and stigmatizing language (Holliday *et al.*, 2004). The hidden message (Sue, 2010) could be that the English trader may not be honest with young French students travelling to Great Britain. This point of view of Michèle implies something that is rigid and restricting, and I take the question of teaching to young students such ways of judging the other. If so, will the students be able to measure the gap between the identity attributions imposed by the teacher and the elements of the other's identity that will emerge from a real-life meeting?

Finally, the notion of stereotypes, if it crosses the discourse of some teachers in the different focus groups, differs according to the positionings of the teachers of the Frankfurt-am-Main group and a group from French Flanders. On the one hand, for the teachers in Frankfurt-am-Main, stereotypes are declared to be almost non-existent among pupils, and German teachers do not then offer any specific work in class on stereotypes, especially since many children have already been to France. They explain that they have observed French and German children who shared themes such as football and song stars (linguistic elements in bold in the excerpt below). The German teacher Tom exchanges with his colleagues about his perception of students' representations of other:

Tom (Frankfurt): Also ***einige Kinder waren schon in Frankreich durch den Urlaub*** *...Deswegen, also ich kann mich jetzt nicht erinnern, uns ein bisschen exp... eum deutlich zu sein:* ***Die denken nicht an Baguette, Beret...***

Daniela: Nee, die haben kein...

Tom: Und eine Gauloise und so etwas, so klassische Cliches glaub' ich sind nicht verbreitet. Eum, was die Kinder immer sagen oder erzählen sind oft solche Bereiche wie du schon genannt hast: wie, zum Beispiel, aus dem ***Bereich Fußball*** *dann kennen sie, euh wie heißt er?* ***Zinedane euh Zidane...***

Annette: Zidane ja

Tom: Ja ***Fußballspieler*** *oder sie kennen einen* ***Sänger*** *so etwas*

Daniela: Ja, genau

Tom: Und damit: das ist für sie Frankreich

(Tom: So **some children were already in France by the vacation** ... Therefore, so I cannot remember now, us a little exp... eum be clear: **They don't think about baguette, Beret...**

Daniela: No, they have no...

Tom: And a Gauloise and such a thing, I believe that so classic Cliches are not widespread. Eum, what the children always say or tell are often /such areas as, as you have already called: how, for example, from the **field of football** then they know, euh what is he called? **Zinedane euh Zidane** ...

Annette: Zidane yes

Tom: Yes **football player** or they know **a singer** something like that

Daniela: Yes, that's right.

Tom: And with that: this is France for them)

On the other hand, in a French focus group, stereotypes are said to be prominent and rooted in Franco-German history. Noiriel (2007) explains history 'carries an incalculable number of representations, impressions, memories and interpretations' (2007: 25). A French teacher stresses the association of the words Germany/German with war and gives her point of view:

Cécile (Bailleul): L'allemand c'est considéré comme ceux qui ont fait la guerre et machin bidule ... mais la guerre, la seconde enfin je crois qu'on peut pas aller plus loin dans l'horreur que ce qui a été fait dans la seconde guerre mondiale, il reste un...c'est lourd, c'est un passif

(Cécile: German is considered as those who fought the war and whatnot... but the war, the second one I think we can't go any further in the horror than what was done in the Second World War, there is still a... it's heavy, it's a liability)

Or another French teacher Michèle says she is tackling prejudices and seems to be replacing them with others: the so-called typically German consumer objects. She explains that Germany is nice for shopping: 'You can buy Haribo,' 'you can eat Brezel,' 'At McDonald's, there are high tables because the Germans have lunch standing up.' The teachers explicitly insist on teaching key sentences in class that would tend to minimize language problems in order to communicate when students are in a foreign country, especially when shopping. This approach has a pragmatic-communicative orientation, which 'leads to a tourism vision' (Byram, 1992: 87). She believes she dispels some stereotypes, but at the same time, she feeds others. Prejudices are erected against the other: here in speeches, the English in commerce are seen as a potential threat by French teachers. This reveals a certain vision of the identity of the other as a fixed category, but also of the self that arises *versus* the other. It is a posture that questions even if, according to Billig (2008: 451), 'pre-judgment does not lead on every occasion to pre-judgment'. In other words, it is possible for the teacher who expresses negative prejudices towards a particular person or group will not automatically have negative behavior in contact with the other.

The approach shows findings by variations and not in Franco-German binarity that would fix identities by a national group. Findings show that teachers are both similar to some points of discussion (interculturality is culture) and different on other points (views on children's stereotypes). Some want to enact their identity as native, as an expert or declare themselves incompetent in the language (because of French).

Implications and Conclusion

To think that these ideas are going to deconstruct and (re)construct themselves during the exchanges is to accept that the truth in itself does not exist. As we have seen, the findings show that the group identity – in this study teachers in primary school – cannot be reduced to representations the teachers have of them teaching (inter)cultural contents since social and professional practices play an important role in definition, redefinition and reproduction (De Fina, 2006: 356). This stance prevents stigmatization and allows us to see the problem in a dynamic dimension without judging the practices. The study shows, by way of the focus group, the tensions between culturalist tradition and attempts at renewed methods the teachers could produce by a reflexive posture before inventing devices to work on meeting themselves and the others. As such, the culturalist paradigm can no longer function in the teaching of languages in the light of such strong social demands. There is an erosion of articulation between the content, the references and the purpose, seen as a mismatch, which begs the question of educational content and language training for a 'renewed interculturality' at school (Dervin, 2010: 35).

Although teachers work in the same profession, people do not have a single identity correlated to that profession. Findings show that they introduce themselves to others, represent themselves by choosing from a range of possibilities: they sometimes want to be compatible with the group and feed conversations that touch on the culturalist aspects of (inter)cultural education; they sometimes want to define themselves in contrast to others: linguistic experts, native speakers, experts in school exchange routines. We can say that they choose 'within an inventory of more or less compatible identities that intersect and/or contrast with each other in different ways and in accordance with changing social circumstances and interlocutors' (De Fina, 2006: 353). The recognition of this polyphonic character of identity does not imply that the identity (co)construction is a total creation that would emerge from interactions. Indeed, it is necessary to take into account the teachers' representations, the knowledge already in place ('*les savoirs déjà-là*'), the beliefs that form their convictions and the institutional obligations of education professionals. In other words, it is interesting for intercultural training to take into account the subjection of the teacher: the latter is indeed a reflective subject in activity but also a professional subject to the obligations related to his or her teaching context. In the final, this allows us to consider a reversal of point of view when observing teaching practices, namely to question teaching practices in order to understand what is problematic rather than to judge them in terms of good or bad practices in teaching (inter)cultural content.

Notes

(1) Students are 6 to 10 years old.
(2) Students are 6 to 11 years old.
(3) Selvi (2014), among many other scholars, denounces the myth that the native is a better teacher than the nonnative which tends to become discrimination.
(4) First names are not real in order to preserve the anonymity of study participants.
(5) Discourses are presented in the speaker's language to maintain the authenticity of the content. The English translation is inserted just after, in order to make it easier to read.

References

Adelswärd, V., Linell, P. and Wibeck, W. (2004) Comprendre la complexité: les focus groups comme espaces de pensée et d'argumentation à propos des aliments génétiquement modifiés. *Bulletin de Psychologie* 57 (3), 253–261.

Aneja, G.A. (2016) (Non)native speakered: Rethinking (non)nativeness and teacher identity in TESOL teacher education. *TESOL Quarterly* 50 (3), 572–596.

Billig, M. (2008) Racisme, préjugés et discrimination. In S. Moscovici (ed.) *Psychologie Sociale* (pp. 449–471). Paris: PUF.

Bucholtz, M. and Hall, K. (2005) Identity and interaction: A sociocultural linguistic approach. *Discourses Studies* 7 (4–5), 585–614. London: Sage Publications.

Byram, M. (1992) *Culture et Education en Langue Etrangère*. Paris: Didier.

Byram, M. (2000) Mehrkulturalität, Begriffsanalyse und sprachpolitische Schlussfolgerungen. In K. Aguado and A. Hu (eds) *Mehrsprachigkeit und Mehrkulturalität*. Dokumentation des 18. Kongresses für Fremdsprachendidaktik. Dortmund, 4–6 Oktober 1999, DGFF.

De Fina, A. (2006) Group Identity, narrative and self-representations. In A. De Fina, D. Schiffrin and M. Bamberg (eds) *Discourse and Identity* (pp. 351–375). New York: Cambridge University Press.

Delamotte-Legrand, R. (1997) Langage, socialisation et constitution de la personne. In R. Delamotte, F. François and L. Porcher (eds) *Langage, Ethique, Education. Perspectives Croisées* (pp. 65–115). Rouen: Publications Université de Rouen.

Dervin, F. (2009) Les canulars de l'interculturel, mettre fin à la quasibiologisation. http://users.utu.fi/freder/quasibio_dervin_0703-3.pdf (2019/03/18)

Dervin, F. (2010) Pistes pour renouveler l'interculturel en éducation. *Recherches en Éducation* 9, 32–42.

Dervin, F. and Fracchiolla, B. (2012) *Anthropology, Interculturality and Language Learning-Teaching. How Compatible are They?* Berne: Peter Lang.

Fairclough, N. and Wodak, R. (1997) Critical discourse analysis. In T.A. Van Dijk (ed.) *Discourse Studies: A Multidisciplinary Introduction* (pp. 258–284). London: Sage.

Gee, J.P. (2015) Discourse, small-d, Big-D. In K. Tracy, C. Ilie and T. Sandel (eds) *International Encyclopedia of Language and Social Interaction* (pp. 418–422). Malden, MA: Wiley-Blackwell.

Goffman, E. (1967) *Interaction Ritual: Essays in Face-To-Face Behavior*. Chicago: Aldine Pub.

Gohier, C., Anadón, M., Bouchard, Y., Charbonneau, B. and Chevrier, C. (2001) La construction identitaire sur le plan professionnel: un processus dynamique et interactif. *Revue Des Sciences De L'éducation* 27 (1), 3–32.

Hofstede, G., Hofstede, G.-J. and Minkov, M. (2010) *Cultures and organizations. Intercultural Cooperation and its Importance for Survival*. New York: McGraw-Hill.

Holliday, A., Hyde, M. and Kullman, J. (2004) *Intercultural Communication. An Advanced Resource Book*. London: Routledge.

Holmes, P. (2006) Workplace narratives, professional identity and relational practice. In A. De Fina, D. Schiffrin and M. Bamberg (eds) *Discourse and Identity* (pp. 166–187). New York: Cambridge University Press.

Jovchelovitch, S. (2004) Contextualiser les focus groups: Comprendre les groupes et les cultures dans la recherche sur les représentations. *Bulletin de Psychologie* 57 (3), 245–252.

Kerbrat-Orecchioni, C. (1999) *L'énonciation*. Paris: Armand Colin.

Lipiansky, E.M. (1992) *Identité et Communication*. Paris: PUF.

Ministerium für Schule und Weiterbildung des Landes Nordrhein-Westfalen. Rechtlinien und Lehrpläne für die Grundschule in NRW, Lehrplan English (2015).

Ministère de d'éducation nationale (2015) Programmes à L'école Primaire. (Publication BO hors-série n°11 du 26 novembre 2015).

Müller, R. (2008) *Französisch in der Grundschule, ein interkulturelles Unterrichtsdesign*. Marburg: Tectum Verlag.

Noiriel, G. (2007) *Racisme: La Responsabilité des Elites*. Paris: Textuel.

Perrin, L. (2010) Présentation. La question polyphonique en sciences du langage. In M. Colas-Blaise, M. Kara, L. Perrin and A. Petitjean (eds) *La Question Polyphonique ou Dialogique en Sciences du Langage* (pp. 3–13). Metz: Université Paul Verlaine.

Portine, H. (2011). Le natif comme enseignant de langue: mythes et réalités. In F. Dervin and V. Badrinathan (eds) *L'enseignant Non Natif: Identités et Légitimité dans L'enseignement-apprentissage des Langues Etrangères* (pp. 51–73). Bruxelles: Proximités E.M.E.

Prairat, E. (2017) *Éduquer Avec Tact*. Paris: ESF Sciences humaines.

Rampton, B. (2003) Displacing the native speaker: Expertise, affiliation and inheritance. In R. Harris and B. Rampton (eds) *The Language, Ethnicity and Race Reader* (pp. 107–111). London: Routledge.

Rudolph, N., Yazan, B. and Rudolph, J. (2018) Negotiating 'ares,' 'cans,' and 'shoulds' of being and becoming in English language teaching: Two teacher accounts from one Japanese university. *Asian Englishes* 21 (1), 22–37.

Selvi, A.F. (2014). Myths and misconceptions about the non-native English speakers in TESOL (NNEST) Movement. *TESOL Journal* 5 (3), 573–611.

Sue, H.D. (2010) *Microaggressions in Everyday Life*. Hoboken, NJ: John Wiley and Sons.

Taylor, A. and Manes-Bonnisseau, C. (2018) *Propositions pour une meilleure maitrise des langues étrangères. Oser le monde*. Rapport ministère de l'éducation nationale.

Van Der Maren, J.M. (2010) La maquette d'un entretien. Son importance dans le bon déroulement de l'entretien et dans la collecte de données de qualité. *Recherches Qualitatives* 29 (1), 129–139.

Van Dijk, T.A. (2015) Critical discourse studies: A sociocognitive approach. In R. Wodak and M. Meyer (eds) *Methods of Critical Discourse Studies* (pp. 63–85). London: Sage Publications.

Vasseur, M.T. (2000) Apprendre à être professeur de langue dans un pays étranger. Déplacement, imaginaire et réflexivité. *Recherches et Formation* 33, 45–61.

Yazan, B. (2018) A conceptual framework to understand language teacher identities. *Journal of Second Language Teacher Education* 1 (1), 21–48.

5 English in Cuba: Reflections on a Study of Cuban Teachers' and Students' Relationships to English

Jeremy R. Gombin-Sperling and Melanie Baker Robbins

Introduction

In February 2017, we embarked on a week-long international research program to Cuba. This program represents a longstanding partnership between students, scholars and educators in the United States and the Asociación de Pedagogos de Cuba (APC; Association of Cuban Educators). The purpose of the exchange was to foster mutual learning and stronger US–Cuban relations despite the US blockade. Throughout the week, we participated in lectures, workshops and roundtables with Cuban colleagues and discussed issues in the education systems of both countries. Prior to arrival, each US-based participant designed a qualitative research project built around an aspect of the program. For our project, we explored how the English language operated in Cuba, ultimately focusing on two aspects: the relationships that Cuban English teachers and students have with the language, and the pedagogical practices inside Cuban English-language classrooms, with a specific focus on critical pedagogy. We arrived at these topics primarily due to our backgrounds as English teachers. Our experiences teaching English in the United States and other countries inspired us to understand how English teachers in different cultural and linguistic contexts approach their work. Additionally, we have observed how English has spread dramatically around the world, and how governments and private enterprises have pushed the study of English in places where it is not predominantly spoken (Ives, 2009). Having had these experiences, we wanted to use our research as a way to better understand how Cuban English teachers and students related to English and what the culture of English language teaching (ELT) in Cuba was like.

Our interest was further piqued after learning about recent policy changes to graduation requirements in Cuba. In 2015, the Cuban Ministry of Higher Education (Ministerio de Educación Superior) announced that beginning in 2016–17, students would need to demonstrate proficiency in English in order to graduate from university (Casals Pierre *et al.*, 2017). The new standards seemed to reflect the recent relaxation of US–Cuban relations, government-encouraged support for the tourism industry and an effort to enhance Cubans' abilities to engage in a globalizing world (Pinto Pajares, 2016; Sanchez & Adams, 2008). We were curious how Cuban English educators navigated these changes, their reflections on the significance of these new policies and how, if at all, it impacted their identity as educators, students and Cubans.

The historical tensions between the governments of our countries also became increasingly salient throughout our time in Cuba. The story of US–Cuban relations, especially in the post-1959 revolutionary period, has been complicated. The Cuban government has worked to demonstrate it can embrace a political and economic ideology that runs counter to the hegemonic capitalist ideologies of US institutions, despite the damage that the US blockade has caused for many Cubans (Perez, 1995). It became important for us to consider these power struggles, and to think through what it meant for us as US researchers to 'do research' in Cuba about Cuban educators, knowing that the narratives we learned of Cuba in our upbringing as White middle-class US citizens was one of deficit, of Cuba as enemy rather than ally (Franklin, 2016). How were the assumptions and lenses we brought to our study and our US identities informing how we interacted with participants, asked questions, interpreted data and formed relationships?

Upon analyzing and reflecting on our data, we realized our research questions carried many assumptions. Although we learned much from our participants about their understanding of their identity as English educators, students and Cubans, we struggled to unhinge the biases informed by our identities and background that we brought with us to Cuba. Our chapter, therefore, is about reflection. Through it, we wish to share what we have learned about our participants and ourselves, to expand on how the English-language classroom can be a space for negotiating and developing one's sense of who they are in a globalized world, and to emphasize how important it is for researchers in this field to practice a critical self-reflection on their own relationship to English.

Thinking through the History of English in Cuba

When planning our research, we reviewed the literature on current trends in English in Cuba. What we have realized in this revisit to our study is the importance of tracing the genealogy of English in Cuba – its history and development within the country. This context has allowed us to better understand and situate responses we received from our participants within the dynamics of Cuba's educational history and its present.

Although English existed on the island prior, the United States' militaristic takeover of Cuba in 1898 after the Spanish-American War was the first time English was instituted nationally (Epstein, 1987; Smith, 2012). From 1898–1902, the United States implemented a cultural and linguistic assault *vis-a-vis* the Cuban education system, introducing a US-centric history curriculum translated into Spanish, and then making the study of English mandatory (Corona & García, 1996). This occurrence was not new; Anglophone Western nations had utilized English as a tool of oppression and domination throughout their imperial projects during the 19th and 20th centuries (Canagarajah, 2006; Imam, 2005). Although there were those who due to their race, class and proximity to US elites benefitted from this regime, the weaponization of English also fostered anti-US and anti-English sentiment for many Cubans (Irizar, 2001).

One may assume that after the 1959 revolution, the Cuban government under Castro would abandon English; however, this is precisely when English education began to spread further (Smith, 2012). As Irizar Valdes and Chiappy Jhones (1991) note, the Cuban government recognized the importance of English for international communication and forged a new pedagogical system for teaching the language that was based on the values of the revolution. By the 1960s and 1970s, the government had constructed several pedagogical institutes focused on English language learning and teaching throughout the country (Corona & García, 1996). Thus, English gained a foundation within the post-1959 revolution's educational infrastructure.

English also had economic worth in the eyes of the revolutionary government, being seen as a vital skill to support the Cuban tourism industry. Pupo-Ferrás *et al.* (2012), in conducting a review of the academic discipline English for Specific Purposes (ESP; *Ingles con Fines Especificos*) in Cuba found that one of the first ESP programs was created in Matanzas for students pursuing degrees in Tourism Economics (*Economía de Turismo*); since then, English programs and centers focused on teaching English for tourism have only grown (Martin, 2007). Tourism and English took center stage after the fall of the Soviet Union in 1991. The Soviet Union had been one of Cuba's largest trade partners, and, upon its collapse, the Cuban economy sunk by 33% (Smith, 2012). During this time known as the Special Period (*El Período Especial*), the Cuban government initiated massive economic reforms and opened itself to foreign investment to boost its tourism industry (Sanchez & Adams, 2008). In order to provide a workforce that could accommodate new waves of tourists, the Castro administration established the National Tourism Institute and trained over 300 English teachers (Martin, 2007). English learning became a foundational skill associated with the revival of the Cuban economy.

It must be noted that the post-1959 Cuban government worked with the resources available to persevere and recreate themselves; at the same time, this utilization of tourism also speaks to historical exploitation of Global South countries like Cuba. When looking at tourism, much can be attributed to corporate forces in the Global North utilizing a neoliberal narrative to convince governments and civil society in the Global South that tourism is a viable investment that will bring greater wealth, reduce inequality and improve economic outcomes (Brown & Hall, 2008; Christian, 2013). Sanchez and Adams (2008), in a study of Cuban tourism, found evidence of these dynamics, where capitalist enterprises with government support had carved out tourist enclaves to boost economic growth throughout the island during the 1990s and 2000s. Although some Cubans benefited economically from these changes, most did not. Tourism was unequally distributed, favoring coastal areas, and offering employment mostly to light-skinned and White Cubans over Black Cubans (Sanchez & Adams, 2008). This is what led the researchers to argue that tourism was 'an uneasy yet frequently resourceful fusion' (Sanchez & Adams, 2008: 29).

Tourism and its relationship to English also point to the neoliberal domination of English education prevalent throughout the second half of the 20th century (Hyslop-Margison & Sears, 2006). Transnational bodies and corporations from Global North, predominantly White, English-speaking nations, have supported a narrative that identifies English language proficiency as needed for economic participation (Ricento, 2015; Rossi, 2007). As a result, many governments in non-predominantly English-speaking countries have pressured their education systems to ensure students learn the language (Shin, 2016; Vavrus, 2002). Mastering English, according to Park (2010), therefore, creates individuals who become 'the linguistic version of the neoliberal subject' (2010: 23), in that they have gained the language needed to participate in dominant economic and political discourses. In a country like Cuba where the education system is free and open to all citizens, it is important to consider that there may still be Cuban nationals and non-Cubans living on the island who encounter barriers to accessing English language education, and therefore, the privileges and opportunities that could come with it (Pennycook, 1994). Considering these histories of English in Cuba – from its initial iteration as colonial oppression, to the Castro administration's re-appropriation of the teaching and learning of the language, and now in this neoliberal globalized period – has helped us understand the relationships and perspectives of the Cuban English teachers and students that participated in our study with greater depth.

This level of nuance is expressed in other studies that have explored the relationships of Cuban English teachers and students with English and how it informed their identity. Pinto Pajares (2016) conducted a qualitative study in Havana looking at Cuban youth's ideas towards English and found that participants believed learning the language provided multiple benefits. While they acknowledged English's 'economic value,' they valued English more as a tool for intercultural engagement, one that could allow them to connect with people and cultures worldwide (Pinto Pajares, 2016). In Smith's (2012) research on Cuban English teacher identity, he found that his participants had a multifaceted relationship with English. They appreciated how it provided students access to different cultures and media, and some saw it as an essential skill for forging bonds with other Global South nations through Cuba's justice-based aid program. Simultaneously, they rejected certain cultural values embedded in English that they felt went against these values of community and solidarity. While the economics of English was understood, teachers and students valued other things more highly. As we reflected on our study, it was critical to consider all these dynamics and to examine our own assumptions of how we expected our participants to speak about their relationship to English, while also making space to think through these historical tensions of English in Cuba. From this standpoint, we continued to think through how Cuban English teachers' and students' identities were informed by their relationships to English, their relationships to Cuba, and the intersections within.

Critical Pedagogy in English Language Teaching

When we first considered what ELT might look like in Cuba, we mostly thought about it through a relationship to neoliberal globalization. Given recent Cuban history, we wondered to what extent Cuban English teachers employed practices that intended to question and resist the neoliberal impulse of English in their classrooms, and how critical perspectives informed how Cuban teachers and students constructed their identities. We were particularly interested in critical pedagogy, as it has frequently been used by educators seeking to bring conversations on structural issues into the classroom. Given the global and neoliberal power dynamics associated with the proliferation of the English language, the emphasis on social equality in Cuba, and the history of tense relations between Cuba and the US, we thought it likely that critical pedagogy would be present. At the same time, as Americans, we were unsure if a pedagogy encouraging critiques of power relations would be encouraged, considering the lessons we had been taught, suggesting the Cuban government's desire to control the opinion and potential dissent of the Cuban public.

Freire's (2000) work on critical pedagogy informed our understanding of its application to ELT. From his perspective, education is an inherently political act that is never neutral (Freire, 2000); when this lack of neutrality is not acknowledged, education can actually 'surreptitiously legitimize and reproduce the politics of the dominant classes, perpetuating social inequalities' (Cox & de Assis-Peterson, 1999: 435). Critical pedagogy argues for an education that acknowledges and reveals social inequalities and seeks to empower students to make positive changes in their lives, communities and societies (Freire, 2000; Shor, 1993). It asks students to critically consider the contents of their curriculum and interrogate what is known as the 'hidden curriculum,' i.e. the assumptions and dominant narratives embedded in the material that is taught and how it is taught (Jay, 2003). Critical pedagogy promotes a classroom that is student-centered, participatory, democratic, dialogic, multicultural and affective. The teacher is not seen as the possessor of knowledge or as a domineering authority but is instead a facilitator who encourages classroom discourse that is co-constructed by students and teachers (Shor, 1993). Such practices challenge hegemonic teacher-student formations by interrupting these power relations.

The literature we found on critical pedagogy in ELT classrooms suggested that it was less developed, but that there was potential for its incorporation to study language in order to promote equity and justice (Crookes, 2013). One study investigated critical pedagogy in English language teaching in Brazil. In this study, Cox and de Assis-Peterson (1999) interviewed 40 Brazilian English teachers to understand 'what English teachers know about and think of critical pedagogy' (1999: 439). Interestingly, they found that teachers were unfamiliar with critical pedagogy and tended to hold the dominant view of ELT as an unproblematic practice. Another study in Iran examined the impact of integrating critical pedagogy into pre-service EFL teacher education programs on teachers' identity construction. In this study, Sardabi *et al.* (2018) found that integrating critical perspectives into the program helped teachers expand from having a more 'compliant' and 'narrow' view of ELT to having a more complex view. As a result, they recommended teacher education programs incorporate more critical, dialogic and reflexive components into their programs.

Entering our study, we assumed that finding elements of critical pedagogy in Cuban ELT spaces would indicate that Cuban teachers and students were approaching English with a critical lens; if we did not find evidence, we would assume this meant that there was a space to fill with new teaching practices. What we now realize is how this mentality reflected a neocolonial approach to research that reified a power dynamic in which we as White researchers from the Global North implied that we knew better than our participants what was best for their teaching (Sriprakash & Mukhopadhyay, 2015). As Tikly and Bond (2013) note, in order to decenter comparative educational research away from reproducing inequality, we as researchers must interrogate the power differentials embedded in our process: 'Who defines the research questions and in whose interests? What are the theoretical and methodological assumptions guiding the research? Who benefits from the research findings' (Tikly & Bond, 2013: 437)?

By not self-interrogating, we run the risk of ignoring the histories of knowledge and practices within the community we claim to wish to know, which in the case of Cuban education is a deep history (Sobe, 2017; Turner Martí & Pita Céspedes, 2001). The education system was and continues to be a critical priority of the post-revolutionary Cuban government. Cuban educators are trained to be not only practitioners but also researchers, meaning that there is a plethora of work on pedagogy and its impact within Cuban scholarship (Smith, 2012). This is not to say that we could not still explore how critical pedagogy manifests in the Cuban ELT classroom; however, we also needed to ask more about the pedagogical frameworks and histories that informed our participants' relationships to English education and their identities as teachers and students. Our return to our research in this chapter is an effort to better represent the fullness of what our participants shared with us, knowing that our lenses and positionalities always interact with how we interpret and tell stories (Pillow, 2003). We, therefore, intend in this chapter to more accurately depict the values, goals and pedagogical philosophies that we believe emerged from our participants' responses.

The Study

Methodology

For this study, we employed a variety of resources and techniques within the context of our exchange program with the *Asociación de Pedagogos de Cuba* (APC, Association of Cuban Educators). We spent approximately seven days in Cuba for the study, beginning and ending our program in Havana, while spending the majority of the time in Holguín, a city in eastern Cuba. It was the first time that either of us had visited the country. In Holguín, we participated in an educational symposium at a local higher education institution. The purpose of the symposium was to build solidarity and mutual understanding of educational issues between Cuban and US participants vis-a-vis a series of formal presentations given by educators, panel presentations and roundtable discussions. One example of a panel was 'Contemporary Education in Cuba and the United States: Challenges and Perspectives for the Future.' Roundtables had themes such as 'Internationalization and Higher Education,' 'School–Family–Community,' 'Transformations in Teacher Training,' and 'Education for Coexistence and a Culture of Peace.' Finally, site visits were made to different educational institutions, including a primary school, a special education school, a teacher training institute and a research center.

Because of the time spent there, this symposium in Holguín became our primary site for data collection.

We collected our data through semi-structured interviews with Cuban English language students and teachers who we recruited at the symposium. These participants joined the symposium by either applying to the APC, being invited by the APC due to expertise in relevant research, or, in the case of two of our participants, serving as translators throughout the event. Criteria for participation in our study included being above the age of 18, being current or past ELT students, teachers, or administrators in Cuba, and giving written consent to participate in the study. The three people we interviewed (see Table 5.1) were those with whom we had worked the most during our time in Holguín. We felt that we had established rapport with these colleagues and that there was sufficient trust to request an interview within the limited timeframe of our program.

We conducted interviews once with each participant; two of the interviews were conducted in English, while the third was conducted in Spanish. One of the researchers translated this interview. We audio-recorded the two interviews done in English and took written notes for the third. Each interview lasted between 30–45 minutes. Our questions asked about formative experiences with the English language, motivations for studying and/or teaching English, participants' reflections on their classroom experiences, and what they learned from their academic studies. Sample interview questions include: (1) Describe the first time you experienced English. (2) What messages do you remember receiving about the English language from parents, teachers, or friends? (3) How, if at all, have students' motivations for learning English changed over time? (4) To what extent and in what ways are topics discussed in English classes connected to the lives of students? (5) How, if at all, has your experience with English affected how you see your identity as a Cuban national and your relationship to the rest of the world?

Originally we utilized deductive and inductive coding methods to develop our themes. Saldaña's (2015) concept of in vivo coding informed our process. In vivo coding places heightened importance on the words and phrases spoken by interviewees, and is often a first step towards building larger themes from the data. For the deductive process, we looked for words and phrases that came from our research questions, such as

Table 5.1 Demographics of study participants

Name (pseudonyms)	Profession	Location	Age	Language of Interview	Recorded or Written?
Daniela	English Teacher	Holguín	22	English	Recorded
Isa	English Student	Holguín	19	English	Recorded
Emmanuel	English Teacher	Havana	56	Spanish	Written

'pedagogy,' 'relationship' and 'values,' and characteristics associated with critical pedagogy. The inductive method was more open; we noted and compared it when participants' responses contained similar language and analyzed them together to build conceptual themes.

In revisiting our data, we realized how our deductive codes had limited our interpretations by imposing what we wanted the data to say, rather than letting it speak for itself. Through conversation with one another and the editors of this text, we identified new themes from this process: 'developing a relationship and history with English,' 'the multi-layered values of English,' 'the construction of community in Cuban ELT classroom practices,' and 'the evolving dynamics of English and identity in Cuba.'

Researcher positionality and relationship to findings

In discussing our positionality in this chapter, we want to talk about accountability – to recognize who we are, and our role in perpetuating and/or interrupting dominant narratives of places and people. We felt we understood this role and entered Cuba with 'good intentions' of wanting to strengthen US–Cuban relations within our locus of control. We knew in the context of international ELT research, we as White, L1 English-speaking US citizens and doctoral students inhabit identities most associated with power – the voices that are often heard the loudest and questioned the least (Ruecker, 2011). Despite this, we brought our own conceptualizations around English and ELT pedagogy into our research without questioning our assumptions. What we see now is how ingrained our senses of knowing were; we conducted our research, made our conclusions, and did not see a need to go back and critically reflect on the narrative we constructed. Our first writings essentialized aspects of Cubanness and, through our focus on critical pedagogy, we often painted Cuban teaching via a deficit lens, i.e. by what it lacked vis-à-vis our understanding of critical pedagogy.

In retrospect, we see the act of not revisiting our data as a reflection of our social power and privilege – the ability to use our good intentions to absolve any need for critical conversations on the impact of our work. In no way do we consider our current writing or method perfect; however, we do believe that we have made significant strides to move away from what Motha (2014) would call reproducing empire in ELT, i.e. reifying a power relation that depicts us, White Western persons, as knowing more about our participants of the non-West (read often as Global South, developing world, non-White spaces) than they know about themselves. Our discussion on positionality is, therefore, a reminder to us and other US researchers who share a similar positionality to continue the work of decentering our ways of knowing and being and to critically question what we bring with us into research.

Our Findings and Reflections

Developing a history and relationship with English

The origins of our participants' relationships with the English language varied depending on their individual circumstances. Isa encountered the language in primary school as one of her subjects when she was eight. It was then that she began to gain interest in further study. Daniela and Emmanuel had more intimate beginnings with the language. Daniela first experienced English through her parents, who were both English teachers themselves. Her parents played music in English by groups such as The Beatles and Queen, showed movies and communicated with her in the language – not so that she would be forced to learn, but rather so that she had exposure and familiarity.

In asking Daniela more about how her parents came to be English teachers, we found interesting commonalities between them and Emmanuel. For Daniela's parents, the music she grew up with was a key factor in her father's interest in English. He was a guitar player and learned the instrument during a period when English-singing bands were very famous: 'When they went to parties, they wanted to sing songs in English that were popular, so he started learning English individually, and then he became a teacher because he really loved it.' According to Daniela, her mother also followed this path. When we interviewed Emmanuel, who is close in age to Daniela's parents, he reported an analogous story of growing up in a time when English media was popular in the country. Learning English allowed him to connect with other Cubans who had similar interests.

In addition to the social aspect, the Cuban government during the 1970s made a call for more English teachers. A large proportion of those who left Cuba either voluntarily or involuntarily during or after the revolution had made up the majority of English speakers in the country, meaning the Castro government needed to educate a new generation of ELT practitioners (Corona & García, 1996; Smith, 2012). In this period, the government offered an expedited English certification program. As Daniela recalls, 'the country made a call for teachers…because we needed more teachers of English, and they all of a sudden (snaps) decided to go.' Emmanuel also became an educator during this critical period.

Although this may seem like English teaching was an imposition, our participants saw this as an opportunity to support their country while also developing a profession. When discussing her motivations for studying English, Daniela shared:

> From my parents, they didn't tell me, 'You have to study English,' no. But… it would be like 'It's really important for you, whether you decide to make it your own major, it is important that you learn how to speak another language apart from our mother tongue because it would help you in the future to communicate with others, not only in Cuba, to learn

> from others' experiences, and to know more about the world in general, and that would be the key to communicate, so it would be great if you learn.'

We note here how much of a relational aspect was inherent in participants' connection to English. The desire and foundations for learning English were built around how it supported significant relationships in their lives – whether to family or Cuba as a nation-state. This is not to say that participants did not also find personal fulfillment, but rather to recognize that part of building a relationship with English was this deep consideration of the community.

The multilayered values of English

We also see this relational aspect of how participants discussed the value of English. All participants expressed that English was a powerful tool for intercultural engagement and community building. When Isa was asked about how learning English has impacted her, she responded,

> When we learn a different language, we learn the cultures of those countries speaking that language...I learn what is going on in the rest of the world, what good things my country has, what things are not so good, what things I would like to change.

For Emmanuel, learning English has become a symbol of international collaboration and solidarity. Since 2000, he has been part of a series of diplomatic projects to support English language learning in Haiti, Venezuela, Nicaragua, Bolivia and other countries in the region. He saw his work as an opportunity to use his language abilities as a way to strengthen his relationship with other Latin American and Caribbean communities. This perspective reflects the social justice approach to aid that has been harnessed in the rhetoric and practice of the post-revolutionary government, what Hickling-Hudson *et al.* (2012) identify as a form of Cuban solidarity in education. We can also see this value of community in how Daniela spoke about English and the United States:

> I know English will help me and it is helping me a lot as a professional to know more – to know more about the realities of everything. Because...we have some ideas, for example, our relationship between the United States and Cuba, so now I can speak English and know what you think, what you do...and it helps me see the reality from my point of view for myself.

Our interviewees did address the economic attributes of English and named how people were attracted to the language in order to find work in the tourism industry; however, this aspect of English was not central to their responses. Community building and intercultural engagement are what they primarily discussed, and it is where we felt the most enthusiasm.

The construction of community in Cuban ELT classroom practices

In returning to our research without a narrow focus on critical pedagogy, we better identified the importance of community in the classroom and how this contributes to our participants' identities not only as English language teachers and learners but also as Cubans. Building community in the classroom helped mitigate power differentials that often characterize the teacher–student binary. Participants emphasized teachers as co-learners and depicted a warm relationship between teachers and students. As Isa explained, the relationship between students and teachers 'could be described as warm because, not only English teachers, all teachers, try to make this very close interaction with the students.' Daniela elaborated, adding,

> In my case, I don't like it to be... a wall between students and teachers... I like us to be combined... The teacher must not be just this presence that you have to respect; no, it can be someone that will help you in any case, and that's what we try to do... I'm learning from you, as well as you're learning from me.

Daniela's assertion that she does not want there to be a 'wall' between students and teachers illustrated a concern with forming relationships with students and with fostering trust. Additionally, Daniela's emphasis that she learns from her students as they learn from her further demonstrated a valuing of students as active possessors and sharers of knowledge.

Isa and Daniela also depicted English classes in Cuba as generally dialogic, cooperative, and participatory in terms of teaching methods used and students' roles in the selection of course materials. For example, although Isa described the classroom as teacher-centered, she also indicated some complexities in the dynamics, sharing with us that teachers make room for students to share their ideas and challenge them to think more deeply about their perspectives. Her example reflects a classroom that encourages students to express their ideas and allows room for contradictory opinions and debates.

Similarly, Daniela emphasized how, even in her written translation courses, she seeks to promote dialogue and collaboration during class sessions. She explained,

> If you enter my classroom when I'm teaching, you can't tell whether I'm the teacher at some points because we're all talking... we are all working together... When I bring a text to the classroom, we have several activities to extract some information from the text in general... we'll try to give first a general idea about what the text is about; and we do that together because they give me ideas and I'm like, okay, that's okay, but let's listen to others, so we are talking, all of us... So just like that, we are working together.

Here, Daniela's repeated use of the plural pronouns 'we' and 'us' (rather than sole usage of singular 'I,' 'me,' and 'my') reveals her emphasis on collaboration, indicating how she views herself not as a powerful authority in a position above her students, but rather as part of a greater collective educational body.

Daniela also explained that she teaches a university-level English/Spanish translation course, and that policy required her to include texts pertaining to specific topics (e.g. medicine, science and technology); however, she is free to select which texts are used to explore those topics. With this in mind, Daniela tries to learn students' interests at the beginning of the term so that she can find texts related to those interests. This, in effect, gives students a degree of decision-making power and reflects the teacher's interest in incorporating topics that are relevant and interesting to students. Isa complemented Daniela's remarks noting how as a student, she often had the opportunity to choose topics for her English assignments that resonated with her interests and goals, giving her a sense that her teachers trusted her.

The evolving dynamics of English and identity in Cuba

When it came to discussing how English was changing in Cuba, participants pointed to the recent policy reforms. Isa noted that when she first learned English, there was less pressure; rather, students and teachers treated it as just 'another subject.' As she informed us, 'sometimes we students would take this in not a serious way… it was like "ok, I am going to take this test and if I get a low or a good grade, that's good for me."' This, however, had changed greatly in the year leading up to our study, not only because of the policy change but also because 'of the new relation with the United States.' From her perspective,

> Here in Cuba, every day those who can speak English or those who can teach others how to speak English are taken more and more importance. And all the people are considering the possibility of learning English. It was not like before that just those people study a foreign language because they like it…now most people consider this as a need.

Emmanuel also commented on this in his discussion of the five pillars of learning English. This framework was originally composed of four pillars that included reading, writing, speaking, listening, and now has a fifth one entitled interaction. Interaction, according to Emmanuel, 'is a symbol of the changes in Cuba…students are now being trained more actively on how to interact with people from different cultures.' He identified these skills as a needed part of Cuba's continued development. The institutionalization of 'interaction' in ELT could be seen as contributing to what Isa had observed – the new meanings Cubans were attributing to English. Through Emmanuel and Isa, we began to see how the Cuban government, in reaction to globalization and changing relationships with the United States, were reimagining the symbolic role and practical application of English.

When asked if they had concerns about the influence of English, Daniela addressed this concept with what she labeled 'the line.' She wanted her students to be exposed to new cultural perspectives through language study and for them to develop their own relationship with English. Daniela, however, had developed a clear and personal understanding of her own boundaries:

> I have this line that I love my country – even though I don't like to talk about politics – we all know that we have some troubles...but, we, many people – most of us – love our country as a general culture, traditions, so we have a difference. And that's it. There's the line.

Daniela exhibited her agency by constructing borders around the values of English that allowed her to show pride and love of her English teaching without compromising her identity as a Cuban national. One could see this as an act of resistance, of realizing the power and agency she had to ensure her English teaching reflected her Cubanness. What these reactions and responses allude to is how our participants were adapting to the evolutions of English's place in Cuba, while also developing parameters that preserved the values that most defined their identities as Cuban teachers, students and citizens.

Discussions, Limitations and Final Reflections

Our reengagement with our study has allowed a deeper understanding of the topics we explored and the people we had the privilege of knowing in Cuba. Our participants' relationships and values of English were revealed to be historical, multifaceted, and evolving – shifting with the changing position of English in Cuban education and society. When we first evaluated our data, we noted the collective nature reflected in the ways Cuban educators spoke about the value of English, as well as in how they experienced the Cuban English classroom. It is not that our participants did not express appreciation for how they benefited individually from learning and teaching English, but rather that the primary emphasis was on how these skills supported a community – within and outside the Cuban education system.

Our original focus on critical pedagogy hindered our ability to recognize how deep these concepts and values of the community were embedded in participants' reflections on their teaching practices. We saw things like the use of 'we' and the desire to dismantle barriers between teachers and students as snippets of critical pedagogy, rather than questioning if these expressed values were a reflection of a pedagogical framework indigenous to or founded within the Cuban context. After returning from our program, we were introduced to the 'pedagogy of tenderness' ('*la pedagogía de la ternura*'), a teaching practice credited most notably to Afro-Cuban educator Lidia Turner Martí (see Turner Martí & Pita

Céspedes, 2001). Smith (2016: 102) provides a brief but helpful description of this practice:

> The pedagogy of tenderness arose from the educational philosophy implemented in 1961 during the Cuban National Literacy Campaign, and the subsequent Cuban 'Yo, Si Puedo' and 'Yes, I Can' adult literacy programs in many countries. Taken up and developed further in Freire's *Pedagogy of the Oppressed* (Freire, 2000), it considers that significant learning requires significant relationships and emphasizes the role of the family and community in each student's education. Teachers are expected to know each student, 'their needs, and the material and social conditions of their home lives' and work with them as partners' (Lutjens, 2007: 185).

In retrospect, the pedagogy of tenderness would have been a supportive lens to approach Cuban English teachers' and students' sense of identity through because of its historical relationship and grounding in the Cuban education system (Schultz *et al.*, 2011). The pedagogy of tenderness demonstrates the value placed on collaboration and collectivism in Cuban education (and society) and stands in stark contrast to Western neoliberal values such as competition and individualism, which are often perpetuated through our education structures (Smith, 2016).

This is what makes Daniela's concept and discussion of the 'line' so powerful. Seen through the pedagogy of tenderness, the line delineates the pedagogical and personal values that either contradict or struggle to coalesce with some of the neoliberal baggage embedded in ELT. This is not to suggest a binary of pedagogy of tenderness against. neoliberal capitalism, but rather to recognize the prominent belief among our participants of education's power and purpose to build empathy, trust and community. This stands in contrast to many of our experiences in the United States, where education is becoming a primarily corporate and marketable commodity (Saunders & Blanco Ramirez, 2017).

While we learned much from our participants and experience, we recognize the limitations of our study and lack of generalizability across Cuba. Our study would have benefitted from more time in-country, interviews with a wider array of teachers and students, time to review classroom materials, and, if possible, conduct classroom observations. ur trip was also in the context of an official conference, co-organized by Cuban and American educators, and where representatives of the Cuban government were present. It is possible that our conversations with our Cuban colleagues may have been different in another context or venue. We highlight this because our participants did not provide much critique about social issues or issues with the government, outside of Daniela's brief mention of 'some troubles' in Cuba. We do not believe that participants sought to hide information; instead, we recognize the precarious dynamics and the possible risk involved in sharing criticisms of Cuba with representatives of the United States, considering the imperial history and neocolonial damage our government continues to cause with the ongoing blockade.

What we can say about our research and our subsequent process of critical reflection is that it has informed our thinking on the need to understand identity as an ongoing sociocultural process embedded in relations of power and resistance. Our inability to recognize the impact of our own identity in relation to Cuba limited our capacity to see our participants, hear their stories, and do more to understand the context of where we were conducting research. Through our participants, we now visualize the English language classroom as a site of identity negotiation, construction and resistance, framed within the interplay of governmental policy, pedagogical agency, neoliberal globalization and the histories of English's various roles and social positions within a place. It is with this understanding that we see the English language classroom, or the language classroom in general, as a site of contestation where assumptions about the values and relationships we and others have to language can be challenged and reassessed.

References

Brown, F. and Hall, D. (2008) Tourism and development in the global south: The issues. *Third World Quarterly* 29 (5), 839–849.

Canagarajah, A. (2006) TESOL at forty: What are the issues? *TESOL Quarterly* 40 (1), 9–34.

Casals Pierre, F., Houelly Pérez, E., Rey Rivas, P. and Tardo Fernández, Y. (2017) Experiencias y resultados preliminares sobre la nueva estrategia de idioma inglés para la educación superior en la universidad de oriente. *Medisan* 21 (9), 2068–2075.

Christian, M. (2013) '... Latin America without the downside': Racial exceptionalism and global tourism in Costa Rica. *Ethnic and Racial Studies* 36 (10), 1599–1618.

Cox, M.I.P. and de Assis-Peterson, A.A. (1999) Critical pedagogy in ELT: Images of Brazilian teachers of English. *TESOL Quarterly* 33 (3), 433–51.

Corona, D. and García, O. (1996) English in Cuba: From imperialist design to imperative need. In J.A. Fishman, A. Conrad and A. Rubal-Lopez (eds) *Post-Imperial English: Status Change in Former British and American Colonies*. Berlin: Mouton de Gruyter.

Crookes, G. (2013) Critical pedagogy in language teaching. In C.A. Chapelle (ed.) *The Encyclopedia of Applied Linguistics* (pp. 1–4). Oxford: Blackwell/Wiley.

Epstein, E. (1987) The peril of paternalism: The imposition of education on Cuba by the United States. *American Journal of Education* 96 (1), 1–23.

Franklin, J. (2016) *Cuba and the U.S. Empire: A Chronological History*. New York: Monthly Review Press.

Freire, P. (2000) *Pedagogy of the Oppressed* (30th anniversary edn). New York: Continuum.

Hickling-Hudson, A., Gonzalez, J. and Preston, R. (2012) *The Capacity to Share: A Study of Cuba's International Cooperation in Educational Development*. New York: Palgrave Macmillan.

Hyslop-Margison, E. and Sears, A. (2006) *Neo-Liberalism, Globalization and Human Capital Learning: Reclaiming Education for Democratic Citizenship*. Dordrecht: Springer.

Imam, S. (2005) English as a global language and the question of nation-building education in Bangladesh. *Comparative Education* 41 (4), 471–486.

Irizar, T. (2001) English language education in Cuba. *ESL Magazine*, 4 (1), 26–28.

Irizar Valdes, A. and Chiappy Jhones, A. (1991) Introduction of communicative language teaching in tourism in Cuba. *TESL Canada Journal* 8 (2), 57–63.

Ives, P. (2009) Global English, hegemony and education: Lessons from Gramsci. *Educational Philosophy and Theory* 41 (6), 661–683.

Jay, M. (2003) Critical race theory, multicultural education, and the hidden curriculum of hegemony. *Multicultural Perspectives* 5 (4), 3–9.

Lutjens, S. (2007) (Re)Reading Cuban educational policy: Schooling and the third revolution. In I. Epstein (ed.) *Recapturing the Personal: Essays on Education and Embodied Knowledge in Comparative Perspective* (pp. 163–194). Charlotte, NC: Information Age Publishing.

Martin, I. (2007) Some remarks on post-1990 English language teaching policy in Cuba. *TESOL Quarterly* 41 (3), 551–557.

Motha, S. (2014). *Race, Empire, and English Language Teaching: Creating Responsible and Ethical Anti-Racist Practice.* New York: Teachers College Press.

Park, J. (2010) Naturalization of competence and the neoliberal subject: Success stories of English language learning in the Korean conservative press. *Journal of Linguistic Anthropology* 20 (1), 22–38.

Pennycook, A. (1994) *The Cultural Politics of English as an International Language.* London: Longman.

Perez, L. (1995) The imperial design: Politics and pedagogy in occupied Cuba, 1899–1902. In L. Perez (ed.) *Essays on Cuban History: Historiography and Research* (pp. 35–52). Gainesville, FL: University Press of Florida.

Pillow, W. (2003) Confession, catharsis, or cure? Rethinking the uses of reflexivity as methodological power in qualitative research. *International Journal of Qualitative Studies in Education* 16 (2), 175–196.

Pinto Pajares, D. (2016) Ideologías y actitudes lingüísticas de la juventud cubana hacia el inglés. *En Diálogo de la Lengua* VIII, 97–117.

Pupo-Ferrás, S., Faedo-Borges, A. and Ortigoza-Garcell, C. (2012) Tendencias curriculares del inglés con fines específicos: Surgimiento y evolución para el turismo en Cuba *Ciencias. Holguín* 18 (2), 1–11.

Ricento, T. (ed.) (2015) *Language Policy and Political Economy: English in a Global Context.* Oxford: Oxford University Press.

Rossi, I. (2007) *Frontiers of Globalization Research: Theoretical and Methodological Approaches.* New York: Springer Science Business Media.

Ruecker, T. (2011) Challenging the native and nonnative English speaker hierarchy in ELT: New directions from race theory. *Critical Inquiry in Language Studies* 8 (4), 400–422.

Saldaña, J. (2015) *The Coding Manual for Qualitative Researchers* (3rd edn). Thousand Oaks: Sage Publications.

Sanchez, P.M. and Adams, K.M. (2008) The Janus-faced character of tourism in Cuba. *Annals of Tourism Research* 35 (1), 27–46.

Sardabi, N., Biria, R. and Golestan, A. (2018) Reshaping teacher professional identity through critical pedagogy-informed teacher education. *International Journal of Instruction* 11 (3), 617–634.

Saunders, D.B. and Blanco Ramírez, G. (2017) Against 'teaching excellence': Ideology, commodification, and enabling the neoliberalization of postsecondary education. *Teaching in Higher Education* 22 (4), 396–407.

Schultz, L., Tiner, K., Sewell, D. and Hirata, L. (2011) Towards a pedagogy of tenderness: Reflections on Cuban education. *International Journal of Humanities and Social Science* 1 (10), 55–58.

Shin, H. (2016) Language 'skills' and the neoliberal English education industry. *Journal of Multilingual and Multicultural Development* 37 (5), 509–52.

Shor, I. (1993) Education is Politics: Paulo Freire's critical pedagogy. In P. McLaren and P. Leonard (eds) *Paulo Freire: A Critical Encounter* (pp. 25–35). London: Routledge.

Smith, S. (2012) English Language Teacher Education in Cuba: Context, Pedagogy and Identity. Queensland University of Technology, Brisbane.

Smith, S. (2016) Cuban voices: A case study of English language teacher education. *International Education Journal: Comparative Perspectives* 15 (4), 100–111.

Sobe, N.W. (2017) Travelling researchers, colonial difference: Comparative education in an age of exploration. *Compare: A Journal of Comparative and International Education* 47 (3), 332–343.

Sriprakash, A. and Mukhopadhyay, R. (2015) Reflexivity and the politics of knowledge: Researchers as 'brokers' and 'translators' of educational development. *Comparative Education* 51 (2), 231–246.

Tikly, L. and Bond, T. (2013) Towards a postcolonial research ethics in comparative and international education. *Compare: A Journal of Comparative and International Education* 43 (4), 422–442.

Turner Martí, L. and Pita Céspedes, B. (2001) *A Pedagogy of Tenderness*. Caracas, Venezuela: Asociacion de Educadores de Latinoamérica y el Caribe.

Vavrus, F. (2002) Postcoloniality and English: Exploring language policy and the politics of development in Tanzania. *TESOL Quarterly* 36 (3), 373–97.

Part 2

Teacher Identity as/in/ Beyond Practice

6 From Being a Language Teacher to Becoming a Graduate Student-Teacher: In the Midst of Professional Identities

Şeyma Toker

Introduction

A growing line of research on second language (L2) teacher identity has examined identity construction of pre-service and novice teachers in their developmental process during their graduate studies, typically at MA Teaching English to the Speakers of Other Languages (TESOL) programs in North American contexts. In these contexts, the population of so-called 'non-native' English-speaking teachers ('NNESTs') has drawn the most attention. A large body of studies on L2 teacher identity has engaged in understanding the experiences of being an 'NNEST' and attempted to empower 'NNESTs' as legitimate teachers as they construct their professional teacher identities (Golombek & Jordan, 2005; Park, 2012).

One common trajectory of L2 teacher identity development mapped out in these studies is the transformation of 'NNESTs' from language learner/student identity to legitimate language teacher identity (Johnson, 2001; Reis, 2012; Samimy *et al.*, 2011). There is, however, an underrepresented group of graduate students (regardless of their 'nativeness') in MA and PhD programs in education, TESOL and applied linguistics (AL) who come with some teaching experience and already identify themselves as professional language teachers. Contrary to the expanding understanding of novice L2 teachers' construction of emerging teacher identities, identity re-negotiations of more experienced L2 teachers during graduate study have not been much researched.

Literature Review

Research on identity negotiations and academic socialization of graduate students in AL is surprisingly limited (Cho, 2013; Donato *et al.*, 2015; Herath & Valencia, 2015; Ortaçtepe, 2015) despite the large number of graduate students in this field who typically come from teaching professions or assigned teaching positions during their study. In an auto-ethnographic study, Herath and Valencia (2015), doctoral students working in tertiary institutions for a decade, discussed how they negotiated their multiple and shifting identities as teacher-researchers. They found that they enacted diverse identity positions in relation to micro and macro level sociopolitical contexts of their communities. In addition, Donato *et al.* (2015) analyzed the professional identity trajectories of ten female AL scholars after their doctorate. They concluded that the apprenticeship model enabled students to transform their professional identities in their professions; however, they also faced certain challenges in their new institutions. Some participants, for instance, reported a lack of alignment between their research goals and those of the new community of practice, which created struggles for maintaining their professional identities. Similar issues regarding the institutional acknowledgment of professional identities of newcomers in academic communities were also echoed in Cho's (2013) study on the disciplinary enculturation processes of three Korean students in MA TESOL programs. Cho (2013) found that one 'NNEST' graduate student who was an experienced English as a foreign language (EFL) teacher in Korea resisted taking ownership of his graduate TESOL community since he believed that the master's program focused heavily on teaching English as a Second Language (ESL) rather than EFL, which was central to his professional identity in Korea. Non-recognition of his EFL teacher identity within the larger curriculum contributed to his isolation from the graduate community, hindering his disciplinary enculturation in the US.

Adopting a language socialization perspective, Ortaçtepe (2015) further explored the experiences of AL graduate students with prior teaching experience in graduate programs in the US. In a narrative inquiry with two experienced EFL teachers from Turkey, she examined the relationship between studentship and professional teacher identities in professional identity construction of emerging applied linguists. The findings revealed that participant's identities as (1) an experienced EFL teacher, (2) an L2 user and (3) a burgeoning scholar were compatible with each other, facilitating their academic socialization. Highlighting the significance of understanding the identities of L2 teachers in academia, Ortaçtepe (2015) calls for expanding the research in this field to more experienced L2 teachers. This study addresses such a gap in the literature by examining the professional identity negotiations of Zeynep across multiple professional communities over her four-and-a-half-year career.

It maps out the complexity of her professional identity trajectories drawing on and expanding the Communities of Practice (CoP) framework (Wenger, 1998).

Theoretical Framework

Conceptualizing 'non-nativeness' and professional teacher identity

The view of identity and 'non-nativeness' adopted in this study is situated within the critically oriented, poststructuralist paradigm (Aneja, 2016; Rudolph *et al.*, 2015) to researching L2 teacher identity. As Norton (2013) defines, identity construction is one's attempt to understand their 'relationship to the world, how that relationship is structured across time and space, and how the person understands possibilities for the future' (2013: 45). Moreover, identity is multiple, shifting and contradictory across time and space. Likewise, in the current study, teacher identity is conceptualized as one's making sense of self in relation to his/her past, present and future selves as well as others in social contexts. Along the same paradigm, 'non-nativeness' is viewed as 'mutually constitutive subjectivities that are produced through a dynamic, discursive process' (Aneja, 2016: 573) rather than an assigned identity inscription in reference to the native speaker.

Professional teacher identity manifests itself through both teaching practice and discourse, which Varghese *et al.*, 2005 call 'identity-in-practice' and 'identity-in-discourse.' The former refers to the process of professional identity construction through shared practices of professional teaching communities, starting from teacher preparation programs to classroom and school settings while the latter foregrounds the role of power relations and available discourses in a particular teaching context (Varghese, 2017). This study mainly draws on Wenger's (1998) CoP to conceptualize professional teacher identity, where identity is defined as a negotiated experience of self through participation in the practices of a professional community. In this sense, it aligns with the 'identity-in-practice' perspective; however, as Varghese *et al.* (2005) pointed out, CoP underestimates power dynamics and ideologies in the community. Thus, acknowledging this limitation, the present study also attunes to the role of ideologies and power within and beyond the local CoP.

Communities of Practice: Identity trajectories and the nexus of membership

I draw on Wenger's (1998) framework of identity formation, CoP, in particular the notions of *trajectories* and *the nexus of membership* to analyze Zeynep's professional experiences. According to Wenger's (1998) framework, various degrees of participation in CoPs may result in five different identity trajectories. In *peripheral trajectory*, one has access to participate in the CoP, and this affects their identity positively; however, it never leads to full participation. If a newcomer's present participation is at peripherals, yet they invest in future full participation, then they form an *inbound trajectory*. As for *insider trajectory*, full participation allows full membership, but the identity negotiations do not end with full membership, instead, inbound trajectory shifts to insider trajectory where identity renegotiations continue as the practice evolves over time. Regarding *boundary trajectory*, Wenger explains that some individuals maintain their identity across the boundaries of several CoPs instead of being a complete insider of one. They become brokers shuttling between CoPs on a boundary trajectory. Lastly, the *outbound trajectory* entails movement out of the community.

Wenger (1998) acknowledges that every individual does not belong to a single CoP, but is a member of many CoPs with various forms of participation. Some CoPs may be central to an individual's identities, while some others may have a slight influence. Therefore, identity is viewed as 'an experience of multimembership' and it involves 'the work of reconciliation to maintain one identity across boundaries' (1998: 159), which Wenger (1998) calls *nexus of membership*. This notion brings multiplicity to individuals' identity trajectories in a CoP. A nexus does not sum the single identity trajectories in several communities into one; neither does it split a single identity into several trajectories. Indeed, it is the intersectionality of multiple trajectories where each trajectory becomes a part of each other, whether they conflict or support each other.

Despite being one of the most comprehensive and influential frameworks to explain social learning, CoP has been criticized in certain aspects. Many applied linguists have addressed the limitations of this theoretical framework in empirical studies (Canagarajah, 2012; Li & De Costa, 2018; Liu & Xu, 2013). Overall, CoP has been critiqued to:

- assume the static and homogeneous profile of newcomers who endeavor to become expert participants (Morita, 2004; Toohey, 1998);
- be too optimistic about the inextricable relationship between learning and participation and lack critical analysis of different learning types (Haneda, 2006; Harris & Shelswell, 2005);
- ignore the issues of 'illegitimate peripheral participation' and 'legitimation conflicts' (Harris & Shelswell, 2005);
- disregard power relations with regards to who can assign certain roles and identities in the CoP, which control identity trajectories (Toohey, 1998; Varghese *et al.*, 2005);
- overlook issues of power and conflict-driven by broader social contexts (Barton & Tusting, 2005).

Therefore, applying a CoP framework requires careful consideration of its limitations, especially with regards to the role of power relations and ideologies in professional identity construction in CoPs, which are further examined in the 'Discussion' section.

The Study

The participant and the context

Zeynep is a 26-year-old female first-year PhD student in a mid-western university in the US. She is an L1 speaker of Turkish and a proficient user of English. During the first half of the study, Zeynep was a second-year master's student and a graduate teaching assistant (TA) in the composition program of a university in the southwestern US. She had been teaching first-year undergraduate composition courses to a mix of American and ESL students for two years. During the second half, she was in her first year as a PhD student in a mid-western university and a graduate TA in an intensive English program (IEP). She had been teaching ESL communication and grammar courses for one semester. Before coming to the US, she had two years of EFL teaching experience in a large private university in Turkey. She taught academic English courses in an IEP program. Although this study lasted two academic semesters (Spring and Fall 2016), Zeynep's stories of teaching and learning encompass her four-and-a-half-year career teaching EFL and English composition.

Researcher's positionality

I met Zeynep in college as a classmate eight years before the time of this study. She graduated from college one year earlier and started working in an IEP program in a private university in Turkey, where we worked together for one year as English language instructors before she moved to the US for graduate study. When she was in her second year in an MA TESL program in the US, I moved to the US for my master's in TESL. Since then, we often times shared our academic experiences in informal conversations over phone or Skype. Our sharing took a more formal and systematic shape with this narrative inquiry starting in Spring 2016. Due to my established rapport with my participant and our shared educational and teaching background, I see my positionality as a total insider of her teaching experience in Turkey and a partial insider of her teaching contexts during her graduate study.

Narrative inquiry

Zeynep's professional identity construction was examined through a narrative inquiry approach (Connelly & Clandinin, 1990). Connelly and

Clandinin (1990) see narrative inquiry as 'a process of collaboration as mutual storytelling and re-storytelling' (1990: 4) by the participants and the researcher. They emphasize that the researcher's relationship with the participants is key in narrative inquiry since the participants should feel cared for and trusted so that they can openly tell and re-tell their stories. Given my shared identities with Zeynep, this narrative inquiry served as a mutual space for both of us to make sense of and re-construct our emerging professional teacher identities. Nevertheless, since the focus of this study is to examine Zeynep's stories of teaching and learning and trace the trajectory of her professional identity construction, only her narratives, which were recounted from her perspective, are included in the analysis.

Data collection and analysis

The data for this inquiry were collected in two academic semesters over five semi-structured Skype interviews in Turkish, and each lasted from 60 to 90 minutes. Three of the interviews took place in Spring 2016, and the other two were conducted in Fall 2016. The first three interviews were designed adopting Seidman's (2013) Three-Interview Series protocol of qualitative interviewing, which 'allows both the interviewer and participant to explore the participant's experience, place it in context, and reflect on its meaning' (2013: 20). They focused on her stories of English language learning, becoming a teacher and teaching in Turkey and the US. The last two interviews corresponded with her first semester in the PhD program. They aimed to elicit stories about her experience working in an IEP and being a PhD student as well as reflections on her professional identity construction and participation in her professional communities.

The interview data were verbatim transcribed and analyzed recursively at three levels. First, the stories were ordered chronologically. Second, they were sorted out according to key events in each professional community. Finally, the data were analyzed according to the trajectories of learning (*peripheral, inbound, insider, boundary* and *outbound*) in Wenger's (1998) CoP. After the analysis, I member-checked the trajectory maps and English translation of the selected excerpts with Zeynep to ensure that they represent her experiences (Loewen & Plonsky, 2016).

Zeynep's Identity Trajectories

In this section, I recount Zeynep's narratives of professional identity negotiations from pre-service education to her first semester in the doctorate program. I map out the identity trajectories in her CoPs over her four-and-a-half-year professional career, adapting the visual representation of identity trajectory designed by Liu and Xu (2013) based on Wenger's CoP (Figure 6.1). I highlight the key events that gave a distinct shape to her trajectories.

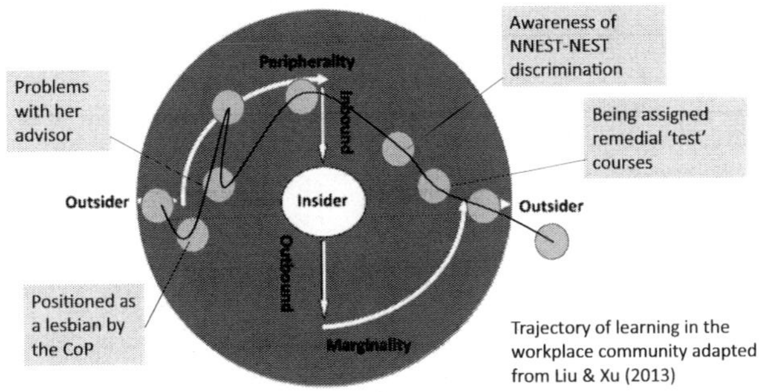

Figure 6.1 Zeynep's trajectory in her workplace in Turkey

Pre-service teacher identity: 'I want to be a professor'

I met Zeynep on the first day of classes at college in an English literature class. The professor asked us about our imagined professions, and most of us replied: 'English language teacher,' but I remember that moment when Zeynep said: 'I wanted to be a professor.' She recalled this when I asked her what kind of teacher she aspired to be during her pre-service education.

> I think the things I wanted to do weren't totally different from what I want to do now. I had frustration about my middle school and high school learning experience. I really wanted to change that. I believed one way to achieve this was research. Do you remember on the first day, one of the professors asked us what we wanted to be after 4 years of university education? I said that I want to be a professor… I wanted to increase my agency… Of course, as a regular teacher, I could change something, but to make great changes and to change educational policy, I needed to be more knowledgeable and I knew that I need to continue studying after college. (Interview 1, 3/6/16)

In order to be placed in an English language teaching (ELT) program, Zeynep had to go through a test-dominated language education, which she described as a constraint on her learner agency. She was more interested in the communicative aspect of language, which had no place in the nation-wide English language test. This situation created some frustrations for Zeynep in middle and high school. It compelled her to study ELT so that she could change the system from which she suffered. As evident in the above excerpt, early in her pre-service teacher education, Zeynep started to develop an agentive teacher identity with fragments of her learner self and imagined teacher self. Upon completing her degree, she preferred to gain teaching experience.

Working as an English language instructor in Turkey

Although teaching in a university as an instructor was not Zeynep's ultimate goal, she was invested in gaining experience to improve her teaching skills before pursuing a master's. When she stepped in her new teaching CoP, her future participation was reified by orientation sessions where Zeynep and her cohort analyzed textbooks, course syllabuses from various levels, lesson plans and student writing samples. Both the orientation and ongoing in-service Cambridge teacher training program enabled her to professionalize herself into the new community through her emerging *shared repertoire* (Wenger, 1998). However, in her first two months, her colleagues in the unit prevented her full participation in the CoP by positioning her as a lesbian.

> Seyma: Did you feel a part of your unit when you first started?
>
> Zeynep: No, not immediately. It was an interesting story. There was an American teacher in my cohort. We were in the same unit. She found me interesting and always wanted to spend time with me. This girl was different, though. She would go against many Turkish norms. She was kind of weird and too casual at work. Her contract was ended at the end of the year due to some ethical concerns. Anyway, they [colleagues in the unit] thought I am a lesbian because I hung out with her. You would call them open-minded people, but their attitudes towards me changed because of that. I didn't realize that because I was too busy adapting to workload and training. At the end of my second month, I noticed that when one of my colleagues shared this with me. (Interview 4, 11/11/16)

This excerpt illustrates the importance of shared cultural values between newcomers and old-timers in the CoP. As evident in Zeynep's co-workers' reaction to her friendship with a lesbian American colleague, heteronormativity as a dominant norm in Turkish society seemed to have substantially shaped the attitudes and behaviors of local teachers in the CoP. The power of heteronormative ideologies combined with the power old-timers hold due to their status as experienced members of the CoP initially prevented her acceptance in the unit. She was not allowed to gain membership of the CoP until that instructor was dismissed from the institution. Another event that kept Zeynep in the peripheries in the first year was a conflict with her advisor, an old-timer in the CoP assigned to her as a part Cambridge training certification, which was required for all new instructors in the institution. She had an argument with her advisor about one of the written assignments.

> She required a 1000-word limit, and I wrote in around 1200 words. She told me that she had no time for people with low writing skills like me. I was recruited as a teacher, you know. I got 28 on TOEFL writing. I asked her for specific constructive feedback, and she just told me to write within the word limit. I did so, but I didn't find any meaning in what I was doing. Later, I learned some people wrote in 1300-1400 words, especially a few Americans were way above the word limit like 1600. They asked for extensions on deadlines. She was all okay with them, but not me. (Interview 4, 11/11/16)

What is striking here is how Zeynep's advisor exercises her power as a Cambridge-certified trainer to legitimize the double standard she employs in the word count requirement for Zeynep vis-à-vis other American teachers, and how Zeynep, in juxtaposition, portrays herself as a 'competent' L2 writer and teacher by citing her diploma in ELT and her TOEFL score in her recount of the story. Although Zeynep displays an agentive teacher identity within the interactional context of the interview, it appears that she was unable to voice the institutional discrimination she faced as a newcomer in the peripheries, whose full participation in the CoP was bond to the successful completion of the Cambridge certification. In the second semester, however, she was assigned a new advisor, who she reported valued her teaching and enabled her to align more with the CoP. This alignment, however, never led her way towards the center of the community.

One reason why her trajectory remained stable at the peripheries was her resistance to internalize the shared repertoire of the community shaped by a test-dominated curriculum. Having gone through a test-dominated English learning experience that took her agency away as a language learner, she did not want to make a test-based curriculum as a part of her practice. When she was assigned a remedial class, nevertheless, she had no choice but to 'defend the system' and teach the test to students for whom she used the analogy of 'the litter of the test-governed system.' She was frustrated by the position she was put into:

> I was expected to *defend* (emphasized) this system to those students. The whole system was built on over-assessment. I never approved of that. I wasn't approving of it in my first year too, but it never became that visible to me. (Interview 4, 11/11/16)

The only way she could deal with the tension between her beliefs and students' needs was to be 'professional' – putting on a smile, teaching the test for five hours and leaving the last hour for 'real-life English.' At the peripheries of the community, she was still able to negotiate her professional identity by appropriating the practice of the community within a strict structure.

Another reason why she could not fully align with the institution was native English-speaking teachers ('NEST')–'NNEST' discrimination reified as a salary and benefit gap. In addition, due to the prevalent perception of 'NESTs' as 'fact-checkers' vis-à-vis 'NNESTs' as 'hard workers' and the institution's strict adherence to Cambridge teacher training programs as the only legitimate form of professional development, she had no space to negotiate a more personalized professional development path for her career.

> I think such kind of professional development was necessary regardless of new teachers' teaching experience or native-non-native status. The way it was handled, and formatted was wrong. It was uniform. There was no room for negotiation and trust...The whole thing was imperial. Why

> didn't we talk about native speaker non-native speaker issues during this training?... I got training to be conformed to inner-circle countries. (Interview 4, 11/11/16)

As this excerpt shows, Zeynep was particularly uncomfortable with the discriminatory practices against 'NNESTs' that were normalized in the institution and how they were further perpetuated through the Cambridge teacher certification, which she believed lacked criticality and focused heavily on teaching methods. As she became more aware of the *native-speakerism* (Holliday, 2006) dominating the institutional discourse and practices, she resisted fully participating in the CoP.

Starting from her second year, imagination played an important role in finding meaning in her teaching. Instead of participating in extra-curricular professional development activities, she spent most of her time searching for master's programs in the US and preparing the application documents, imagining herself as a future master's student. She nevertheless, always performed her assigned duties as a 'professional language teacher,' but did not strive to make any further contribution to the CoP. She stated, 'In the first year, I didn't really think about whether I was an insider or outsider. But in the second year, I was so out' (Interview 5, 11/24/16). Situated at the peripheries of the CoP that never led to full membership, Zeynep placed herself on an outbound trajectory, imagining her new CoPs in the US.

Graduate school and teaching assistantships in the US

Two years in the MA program

Being immersed into the perceived discourse of *native-speakerism* in Turkey led Zeynep to create an imagined boundary between NS-NNS that was impossible to transcend. This was manifested in her reaction when she was given legitimate access to teach composition to predominantly American first-year students as one of the few international TAs in her new CoP in the composition program, which was in stark contrast with her experience with her first advisor in Turkey who positioned her as an incompetent L2 writer.

> I was afraid. They [the department] told me, 'You are going to teach academic writing to Americans.' I e-mailed them three times to confirm that. I asked: 'Am I going to teach native speakers?' They said: 'Yes, you will teach Americans.' I asked again and again if I wasn't going to work in IEP. I couldn't believe that for a while. That was my reaction. Then, I asked: 'But, what can I teach them?'. I overestimated them...I wasn't self-confident at first. I was wondering if our writing level was equal. But during the orientation, the mentors always reassured me. We analyzed students' writing samples, and I couldn't believe my eyes. I said: 'Are they really native speakers?' (Interview 2, 3/19/16).

Orientation provided a space for her to deconstruct the ideology of '*native-speakerism*' deeply embedded in her language teacher identity. As she went through American students' writing samples, she compared them to her 'non-native' English-speaking students in Turkey and became conscious that writing competence was not a default for being a 'native' speaker. Moreover, her colleagues' and program director's welcoming approach situated her on an inbound trajectory. However, her inbound trajectory, as projected in Wenger's (1998) framework, did not lead to an insider trajectory since Zeynep considered composition program as secondary to her professional identity construction. She was first a master's student, and she aligned herself more with the graduate school community (Figure 6.2).

> That's how I dealt with all those different roles. I needed to prioritize one of them, and it had to be my role as a master's student. I saw myself as an academic in progress. I wasn't there to learn how to teach and how to be a writing teacher. (Interview 5, 11/24/16)

Imagination, being a primary source of her professional identity construction, moved her to the center of the graduate community as a full member of the graduate school community in her master's program. She was fully invested in her graduate studentship. She developed her research interests and engaged in research with the support of the faculty. Both the resources provided by her master's program and her investment in her graduate studentship made it conducive for Zeynep to place herself in the center of the local applied linguistics community in her master's program.

Zeynep never doubted whether or not she wanted to proceed with her graduate studies. Having positive teaching and graduate school experience, in her words, with her 'family' in the master's program, had an immense impact on her enthusiasm to continue her insider trajectory within the larger CoP of applied linguistics through her PhD studies.

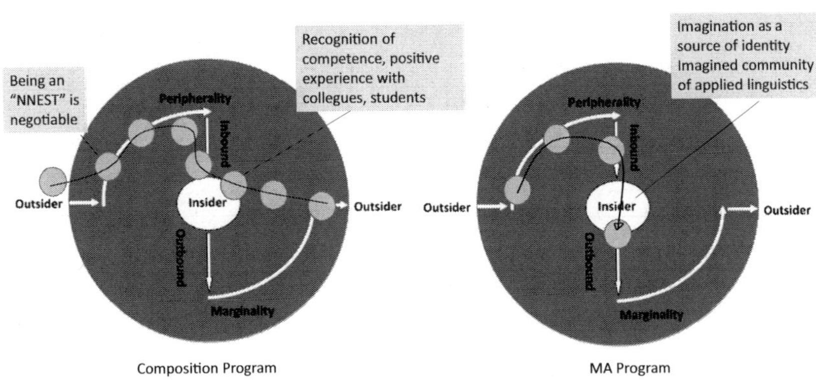

Figure 6.2 Zeynep's trajectories in her teaching and graduate school communities in MA

First semester in the doctorate program

Among her many options, Zeynep decided to pursue her PhD in a mid-western university in the US. She attended the departmental orientation hoping that she would meet her new 'family.' Contrary to her expectations, however, her by-default inbound trajectory in her new two CoPs, teaching, and graduate school communities, gave its way to a form of non-participation in both (Figure 6.3).

> I couldn't find the community I was hoping for here. I said, 'What have I done?' ... I noticed the tension between the professors in the orientation. That was not professional. Also, I got the message: this is not a family... The IEP program here – the program has many issues about curriculum, courses, assessment, etc. It is not an established program yet. (Interview 4, 11/11/16)

Zeynep's non-participation was mediated by the institutional arrangement of her teaching assignment. Being assigned weekly 10-hour teaching load in the IEP as the only new PhD student despite her request to be a research assistant, she believed, prevented her access to the community of researchers in the PhD program. Although she loved her students, she thought her program did not recognize her research competence.

> I told them [the department] that I wanted to be an RA. It's my fifth year of teaching. I already have some teaching experience. I know you always learn something new as you teach, but I also need to learn so much about research too. There is a lot to learn, and I am on my own. I need to put so much effort into this. This school doesn't teach me anything new about research. My advisor doesn't reach out to me. I am all alone here, and I have to keep reading more articles on my own. I could have been in a different university and writing research grants, you know. I made a huge mistake by coming here. (Interview 5, 11/24/16)

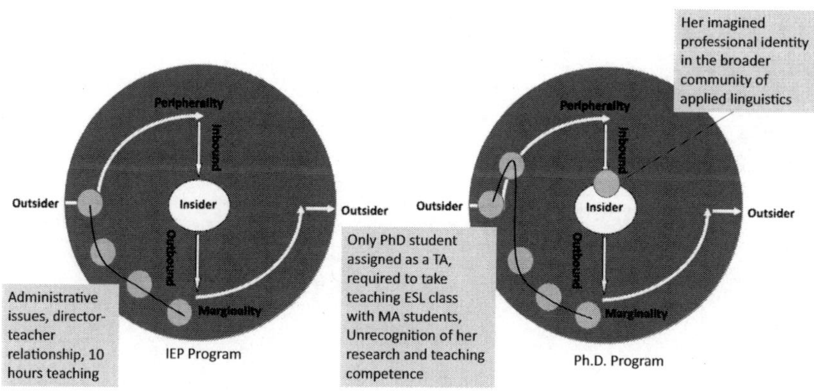

Figure 6.3 Zeynep's trajectories in her teaching and graduate school communities in PhD

Moreover, as a TA, she was required to take a course about teaching ESL with master's students, which she interpreted as unrecognition of her teaching competence. Neither her research competence nor her teaching experience was recognized by the PhD program in her account. In other words, Zeynep was not positioned as 'a PhD student first' by the department, which was what she identified herself with but was not allowed to negotiate in her local context. This further contributed to her non-participation in her CoPs. However, this form of non-participation did not necessarily mean that she stopped constructing her professional identity. Positioning herself as a broker between her students and larger applied linguistics community, she used her own classroom to enact her imagined professional identity by making language learning-language research connection visible to her own students. She made her non-participation or marginality as an integral part of her professional identity construction in the margins of both communities.

> Here I found myself many times sharing my research with my students. I questioned why I am doing this right here right now. I didn't use to do that with my previous students. I allocate the last 5 minutes of my lessons to share what I learned from my graduate classes with my students. It's kind of metacognitive, but they enjoy listening to me talking about their learning drawing on my research interests. (Interview 5, 11/24/16)

The excerpts in this section suggest that institutional recognition of professional identities and goals of new PhD students plays a particularly important role in identity investment and trajectory of PhD students with prior teaching experience. They also illustrate the importance of imagination as an integral resource in professional identity construction, even in the case of marginalization in a new CoP.

Discussion

Agency and imagination

Zeynep's stories show that agency and imagination are central to her identity construction process as a language teacher and a graduate student. Despite the structural constraints in her CoPs, her agency and imagined professional identity as a prospective applied linguist is what enabled her to transcend time and space in her CoPs. In line with Bakhtin's (1993) concept of *act* as involving human consciousness, Zeynep enacted her agency by making a conscious decision about to what extent to participate in the practices and discourses of her CoPs. Her intentional integration of communicative activities in her remedial test class in Turkey as well as sharing her research with the IEP students in her first semester in the PhD program are two examples of how she used her agency to create a space for her imagined professional identities in the peripheries or margins of the CoPs.

However, the concept of imagination in Zeynep's narratives differs from that of Wenger (1998). In the CoP framework, imagination is described as a concept that reinforces an individual's participation in the CoP, which, in return, benefits the local community. What happens when one's imagined self-conflicts with the practice of the community? What if such imagination does not benefit the community itself contrary to how it is portrayed in Wenger's theory? As Kanno and Norton (2003) acknowledge, imagined communities are not necessarily restricted to a particular locale, thus, an individual's practice might as well be driven by an imagined community beyond the territorial context whose practices may or may not be similar to the local community as in the experiences of Zeynep. Likewise, the conflict between one's imagined identity and possible imagined identities a CoP offers does not lead to the marginalization of an individual, as Wenger (1998) puts. Especially, if one can find commonalities between their current practice and the imagined CoP, imagination can serve as a resource for identity construction even in the margins of a community.

Identity trajectories as a nexus of multimembership

Unlike a traditional progressive trajectory of participation in a CoP from peripheries towards its center, Zeynep's identity trajectories both as a language teacher and teaching assistant demonstrate a distinct pattern due to her continuous reconciliation of her multiple professional identities and forms of participation into one nexus, which Wenger (1998) calls *nexus of multimembership*, that is, 'all the subtle ways in which our various forms of participation, no matter how distinct, can interact, influence each other, and require coordination' (1998: 159). Navigating this nexus of multimembership, however, was not a linear process for Zeynep as it was in the case of graduate students in Ortaçtepe (2015) whose L2 learner, teacher, and emerging scholar identities were compatible with each other. Zeynep's experiences show that institutional arrangements such as assistantship assignments as well as the recognition of academic goals of individual graduate students play a significant role in how graduate students navigate their multiple professional identities during graduate school. Other studies also discussed the role of institutions in professional identity trajectories in terms of their power to provide or prevent the *legitimacy of access to practice* (Tsui, 2007) and supporting network (Cho, 2013). Zeynep's experiences provide further evidence that navigating a nexus of multimembership is not solely an identity work at an individual level, but it is also institutions' responsibility to address the needs of graduate students to support their professional development.

Participation and learning in the margins

Wenger (1998) distinguishes between the notions of peripherality and marginality and explains how they shape the participation and learning of community members. In the former concept, non-participation is an enabling force for full participation, while in the latter, the form of non-participation prevents full membership. In Zeynep's experiences, her trajectories of learning and participation across her CoPs (Figure 6.1, 6.2 and 6.3) does not necessarily match Wegner's definition of peripherality and marginality and the equation of learning with full participation.

Two findings problematize the concepts of learning through participation, peripherality and marginality. The first contradictory finding is that peripheral trajectory does not necessarily mean engaging in learning and practice, and it does not predict full participation in the community. For example, Zeynep's peripheral trajectory in her teaching and graduate school CoPs during her master's led to full membership in the latter CoP, while it did not in the former because she opted to be a full member of one and not the other.

The other finding that complicates the distinction between peripherality and marginality is relevant to what I call *legitimate learning in the margins*. Marginality in Wenger's (1998) framework is defined as a form of non-participation that leaves no room for learning. Zeynep's experiences in the first semester of her PhD program, nevertheless, cast doubts on how learning should be viewed in the margins. Situated in the margins of both of her teaching and graduate school communities in her PhD, Zeynep kept engaging in a type of learning that she believed was legitimate. Her learning was not driven by her local CoPs, nor was it towards the center of these local CoPs, but that of her broader imagined community of applied linguistics. To illustrate, even though she was in the margins of both CoPs, she continued to invest time and effort in her research, sent papers to journals, presented her studies at local and international conferences. Moreover, she used her classroom as a space where she could continue developing her imagined professional identity by sharing research with her students. It seems that despite being on her own, Zeynep was still engaging in *legitimate learning in the margins*, which suggests that margins do not necessarily imply a lack of learning.

Power dynamics

My discussion thus far has highlighted the power of agency Zeynep could exercise in her professional identity negotiations across several CoPs. However, our understanding of Zeynep's experiences remains incomplete without an examination of power dynamics in these CoPs, which is not quite discussed in Wenger's (1998) CoP. Although the notion of negotiability is rigorously elaborated in the framework, as Haneda (2006) states, Wenger (1998) 'does not provide any critical analysis of unequal participatory opportunities' in the framework (1998: 811). Below, I identify salient power dynamics in Zeynep's CoPs, all of which also marked the key points in her trajectories (Figure 6.1, 6.2 and 6.3).

Institutional power

Institutional power and ideologies embodied in practices of the communities played an important role in Zeynep's participation in her CoPs in Turkey and the US. They appear to be disguised in (1) institutional practices of *native-speakerism*, (2) course assignments and (3) professional development activities. First of all, Zeynep's identity negotiations as a 'non-native' English teacher were closely tied to how the institutions took up the ideology of *native-speakerism*. While Zeynep was subject to institutional racism (Kubota & Lin, 2006) through the legitimization of *native-speakerism* in her workplace in Turkey, resulting in her deficit understanding of herself as a 'non-native' teacher, she was able transform her conceptualization of 'non-nativeness' in her new teaching CoP during her master's when given legitimate access to teach 'native' speakers of English in the US. Another example of institutional power is obligatory course assignments in the IEP programs in Turkey and the US during her PhD. In both contexts, this appeared to affect her investment and participation negatively. Lastly, a strict model of professional development that pre-conditioned her to complete a set of Cambridge certificates to be able to do a master's was another form of institutional power intersecting with language ideologies that idealize only Inner Circle varieties of English and professional development.

Advisors, mentors and old-timers

Advisors, mentors and old-timers in Zeynep's CoPs were other important agents of power who had the right to assign roles, evaluate her competence, and thus mediate her participation and non-participation (Toohey, 1998). For example, one key crisis in Zeynep's trajectory of participation in her CoP in Turkey was the 'legitimation conflict' (Harris & Shelswell, 2005) with her advisor about her writing competence, which appears to pull her back from her peripheral trajectory and her engagement in the CoP. Similarly, when she started to work in the IEP in Turkey, old-timers in her teaching unit prevented her access by labelling her 'lesbian' based on her close relationship with an American lesbian teacher. These examples suggest that community members, who are idealized as having equal power in Wenger's (1998) framework, may create conflicts that have serious consequences for the trajectory of newcomers, especially when they exercise their power to justify dominant ideologies in the workplace and larger sociocultural and sociopolitical context.

Conclusion

Using Wenger's (1998) CoP, this chapter analyzed the complexity of Zeynep's professional identity trajectories across her teaching and graduate school CoPs. Findings showed that Zeynep's identity trajectories demonstrated a complex pattern, reconciling multiple professional identities into one nexus. The findings also problematized the notion of learning in the margins, suggesting that the margins of a community can as well be resourceful for professional identity construction. *Legitimate learning in the margins* is still possible if an individual has a strong investment in and connection with the practices of a broader imagined community beyond the local context. This study also provided further evidence regarding the non-negligible role of power and ideologies in the CoPs and the broader social context in shaping the identity trajectories of graduate students. Future studies that use CoP to investigate academic professionalization should continue to attune to the macro context of socialization to uncover the complexity of professional identity construction. Although the scope of this study expanded beyond the marginalization in professional communities, future studies that are particularly concerned with participation and marginalization in CoPs may also benefit from a complementary framework, *Individual Network of Practice* (Zappa-Hollman & Duff, 2015), to unpack the social processes and networks or lack thereof in individual's professional trajectories.

References

Aneja, G.A. (2016) (Non)native speakered: Rethinking (non)nativeness and teacher identity in TESOL teacher education. *TESOL Quarterly* 50, 527–596.

Bakhtin, M. (1993) *Toward a Philosophy of the Act*. Austin: University of Texas Press.

Barton, D. and Tusting K. (2005) Introduction. In D. Barton and K. Tusting (eds) *Beyond Communities of Practice: Language, Power and Social Context* (pp. 158–179). New York: Cambridge University Press.

Canagarajah, A.S. (2012) Teacher development in a global profession: An autoethnography. *TESOL Quarterly* 46 (2), 258–279.

Cho, S. (2013) Disciplinary enculturation experiences of three Korean students in US-based MATESOL programs. *Journal of Language, Identity & Education* 12 (2), 136–151.

Connelly, F. and Clandinin, D. (1990) Stories of experience and narrative inquiry. *Educational Researcher* 19 (5), 2–14.

Donato, R., Hendry, H. and Tucker, G.R. (2015) Developing professional identities in applied linguistics: from doctoral study to professional practice. In Y.L. Cheung, S. Ben Said and K. Park (eds) *Advances and Current Trends in Language Teacher Identity Research* (pp. 217–234). New York: Routledge.

Golombek, P. and Jordan, S. (2005) Becoming 'black lambs' not 'parrots': A poststructuralist orientation to intelligibility and identity. *TESOL Quarterly* 39, 513–534.

Haneda, M. (2006) Classrooms as communities of practice: A reevaluation. *TESOL Quarterly* 40, 807–817.

Harris, S.R. and Shelswell, N. (2005) Moving beyond communities of practice in adult basic education. In D. Barton and K. Tusting (eds) *Beyond Communities of Practice: Language, Power and Social Context* (pp. 158–179). New York: Cambridge University Press.

Herath, S. and Valencia, H. (2015) Neither 'a complete insider' nor 'a complete outsider': Autoethnographies of two teacher-educators-in-the-making. In Y.L. Cheung, S. Ben Said and K. Park (eds) *Advances and Current Trends in Language Teacher Identity Research* (pp. 86–101). New York: Routledge.

Holliday, A. (2006) Native-speakerism. *ELT Journal* 60, 385–387.

Johnson, K. (2001) *Social identities and the NNES MA TESOL student*. Retrieved from https://files.eric.ed.gov/fulltext/ED457682.pdf

Kanno, Y. and Norton, B. (2003) Imagined communities and educational possibilities: Introduction. *Journal of Language, Identity, and Education* 2 (4), 241–249.

Kubota, R. and Lin, A. (2006) Race and TESOL: Introduction to concepts and theories. *TESOL Quarterly* 40 (3), 471–493.

Li, W. and De Costa, P.I. (2018) Exploring novice EFL teachers' identity development: A case study of two EFL teachers in China. In S. Mercer and A. Kostoulas (eds) *Language Teacher Psychology* (pp. 86–104). Bristol: Multilingual Matters.

Liu, Y. and Xu, Y. (2013) The trajectory of learning in a teacher community of practice: A narrative inquiry of a language teacher's identity in the workplace. *Research Papers in Education* 28 (2), 176–195.

Loewen, S. and Plonsky, L. (2016) *An A-Z of Applied Linguistics Research Methods*. London: Palgrave.

Morita, N. (2004) Negotiating participation and identity in second language academic communities. *TESOL Quarterly* 38, 573–603.

Norton, B. (2013) *Identity and Language Learning: Extending the Conversation* (2nd edn). Bristol: Multilingual Matters.

Ortaçtepe, D. (2015) EFL teachers' identity (re)construction as teachers of intercultural competence: A language socialization approach. *Journal Language, Identity and Education* 14, 96–112.

Park, G. (2012) 'I am never afraid of being recognized as NNES': One woman teacher's journey in claiming and embracing the NNES identity. *TESOL Quarterly* 46, 127–151.

Reis, D.S. (2012) 'Being underdog': Supporting nonnative English-speaking teachers (NNESTs) in claiming and asserting professional legitimacy. *Journal of Excellence in College Teaching* 23 (3), 33–58.

Rudolph, N., Selvi, A.F. and Yazan, B. (2015) Conceptualizing and confronting inequity: Approaches within and new directions for the 'NNEST movement.' *Critical Inquiry in Language Studies* 12 (1), 27–50.

Samimy, K., Kim, S., Lee, J.-A. and Kasai, M. (2011) A participative inquiry in a TESOL program: Development of three NNES graduate students' legitimate peripheral participation to fuller participation. *Modern Language Journal* 95, 558–574.

Seidman, I. (2013) *Interviewing as Qualitative Research*. New York: Teachers College.

Toohey, K. (1998) 'Breaking them up, taking them away': ESL students in Grade 1. *TESOL Quarterly* 32, 61–84.

Tsui, A.B.M. (2007) Complexities of identity formation: A narrative inquiry of an EFL teacher. *TESOL Quarterly* 41, 657–680.

Varghese, M.M. (2017) Language teacher educator identity and language teacher identity. In G. Barkhuizen (ed.) *Reflections on Language Teacher Identity Research* (pp. 43–48). New York: Routledge.

Varghese, M., Morgan, B., Johnston, B. and Johnson, K.A. (2005) Theorizing language teacher identity: Three perspectives and beyond. *Journal of Language, Identity, and Education* 4, 21–44.

Wenger, E. (1998) *Communities of Practice: Learning, Meaning and Identity*. Cambridge: Cambridge University Press.

Zappa-Hollman, S. and Duff, P.A. (2015) Academic English socialization through individual networks of practice. *TESOL Quarterly* 49 (2), 333–368.

7 Who Am I and Where Do I Fit In: A Narrative Analysis of One Teacher's Shifting Identities

Naashia Mohamed

Introduction

Becoming a teacher is not simply a matter of adopting a role, but rather, a dynamic 'identity forming process' (Danielewicz, 2001: 3) that is co-constructed by the individual and the people the teacher interacts with during the course of her career (Beijaard *et al.*, 2004; Connelly & Clandinin, 1999; Jenlink, 2014). Teacher identity is not a static, unitary, internally coherent phenomenon (Varghese *et al.*, 2005). It is multi-faceted (Han, 2017), in a state of perpetual shift, shaped by multiple trajectories (Trent & Gao, 2009). The socially constructed process of identity development involves tensions and conflicts (Block, 2006; Kanno, 2003) and is often characterised as a struggle over positionality (Norton & Toohey, 2011) as teachers attempt to establish and negotiate their positioning and membership within their educational context. Norton (2010) describes that 'every time we speak, we are negotiating and renegotiating our sense of self in relation to the larger social world, and reorganizing that relationship across time and space' (2010: 350). This repositioning of the self is dependent not only on teachers' personal values and on belief structures, but also on the complex social, cultural, political and institutional contexts within which they work (Yazan, 2018). Tsui (2007: 33) takes this a step further, maintaining that 'identity is not just relational (i.e. how one talks or thinks about oneself, or how others talk or think about one), it is also experiential (i.e. it is formed from one's lived experience).'

One significant aspect that contributes to the relational aspect of identity construction is language (Pavlenko, 2002). Norton (2010) encourages us to think of language not simply as a linguistic system, but as a social practice where our experiences lead us to resist, negotiate and accept different identity positions. The multiple identities that multilingual speakers enact may be diverse, contradictory and dynamic (Donato, 2016; Jenkins, 2007), continually affected by their experiences that may privilege or marginalise them in a particular context. Studies (e.g. Lee, 2003; Su Kim, 2003) have shown that individuals draw on their linguistic resources to fit in, by downplaying the use of languages deemed to be unacceptable within a community, or incompatible with the identities they wanted to enact, while consciously adopting language practices that gave them validation. In relation to language teacher identity, the way in which a teacher uses language may serve to validate their membership within their teaching context or allow others to exclude them from affiliation.

The close interrelationships that exist between teacher identity, teacher learning and teacher practices (Hanna *et al.*, 2019; Vanassche & Kelchtermans, 2016) and the impact of these teacher-related aspects on student learning (Yazan, 2018) highlight the importance of teacher identity as a phenomenon for further study. As Donato (2016) states, although much has been written about identity from various theoretical perspectives, research remains to be done to understand fully the role and importance of teacher identity to language teaching professionals. One aspect of teacher identity that remains to be fully investigated is the impact of one's past experiences as a language learner on the teacher's professional identity and teaching practice. By connecting the visceral feelings, attitudes and emotions that arose during past language learning experiences to the shifting nature of a teacher's identity as she progresses in her career, this chapter aims to capture how identity construction is entangled with perceptions of language, power, and expertise. Through an in-depth analysis of a single case, this study presents an analysis of one individual's struggle to establish her identity and achieve a sense of belonging in different periods of her life as she progressed from student to school teacher to college lecturer.

Theoretical Framework

This study draws on Kelchtermans' (2009) personal interpretative framework and Davies and Harré's (1990) positioning theory to examine the ways in which one teacher's self-image, language competence and her interactions shape her sense of self.

The personal interpretative framework

The personal interpretative framework refers to the set of cognitions and beliefs that operates as a lens through which individuals perceive their job situations, give meaning to and act in them (Kelchtermans, 2009; Vanassche & Kelchtermans, 2014). This framework is based on two domains: professional self-understanding and subjective educational theory. Professional self-understanding is composed of five components: self-image, self-esteem, task perception, job motivation and future perspective.

The second domain within the personal interpretative framework is the subjective educational theory. It includes the personal system of knowledge and beliefs on teaching and how to enact these. This comprises the technical know-how and the theoretical underpinnings which guide their professional decisions. This framework guides teachers' interpretations and actions in particular situations and is modified by the interactions that occur within that context. Kelchtermans (2009) describes it as representing the 'mental sediment' of teachers' learning and developing over time. Because the study is primarily interested in exploring how the teacher perceives herself and her role within her context, I will draw primarily from the first domain of the framework, by exploring how the teacher constructs her self-image, and how her interactions throughout the course of her career affect her self-esteem and job motivation. I will also consider how her task perception influences her future perspective.

Positioning theory

The metaphor of positioning is a complex, multi-faceted, dynamic construct associated with the ways in which people construct their sense of self in relation to others through discursive practices. Originating in the field of social psychology, positioning theory is based on the work of Davies and Harré (1990) and considers how communication shapes identity. It addresses 'how people use words (and discourse of all types) to locate themselves and others' (Moghaddam & Harré, 2010: 2). Inherent in the storylines that individuals construct and enact, positions not only involve rights, duties and obligations but also expectations about how an individual will enact these. As Harré and van Langenhove (1999) observe:

> One can position oneself or be positioned as e.g. powerful or powerless, confident or apologetic, dominant or submissive, definitive or tentative, authorized or unauthorized, and so on. A 'position,' can be specified by reference to how a speaker's contributions are hearable with respect to these and other polarities of character, and sometimes even a role. (1999: 17)

Two modes of positioning are relevant to the study. The first mode is reflexive positioning or intentional self-positioning, 'in which one positions oneself' (Davies & Harré, 1990: 48). Self-positioning occurs in every conversation where one wants to express his/her professional identity. For teachers, this links to their beliefs and assumptions about good teaching and the grounding upon which they make professional judgements. The second mode of positioning, which Davies and Harré (1990) define as interactive positioning, is where 'what one person says positions another'

(1990: 48). Interactive positioning may occur intentionally or unintentionally, and individuals may reject or contest the ways in which others may attempt to position them.

This study will explore the ways in which the teacher participant positions herself as a teacher and language user in her professional contexts (reflexive positioning), and how she is affected by the ways in which others within the context attempt to position her (interactive positioning). It must be noted that as the study is based on the narrative of the teacher, the interactive positioning of others will be explored from the point of view of the teacher, through the interactions reported in her narratives.

Participant and setting

Hawwa,[1] the teacher participant of the study, is from the Maldives, where Dhivehi has exclusive native language status. Although Dhivehi is the language of communication in society, English presides over all educational institutions, and consequently, Dhivehi is often relegated to second-class status in schools (Mohamed, 2013). Dhivehi and Islam lessons are the only times that Dhivehi is likely to be used as all other subjects are taught in English. This situation of English language dominance in the education sector (Mohamed, 2019) has many implications for the identity construction of particularly those teachers who teach subjects in Dhivehi, as these teachers are often viewed as being less competent in English, the dominant language of the education system.

Hawwa was born on a rural island of the Maldives. Growing up in a large family, typical of the 1980s, Hawwa was aware of the need to succeed academically to secure a 'good job' that would allow her the opportunity to help her parents in raising her younger siblings. Her family was 'an ordinary one, and not very well off,' but Hawwa remembers her childhood as being a very happy one. The family spoke a dialect variety of Dhivehi that was particular to her island. But through school, she became confident using the standard variety of Dhivehi as well as English. As was typical of the community, Hawwa learned to read and write in Arabic when she was about three years of age, to allow her to read the Qur'an.

Hawwa described herself as being 'a good student, always keen to learn and excel.' She completed her schooling in her island school, achieving awards for being the best student in her year. This allowed her the opportunity to obtain a place in the teacher training institute in Malé, the capital city, to study for a Diploma in Primary Teaching. This was the basic qualification for a teacher to be employed in a primary school, and was, at the time, the most common one.

The decision to join the teacher training programme was a pragmatic one, because there were few career options for women on a rural island and teaching seemed to be 'the easiest option that would guarantee a job on the island.' Hawwa's priority at this stage was to complete her training and return home to help her family. This was what her family expected from her, and Hawwa was eager to fulfil these expectations, which she regarded as an honour. Being selected into the teacher training programme was a source of pride for Hawwa as she became the first in her family to complete secondary school and attend college.

Following her graduation, Hawwa went on to take up a position as a primary teacher in her island school – a position that enhanced her and her family's pride in her achievement. Her career, spanning over a decade, saw many changes to her role as an educator. As will be evident in the following sections, Hawwa moves from being a primary teacher in an island school, teaching in the medium of English, to a Dhivehi teacher in a Malé school, and eventually, to a lecturer in a higher education college.

Method

Hawwa was purposefully selected for the study, and being a single case study, there are no aspirations to claim representativeness of her narrative. Rather, her case is used to exemplify how a teacher's professional identity evolves over time as a result of her interactions with those around her. Hawwa's story was constructed over a period of six months, using two main methods that collected what Kelchtermans (2009) refers to as narrative-biographical data. These data captured the stories through which Hawwa made sense of herself and her work as a teacher and formed the best way to reconstruct her thinking about teaching and teachers. Due to the geographical distance between Hawwa and myself during the period of data collection, her stories were captured using email and phone interviews. Prior to the study, I had known Hawwa professionally. We both shared similar cultural and linguistic backgrounds and were both educators with a keen interest in language. Knowing Hawwa prior to the study, and coming from similar backgrounds, I was able to develop rapport with Hawwa and create a safe context in which she could candidly share her stories. Initially, I conducted a semi-structured phone interview lasting about an hour. This interview focused on (1) Hawwa's beliefs about teaching, teachers, and the role of language in positioning teachers; and (2) Hawwa's professional self-understanding, focusing on aspects of the five questions related to that domain (Vanassche & Kelchtermans, 2014).

Over the next few months, I engaged with Hawwa in a series of emails to elicit narratives about her experiences as a teacher. Each of these emails consisted of about five open questions to encourage narrative stories of her professional history. These questions were informed by the theoretical framework of the study and included the following:

> *How did your interest in teaching come about? Do you recall any particular incidents or stories at any point in your life that led to creating this interest? If so, please describe these incidents and how they made you feel* (Q3, Email 1).

Subsequent emails introduced new questions and built on the responses of the previous emails. For example:

> *In your previous email, you referred to feeling demotivated at Hameediyya School. Can you share some examples of specific incidents, and/or things that people said at the time that contributed to how you felt?* (Q2, Email 2).

In this way, the series of email exchanges, taken together, operated like an extended semi-structured interview. They elicited stories from her past and present and allowed her to share her hopes for her future. At the end of the email exchanges, I interviewed Hawwa over the phone again, lasting about an hour. This interview was conducted to clarify issues raised in the email responses, and allow the opportunity to narrate stories that she felt were better told than written. Both the email responses and the phone interviews were conducted mainly in Dhivehi because this was Hawwa's preferred language.

At the end of the data collection period, I transcribed and translated the two phone interviews, and together with over 10 email exchanges, began the analysis process. For the analysis, the data were sorted in two ways. First, the data were arranged chronologically, from her experiences as a student to her current status as a lecturer, to construct a life story (Lieblich *et al.*, 1998). I then repeatedly read the data to identify the ways in which Hawwa positioned herself. I then re-read the data to locate turning points in her narrative that indicated shifts in her identity positioning. I operationalised turning points to be episodes in Hawwa's narratives, which led to a clear change in the way she positioned herself. Bruner (1994) suggests that turning point memories are examples of the process of self-development, and are important to understand shifts in participants' self-image and positioning.

Table 7.1 shows how her identity evolved over time and how she positioned herself within each stage of her career. There were four notable stages in Hawwa's identity construction. The years she spent as a student and in her first role as a primary teacher could be seen to be her stage of establishing her professional identity. The next four years, when she was forced to take on the role of a Dhivehi teacher saw her lose her sense of belonging. The two years Hawwa spent as a graduate student showed a shift in her identity as she began to explore new avenues and gain new understandings. The last year of her career, at the time of data collection, when she was employed as a lecturer at a college could be described as a stage when she rebuilt her expertise.

I conducted a thematic analysis for the data for each of these four stages of her career to describe how her identity construction evolved over time and what shifts were evident, particularly in relation to her emotions at each stage. This process of analysis involved going over the data, assigning descriptive codes in the first instance and then, later,

Table 7.1 Stages in identity construction

Identity stages	*Establishing a professional identity*	*Losing a sense of belonging*	*Shifting identities*	*Re-building expertise*	
Role(s)	Student-teacher	Primary school teacher	Dhivehi teacher at school	Graduate student at college	Lecturer at college
Duration	2 years	3 years	4 years	2 years	1 year
Themes	• Ease of success • Fulfilling expectations	• Loss of recognition • Sense of inadequacy	• Self-exploration • Vulnerability	• Significant others • Hopes and dreams	
Self-positioning	student teacher □ expert teacher; language learner □ language expert; community leader	language expert □ mediocre language user; expert teacher □ inferior teacher	language learner; novice researcher	language expert; researcher; lecturer	

grouping these into overarching themes. Two themes were identified for each identity stage.

The final row of the table shows the different ways in which Hawwa positioned herself within each stage. In some cases, it was evident that a shift occurred in the way she positioned herself. For example, during the initial stage of establishing her professional identity, Hawwa first talked of being a student teacher, but later described herself as an expert teacher. The □ indicates this shift in positioning within each stage.

In the following four sections of the chapter, I will present Hawwa's story, progressing chronologically to show how her professional identity and self-positioning evolved over time.

Establishing a professional identity

The first stage of identity construction focused on establishing a professional identity. During the course of five years, Hawwa positioned herself in three different ways, progressing from a student teacher to a novice teacher and to an expert teacher.

Hawwa characterised the two years of teacher training as a time of 'fun and freedom' when she felt that 'success came easily, without much effort.' However, she remained focused on achieving the top marks in her cohort. She revelled in the praise of her lecturers, and sought their advice on all matters 'from how to pronounce a new word to how to study for an exam on how to land a part on a TV commercial.' For Hawwa, her lecturers held the keys to her success, and building a good relationship with them was one of the ways in which Hawwa found it easy to succeed.

Hawwa did not feel the learning experience to be any more challenging than her experience of school, but she describes how she mentally shifted from being a student to being a teacher just before her first practicum teaching.

> *It was then that I realised that I needed to exhibit a certain demeanour. I had to both act the part and look the part. It was no longer about just studying and trying to be the best in the class. I had to try and be a teacher.*

This was the first time that Hawwa first positioned herself as a teacher. From then onwards, Hawwa describes her self-image as a teacher. Hawwa recalled that prior to the practicum, she had 'focused mostly on the content of what to teach' and in 'improving English,' assuming that the skill of teaching would 'happen naturally' as it was something she felt she knew, having 'watched teachers in action.' Hawwa explained that after the practicum, she began to reflect deeply on how she needed to prepare for her lessons, strategies she could employ to engage students, and what she could do to manage behavioural incidents in her classroom.

Hawwa went on to achieve the award of the best student on the programme. A few weeks after her graduation, Hawwa returned to her island, back to the school where she herself had studied, and began a new role as a primary teacher. The role of a school teacher was a respected one in her small community and one that would earn her a higher than average salary in that rural island. As a result, it was a great source of pride for her parents.

She received a lot of support and praise for her work from the school and especially from its parent community. They noted her skills in managing her class, the ease with which she taught and encouraged all her students, her friendly personality and her proficiency in English. Hawwa found this support from parents to be very rewarding and satisfying, and as a result of how her school community positioned her, her self-image changed. She 'went from being a student teacher to being an expert teacher within the course of a few months.'

Hawwa noted that being a teacher raised her status in the community. She was regarded as a learned member of the community, and people came to her for help with many issues, ranging from assistance with schoolwork to filling forms and writing letters for members of the wider community. Hawwa felt that these requests for help were a recognition of her education, and enjoyed the sense of being wanted. The high regard the community had for her, clearly helped to raise her self-esteem, allowing her to position herself as an expert in the English language and as a leader of her community.

This period of her career was, as Hawwa put it, 'the golden era' when everything was easy, and her career was on an upward trajectory, and she felt like she was able to fulfil everyone's expectations of her.

Losing a sense of belonging

Buoyed by her career success till then, Hawwa was encouraged by her family and colleagues to further her knowledge and skills. She decided to undertake a bachelor's degree in education as this would lead to better career prospects. However, such a programme was only available for students resident in Malé, so Hawwa decided to move to the city and finance her studies by taking up a teaching position there. This is indicative of the future perspective she had at the time, and her high level of motivation to excel as a teacher.

> *I didn't even once doubt that I would get a job. Everyone was encouraging me to go to Malé and do my degree, even hinting that I could one day be the headmistress when I returned to the island. I was on cloud nine.*

The next stage of Hawwa's career saw her well-established identity of expert teacher and proficient English language user become fragmented due to the ways in which others within her new context positioned her. She realised that although she viewed herself as an expert teacher and as a skilled user of English, others did not share this view. During this stage, the most difficult time in her career, Hawwa felt inadequate and like an outsider, no longer recognised or valued in her school community.

This initial dent in her high self-esteem occurred when she began seeking a job in Malé. She had sent applications to many schools but received no responses. She decided to be proactive and follow up on her application to Hameedhiyya School. This resulted in being invited to a meeting with the Deputy Principal – a meeting that turned out to be another turning point for Hawwa. The meeting was conducted in English, and Hawwa felt intimidated by the way in which the Deputy Principal's English appeared 'fluent and natural-sounding' against which her own English sounded 'stilted and anything but smooth.' The Deputy Principal explained that there were no available positions for a primary teacher, but that they did need a Dhivehi teacher. This, Hawwa felt, was 'like a slap across the face' because it undermined her status of a primary teacher, which she had projected to be a level higher than a Dhivehi teacher. Hawwa 'did not have any interest in being a Dhivehi teacher' because she felt that it was 'second best.' But, without rejecting the offer, she agreed to think it over and get back to them within a week.

During that week, Hawwa followed up with all the schools she had applied to, and not having had any other offers elsewhere, Hawwa realised that if she wanted a teaching position, the Dhivehi teacher position at Hameedhiyya School was her best option. If she was to remain in Malé to complete her education, she needed a job to finance her stay. The following week, she began working at the school as a Dhivehi teacher. Hawwa describes how the implicit hierarchy system in schools, based to a large extent on the language of instruction and whether or not the teacher was

Maldivian in origin, affected her own self-image and positioning of a teacher.

> *That experience showed me that in our schools, there is a certain pecking order. Teachers who are Maldivian but teach only English are at the top. This is the crème de la crème of teachers, the ones that everyone looks up to. Then, there are the teachers who are Maldivian but teach other subjects in English. This includes primary teachers who teach all subjects and secondary subject teachers. Next in line would be expatriate teachers, regardless of what subject or level they taught. At the bottom would be the Islam and Dhivehi teachers. These were teachers who were not very highly regarded by either the students, their colleagues, or the parents. I was one of these in the bottom group.*

The hierarchy system that Hawwa refers to here is an implicit one that Dhivehi teachers allude to, suggesting that those who teach English or subjects other than Dhivehi or Islam get preferential treatment within the school. Consequently, Hawwa felt inferior. Hawwa realised that Dhivehi teachers had a higher workload and were not usually involved in extracurricular activities in the school. There were four other Dhivehi teachers in the school, and when they were not teaching in class, they would often sit together in the staffroom and mark books. The school management expected teachers to mark every single piece of work every week, so with about 150 students in her classes, marking became 'a boring chore.' This did not leave much time to be involved in other activities in the school. As someone who has relished the opportunity to run clubs and sports activities for students, Hawwa felt disappointed and isolated.

In the classroom, too, Hawwa felt that she was struggling. She had never taught Dhivehi, and had not studied the language beyond school. She recognised that knowing Dhivehi alone was insufficient to teach it, and having had no training as a Dhivehi language teacher, and she felt unprepared and insecure as a teacher. But Hawwa was grounded in her commitment to improve herself. She found the content of the assigned lessons 'dry and boring' and began to suggest to her colleagues ways to make them more interesting by introducing more communicative activities. This was not welcomed by her colleagues.

> *One teacher told me that Dhivehi could not be taught in the ways I suggested. They found some of my suggestions amusing, sometimes laughing at me. I felt unsure of my knowledge and began to question my decisions.*

After several attempts to offer her opinions on lessons, and being rejected or criticised every time, Hawwa felt as if she was losing her sense of belonging in the school community. She felt 'like an outsider who did not really belong' there.

This feeling of professional isolation was exacerbated by an incident that happened in her classroom, about six months into her new job. The example of interactive positioning demonstrates how her students viewed Hawwa as lacking the linguistic skills required to be a teacher and how this caused Hawwa to reassess her professional identity. A student had asked if Hawwa knew English, and she had explained that she had taught English in her previous school. The child had asked her to name in English some items from a set of picture cards. Good naturedly, Hawwa had done so but ended up mispronouncing several words. She had pronounced 'bird' as /bɑːd/, 'girl' as /gɑːl/ and 'nurse' as /nɑːs/. Hawwa stated that she had always had difficulties with the /ɜː/ sound, and it had become a 'fossilised error' that she did not even notice. But her students did notice, and their peals of laughter dented her confidence further. She heard one student comment *'She can't even talk in English! How can she be a teacher?'* This statement was the point when Hawwa felt that her long-held perception of herself as a good English speaker and an expert teacher had been fragmented. The students' implication that she was incompetent as a teacher and English speaker led her to question her professional self-understanding. Hawwa described how this made her feel 'like an imposter' as if she was 'simply pretending.' While teaching had previously felt natural and enjoyable, it had now become tedious. Hawwa felt inadequate and in a constant struggle to prove herself.

Shifting identities

The third stage of her identity construction showed evidence of Hawwa's determination to take control of her career and steer herself toward success. This conscious shift in her identity was brought about in an effort to salvage her self-esteem and showed evidence of several fluctuations in her self-positioning as well her agentive role in re-constructing her professional identity.

Every two years, teachers at Hameedhiyya School were observed at least once by a school leader or an external teacher educator. Hawwa was observed when she was at the end of her second year of teaching in the school. This was a time when she was at a low point. But the visiting teacher educator who observed her commented positively on her teaching, and particularly her use of language. Hawwa notes this as a significant point in her career because it was 'the first time that [she] gave serious thought to [her] own use of the Dhivehi language.' She spent the next few weeks reflecting on the language. Hawwa recognised it as a turning point in her identity narrative:

> *I realised that this may be an opportunity for me. That this may be something I could explore to see what kind of niche options focusing on the Dhivehi language could lead to. I made a conscious decision to change my focus and my attitude. I wanted to be proactive in bringing about change.*

Encouraged by her family to turn things around, Hawwa decided to focus on being a learner and improve her communicative skills. Hawwa's recognition that she needed to invest in language learning in order to re-position herself suggests her agency in re-establishing her identity. She recalls that she enrolled in an English language course for adults, which she took in the evenings. This was to re-build her confidence in using English and address the difficulties she had always had with pronunciation and speaking. Next, she contacted a renowned Dhivehi scholar and requested for private lessons to study the language in depth. She wanted to understand the language, and particularly its syntax. In describing this study as stimulating as well as frustrating, Hawwa shows her vulnerability in taking on a new learner role, and her strong determination to succeed.

> *I had previously assumed that being a native speaker of Dhivehi I knew all there was to know about it. But once I started studying it, there was so much more to learn. I was excited. Learning has always been very exciting, and knowing that the study of Dhivehi in this way is not something that many people do, I was even more encouraged.*

Around this time, Hawwa completed her bachelor's degree, inspired by her new experiences of learning Dhivehi, and embarked on a new learning venture by enrolling in a master's programme specialising in Dhivehi language. This introduced her to the field of academic research. With her interest in exploring Dhivehi, Hawwa felt herself considering how well she fitted into other career pathways.

> *One of my lecturers suggested that I should take up teaching at the college. She would often get us to do peer teaching in her classes and was always very encouraging. She told me that I was a born teacher. That boosted my morale.*

Taking up a part-time position as an assistant lecturer at a small private college, Hawwa worked hard to negotiate her positionality within her new professional domain by familiarising herself with her allocated tasks and ensuring that she met the expectations of both her superiors and her students. Hawwa realised that college students were more critical than school children, and felt vulnerable, often on edge. Even though she remained positive and calm in class, Hawwa recalled that the smallest things would trigger intense emotional responses within herself. But she was adamant that she was going to succeed in her new role.

Hawwa recalls that she actively chose to alter her goals and learned to focus on her strengths. She realised that she had 'always been a good teacher' but that she had been too fixated on her linguistic limitations and too easily affected by others' positioning of her, to work on building her own strengths.

> *I realised that I don't have to have all the answers that it's okay for me to be able to say that I don't know anything. … I also realised that I would*

never have perfect English, but then again, nobody speaks perfectly, so it's not the end of the world.

Re-building expertise

This was the fourth stage of Hawwa's ongoing identity construction. It showed evidence of her attempt to re-build her self-image and depict herself as an expert in a way she had not imagined before. This stage also showed her recognition of the evolving nature of knowledge and her hopes for her future.

By the time Hawwa had completed her master's studies, Hawwa had left both her permanent position at Hameedhiyya School as well as her part-time role as an assistant lecturer at the college, as she was offered a lectureship position at Prosper College. She was so focused on excelling as a lecturer that initially, her work consumed her whole life. She spent many hours preparing stimulating content for her students and made a special effort to establish a good rapport with them. She sought the advice of her mentoring lecturer and was encouraged by the support from her family.

Hawwa explained that she spent close to 12 hours at work every day – an anomaly for the context where 6-hour workdays were the norm – and was constantly available to students and colleagues on her phone. She felt that her efforts paid off, as her superiors commented on her dedication, and her colleagues were inspired by her commitment to studying Dhivehi. Hawwa wanted to 'make teaching Dhivehi cool' and remove the stigma she had experienced as a Dhivehi teacher in Hameedhiyya School.

> *In the time I have been here, I feel respected and valued. Colleagues come to me to ask about language matters. I am often asked to proofread reports or write speeches for special days. My students appreciate the work I do, and I am starting to feel like I belong here.*

Hawwa attributes the change in her sense of self and self-positioning to how others treated her.

> *When others treat me as if I matter, as if what I have to say is also important, then I feel valued. Even little things like using respectful language to talk to me, or copying me into an email, or asking my opinion in a meeting. They all add up to make me feel like [I belong here].*

Looking ahead to the future, Hawwa explained that she wanted to continue to learn to do research and go on to do a PhD. Hawwa noted that although fascinating, research was 'difficult' because 'no such culture' existed at her college. But she was hopeful that she would find opportunities to work with and learn from others with shared interests.

> *I am focused on becoming the best version of myself, so it is a continuous process. Learning never stops.*

Discussion and Conclusion

This chapter has discussed one language educator's evolving identity as she progressed from student to school teacher and then to college lecturer. Focusing on one single case study has allowed the presentation of rich data that shows the complex nature of how identity is perpetually co-constructed by the individual and those around her. Through presenting narrative-biographical data, this study broadened understandings of the influences on teacher identity in pre- and in-service teaching. Hawwa's stories articulate the ongoing process of identity shaping and re-shaping, and revealed that her teacher identity was influenced by multiple factors, particularly her interactions with others – her colleagues, the parents and wider community, and the students themselves.

Examining Hawwa's identity negotiation and construction in terms of narrative-biographical data is beneficial as it showed multiple aspects of her work that were constitutive of her existing and evolving identity. It is clear that Hawwa's identity construction and negotiations included intellectual and emotional aspects, and related to how she gained a deeper understanding of herself as a teacher, of herself as a language user, and of her professional responsibilities. Her case has furthered our understanding of how experiencing crises during one's teacher education can assist one in developing a strong teacher identity (Beijaard *et al.*, 2004). Over the course of her career, Hawwa's emotional state fluctuated quite significantly and influenced her ability to function as an effective teacher. Although Hawwa was a trained teacher and had ideas about how to apply her understanding of pedagogy to her role as a Dhivehi teacher, due to the vulnerability she felt at the time, she was not able to apply this, suggesting that knowledge of effective pedagogy is inadequate to shape practice and create change. As Varghese (2006) reminds us, teacher education will do well 'to address and formulate what teachers should become ... rather than solely what they should know' (2006: 223).

While this study has presented how teachers struggle over positionality (Norton & Toohey, 2011), these findings provide evidence of the important role of self and others in negotiating identity. In each of the four stages of her career, Hawwa's self-positioning was directly influenced by how she was positioned by others. Where Hawwa experienced supportive collegial relationships, she flourished, identifying herself as a competent, skilled, and appreciated teacher and language user. Conversely, when the professional context was hostile and unsupportive of her professional learning and practice, Hawwa felt not just ousted from the community, but began to question her self-worth and pedagogical knowledge, seeing herself as being inferior in her professional practice. As a result of the interactions with others, Hawwa is sometimes forced positioned (Harré & van Langenhove, 1999) to take up an identity that she would not have chosen for herself.

These findings reiterate the essential role of supportive and welcoming professional communities and serve as a reminder that teacher identity cannot be reduced to a teacher's content and pedagogical knowledge alone. Instead, it corroborates Danielewicz's (2001) assertion that becoming a teacher 'requires engagement with identity, the way individuals conceive themselves so that teaching is a state of being, not merely ways of acting or behaving' (2001: 3). This narrative framework is also a reminder of points of continuity and change, which are evident in how Hawwa positioned herself at different stages of her work from a pre-service to an experienced teacher.

Hawwa's case lends support to Yazan's (2017) assertion that the way teachers position themselves is intertwined with their beliefs and values. Hawwa's belief that teachers must have expertise not just in their skill of teaching but in their knowledge of the subject content and, most especially, the language of instruction was evident in the way in which she continued to position herself. This highlights the need for teacher education programmes to explicitly address teacher's beliefs and values and provide opportunities for reflection.

Two strands of positioning were evident in Hawwa's journey: one which related to language competence and one which related to her competence as a teacher. At the start of her teaching career, Hawwa was put on a pedestal by her colleagues and island community. This led her to believe that she had graduated from a novice to an expert teacher in the course of months. Her self-esteem was at an all-time high; her competence as a teacher, and her expertise in English were being constantly validated through social recognition and support. This serves as a powerful testament to the dynamic and fluid conceptualisation of language proficiency and pedagogical expertise within her professional context. As Vanassche and Kelchtermans (2016) note, the acknowledgement of competence from significant others serves as the actual validation of one's self-judgement. When, during her period at Hameediyya School, Hawwa experienced a lack of acknowledgement of both linguistic and professional competence, it created feelings of uncertainty and self-doubt, leading to professional isolation and withdrawal. When impacted by external criticism, Hawwa described herself as being fragmented. Her self-esteem was fragile, fluctuating over time, and needed to be re-established through social recognition by others.

Through these identity shifts, the significance of emotions in a teacher's identity construction has been highlighted. As Zembylas (2003) suggests, emotions provide meaning to experience and are essential for forming an identity. This study suggests that due to the continuous and emotional nature of identity development that spans over the course of a teacher's career, teachers must be provided with learning opportunities to support their career development. Hawwa's story has suggested the powerful influence of a supportive mentor in adapting to a new role. Teachers must be guided on how to adjust to changes in their professional lives, thereby helping to develop their resilience and wellbeing, reducing attrition rates as a result (McKay & Manning, 2018).

While this study has explored one teacher's identity construction and self-positioning based on data sourced directly from the teacher alone, it would be interesting to explore (in)congruencies in the positioning between several individuals within one context. Despite this being a single case study, the findings are significant because they contribute to our understanding of how language teachers develop and shift their identities according to their contexts, as a result of interaction. The pressures that Hawwa faced served to strengthen her identity eventually, and shows the complex interplay between the processes of modification and continuity in the construction of teacher identity, and exemplifies the sense-making processes of an individual with a strong sense of agency.

Note

(1) Every measure was taken to ensure confidentiality in the research process and reporting. Pseudonyms are used for all people and institutions reported here. Other information that could lead to the identification of institutions or related individuals has either not been reported in this research or has been altered to reduce the risk of identification. Some of the details of the participant's background has been deliberately kept vague at the request of the participant, who was provided with a copy of an initial draft of the paper.

References

Beijaard, D., Meijer, P.C. and Verloop, N. (2004) Reconsidering research on teachers' professional identity. *Teaching and Teacher Education* 20 (2), 107–128.

Block, D. (2006) Identity in applied linguistics. In T. Omoniyi and G. White (eds) *The Sociolinguistics of Identity* (p.34–49). London: Continuum.

Bruner, J.S. (1994) The remembered self. In U. Neisser and R. Fivush (eds) *The Remembering Self: Construction and Accuracy in the Self-Narrative* (pp. 41–54). New York: Cambridge University Press.

Connelly, F.M. and Clandinin, D.J. (1999) *Shaping a Professional Identity: Stories of Educational Practice*. London, Ontario: Aithonse Press.

Danielewicz, J. (2001) *Teaching Selves: Identity, Pedagogy, and Teacher Education*. Albany, NY: State University of New York.

Davies, B. and Harré, R. (1990) Positioning: The discursive production of selves. *Journal for the Theory of Social Behaviour* 20, 43–63.

Donato, R. (2016) Becoming a language teaching professional: What's identity got to do with it? In G. Barkhuizen (ed.) *Reflections on Language Teacher Identity Research*. New York. Routledge.

Han, I. (2017) Conceptualisation of English teachers' professional identity and comprehension of its dynamics. *Teachers and Teaching: Theory and Practice* 23 (5), 549–569.

Hanna, F., Oostdam, R., Severiens, S. and Zijlstra, B. (2019) Domains of teacher identity: A review of quantitative measurement instruments. *Educational Research Review* 27, 15–27

Harré, R. and Van Langenhove, L. (eds) (1999) *Positioning Theory: Moral Contexts of International Action*. Oxford: Wiley-Blackwell.

Jenlink, P. (2014) *Teacher Identity and the Struggle for Recognition: Meeting the Challenges of a Diverse Society*. Lanham, MD: Rowman and Littlefield Education.

Jenkins, J. (2007) *English as a Lingua Franca: Attitude and Identity*. New York: Oxford.

Kanno, Y. (2003) *Negotiating Bilingual and Bicultural Identities: Japanese Returnees Betwixt Two Worlds*. Mahwah, NJ: Lawrence Erlbaum.

Kelchtermans, G. (2009) Who I am in how I teach is the message. Self-understanding, vulnerability and reflection. *Teachers and Teaching* 15 (2), 257–272.

Lee, S.K. (2003) Multiple identities in a multicultural world: A Malaysian perspective. *Journal of Language, Identity and Education* 2, 137–158.

Lieblich, A., Tuval-Mashiach, R. and Zilber, T. (1998) *Narrative Research: Reading, Analysis and Interpretation*. Thousand Oaks, CA: Sage Publications.

McKay, L. and Manning, H. (2018) Do I belong in the profession? The cost of fitting in as a preservice teacher with a passion for social justice. *Journal of Teacher Education* 70 (4), 360–371. https://doi.org/10.1177/0022487118811326

Mohamed, N. (2013) The challenge of medium of instruction: A view from Maldivian classrooms. *Current Issues in Language Planning* 14 (1), 185–203.

Mohamed, N. (2019) From a monolingual to a multilingual nation: Analysing the language education policy in the Maldives. In A. Liddicoat and A. Kirkpatrick (eds) *The Routledge International Handbook of Language Education Policy in Asia* (pp. 414–426). New York: Routledge.

Moghaddam, F. and Harré, R. (2010) Words, conflicts and political processes. In F. Moghaddam and R. Harré (eds) *Words of Conflict, Words of War: How the Language We Use in Political Processes Sparks Fighting* (pp. 1–29). Santa Barbara, CA: Praeger.

Norton, B. (2010) Language and identity. In N. Hornberger and S. McKay (eds) *Sociolinguistics and Language Education* (pp. 349–369). Bristol: Multilingual Matters.

Norton, B. and Toohey, K. (2011) Identity, language learning, and social change. *Language Teaching* 44 (4), 412–446.

Pavlenko, A. (2002) Poststructuralist approach to the study of social factors in second language learning and use. In V. Cook (ed.) *Portraits of the L2 User* (pp. 277–302). Clevedon: Multilingual Matters.

Su Kim, L. (2003) Multiple identities in a multicultural world: A Malaysian perspective. *Journal of Language, Identity, and Education* 2, 137–158.

Trent, J. and Gao, X. (2009) 'At least I'm the type of teacher I want to be': Second-career English language teachers' identity formation in Hong Kong secondary schools. *Asia-Pacific Journal of Teacher Education* 37 (3), 253–270.

Tsui, A.B.M. (2007) Complexities of identity formation: A narrative inquiry of an EFL teacher. *TESOL Quarterly* 41 (4), 657–680.

Vanassche, E. and Kelchtermans, G. (2014) Teacher educators' professionalism in practice: positioning. theory and personal interpretative framework. *Teaching and Teacher Education* 44, 117–127.

Vanassche, E. and Kelchtermans, G. (2016) A narrative analysis of a teacher educator's professional learning journey. *European Journal of Teacher Education* 39 (3), 355–367.

Varghese, M.M. (2006) Bilingual teachers-in-the-making in Urbantown. *Journal of Multilingual and Multicultural Development* 27 (3), 211–224.

Varghese, M., Morgan, B., Johnston, B. and Johnson, K.A. (2005) Theorizing language teacher identity: Three perspectives and beyond. *Journal of Language, Identity, and Education* 4 (1), 21–44.

Yazan, B. (2017) 'It just made me look at language in a different way': ESOL teacher candidates' identity negotiation through teacher education coursework. *Linguistics and Education* 40, 38–49.

Yazan, B. (2018) A conceptual framework to understand language teacher identities. *Journal of Second Language Teacher Education* 1 (1), 21–48.

Zembylas, M. (2003) Emotions and teacher identity: A poststructural perspective. *Teachers and Teaching* 9 (3), 213–238.

8 *Suntem profesori* / We Are Teachers: Self-exploration as a Pathway to Language Teacher Education

April Salerno and Elena Andrei

Introduction

We have a rare gem of a relationship: one of those professional friendships that comes along once in a blue moon. When we work together, things click. Our questions to each other improve our writing and thinking, even through online collaboration, across long distances (see Andrei & Salerno, 2018). Not only do we have a lot in common professionally – both longtime teacher educators, interested in how we can help teachers improve their instruction of English learners (ELs) and coordinators of Teaching English to Speakers of Other Languages (TESOL) programs at separate US universities – we also have a lot in common personally. We are 'inverse language partners,' meaning we speak the same two languages but in opposite first language (L1)/second language (L2) order. April's L1 is English, with Romanian as an L2; Elena's L1 is Romanian, with English as an L2. We talk together in both languages, often at the same time (see Palmer & Martínez, 2016, on hybrid language use). And we are friends. We take our families with young children on joint vacations (and amid complaints from our partners, we huddle together over work during our children's afternoon naptimes). In Romanian, we perhaps would be called *nănași*, people who are family not by blood, but through friendship.

So with all that professional and personal history between us, it might be an understatement to say that we found the discoveries we made during a dialoguing project between the two of us to be 'surprising.' Our project consisted of a back-and-forth-style written discussion between the two of us about our experiences as language learners and teacher educators. We created our dialogue over several months by reading each other's answers and asking additional and clarifying questions. We hope dialoguing might be a way to help teachers we teach discover the complexities of their language learning experiences and identities through interaction with each other and then to apply these understandings to their classroom practices, helping them better understand the complex identities of language learners they teach. Aligned with the goals of this volume, we seek to equip language teacher educators with a tool for supporting teachers' exploration of their own identities and interactions in the diverse spaces and communities where they teach or will teach. We do this through self-study of our own experiences as language learners and teacher educators (Russell, 2007). We draw from Korthagen and Verkuyl's (2007) idea that: 'One cannot help others look more closely at their own inner selves if one has not done this oneself and become acquainted with the fears, obstacles, and joys inherent to such a quest' (2007: 107). Here we explain our process, followed by a proposed assignment that other language teacher educators can use and modify toward these ends.

What is dialogue?

Certainly, dialogue is a word that means many things to different people. In using narrative and dialogue as approaches for teaching teachers about cultural diversity, McVee and Boyd (2016) explain two ideas that dialogue is *not*: 'Dialogue is not mere argumentation' (2016: 47). And 'dialogue is not merely talk' (2016: 48). Instead, they quote Burbules (1993):

> Dialogue is an activity directed toward discovery and new understanding, which stands to improve the knowledge, insight, or sensitivity of its participants. ... Dialogue represents a continuous, developmental communicative interchange through which we stand to gain a fuller apprehension of the world, ourselves, and one another. (Burbules, 1993: 8; McVee & Boyd, 2016: 48)

We draw on this dynamic idea of dialogue, that dialogue moves and changes, lives and breathes, as it is created. And that in the process, dialogue also changes those who are living and breathing and creating it. Fecho and Clifton (2016) wrote:

> As people share lives, experiences, concerns, and resources with others near and distant, they are shaped by and, in turn, shape what they share – values, materials, ways of being, relationships, institutions, and practices – and the ways they share these things with others. What is shared and how it is shared with others are what give rise to cultures that people find themselves part of, sometimes by choice, sometimes of necessity, sometimes by a bit of both. (2016: 4)

We believe that dialogue (which uses language) affects cultural and individual identity. Gee (2014) wrote of language 'as saying, doing, and being' (2014: 2). In his view, language is not only about saying and accomplishing things, but also 'language allows us to be things. It allows us to take on different socially significant identities' (2014: 2). Through the language of dialoguing, we believe we can both project ourselves and explore and develop our identities as teachers and as bi- or multi-linguals.

Fecho and Clifton (2016) asked important questions about humans in general and their own dialoguing in particular:

> What, then, do we who engage across cultural boundaries – that is to say, all of us – do when certain contexts or cultural stances or cultural experiences or cultural histories shape our transactions in a particular way – sometimes in predictably scripted ways – and yet there is some exigency to try to reconfigure those stances and those transactions? What might it mean in these contexts to reconfigure our ways with words by seeing our selves and the selves of others as dialogical – as multiple, in flux, in dialogue, unfinished? (2016: 5)

We, too, believe our dialogue is situated within this idea that our dialogue is shaping our selves – and that the dialogues of teachers might also help in shaping their selves.

A note about two specific identities: Bilinguals and language teacher educators

We identify as bilingual and bicultural language teachers and language teacher educators. Our identities and varied language learning and teaching experiences sparked our dialogue and lead us to explore and later discover surprising aspects of ourselves. It is well outside the scope of this chapter to thoroughly review the vast literature on identity and language teacher identity (see Yazan, 2018) as it relates to bilingualism (or multilingualism, as the case may be) and as it relates to teaching. Still, it is difficult to proceed without first considering at least that these two specific identities might cause dissonance for individuals grappling with them. Related to bilingualism, Grosjean (2013) considered a Czech proverb: 'Learn a new language and get a new soul.' The proverb itself speaks to the inner depth with which bilinguals, or as Grosjean makes the distinction 'biculturals,' have regarded their identities. Grosjean goes on to explain that the phenomenon of bilinguals' feeling different across languages is an indication of 'a shift in behavior and attitudes corresponding to a shift in situation or context' (2013: 23). Further, Grosjean (2010) writes of biculturalism as closely linked to identity: 'Their dilemma is that monocultural members of their different cultures want to know if they are members of culture A or culture B, or of a new culture, when biculturals just want to be accepted – consciously or unconsciously – for who they are: members of two or more cultures' (2010: 116).

Second, regarding teacher education, many have written about teachers, particularly novice teachers, having to assume new identities when they enter classrooms. Back in 1977, Harris wrote of 'the teacher as actor,' taking on responsibilities usually assumed in the theater, including, according to Harris, speech, pantomime and characterization, as well as 'the classroom equivalent of the duties of playwright, director, stage manager, crew, and producer' (1977: 187). Relatedly, teachers are frequently described as adopting a 'teacher persona' (Kincheloe, 2005: 155). Sadoski (1992) explains, 'Persona derives from the Latin word for mask – the theatrical masks worn by Greek and Roman actors to represent particular characters such as tragedy and comedy to an audience' (1992: 272). Such roles, or identities, can be particularly difficult for language teachers, and language teacher educators, who might be adopting teaching roles and straddling cultures simultaneously. Teachers commonly referred to as 'NNESTs,' or 'non-native English-speaking teachers,' have been viewed at times as not equally qualified as 'native English-speaking teachers' (NESTs) by not being fully fluent in the language and culture (Selvi, 2014). More recent scholarship on NNEST moves away from apprehending identity and experience categorically (e.g. the NEST/NNEST dichotomy) (Yazan & Rudolph, 2018) to explore a more complex and fluid identity of multilingual teachers of English (Matsumoto, 2018). Understanding these complexities is essential as we view our own identities as bilinguals and as language teacher educators.

Research Questions

This study considers: (1) How are we, as two teacher educators with inverse L1s and L2s, identifying and describing our language identities? And (2) how are these identities and experiences influencing our teaching philosophies and classroom practices?

Methods

We began by keeping our own back-and-forth-style dialogue initially answering the question, 'Can you tell me about your language learning and teaching background?' April wrote first via email and sent it to Elena with additional specific questions related to our backgrounds and personal experiences with language learning and teaching. We wrote to each other regularly (approximately every two weeks) for about four months. In each reply, we answered the other's previous questions and posed additional ones, to extend the conversation and to learn more about the connections and/or disconnections between us. We expected that teaching in our L2s would be a primary focus of our dialogue, but just as questions often shift in qualitative work (Agee, 2009), we found that our dialogue questions evolved across entries and over time. Because our dialogue was not chronological, we also individually constructed timelines of our language learning and teaching. We shared these with each other to help place the 'critical events' or key moments of personal change (Webster & Mertova, 2007: 73), in time. Our back-and-forth dialogue and our timeline became our central data. We then asked two critical friends (Heath & Street, 2008) to read our dialogue, to comment on themes they saw emerging, and to provide guidance on how to proceed with analysis.

As noted above, we believe dialoguing is a dynamic, interactive process. We came to view our dialogue as a sort of narrative that we co-constructed and as data for much-needed teacher-education self-study in the TESOL field (Sharkey & Peercy, 2018). Drawing from self-study principles within narrative inquiry of listening carefully to one another, co-constructing the narrative, and sharing our lived stories (Connelly & Clandinin, 1990), we began the analysis by considering the entire story of the dialogue. We found that this analysis required several readings. We first read the dialogue independently in its entirety. We made notes and wrote questions in the margins, and posed these to each other, a process which extended the dialogue for several months. We then came together and read the entire dialogue in a performance-style, oral reading, influenced by Ericksonian ideas of analyzing qualitative data after first reading it all entirely (Erickson, 1986). This reading required several hours, but while reading aloud, we found that the words took on new meaning, and whereas we had previously written comments back and forth, we were able to engage in real-time discussion and oral dialogue about our experiences and possible interpretations. Through this process, we developed inductive qualitative codes (Miles *et al.*, 2014) for themes that emerged; we identified critical events, and we considered interpretations. In our analysis, we were attentive to Connelly and Clandinin's (1990) warnings of the 'risks, dangers and abuses of narrative' (1990: 10). In ensuring quality, we followed their advice in two areas. First, they tell 'narrative inquirers to listen closely to their critics' (1990: 10). After drafting our findings, just as we had done after drafting the initial dialogue, we invited two critical friends to read our work and to point out missteps. Second, we were on guard against 'narrative smoothing' (Spence, 1986), which Connelly and Clandinin (1990) explain happens as in a 'Hollywood plot,' where 'everything works out well in the end' (1990: 10). They advise inquirers to be 'as alert to the stories not told as to those that are' (1990: 10). Our process of reading aloud helped us pause and press each other at points where stories might have been 'not told.' This work resulted in notes in the margins and additions to the timeline and helped us ensure that we were not 'smoothing' out important details.

Findings

First, to provide context, we give quick summaries of our language learning and teaching timelines. April grew up speaking Southern English in a mostly monolingual, Southern US environment. She studied French in high school and at the university. She visited France and, as an adult, had a French conversation partner, a French teacher with whom she regularly conversed. She first learned Romanian through immersive training with the US Peace Corps in Moldova in the early 2000s. She lived two years in a small village with a Moldovan family, while working as a 5th–12th-grade English as a Foreign Language (EFL) teacher. After returning to the US, she worked as a high school English teacher in New Mexico, where she taught students whose L1s were Navajo and Zuni. She met Elena during her doctoral studies five years after Peace Corps. After graduate school, she returned to Moldova to teach at the university level for one academic year. Both times while she lived in Moldova, she taught some lessons in Romanian, but not as her primary teaching assignment. She now lives in the US and works as a TESOL teacher educator.

Elena grew up in Romania, speaking Southern Romanian. She learned English from a tutor in first grade and, in second grade, began taking English in school with her classmates. She also studied French in school, but English was a greater focus. She studied English throughout high school and university, eventually becoming an EFL K-12 teacher in her hometown. Soon after, she accepted a position as an EFL teacher in Bucureşti, while pursuing a master's in English language teaching. In the late 2000s, Elena moved to the US to become an English as a Second Language (ESL) teacher. She then pursued a second master's degree and later a doctoral degree. Like April, she now lives in the US, working as a TESOL teacher educator.

Although we knew each other well, seeing our timelines helped us understand the pathways we each had followed, especially before we met each other in language learning and teaching. It is important to note that our dialogue also included discussion of various aspects of language varieties and how they affected us; for example, how speaking a Southern variety of English affected April, how Elena's regional variety of Romanian was perceived when she moved to Bucureşti, or how Moldovan and Romanian varieties themselves are different from each other. These are important aspects of language diversity, but fully exploring them is outside this chapter's scope. Here, we focus instead not on varieties we speak of our L1s but on how being bilingual affected our identities.

Critical events

As we moved deeper into the dialogue, we found it was the stories we told each other that revealed the most about our bilingual identities. As we initially dialogued, we did not realize we were working through such deep identity questions or even that we were talking about identity. The idea emerged through our dialoguing. Here, we explain that emergence as we present several critical events.

'Invisible' bilingualism

The first of these events occurred for April just after she had returned to the US from her first time living in Moldova. She told this event while remembering how she met Elena:

> **April:** I was really happy [when I met you]. I had been looking for someone who I could speak Romanian with at the university, and so far, I hadn't found anyone. In fact, I had been to the international center the day before to ask if they knew of someone. I also hadn't met too many Romanian speakers in the US before I met you. The one longest conversation I had had with someone happened one day when I was on lunch break in Washington, D.C., from chaperoning students who were touring the city. A homeless man approached me with an English sign asking for money, but I happened to hear him say very quietly '*Vă rog*' ('Please') in Romanian. I immediately switched to Romanian and began talking with him and was delighted to find out that he was Romanian. I invited him to share my lunch, and we talked for my entire hour break. After that break, my colleagues from the faculty commented and laughed at what a strange experience it was for them to see me shift into Romanian and spend my lunch break with a homeless man. I realized then that they didn't really understand part of who I am, and I felt a little embarrassed or awkward in front of them, given their reaction. I asked him to meet me at the same spot again the next week, but I never saw him again. I'm sure there are many reasons why he might have been afraid to meet me. It was such a great experience meeting you because I felt that it was validating to part of my identity that wasn't really known in the US.

April's mention of identity is the first time in the dialogue where the word 'identity' appears. In discussing the events afterwards, April revealed that there were not many other moments when she used Romanian around Americans who normally saw her using English. One other similar event was this one from the timeline:

> Around fall 2008: I had an experience in South Carolina where a Moldovan man visited my parents' church. I talked with him extensively throughout the church dinner, which followed the church service, and my family was surprised because they had never seen me talk to someone in Romanian before. They said they were proud, and I realized that they really didn't know that side of me. My niece, who was about four years old at the time, was offended, however, because she thought I was talking a funny way on purpose as a joke so that she wouldn't understand. I explained to her what it means to talk two languages, but I'm not sure that she understood then.

We discussed that both of these experiences occurred after April returned from Moldova the first time, when maybe her L2 identity was still in a formative stage, in that she was developing what that identity would look like in the US. Our coding marked both of these events for their importance in others' perceptions. For April, these events revealed that she felt others did not see her L2 identity in the US and that most times, her bilingualism was invisible because there usually were not opportunities such as this for her Romanian use to be seen by others. Gkaintartzi *et al.* (2015) explain how the bilingualism of immigrant students in Greece was 'invisible' to their teachers in that teachers did not expect students to use their L1s in school. April's colleagues, likewise, did not appear to understand her conversation and immediate bonding with the man. Taken from a class perspective, their reaction makes sense. She was a professional faculty member in an upper-middle-class environment inviting a homeless man, who had been begging, to share lunch and conversation with her. Had the man been speaking English, it is unlikely she would have had this reaction to him. But in the moment, the man presented her an opportunity to validate and reconnect to her L2 and her L2 identity. Also, she applied her cultural understanding to the situation: it is impolite in Moldova to eat in front of someone, no matter how poor, without inviting him/her to join you, so her response was somewhat automatic in inviting him. In the South Carolina event, her family expressed pride in her interactions with the Moldovan man but was surprised to see her speaking fluently in Romanian. Her niece's reaction is understandable, given her childhood and sole experiences with monolingualism. Still, April further dialogued about how it was important to her that a family member did not recognize her bilingual identity.

In the same sense, Elena noted, related to her bilingualism:

> **Elena:** But when I was in the US, I became the bilingual person or the NNEST. Of course, my [English] language has improved tremendously, especially in terms of vocabulary, pronunciation and expressions. Listening was my weakest skill as an EFL learner, and it might still be, but I am not sure.

It is interesting in this excerpt, that Elena calls herself 'the bilingual person or the NNEST.' The presence of the article 'the' suggests this is a role that she was expected to play, in a part of the US where there were not many other bilingual Romanian-speaking teachers and few opportunities for her bilingualism to be visible. She later commented about how she assumed that identity and how the privilege of English had affected us both in different ways.

English as a Privileged Language (EPL)

The topic of English privilege was a backdrop for our discussion of teaching in our L2s. In the following passage, our discussion focused on language privilege:

> **April:** ...My experiences teaching in Romanian were generally for teaching other things than the language itself or teaching Romanian. I taught general pedagogical practices to teachers, and I also taught

extra-curricular health and safety lessons to high school students. I always felt like my students were so excited that I was speaking Romanian, that they quickly overlooked any mistakes that I made (of which I'm sure there were plenty). In fact, if I started speaking unexpectedly, I was often met with awes of surprise and frequently applause. My thinking is that this is related to English being a language of privilege. I heard people say they were very honored to meet an American who spoke Romanian. Sometimes people would add that's because American society is so advanced or superior. I reject these ideas of one culture being superior to another. But sometimes it seemed that even opening my mouth put me at the center of this kind of thought. Elena, what was it like for you when you teach in English? Was it different when you first started than now? Was there a difference in teaching in Romania in English versus teaching in the US?

Elena: April, I liked your comment about English as a language of privilege, and this relates to my answer about my learning of English. In Romania, when I grew up, parents, or at least the parents that I knew, wanted their kids to learn English. English was still perceived to be needed to be successful in life. Later on, by the time I graduated from high school, and it is still valid now in 2018, you need to pass a foreign language proficiency oral exam as part of your high school graduation. Informally in my generation and my high school, which was one of the three best high schools in my native town, everyone passed that test, but I do not think that is still the case or was the case with other high schools. Yes, English was perceived as a language that will move you forward economically. I am not sure I would say privileged, but if you knew English you would have advantages; thus, you will be privileged.

We went on to discuss that the privilege of English is seen in the value that is placed on its learning and the expectation that English should be learned 'perfectly', while mistakes in Romanian as an L2 made by April were more easily forgiven. We also talked specifically about English's privilege and how it related to teaching:

April: Also, did anyone (students or a colleague or anyone else) ever comment on your accent? How did they respond?

Elena: I do not remember vividly specific examples when people commented on my accent. I get that pretty often in a variety of settings, so I do not remember examples. I know at times I had gotten offended when they asked me if I came from Russia, and I get that a lot, and it makes sense to get that. Romanian has a lot of Slavic influences because we are surrounded by Slavic languages such as Russian, Bulgarian, Serbian. That is why I sound Russian. I sometimes joke with my students and tell them I have a southern accent and not a foreign one. The reason I had gotten offended when asked if I am Russian is historical. We were part of the Eastern Bloc under the influence of the former Soviet Union, and that was not a good period of our history. I didn't get offended when asked if I am from Canada or Italy, which happened only once. I think now I am more sensitive about assumptions, and when I talk with people that sound like L2 speakers of English, I ask them, 'Where are you from?' rather than assuming they are not from here or assume a certain country or language.

While April was greeted with praise for her attempts at Romanian, Elena was expected from an early age to master English. Although she was speaking at a very proficient level as an adult, still her accent was a subject of curiosity for others, often revealing assumptions that she was the speaker of a Slavic language. People who interacted with Elena sometimes unfairly expected her to speak with native-like proficiency, an unrealistic expectation for bilinguals (Mahboob, 2010). Additionally, the assumption that she was Russian was for Elena a microagression (Sue, 2010), given the difficult history between Romania and the former USSR.

Bilingual (in)validation

Perhaps because of English's privilege, and the desire of many Moldovans to be exposed to English as much as possible, April's Romanian proficiency was disregarded, and she was asked specifically to keep her Romanian identity hidden:

Elena: April, tell me about your perception of teaching in your L2.

April: ...Our contexts are pretty different. ... I was generally supposed to be teaching my L1. ... Those who were very serious about learning English wanted me to talk in English all the time. ... The youngest class I taught there were 5th graders, and I do remember that with these younger students, I used more Romanian ... I remember the head student in the class told a classmate that I wouldn't have to speak in Romanian if he and the others would learn English better. This statement alone speaks a lot to me about the privilege of English in that environment. The idea was that English was the target and that resorting to Romanian was a reason for fault in the students.

I remember when I first arrived at the university, my department chair asked me not to tell students that I spoke Romanian. She told me to push them instead to use English. That was a difficult request. Pretending not to speak my L2 felt like it would be hiding part of my identity, and I thought it would hurt my ability to form real relationships with them if I pretended not to understand them when they talked to me in Romanian. So at first, I didn't advertise to students that I spoke Romanian, but I didn't try to disguise it either. Then, I remember there was a day in one of my English teaching methods courses when the jigsaw activity I was trying to orchestrate was falling apart. Students didn't understand the logistics of which group they were supposed to move to, and the whole thing was chaotic. Exasperated, I started calling out explanations in Romanian. There was a silence of shock in the room and then a wave of translations for the many students who spoke Russian but not Romanian.

> **Elena:** I like how you decided to follow the rule of not telling your students you spoke Romanian, but also, you did not do anything to hide that. I think that was the best decision. It took me a little by surprise when you said Romanian is part of your identity. When I think of all your actions and what you did, I am like, yes, why didn't I get to that conclusion? I guess you let your actions speak for you rather than label yourself, which I think is more powerful. Yes, Romanian and Moldova are part of your identity and what you do.

This proved to be a critical event in our dialogue because of Elena's revelation that she had never really considered Romanian to be an essential part of April's identity. Though we had worked together for years and shared memories and stories about Romania and Moldova, we had never verbalized the role that our L2s play in our identities. In this excerpt, April explains two critical events: First, one of her 5th-graders accused another of not knowing English well enough and, therefore, forcing her to speak Romanian. These words, from a 5th-grader, suggested that her L2 use did not belong in the classroom, except when students failed in their work of learning English. Years later, this event was reified when not a child, but the university department chair asked April to refrain from using Romanian in the classroom with pre-service EFL teachers. In that situation, April made an instructional decision that best fits the context and also who she was. In the dialogue, April explicitly cited the idea of identity: 'Pretending not to speak my L2 felt like it would be hiding part of my identity,' she wrote, prompting Elena to reveal that she had never fully considered Romanian as part of April's identity.

In analyzing our dialogue, we considered our experiences as doctoral students and reviewed our timelines of how our language-learning experiences had shaped our identities. As doctoral students, we often talked in Romanian, while walking to class and while working together on in-class assignments. Through dialoguing, we realized that this shared use of Romanian, not only supported us linguistically, providing us opportunities to use both English and Romanian for academic purposes; it also made our Romanian visible to other students, faculty members around us and also to ourselves, as we came to see Romanian as a language we could use for our work. For April, this visibility served as confirmation that she was bilingual. For Elena, this visibility validated her L1 and afforded her the chance to use it in doctoral work that otherwise would have exclusively been in English. Despite that we are both bilingual and have focused our careers on the importance of language learning and multilingualism, our dialogue still revealed to us an added dimension of how useful it was for us to use both of our languages in various settings, including academic ones. We went on to apply this new thought to how we regard English learners as having English as part of their bilingual identities and how we could apply this type of dialoguing to the teachers we work with.

Proposed Assignment: Dialoguing about Language Learning and Identity

Based on our dialoguing, we developed the following assignment for teachers in their first TESOL course. We should clarify that we do not expect students' dialogues to be like ours. No two dialogues are alike. Plus, we have years of experience in TESOL; we are both bilingual in the same languages, and we dialogued over a much longer period of time than the assignment permits. Our students might come from very different backgrounds. They might have bilingual experiences, or they might regard themselves as monolingual or as having failed at learning an L2. All people have their own idiolects (Mihalicek & Wilson, 2011), uniquely linked to their identities and backgrounds. Regardless of their language-learning experiences, we believe the teachers we work with can examine the influences of languages, including English varieties, on themselves and their teaching practices.

Purpose

The purpose of this assignment is for you to explore your own language background with a partner and make connections to your current/future teaching, considering how ELs in your classroom might have different or similar experiences and how to view them from assets-oriented perspectives.

Task

This assignment includes multiple steps. Keep one document where you add work for each step. Submit the assignment after each step, and I will provide feedback with additional questions/ideas to explore. In the end, you will submit a final draft with all the steps.

Step 1: Notify me if you have preferences for who your partner is. If not, I will assign partners.

Step 2: Individually answer the following questions (1–3 pages). Be specific, giving examples whenever possible:

- Describe an early memory you have of learning or using language.
- What varieties of English and/or other languages do you speak? How do you use language differently in different contexts? Why?
- How do you feel about your experiences learning a language (including English and/or other languages)?

  Share your reflection with your partner. If you want to ask your partner questions as he/she reads, include a note to your partner.

Step 3: When you receive your partner's reflection, read it carefully, and ask your partner two follow-up questions. Questions should be open-ended but can ask for clarification or push your partner to think more deeply about an experience or its relationship to teaching. Return the reflection with the follow-up questions to your partner.

Step 4: Answer your partner's two questions and these questions:

- Describe a time when you felt your language did not fit in whatever context you were in. This might have been a travel experience, or a group you joined, where you found others used language in different ways than you (e.g. visiting a physician who used technical terms).
- How might this experience be the same or different from those of ELs you teach/will teach? (Consider their age, school context, and the response of others in your school to ELs). Remember, there is always a danger in essentializing or stereotyping ELs, who come from diverse backgrounds (Wright, 2019). As much as possible, think of one or two specific ELs and how your experiences might differ from theirs. If you haven't worked with or known any ELs, discuss that.

Complete the 'Instructor Check-in' to give your instructor feedback about your dialoguing progress.

Step 5: Read your partner's new reflection and write two new questions you would ask him/her in a meeting.

Step 6: Meet with your partner face-to-face, by phone, or via online conferencing. Allow 30–60 minutes. Ask your questions, and discuss what you learned about yourself and ELs. Look for ways you can move toward assets-oriented language and viewing ELs as a diverse group. Each of you should document how you met and what you discussed.

Step 7: Re-read your entire document and reflect on what you learned. Answer these questions:

- How does your language relate to who you are as a person and your identity?
- How do you think your language learning/speaking experience(s) might influence your teaching of ELs?

Add this reflection to your document.

See the Appendix for a sample rubric.

Discussion and Conclusion

Since we created this assignment, we have recently begun implementing it. We have found in just our initial implementation that the dialogue offers teachers space to reflect on their language learning identities and to connect those experiences with their language teaching and their students' learning. Our dialoguing, and we hope that of our students now and in the future, is 'not merely talk' (McVee & Boyd, 2016: 48); it is a journey. *Suntem profesori* / 'We are teachers,' and at the same time, we are bilingual, bicultural language learners and language teacher educators. As such, our dialoguing was a self-study of our language learning and teaching (Russell, 2007; Sharkey & Peercy, 2018). April recalled having her colleagues watch her interact in Romanian with a homeless man and of having her family watch her speak Romanian with a church visitor. These experiences led us to explore ways in which her bilingual identity was previously 'invisible' to colleagues and family (Gkaintartzi *et al.*, 2015). Elena identified herself as 'the bilingual person or the NNEST,' an identity she realized she assumed when she moved to the US. She identified these two labels, one that moves away from the NEST–NNEST dichotomy as recent scholarship suggests (Yazan & Rudolph, 2018) and one focused on the absence of native-speakerism (Holliday, 2006). We both explored how English as a privileged language interacted with these identities. April, for example, was met with awe when Romanian-speakers discovered she spoke Romanian. Elena felt pushed from an early age that she must learn English for perceived economic advantages. While April was valued as 'cool' for her American accent in Romanian, Elena felt her Romanian accent in English was seen as different, that people noticed it without understanding who she was or where she was from.

In making these discoveries, it became apparent to us that this type of dialoguing could be beneficial for the teachers with whom we work, as well. Though we do not have much data yet from students and their dialoguing assignment, we had seen this type of discussion happening informally on discussion boards in our courses previously. For example, in this excerpt from April's course, Susan, who lived in France as a child, talks with Rebekah, who had recently returned to the US after having taught English in Ukraine:

> Susan: ...As a young girl learning French abroad, I yearned to just fit in. My limited French made it hard for anyone to communicate with me, and I just wanted to stop being the 'American' girl at school who was bad at French. However, I could see how it would also bother me if my identity was completely obscured. Perhaps if I had been more confident in my abilities to communicate, I would have been more proud....
>
> Rebekah: Thank you for sharing your own experience in France, Susan. I can relate to hating being the odd one out or feeling like people didn't see me as more than the label. Reading your post was a great reminder of how other students will feel.
>
> I think especially in the beginning, I wanted to have a good accent, but as my accent did get better and my intonations became more natural, I started to feel like I was developing a split personality. There was an American-style Rebekah and a Ukrainian-style Rebekah...Going back in [sic] forth could be exhausting and also confusing about which Rebekah was the *real* Rebekah...

We recognized in this conversation a connection between the students, as they struggled to make sense of their bilingual identities. The idea of 'split personalities,' and bilingualism is present within the literature (Grosjean, 2010).

In many ways, these students' words echo some of our own dialoguing and suggest the need to explore bilingual identities further through a more formalized process, such as the assignment we suggest. We found that through our dialoguing, our teaching philosophies shifted in an important way. We had always thought it important for teachers to reflect on both their teaching practices and their autobiographies/identities related to those practices. Through this process, however, we came to recognize the importance of having an interactive dialogue about our language learning and teaching experiences and how those shaped who we are. The process of talking with each other helped us consider questions we would not have come to on our own and to explore 'the stories not told' individually (Connelly & Clandinin, 1990: 10). It became part of our teaching philosophies that teachers should have opportunities to process their language-learning experiences with peers as they come to understand their language identities.

References

Andrei, E. and Salerno, A.S. (2018) Collaborative practice in online TESOL methods courses. In G. Kessler (ed.) *Online and Hybrid Classroom Education* (pp. 7–14). Alexandria, VA: TESOL Press.

Agee, J. (2009) Developing qualitative research questions: A reflective process. *International Journal of Qualitative Studies in Education* 22, 431–447. doi:10.1080/09518390902736512

Burbules, N.C. (1993) *Dialogue in Teaching: Theory and Practice.* New York: Teachers College Press.

Connelly, F.M. and Clandinin, D.J. (1990) Stories of experience and narrative inquiry. *Educational Researcher* 19 (5), 2–14. doi:10.3102/0013189X019005002

Erickson, F. (1986) Qualitative methods in research on teaching. In M. Wittrock (ed.) *Handbook of Research on Teaching* (pp. 119–161). New York: Macmillan.

Fecho, B. and Clifton, J. (2016) *Dialoguing Across Cultures, Identities, and Learning: Crosscurrents and Complexities in Literacy Classrooms.* Retrieved from http://ebookcentral.proquest.com. doi:10.4324/9781315658629

Gee, J.P. (2014) *An Introduction to Discourse Analysis: Theory and Method.* London: Routledge.

Gkaintartzi, A., Kiliari, A. and Tsokalidou, R. (2015) 'Invisible' bilingualism—'Invisible' language ideologies: Greek teachers' attitudes towards immigrant pupils' heritage languages. *International Journal of Bilingual Education and Bilingualism* 18 (1), 60–72. doi:10.1080/13670050.2013.877418

Grosjean, F. (2010) *Bilingual: Life and Reality.* Cambridge: Harvard University Press. doi:10.4159/9780674056459.

Grosjean, F. (2013) Bilingualism: A short introduction. In F. Grosjean and P. Li (eds) *The Psycholinguistics of Bilingualism* (pp. 5–25). Hoboken, NJ: John Wiley and Sons.

Harris, R.J. (1977) The teacher as actor. *Teaching of Psychology* 77, 185–187. doi:10.1207/s15328023top0404_7

Heath, S.B. and Street, B.V. (2008) *On Ethnography: Approaches to Language and Literacy Research.* New York: Teachers College Press.

Holliday, A. (2006) Native-speakerism. *ELT Journal* 60, 385–387. doi:10.1093/elt/ccl030
Kincheloe, J. (2005) Critical ontology and auto/biography: Being a teacher, developing a reflective teacher persona. In W. Roth (ed.) *Auto/biography and Auto/ethnography: Praxis of Research Method* (pp. 155–174). Rotterdam: Sense Publishers.
Korthagen, F. and Verkuyl, H.S. (2007) Do you encounter students or yourself? The search for inspiration as an essential component of teacher education. In T. Russell and J. Loughran (eds) *Enacting a Pedagogy of Teacher Education* (pp. 106–123). London: Routledge.
Mahboob, A. (2010) *The NNEST Lens: Non-native English Speakers in TESOL*. Newcastle upon Tyne: Cambridge Scholars Publishing.
Matsumoto, Y. (2018) Teachers' identities as 'Non-native' speakers: Do they matter in English as a Lingua Franca interactions? In B. Yazan and N. Rudolph (eds) *Criticality, Teacher Identity, and (In)equity in English Language Teaching: Issues and Implications* (pp. 57–79). Cham, Switzerland: Springer.
McVee, M.B. and Boyd, F.B. (2016) *Exploring Diversity Through Multimodality, Narrative, and Dialogue: A Framework For Teacher Reflection*. London: Routledge.
Mihalicek, V. and Wilson, C. (2011) *Language Files: Materials for an Introduction to Language and Linguistics*. Columbus: The Ohio State University Press.
Miles, M.B., Huberman, M.A. and Saldaña, J. (2014) *Qualitative Data Analysis: A Methods Resource Book*. Thousand Oaks, CA: Sage.
Palmer, D.K. and Martínez, R.A. (2016) Developing biliteracy: What do teachers *really* need to know about language? *Language Arts* 93, 379–384.
Russell, T. (2007) How experience changed my values as a teacher educator. In T. Russell and J. Loughran (eds) *Enacting a Pedagogy of Teacher Education* (pp. 182–191). London: Routledge.
Sadoski, M. (1992) Imagination, cognition, and persona. *Rhetoric Review* 10, 266–278. doi:10.1080/07350199209388971
Selvi, A.F. (2014) Myths and misconceptions about nonnative English speakers in the TESOL (NNEST) movement. *TESOL Journal* 5, 573–611. doi:10.1002/tesj.158
Sharkey, J. and Peercy, M.M. (2018) Enhancing teacher education for an inclusive pluralistic world: A shared commitment across multiple landscapes. In J. Sharkey and M.M. Peercy (eds) *Self-study of Language and Literacy Teacher Education Practices* (pp. 1–16). Bingley: Emerald Publishing.
Spence, D.P. (1986) Narrative smoothing and clinical wisdom. In T.R. Sarbin (ed.) *Narrative Psychology: The Storied Nature of Human Conduct* (pp. 211–232). New York: Praeger Special Studies.
Sue, D.W. (2010) *Microaggressions in Everyday Life: Race, Gender, and Sexual Orientation*. Hoboken, NJ: Wiley.
Webster, L. and Mertova, P. (2007) *Using Narrative Inquiry as a Research Method*. London: Routledge. doi:10.4324/9780203946268
Wright, W. (2019) *Foundations for Teaching English Language Learners: Research, Theory, Policy, and Practice*. Philadelphia: Caslon.
Yazan, B. (2018) Toward identity-oriented teacher education: Critical autoethnographic narrative. *TESOL Journal* 10 (1). doi:10.1002/tesj.388
Yazan, B. and Rudolph, N. (eds) (2018) *Criticality, Teacher Identity, and (In)equity in English Language Teaching: Issues and Implications*. Cham, Switzerland: Springer. doi:10.1007/978-3-319-72920

Appendix

Evaluation: We include this sample rubric with advice that instructors consider how it can be used flexibly to encourage diverse conversations in multiple directions.

	Exemplary	**Proficient**	**Developing**
Steps	All steps are submitted completely. Assignment criteria are managed with excellence.	Criteria are followed with fidelity.	Criteria are not always followed with fidelity.
Dialogue/ Reflection	The dialogue and reflections explore the student's language experiences in depth and use examples.	The dialogue and reflections explore the student's language experiences but might benefit from additional examples.	The dialogue and reflections do not adequately explore the student's language experiences.
Considering ELs	The dialogue and reflections show a deep understanding of ELs' diverse experiences and apply the student's experiences to teaching in specific, concrete ways showing a depth of reflection.	The dialogue and reflections show an understanding of ELs' diverse experiences and apply the student's experiences to teaching.	The dialogue and reflections depict ELs as a monolithic group or do not apply the student's experiences to teaching.
Language	The writing is free of deficit-oriented language, or grows beyond it by the end. For example, you used deficit-oriented language in the beginning or unintentionally and later explain why your ideas have changed.	The writing might contain occasional deficit-oriented language that goes unchecked.	The writing is characterized by deficit-oriented language.

9 Teacher Identity Construction In Progress: The Role of Classroom Observations and Interactive Reflective Practices in Language Teacher Education

Alfredo Urzúa

Introduction

The relationship between teacher identity and reflection can be said to be well established by now (e.g. Farrell, 2011; Freese, 2006; Izadinia, 2013); however, how the two are connected and the nature of their relationship continues to be investigated, with many questions still unanswered (Beauchamp & Thomas, 2009; Kanno & Stuart, 2011). In this chapter, I highlight ways in which teacher identity and reflection are influenced by interactive practices. In particular, I discuss how practices aimed at promoting reflection reveal attempts by novice teachers to construct an emerging professional identity, as well as how classroom observations relate to this process. The basic premise is that teacher identity emerges from interactions, with peers and others, within the contexts in which teachers operate regularly (Farrell, 2011; Zeichner & Liston, 1996). These interactions influence interpretations and expectations about what teaching and learning are or should be, and what roles teachers adopt or may be assigned to them (Cohen, 2008).

In the field of teacher education, teacher identity has been framed in terms of 'becoming a teacher' or 'fashioning a teaching identity,' a process that involves a myriad of influences and effects on teachers, both personal and professional (Olsen, 2008). It also encompasses values and assumptions about teaching and learning, negotiating between competing ways of being a teacher, and evolving understandings about the roles of teachers and students (Farrell, 2011; Hatton & Smith, 1995; Olsen, 2016; Sutherland *et al.*, 2010). Current sociocultural views of teacher education conceptualize teacher learning as socially negotiated, emerging out of the experiences of participants and dependent to a great extent on their perceptions of themselves (Miller, 2009; Norton, 2010; Varghese *et al.*, 2005). From this perspective, teacher identity involves prior experiences, beliefs, values, aspirations and imaginations about teaching, which comprise an initial 'interpretive frame' for novice teachers (Yazan, 2018a). This frame, in turn, guides evolving understandings of teaching and learning and, most importantly, the identities teachers adopt and enact, which may be revised and reconfigured along the way (Olsen, 2008, 2016). In essence, for educators adhering to this view of teacher development, the process of becoming a teacher is now considered inseparable from constructing a teacher identity (Kanno & Stuart, 2011; Martel, 2018; Varghese *et al.*, 2016; Yazan, 2018b, 2019).

One specific way in which teacher educators can explore the connection between reflection and teacher identity is by creating opportunities for novice teachers to participate in context-specific, problem-based interactions (Korthagen, 2001). Through these, participants can share ideas and concerns, problems and challenges, and talk about how they perceive themselves in their role as teachers. Similarly, Olsen (2016) considers that, by engaging others in conversations of a reflective nature, teachers begin to explore their own teacher identity and help others do the same. Interaction, in this sense, can mediate between identity and reflection. Exploring such interaction constitutes the main goal of this study, which focuses on reflective comments posted by novice language teachers in an online forum, as well as excerpts from subsequent interviews, both resulting from participation in peer and supervisory classroom observations.

Reflection, Teacher Identity and Classroom Observations

The mental process of reflection has been deemed essential for teachers to be able to examine and organize their experiences, knowledge and beliefs in socially relevant ways, as well as considering opportunities and constraints in context (Beijaard *et al.*, 2004; Farrell, 2006, 2011). It is through reflection that teachers can observe and analyze their teaching actions and those of others, in order to guide their development and construct their professional identity (Zeichner & Liston, 1996). However, as Freese (2006) points out, reflection is not necessarily something that participants do willingly and easily. Her longitudinal case study analysis of Ryan, a novice teacher, illustrates some of these challenges, as well as the crucial role that reflection plays in constructing a teacher identity. Her account also demonstrates the extent to which our understanding of how to best help novice teachers to reflect is only partial. More importantly, it suggests that activities that allow teachers to verbalize their reflections can shed a bright and much-needed light into the process of identity construction.

Traditional views that conceptualize identity as unitary and biologically given started to be replaced, at the turn of the century, with notions of identity as fluid and relationally determined (e.g. Woodward, 1997). Scholars utilizing a sociocultural lens increasingly view identity as complex, multifaceted, dynamic and shifting (Miller, 2009; Norton, 1995, 2010; Varghese *et al.*, 2005), and as anchored in interaction and emergent in discourse (Bucholtz & Hall, 2005; Sutherland *et al.*, 2010). From this perspective, individuals 'have multiple identities which they continuously negotiate, reconstruct and enact through discursive tools as they interact with other individuals in different contexts' (Yazan, 2018a: 24). Identity construction is thus seen as embedded in larger social processes and grounded in distinct practices within particular groups (Norton, 1995, 2006; Tsui 2007). This includes ways of talking and interacting in order to become members of a particular community of practice (Tsui, 2007; Wenger, 1998) and to acquire the necessary 'practices, values, and ways of thinking which enable particular identities to be realized' (Singh & Richards, 2006: 158).

The notion that teacher identity emerges from social interactions has been discussed often in the literature. Varghese *et al.* (2005), for instance, proposed that language teacher identity can be viewed in relation to the notions of 'identity-in-practice' and 'identity-in-discourse.' The former is action-oriented and focuses on concrete practices and tasks in interaction with others, while the latter is discursively constituted since identity formation is 'inextricably intertwined with language and discourse, insofar as all identities are maintained to a significant degree through discourse' (2005: 39). Along the same lines, Kanno and Stuart (2011) state that novice teachers engage in the process of becoming members of a community of practice by engaging in such practice. This requires assembling a variety of messages (e.g. from teacher educators, practicum supervisors) about the ways teaching should be enacted and how to integrate these into personal goals (Martel, 2015). As with discourse, identity and practice are so intimately connected that 'one cannot change without affecting the other' (Kanno & Stuart, 2011: 240). Thus, Kanno and Stuart (2011) support examining novice teacher identities through the analysis of verbal expressions depicting the ongoing relationship between the self and teaching practices. Becoming a teacher, then, involves identity work that is influenced by interactive practices linked to particular situated discourse (Connelly & Clandinin, 2006; Kanno & Stuart, 2011; Varghese *et al.*, 2016).

The role of classroom observations

Why focus on classroom observations? A number of studies suggest that observational practices have an important effect on teachers' ability to develop a reflective disposition, which, in turn, supports the emergence of a teacher identity (e.g. Farrell, 2006; McDonough, 2006). Freese's (2005) analysis of Ryan, mentioned above, illustrates the potential impact of guided classroom observations on teachers' processes of reflection and identity construction. Even though Ryan was initially reluctant and skeptical about the value of such an activity, he is 'shocked' by what he observes: 'I realized ... that not all my beliefs are correct or complete,' and claims that his observations constituted 'the starting point of my growth' (2005: 109). Observations, then, have the potential of not only providing concrete evidence that may counter established beliefs, but they can also constitute turning points in terms of being open to self-examination.

The work of Farrell (2006, 2011, 2012) has been seminal in connecting observation and reflection. He has shown that classroom observations, when conducted within a reflective framework, provide language teachers with the means of examining their own teaching. Similarly, McDonough (2006) and Lundy (2011) state that a reflective approach that includes observations and focused discussions with peers and mentors promotes understanding of teaching practices and self-awareness. This chapter, thus, examines the extent to which observations and interactive practices help novice teachers engage in the kind of reflections that facilitate the construction of an emergent professional identity.

The Study

Participants and context

This study focuses on four MA graduate students (three females and one male, all Spanish-English bilinguals) who were, simultaneously, first-time teachers of Spanish in a large public university in California, USA. More specifically, it focuses on their participation in an online forum and semi-structured interviews in relation to peer and supervisory classroom observations. They did not have any previous teaching experience but participated in an intensive teacher training program (36 hours) before starting to teach and enrolled in a teaching methodology course during their first term. This course covers basic knowledge about second language (L2) acquisition and aims at developing the pedagogic skills needed to design, plan and conduct L2 lessons using a Communicative Language Teaching (CLT) approach and high-leverage teaching practices (Glisan & Donato, 2017).

Data collection

Participation in the online forum occurred mid-semester, during the two-week peer observation period that was part of the assignments for the methodology course, with each participant observing two of their peer's sessions. The purpose of the forum was to provide a space in which they could express their thoughts and feelings about observing and being observed. Even though no specific prompts were provided, the assignment guidelines included various suggestions; for example, discuss actions and behaviors that caught their attention, compare the sessions observed with their own and make connections with themes and topics in their methodology course. To facilitate conversations in the online forum, participants were grouped in teams of four, so they read and responded only to their team members. The number of postings by participants ranged between 8 and 13 and were varied in length, from as few as 17 and as much as 564 words per posting (no minimum number or length was required).

The interviews were conducted the following semester, and participation was voluntary. The interviewer was a graduate student (not involved in the teachers' program) who posed questions formulated by the researcher. The interview focused on two main topics: (a) general experiences during the first semester of teaching and (b) the process of classroom observation, including those conducted by the Spanish language program coordinators. The interviews were conducted after these observations were completed, and they ranged between 25 and 60 minutes in length.

Method of analysis

In order to identify instances of reflective comments, which would then be analyzed from the perspective of identity construction, the data were examined first using a rubric developed by Ward and McCotter (2004). This rubric aims to capture a shift of attention from the self to situated teaching and learning issues, changing practices and the adoption of a more critical stance regarding pedagogy. The rubric aims at distinguishing among four levels of reflection, each involving three dimensions: *focus* (e.g. on self, on students), *inquiry* (e.g. considering multiple perspectives) and *change* (e.g. gaining new insights). The data were analyzed by the author and a graduate student, and only excerpts identified by both as reflective are included below.

In Ward and McCotter's (2004) rubric, *routine reflections* are considered low-level reflections that tend to depict self-centered concerns, such as the ability to control or manage students. They also tend to include unanalyzed, definite statements that lack questioning or put the blame on others, and they are not likely to generate change. *Technical reflections* focus on teaching tasks and include discussions of immediate, specific problems. However, they do not question the nature of the problem itself, and there is little indication of a change in perspective. A deeper level of reflection, *dialogic reflections*, involves consideration of the views of others, a focus on the process of learning, and the emergence of new insights. Lastly, *transformative reflection* involves the questioning of established practices, conventional beliefs, and personal assumptions, and, naturally, this is considered the most difficult to achieve, particularly for novice teachers.

The excerpts presented below, identified using Ward and McCotter's (2004) rubric, are analyzed in relation to both teachers' reflections and identity construction. They are presented separately as data were gathered through different modes (online writing vs. oral interviews) and at two points in time: during the first semester when participants were in the midst of the observation process, and the following semester, to gather retrospective reflections. Most postings were written in Spanish, and, for reasons of space, they are presented here in their English translation only (except those originally in English). Pseudonyms are used for each participant.

Data Analysis

Online forum data

In their initial comments, participants expressed feeling nervous and anxious about being observed, as well as excited about becoming observers and being able to see how a class might be perceived when sitting in the back of the classroom. Excerpt (1), by María, illustrates these feelings.

> (1) *I feel nervous because I'm not sure about how my class is going to behave or if the material I have prepared for that day will work. On a previous occasion, what happened to me was that the materials I had prepared did not have the reaction I was expecting. So, I hope that day my students do not cause any problems, but at the same time, I like the idea that the class may not be perfect so that the peer who is going to observe can give me recommendations about how to improve.* (María: 10/5/2016)

María expresses a common concern among novice teachers when being observed, i.e. that the class may not go as planned, and students may not behave as expected. Comments similar to (1) occurred frequently, and they can be related to routine or lower-level type of reflections in that the concerns are mostly self-centered, with students being discussed mostly as a possible source of problems. María also comments on the potential benefits of being observed and getting feedback. Related to this, in excerpt (2), she writes that observing a class can provide her with a new way of thinking about teaching. María also wonders if the perspective of the observer might be similar to that of students in her own class, suggesting she is starting to consider the views of others.

> (2) *Seeing a peer managing the class could give me a new perspective about a Spanish 101 class, [...] to see the class from the point of view of a student because one who sits in the back observing how the instructor*

teaches the class gets an outside perspective. And at the same time, one starts to think about how you would feel when being observed by a student. (María: 10/5/2016)

By considering an alternative perspective, María changes the focus from her, as the instructor, to her students. Although she does not elaborate on this issue, the change of perspective shows a predisposition towards a more dialogic type of reflection. It also shows an attempt at putting herself in her students' shoes, thus shifting her identity position (Martel, 2015).

Another point of concern commonly shared by participants was related to possible 'errors' when teaching, which Luis considers should be viewed as normal and expected (excerpt 3). He also points out that their goal should be to implement CLT lessons, recognizing that this takes time and requires extensive experience.

> (3) *I think we should take into account that there is a space for errors and that this can tend to happen but, oh well, it is part of the process. Having the CLT method in mind should be something very salient in us and also trying to implement it fully. But one is going to learn by doing and with experience.* (Luis: 10/7/2016)

In (3), we see a comment concerned mostly with the self, but also one that relates to the type of teacher Luis believes he is supposed to become, one who is capable of fully implementing CLT lessons. We can identify an attempt at defining an initial teaching identity. For Luis, this means someone who embraces the institutional identity being promoted in his teaching context. There is no indication in the data that Luis or his peers questioned the status of CLT, and whether or not acquiring competence in implementing it should constitute a major goal in their development, which may be related to their status as beginning teachers and newcomers to the field.

During the weeks when peer observations were conducted, online postings tended to focus more on what was happening in the classrooms, as it can be naturally expected. For instance, in excerpts (4) and (5), María and Luis comment on what they perceived as challenging teaching aspects: encouraging participation, engaging students and keeping them on task during group work. In these excerpts, even though there is some discussion of specific problems, challenges are not described as arising from the instructors' actions. Instead, it is the students who do not respond as expected or who misbehave in class, despite teachers' efforts.

> (4)*An aspect that I have noticed is quite challenging when it comes to teaching is making the students wanting to participate and feel engaged during the class, because there are times when, even if you come extremely prepared with materials that you think they might like,* [it] *will not always work.* (María: 10/12/2016)

In (4), Maria expresses frustration since, despite her coming to class 'extremely prepared,' the outcome is not always as expected. However, she does not further analyze the problem nor considers possible reasons why students may not participate, leaving negative outcomes to unspecified factors. Luis also refers to the roles of teachers as managers in (5), which he finds 'quite challenging,' especially when asking students to work in groups, something he believes is not fully under the teacher's control.

> (5) *Up to this point, what I have observed is quite challenging for my peer is keeping adequate control when the students work in groups. Keeping everybody in line and control the structure can be maintained by the teacher only to a certain extent, given that the students, when they finish, they immediately start to talk.* (Luis: 10/12/2016)

Even though excerpts (4) and (5) include elements of technical reflection, dealing with aspects related to planning and management, they were thought to also include elements of routine reflections, given that the instructors focus on issues of control and assigning blame, with comments that tend to be definite and generalized. Frustrations are, of course, common for beginning teachers, but by sharing them, Maria and Luis can realize they are not unique. What is lacking is an analysis of possible underlying factors and potential teaching responses, not only to gain control over these situations but also to re-shape their sense of self as teachers. Olsen (2016), to this respect, considers that teachers need to be able to move beyond management concerns in order to attend to teaching and learning issues.

The excerpts presented above illustrate participants' feelings of nervousness or frustration, as well as their expectations about the observation process. In addition, they share their reactions to instances of teaching, although they tend to be definite and general in their evaluations. Nonetheless, expressing and sharing their thoughts and reactions provides them with an opportunity to build a sense of community and solidarity. This sense of belonging to a community of peers, in turn, supports the emergence of identity as novice teachers who are working together to understand what goes on in the classroom and how this connects to their still-developing pedagogical knowledge. They explicitly define this identity in terms of what can be expected of them as beginning teachers and as members of the local teaching community. In addition, they are able to compare their own teaching to that of their peers, including common challenges and particular strengths or weaknesses. These comments indicate how novice teachers envision their role as teachers, what type of teacher identity they perceive is expected, and what teaching actions may be considered valuable in their context, i.e. what they understand is an appropriate institutional identity. In this sense, peer observations constitute opportunities to verbalize and share early perceptions of teaching and of being a teacher within their context.

On the other hand, for a process of reflection to be more fully developed, teachers need to consider situated problems in light of their beliefs, knowledge and actions, as well as consider these from multiple perspectives in order to develop new insights that can eventually lead to change and improvement. It is quite possible that such reflections are not likely to occur while being in the midst of action. For this reason, participants were also asked to post comments after completing their peer observations. In this phase, an effort to make connections between observations and evolving understandings of teaching and learning was apparent. This can be noted in comments that focus on students and their performance (excerpt 6) or relate theory to actual practice (excerpt 7).

> (6) *What felt most rewarding is that I was able to make a connection between my peers and me (as an instructor) and the students (and me being in that position). I was able to analyze the perspective a student has while class is undergoing. That reinforcement for me was very much needed since I was able to perceive what goes around the class while the instructor is teaching. Are students getting distracted? Are the students lacking interest in the lesson? Questions like these were much clearer when I took on that role of the observer.* (Luis: 10/21/2016)

In excerpt (6), Luis, adopting the perspective of a student while observing, reflects on how teaching actions might affect students' behavior. This can be taken as an example of dialogic reflection, based on Ward and McCotter's (2004) rubric, and of a shift in the positioning of the teacher. The identity being constructed is one of a teacher whose goals center in his students and factors affecting their learning. By being an observer, Luis appears to be able to move from a teacher-centered orientation to a more student-centered one (Olsen, 2008). Similarly, Helen adopts a student-centered perspective when she comments on the need to be flexible in order to make adjustments given particular student needs at specific moments, taking into consideration the resources at hand. In excerpt (7), she not only connects what she is learning in her methodology course to her teaching but also reflects on the unpredictable nature of actual classrooms and students.

> (7) *These observations help us to see from a more objective viewpoint the practical application of the theories we are studying and how each instructor makes practical and/or real-time adjustments, as much for a particular response by a particular student in a particular moment, as for any particular limitations or advantages of space and equipment for a given classroom.* (Helen-10/18/2016)

What is missing in the excerpts above is an examination of specific incidents from a more critical perspective or any questioning of personal beliefs or assumptions about teaching and learning. This type of reflection is what Ward and McCotter (2004) describe as transformative reflections. In the online forum data, no instances of reflection within this category were identified. However, as this was the participants' first semester of teaching, it may be premature to expect such perspective. On the other hand, what can be seen is elements that points towards the construction of an emergent identity, particularly an institutional identity and a designated identity (Sfard & Prusak, 2005) reflecting participants' perceptions of what is expected of them, as well as a shift in orientation from the teacher to the students. Peer observations were followed by supervisory observations, both during the first and second semesters. The data presented below come from interviews conducted after such observations.

Interview data

One of the goals of classroom observations is for teachers to direct their attention to those instructional aspects that may need change and, at the same time, have an opportunity to consider multiple perspectives while focusing on students' learning. By considering how they position themselves in the classroom and what roles they adopt or might imagine themselves adopting, beginning teachers can shape their view of themselves in order to construct an emergent teaching identity. Observations can also aid in assessing and re-assessing teachers' developing knowledge and skills. Indeed, during her interview, Helen comments on how peer observations help her assess her own teaching ability. When asked what she sees as the main purpose of observing classes taught by her peers, she comments that this provides an opportunity for self-examination (excerpt 8).

> (8) *That is very important, I'd say, because at times...as I was saying, we do things that are so natural to us that we really do not notice the good things we do. Yes and...uh...they gave me more ideas...and I also see how...uh...my challenges are common, and that helps me a lot with my confidence, you know? on myself.* (Helen: 4/27/2017)

By observing others, Helen gauges her strengths and weaknesses, and even those teaching actions that seem second nature to her can be seen in a new light. Also, by observing that others have similar problems, Helen is able to keep her teaching in perspective. Similarly, but referring to the classroom observations conducted by her coordinator, María comments that the feedback received boosted her confidence, even though the observer pointed out some aspects in her teaching that needed improvement (excerpt 9).

> (9) *Well, I truly see it as helpful...uh... the two times were...well, it is that in general, it went well for me. So, just...yes, yes, it helped me to realize that up to this point, I am doing a good job, I think, given the comments that I received. So it was helpful to reaffirm my confidence, more than anything else, uh...obviously also, what they pointed to...the the mistakes I made...I was aware of the...that I have those mistakes, but nothing, no, they are not mistakes that can't be fixed. So, it was very helpful the...meeting with the supervisor.* (María: 4/28/2017)

In terms of Ward and McCotter's (2004) rubric, excerpts (8) and (9) can be considered as concerned mainly with the self. On the other hand, Helen and María are also constructing an identity as capable teachers, which is quite important for novice teachers. Despite their lack of experience, Helen and María express a sense of self as language teachers who are having relative success in the classroom. Conway (2001) has argued that the construction of such a teaching identity is extremely important since a sense of self as capable and in control is crucial to continue teaching with a certain degree of optimism and hope. This is particularly true for novice teachers, who must be able to sustain a feasible 'imagined identity' as they project themselves into the future (Urzúa & Vásquez, 2008), especially during the first years of teaching when multiple challenges arise. Thus, excerpts (8) and (9) can also be considered attempts at constructing an emergent professional identity.

Identifying areas in need of improvement was another major topic of discussion emerging from the observations. In the interviews, the participants often commented on this aspect. These reflections were classified as technical in that they focused on teaching tasks, specific problems, or frustrating situations, and there is an attempt on the part of the teachers to respond to the situation. For instance, in excerpt (10), María reflects on her use of the students' native language in class versus using the target language.

> (10) *So definitely...mmh...what I might not been able to see is that perhaps the way I interact with the students in the sense that...and it is, and it is my fault and also because we do it unconsciously, to try to explain everything to them in English, to make it easier for them, and it does not always work. They become dependent on one being able to automatically switch to English so that they can understand. So they use this as a crutch to be able to ... not having to use Spanish as much. So that...so yes... for example, the coordinator has commented on this when she went to observe me, that I speak a bit too much in English, at times. And it is true, there are some classes where I do not speak in English as much and there are days when I do. So take this more into account and be more consistent in the level of English and Spanish.* (María: 4/28/2017)

In excerpt (10), María comments on the difficulty of finding a balance between the use of the L1 and the L2, between facilitating students' comprehension and providing opportunities for them to use the target language, especially when interacting with students. She tries to analyze the reasons why she might turn to use the students' L1, at times 'unconsciously,' and possible consequences; for example, students might become dependent on it. At the same time, María is outlining desired identity as teacher: someone who aims to be 'more consistent' in relation to the use of the L2. This identity may come from her own internalization of established professional guidelines in the field (Glisan & Donato, 2017) or local discourses and expectations regarding possible functions of the L1 in the L2 classroom.

Ana also considers supervisory observations helpful precisely in that they focus on teaching aspects that require change or improvement (excerpt 11).

> (11) *They [program coordinators] are really getting to know if we are putting into practice what we are learning or not, if the activities work or not, if we have the class under control, how we control it, if there are, you know, chaos in the class, how we manage the activities in group, how we maintain order, the time, everything. So really, the observations, the one…I really value the ones by my peers too, but the one I really take more into account and the results at the end, when I have the meeting after the observation, it has always been that of the coordinator, no?* (Ana: 4/27/2017)

In (11), Ana discloses that she values supervisory observations over being observed by her peers, as the former allows her to display what she perceives as expected teacher performance: be able to control her class, manage group work activities, maintain order and organize her time efficiently, all aspects of a teacher's role as classroom manager. This can be an attempt to perform an identity as a competent teacher, one who is fully in control, while at the same time directing attention to the role of the supervisor, who is not only a key member of her community of practice but also one in a position to recognize such identity (Miller, 2009).

Peer observations also generated reflections about different ways of 'being a teacher.' For example, in excerpt (12), María shares how intently she focused on the type of teaching identity that her peers projected in class.

> (12) *But what I really want to see is how they interact in class, the way in which… the way they…uh…make themselves understood and how they project the image of an instructor because that is what is viewed in reality, what you need to do. You have to have the authority, be a figure of authority in front of the students, but it has to be something moderate and not exaggeratedly… authoritarian, right? Not be too extremely strict but flexible enough.* (María: 4/28/2017)

In excerpt (12), María states that she pays close attention to the way her peers interact with students and how this projects a particular teaching identity. She considers this crucial in terms of negotiating the line between being a teacher with authority, yet still flexible, versus being authoritarian, a major concern for many novice teachers. Along the same lines, in excerpt (13) Luis reflects on how one of his peers builds up rapport with students in order to build a more positive class environment.

> (13) *I went to observe and I confess that my peer was more…tried to create connections with the students, asking them…uh…posing some questions…uh… face to face…and and I saw her implementing this technique, when one starts by asking somebody individually, 'hey, how was your day?' and this and that. They answer and …in fact…uh…they*

could be with a face of not being very willing and when you have this interaction with them...uh...it is like a change of face so to speak. So this is this type of dynamics that I observed. (Luis: 4/21/207)

Luis, in excerpt (13) comments on teacher's interactions with students and the effect that showing empathy can have on students' attitudes. This shows elements of dialogic reflections in that the focus is on students and how to help them. At the same time, Luis describes how a teacher negotiates his or her identity through language in the day-to-day interactions with students. Informal conversations, in this way, constitute discursive tools that enact a particular way of being a teacher which is recognized by students. Excerpts (12) and (13) illustrate well the notion that identity is both 'relational,' i.e. how one talks or thinks about oneself, as well as 'experiential,' i.e. negotiated through lived experiences (Tsui, 2007).

Ana also reports that, through peer classroom observations, she can pay attention to aspects of classroom instruction that would be difficult to examine otherwise (excerpt 14).

> (14) *I always pay attention to the kids' attitude, that they are really in sync with the teacher, that they are paying attention, that the teacher engages the students, no? That they do the activities or that they are participating in the topic, that they are not somewhere else. I also pay attention to the activities, how the teacher implements them, no? If they are individual, if they are put into groups...and why, what is the purpose of the activity, no? I am always, always paying attention to this.* (Ana: 4/27/2017)

Ana considers that observing her peers teaching and being observed by supervisors is essential to continue developing her teaching skills and abilities as they prompt her to reflect on her performance and, more importantly, to see herself as an increasingly capable instructor. In (14), Ana constructs an identity as a teacher who is, first and foremost, concerned with her students. She also discusses aspects of teaching such as implementing and assessing the outcome of activities, enacting an identity as an effective, competent teacher who is aware of the effect of her decisions on students' success. Towards the end of the interview, Ana reflects on the experiences related to the process of classroom observations and what they have meant to her (excerpt 15):

> (15) *I take this experience like...learning from them, no? Why? Because in the end, I realize what my level is, in what point I am, what I am missing...to improve as a TA. I had, I think, good evaluations. I am pleased with what... with what I did the day of my two observations that I had last semester and this semester. Then this made me reflect, no? What I am doing well, what I am doing badly, in what way I am doing better, in what way I can...as a TA... evolve, no? To be something quite different than what I am doing right now, for me and for my future students, no?* (Ana: 4/27/2017)

As excerpt (15) shows, Ana considers that classroom observations and related activities, i.e. the online forum and supervisory meetings, provided her with the time and space to reflect on her development and growth as a teacher. She describes her learning as resulting from her interactions with others, which in turn prompted her to assess and reassess her knowledge, skills, and goals as a teacher. She projects herself as a self-confident teacher who is constantly assessing and re-assessing her teaching and who looks to the future with optimism.

Conclusions

Graduate students who are also instructors have two major tasks: to develop the academic skills needed to succeed as students and to acquire the pedagogical skills necessary to be effective as teachers (Farrell, 2012). There is no specific point when they make the transition from student to teacher. Rather, they must negotiate both roles, which involve constructing, early on, an emerging identity as teachers. In the data analyzed here, the participants generated, for the most part, routine and technical reflections, and sporadically engaged in dialogic reflections, with no instances of transformative reflections identified in the data. Obviously, it is unlikely for novice teachers to reach the highest levels of reflection during their first year of teaching. In fact, Ward and McCotter (2004) state that 'the developmental path… suggests that concern for self and gaining competence in teaching tasks is and probably should be the most immediate focus' (2004: 254). On the other hand, engaging in practices that stimulate reflection-in-discourse, whether focusing on themselves, their teaching, or their students' learning, allowed novice teachers to start examining and evaluating the multiple and shifting positions, roles, attitudes, beliefs, concerns and emotions that are part and parcel of becoming a teacher. They can do this with the help of their peers and other key participants in order to arrive at an interpreting framework that can guide their development and growth (Yazan, 2018a). It is through this process of self-examination, interaction and reflection that novice teachers can construct an emergent professional identity.

Any process of self-examination and reflection is influenced by social and cultural discourses that permeate perceptions and interpretations of what is appropriate, expected, conventional, and what is troubling, unexpected or challenging in regards to both the personal and the professional (Rudolph *et al.*, 2018). Novice teachers such as those in this study are thus confronted not only with constructing a viable teacher identity that allows them to negotiate those discourses in context, but also with the challenges of aligning their own very personal sense of self with what they perceive as accepted ways of being a teacher.

By examining interactive practices that prompt various types of reflections, language education researchers can explore how novice teachers start constructing an identity as teachers that conforms to their interpretations of the context in which they operate, from an institutional identity to desired or imagined identities (Yazan, 2018a), from a teacher-centered to a more learner-centered teacher identity (Olsen, 2008), or from perpetuating to challenging established practices, positioning themselves along such continua based on their own goals, aspirations and sense of self and agency (Rudolph *et al.*, 2018). The analysis of the data presented here suggests that the process of identity construction can be supported by classroom observations and related interactive practices. It also highlights the notion that when teachers have space and time to reflect on their practice, they are more likely to achieve a level of awareness that supports their evolving pedagogical knowledge and a better understanding of the self (Akbari, 2007; Fendler, 2003).

Investigations of teachers' identity construction are instrumental to understand how teachers develop as professionals while transitioning from a student self to a teacher self (Yazan, 2018a). From the perspective that learning to teach and constructing a teacher identity are inseparable and crucial to one another, I cannot but agree with the view that considers teacher identity development as 'the central project novice teachers engage in' (Kanno & Stuart, 2011: 250), an endeavor essential to their aspirations in terms of the kind of teacher they want to become.

References

Akbari, R. (2007) Reflections on reflection: A critical appraisal of reflective practices in L2 teacher education. *System* 35 (2), 192–207.

Beijaard, D., Meijer, P.C. and Verloop, N. (2004) Reconsidering research on teachers' professional identity. *Teaching and Teacher Education* 20 (2), 107–128.

Beauchamp, C. and Thomas, L. (2009) Understanding teacher identity: An overview of issues in the literature and implications for teacher education. *Cambridge Journal of Education* 39 (2), 175–189.

Bucholtz, M. and Hall, K. (2005) Identity and interaction: A sociocultural approach. *Discourse Studies* 7 (4–5), 585–614.

Cohen, J. (2008) That's not treating you as a professional: Teachers constructing complex professional identities through talk. *Teachers and Teaching* 14 (2), 79–93.

Connelly, F.M. and Clandinin, D.J. (2006) Narrative inquiry. In J. Green, G. Camili and P. Elmore (eds) *Handbook of Complementary Methods in Education Research* (pp. 375–385). Mahwah, NJ: Lawrence Erlbaum.

Connelly, F.M. and Clandinin, D.J. (1999) *Shaping a Professional Identity: Stories of Educational Practice*. New York, NY: Teachers College Press.

Conway, P.F. (2001) Anticipatory reflection while learning to teach: From a temporally truncated to a temporally distributed model of reflection in teacher education. *Teaching and Teacher Education* 17 (1), 89–106.

Farrell, T. (2012) Novice-service language teacher development: Bridging the gap between preservice and in-service education and development. *TESOL Quarterly* 46 (3), 435–449.

Farrell, T. (2011) Exploring the professional role identities of experience ESL teachers through reflective practice. *System* 39 (1), 54–62.

Farrell, T. (2006) Reflective practice in action: A case study of a writing teacher's reflection on practice. *TESL Canada Journal* 23 (2), 77–90.

Fendler, L. (2003) Teacher reflection in a hall of mirrors: Historical influences and political reverberations. *Educational Researcher* 32 (3), 16–25.

Freese, A.R. (2006) Reframing one's teaching: Discovering our teacher selves through reflection and inquiry. *Teaching and Teacher Education* 22 (1), 100–119.

Glisan, E.W. and Donato, R. (2017) *Enacting the Work of Language Instruction: High-leverage Teaching Practices*. Alexandria, VA: American Council on the Teaching of Foreign Languages.

Hatton, N. and Smith, D. (1995) Reflection in teacher education: Towards definition and implementation. *Teaching and Teacher Education* 11(1), 33–49.

Izadinia, M. (2013) A review of research on student teachers' professional identity. *British Educational Research Journal* 39 (4), 694–713.

Kanno, Y. and Stuart, C. (2011) Learning to become a second language teacher: Identities-in-practice. *The Modern Language Journal* 95 (2), 236–252.

Korthagen, F.A. (2001) *Linking Practice and Theory: The Pedagogy of Realistic Teacher Education*. Mahwah, NJ: Lawrence Erlbaum.

Lundy, M. (2011) The journey towards professional competence: A case study of the reflective process of six Japanese EFL teachers during a professional development programme in Canada. Unpublished PhD thesis, University of Ottawa, Canada.

Martel, J. (2015) Learning to teach a foreign language: Identity negotiation and conceptualizations of pedagogical progress. *Foreign Language Annals* 48 (3), 394–412.

Martel, J. (2018) Three foreign language student teachers' experiences with content-based instruction: Exploring the identity/innovation interface. *Innovation in Language Learning and Teaching* 12 (4), 303–315.

McDonough, K. (2006) Action research and the professional development of graduate teaching assistants. *The Modern Language Journal* 90 (1), 33–47.

Miller, J. (2009) Teacher identity. In A. Burns and J.C. Richards (eds) *The Cambridge Guide to Second Language Teacher Education* (pp. 171–181). New York, NY: Cambridge University Press.

Norton, B. (1995) Social identity, investment, and language learning. *TESOL Quarterly* 29 (1), 9–31.

Norton, B. (2006) Identity as a sociocultural construct in second language education. *TESOL in Context* (special issue), 22–33.

Norton, B. (2010) Language and identity. In N.H. Hornberger and S.L. McKay (eds) *Sociolinguistics and Language Education* (pp. 349–369). Bristol: Multilingual Matters.

Olsen, B. (2016) *Teaching for Success: Developing your Teacher Identity in Today's Classroom*. New York, NY: Routledge.

Olsen, B. (2008) *Teaching what they Learn, Learning What they Live: How Teachers' Personal Histories Shape their Professional Development*. Boulder, CO: Paradigm Publishers.

Rudolph, N., Yazan, B. and Rudolph, J. (2018) Negotiating 'ares,' 'cans,' and 'shoulds' of being and becoming in English language teaching: Two teacher accounts from one Japanese university. *Asian Englishes* 21 (1), 22–37.

Sfard, A. and Prusak, A. (2005) Telling identities: In search of an analytic tool for investigating learning as a culturally shaped activity. *Educational Researcher* 34 (4), 14–22.

Singh, G. and Richards, J. (2006) Teaching and learning in the language teacher education course room. *RELC Journal* 37 (2), 149–175.

Sutherland, L., Howard, S. and Markauskaite, L. (2010) Professional identity creation: Examining the development of beginning preservice teachers' understanding of their work as teachers. *Teaching and Teacher Education* 26 (3), 455–465.

Tsui, A. (2007) Complexities of identity formation: A narrative inquiry of an EFL teacher. *TESOL Quarterly* 41 (4), 657–680.

Urzúa, A. and Vásquez, C. (2008) Reflection and professional identity in teachers' future-oriented discourse. *Teaching and Teacher Education* 24 (7), 1936–1946.

Varghese, M.M., Motha, S., Park, G., Reeves, J. and Trent, J. (2016) In this issue: Language teacher identity in (multi)lingual educational contexts. *TESOL Quarterly* 50 (3), 545–571.

Varghese, M., Morgan, B., Johnston, B. and Johnson, K.A. (2005) Theorizing language teacher identity: Three perspectives and beyond. *Journal of Language, Identity, and Education,* 4 (1), 21–44.

Ward, J.R. and McCotter, S.S. (2004) Reflection as a visible outcome for preservice teachers. *Teaching and Teacher Education* 20 (3), 243–257.

Woodward, K. (1997) *Identity and Difference.* London: Sage Publications.

Yazan, B. (2018a) A conceptual framework to understand language teacher identities. *Journal of Second Language Teacher Education* 1 (1), 21–48.

Yazan, B. (2018b) Being and becoming an ESOL teacher through coursework and internship: Three teacher candidates' identity negotiation. *Critical Inquiry in Language Studies* 15 (3), 205–227.

Yazan, B. (2019) Toward identity-oriented teacher education: Critical autoethnographic narrative. *TESOL Journal* 10 (1), 1–15.

Zeichner, K.M. and Liston, D.P. (1996) *Reflective Teaching: An Introduction.* Mahwah, NJ: Lawrence Erlbaum.

10 Preservice Teachers' Cultural Identity Construction in Telecollaboration

Sedat Akayoğlu, Babürhan Üzüm and Bedrettin Yazan

Introduction

The widespread use of technology and the increasing access to high-speed internet have paved the way for going beyond the physical classrooms and connecting students with others from all over the world. Kern (2006) underscored the importance of 'a shift in focus from single classrooms to long-distance collaborations' (2006: 198), and he argued that there was a renewed focus on the teaching of culture in language classes. Focusing on issues of intercultural competence, cultural learning and cultural literacy, Kern observed that teachers started to initiate collaborations with other educators from different regions of the world, transcending time differences and geographical distance. Recently, numerous telecollaboration projects have provided language learners and teachers with spaces to cultivate their skills of interculturality and negotiate their cultural identities (Guth & Helm, 2010; O'Dowd & Lewis, 2016). These studies focused on enhancing the participants' language learning (Chen, 2012; Dooly & Sadler, 2013) and helping develop their interculturality (Dooly, 2011; Menard-Warwick *et al.*, 2013; Tanghe & Park, 2016). What needs more attention in research is preservice teachers' (PTs') intercultural learning and identity development in telecollaboration projects. Due to PTs' crucial role in developing their students' intercultural competence in their future teaching career, PTs could benefit from networked telecollaboration projects to develop their intercultural competence and imagine the potential use of telecollaboration in their future classes. They could actively participate in these projects to have a first-hand experience during their teacher education programs (Menard-Warwick *et al.*, 2013), instead of theoretical information about the target culture or the importance of integrating of cultural elements in their future classes. Therefore, the chapter reports on a telecollaborative project that included PTs from two teacher education programs in Turkey and the US, who engaged synchronously and asynchronously in small group discussions on topics related to multiculturalism, education, religion and gender. Part of a larger project, this chapter explores how PTs construct and perform their cultural identities through intercultural interactions.

Background Literature

Cultural identity is 'the attribution of a set of qualities to a given population,' and it is mostly associated with ethnic and racial identity in cultural studies (Friedman, 1994: 29). Considering the definitions in the literature, we can infer that all cultural values, ideas, ideologies, practices and attitudes in a community influence the formation of an individual's cultural identity. However, cultural identity construction is not linear. It is a complex and dynamic process that takes place at micro levels as individuals negotiate and enact their identities through discourse and interaction (Bucholtz & Hall, 2005). The cultural identity construction cannot be completed within a specific period of time; this process is continuous and evolves throughout one's life span.

The emergence of Web 2.0 tools provided the individual internet users with more opportunities for intercultural interaction and made possible the crossing of geographical spaces and borders through virtual communication. The advent of user-generated web content and social media, human interactions are not restricted by physical borders across nations, and cultural identities are not considered to be constructed in isolation within specific geographical regions, but are achieved transnationally (Risager, 2007) through the continuous interaction with other individuals living in different parts of the world. Although there are many cultural elements inherited from one's local context, the interaction between individuals and the digital world shapes individuals' cultural identities. From this perspective, interculturality has gained importance as a way of cultural identity construction in online spaces.

Globalization has transformed the nature of interaction, communication, community, culture and identity. The world is now experiencing 'intensified flows of capital, goods, people, images and discourses around the globe, driven by technological innovations mainly in the field of media and information and communication technology, and resulting in new patterns of global activity, community organization and culture' (Blommaert, 2010: 13). As a consequence of these new patterns in education, teachers are now working with students with diverse cultural backgrounds and possibly in a different cultural context from their own upbringing (Haneda & Alexander, 2015; Sercu, 2006). Students are also socialized in culturally diverse classrooms. Beyond the walls of the schools, citizens of this globalizing world tend to interact more with individuals from other cultures for different purposes. Parallel to these changes, the telecollaboration projects mainly focus on the enrichment of the learners' intercultural learning in addition to their improvement of language skills (Kern *et al.*, 2004). As a virtual space for the 'borderland negotiations' of different cultural identities (Yazan *et al.*, 2019), telecollaboration could facilitate participants' working on their intercultural competence. Individuals could learn about their peers' cultural experiences and engage in cultural reflection about their own cultural beliefs and practices. Simultaneously, they negotiate their cultural identities in these online interactions.

Teacher education programs need to attend to PTs' cultural identity negotiation and intercultural competence. Due to the increasing cultural and linguistic diversity in schools, PTs will have to serve students with diverse cultural and linguistic identities and provide instructional spaces for all students to negotiate and enact identities in culturally and linguistically diverse classrooms (Çiftçi & Savaş, 2018; Menard-Warwick *et al.*, 2013; O'Dowd, 2016). Teacher education coursework on intercultural competence, if any, tend to be based on class readings and discussions. However, first-hand engagement with otherness is more effective in developing intercultural competence (Byram, 1997). Therefore, there is a pressing need for PTs' actual interaction with people from different cultures as they are professionally prepared to work with burgeoning student populations from minority (or minoritized) cultures and languages.

Previous telecollaboration projects have examined participants' language learning experiences (e.g. Chen, 2012; Dooly & Sadler, 2013) and intercultural development (e.g. Dooly, 2011; Menard-Warwick *et al.*, 2013). For example, Canto *et al.*'s (2013) study included 34 first-year English language learners and 14 PTs and found that 'networked interactions point towards cultural, linguistic, interpersonal and motivational benefits' (2013: 116). The language learners found this project challenging, motivating and innovative. In Üzüm *et al.* (2020), PTs from Texas and Turkey participated in a telecollaboration focused on multicultural education and developed '(1) awareness of heterogeneity in their own and interactants' culture, (2) nascent critical cultural awareness and (3) curiosity and willingness to learn more about the other culture' (2020: 162). Similarly, in her study on PTs, Dooly (2011) investigated how different modes of communication affected the interaction among the participants, and she claimed that the interactional patterns were influenced by the student teachers' 'previous knowledge, acceptance, experience and willingness to adapt to the different available communication channels and modes' (2011: 334). Menard-Warwick *et al.* (2013) explored the evidence of intercultural learning in virtual intercultural communications between language learners and tutors. They also examined the effect of tutors' cultural identity on intercultural discussions and learning in these online interactions. More recent examples engaged participants in critical service-learning and discussions of social justice issues (Helm, 2016; Porto, 2014; Üzüm *et al.*, 2019). However, further research is still needed on how participants discursively negotiate and enact their identities in telecollaborative interactions.

Theoretical Framework

Theoretically, we drew upon the concepts of imagined identities and communities (Kanno & Norton, 2003), positioning (Davies & Harré, 1999) and identities in interaction (Bucholtz & Hall, 2005), which led us to postulate that individuals construct their identities through discursive positioning guided by their imagination, and concomitantly (re)negotiate their imagination as they enact their identities in their telecollaborative interactions. Kanno and Norton (2003) defined imagined communities as 'groups of people, not immediately tangible and accessible, with whom we connect through the power of the imagination' (2003: 241). These communities can be religious groups, nation-specific groups, age groups and ethnic groups. There are some characteristics attributed to these groups, and individuals prefer to evaluate events and practices within the scope of these images based on their conceptualizations. These imagined identities and communities lead to discursive positioning and the construction of cultural identities.

To understand how PTs perform their identities in telecollaborative interactions, we adopted Bucholtz and Hall's (2005) sociocultural linguistic approach and analyzed PTs' telecollaborative exchanges. This framework defines identity as the 'social positioning of self and other' (2005: 586), and there are five principles for analysis: *emergence, positionality, indexicality, relationality* and *partialness*. First, identity is an 'emergent product' (2005: 588). Although we inherit a linguistic and social background from the culture in which we are raised, we construct identities by interacting with other individuals. Instead of the static and macro classifications of individuals based on social categorizations, Bucholtz and Hall suggest taking identity as a micro and local phenomenon constructed through social interaction.

Regarding *positionality*, Bucholtz and Hall argue that demographic characteristics, such as age, gender and social class provide 'part of the picture' (2005: 593) of identity, and they are important for identity analysis. Thus, the cultural identity can be considered as the combination of macro-level demographic categories, local and specific cultural positions, and interactionally specific positions participants take. Third, Bucholtz and Hall argue identity construction involves 'indexical processes' (2005: 594) in an interaction, which are enacted through linguistic forms. These indexical processes might be the overt use of identity labels and categories, labeling one's and others' positions, and the use of linguistic structures for a group of people or other individuals, such as pronouns. Through these processes, speakers dynamically position themselves and others as part of a particular group.

In this framework, the heart of our identity work is the fourth principle, which is *relationality*. It goes beyond the common perception of identity relations, sameness and difference because identities are constructed on the often-overlapping aspects of *similarities/differences, authentication/denaturalization* and *authority/illegitimacy* during human interactions. Bucholtz and Hall (2005) called similarities *adequation* and differences *distinction* (2005: 599). When the similarities are noticed by individuals, they position themselves as alike, and these similarities are viewed as supportive of immediate identity construction. Differences are often downplayed and deemed unimportant in such alignment, creating a view of 'sufficiently similar', although they may not be identical. For the notion of *distinction*, similarities might be downplayed to emphasize the differences. The second pair in relationality, *authentication/denaturalization*, refers to the processes through which speakers can claim realness and artifice. For example, speakers can authenticate themselves through their right to tell a narrative or can break a stereotypical depiction by enacting an identity that does not align with wide-spread ideologies. The third pair, *authorization/illegitimation* is about the affirmation of identity through existing power structures and ideologies. For *authorization*, an identity can be validated through institutionalized power structures, and for *illegitimation*, these same identities can be ignored, censored, or denied, such as 'one of us' or 'not one of us.' The last principle of the framework is the *partialness* principle. Identity construction is partial and occurs through contextually situated configurations of the self and other. The identity construction might be habitual, deliberate, or the result of others' perceptions. Although identity is considered as a whole, it encompasses multiple dimensions. The identity construction can only be understood when these partial dimensions are analyzed together.

When analyzing the interaction data from the telecollaboration project, we draw from all five elements of this framework to understand how PTs constructed their cultural identities in synchronous and asynchronous interactions. To this end, we use discourse analytic procedures and a sociocultural linguistic approach (Bucholtz & Hall, 2005) to address the research question: How do PTs construct and perform their cultural identities through intercultural interactions in a telecollaborative project?

Methodology

The study is based on an online intercultural exchange between two teacher education classes: a 'Multicultural Education' course at Central City University (pseudonym) in the USA and a 'Language and Culture' course at Northern Anatolia University (pseudonym) in Turkey. These courses were previously conducted in face-to-face classroom settings only. After meeting at a conference, the researchers decided to design the courses as blended so that the PTs could have opportunities to interact with peers from another culture. They thought that such a blended course would help PTs develop intercultural competence and contextualize class readings and discussions more effectively. A total of 48 PTs participated in the project and engaged in asynchronous discussions within groups of six on topics, such as multiculturalism, education, religion and gender. They also participated in one-on-one video-conference interviews and wrote post-project reflections. We randomly selected 20 PTs' discussions, interviews, and reflections as the data source for this chapter.

Data collection procedures

The data were collected between September 2015 and January 2016, according to the approved procedures of human research and participant consent at the university of the second author. The data included discussion board posts, transcripts of video interviews, and post-project reflection papers. Our analysis focused on the discussion board posts since a greater number of identity-negotiation work took place in these asynchronous conversations where PTs had the added ease of time to write detailed posts without the immediacy of synchronous interviews (Chun *et al.*, 2016; Üzüm *et al.*, 2019). The asynchronous discussions took place weekly on a private group on Edmodo (http://www.edmodo.com) and were guided by the prompting questions listed in Table 10.1. To facilitate timely discussions, small groups, consisting of 4–6 people, were formed, and each member was required to make an original post addressing the prompt each Thursday and respond to at least two other members by Sunday. The

Table 10.1 Weekly discussion prompts

Week 1	How do you define multiculturalism in your own life? How do you think your family, friends, or school is multicultural?
Week 2	Please share a memory that you identify as cultural. This could be a cultural item or activity (e.g. places, people, events, books, movies, music and food) that resonates with you on a personal level.
Week 3	How do people in Turkey/the US practice and experience religion? What is its place in schools and people's personal lives?
Week 4	How do you define gender roles of males and females in the workplace, at home, in the society in general? What are some discrimination or privilege examples where one gender might experience privilege or discrimination?
Week 5	What are some current/debated educational issues in your public schools (e.g. challenges, successes, failures)?
Week 6	What did you learn from this experience in general? Was there anything that you found especially interesting or surprising? How do you think learning about another culture like we did in this experience will help you as a teacher in the US/Turkey?

discussions were assigned a weekly completion grade, and the course instructors sent reminders for timely discussions and did not post on the boards to allow unmediated discussions. The one-on-one video interviews took place between PTs and were not monitored or facilitated, and as such, the conversations were unstructured and mostly focused on surface topics and PTs' daily experiences. The synchronous interviews and post-project reflections were used for comparison purposes to understand the discussion board data for an in-depth analysis.

Data analysis

We adopted a qualitative approach and conducted a sociocultural linguistic analysis, focusing on 'the details of language and the workings of culture and society' (Bucholtz & Hall, 2005: 586) to explore how PTs construct and perform their cultural identities as these identities emerge through 'the specific conditions of linguistic interaction' (2005: 588). In the first stage of the analysis, the discussion board posts were independently coded by the researchers by assigning descriptive phrases 'remaining open to all possible theoretical directions' (Saldaña, 2013: 100). Examples of codes included 'explaining one's identity with labels and categories, identifying similarities in a partner's culture, positioning self as different from family and friends, etc.' These codes were later organized into larger categories in the axial coding stage. Once the coding stage was completed, all the data sources were brought together to identify the recurring themes. The excerpts analyzed here are representative examples of the emerging major themes, and they are presented within a larger excerpt to show identity construction in its interactional context. In the selected excerpts, we conducted a sociocultural linguistic analysis and shared our interpretations. This analysis approaches 'identity as a relational and sociocultural phenomenon that emerges and circulates in local discourse contexts of interaction rather than as a stable structure located primarily in the individual psyche or in fixed social categories' (Bucholtz & Hall, 2005: 586). A line-by-line analysis of PTs' interactions helped us explore the many ways they constructed and negotiated their cultural identities and positioned themselves and their interlocutors in relation to the imagined communities.

Findings

The findings suggest that intercultural interactions during telecollaboration opened discursive spaces for 'borderland negotiation' of identities (Yazan *et al.*, 2019), especially when PTs discussed stories and examples from their personal experiences. More specifically, PTs (a) engaged in acts of reflexive and interactive positioning, (b) negotiated their imagined self-communities and other-communities in relation to the dominant social, cultural, and political discourses in their glocal contexts and (c) constructed their cultural identities by contesting, subverting or appropriating these discourses.

Reflexive and interactive positionings

In their conversations, PTs engaged in reflexive and interactive positionings by constantly positioning themselves and their interlocutors in relation to the topics and contexts of the conversations. These positionings sometimes emerged explicitly as PTs explained their personal identities and told autobiographical stories, using first-person pronouns 'I, me, myself' (Harré & Langenhove, 1991; Quirk *et al.*, 1985) or sometimes were embedded in the conversations implicitly, as PTs took the positions of joke teller, student, teacher candidate, etc. For example, in Table 10.2 below, Yesim responds to the prompt[1] 'Introduce yourself and write about your cultural identity' and takes on multiple positionings.

Table 10.2 Explicit self-positioning

Line	Text
1	My name is Yesim. I am a senior in [Northern Anatolia University] and I am a muslim who
2	live in Turkey. I am a coming migrant from Georgia. My family has come in Turkiye from
3	Georgia before a lot of time. Sometimes, we can go to Batum especially festivals and visit
4	our relatives. I attack from their foods and dances of Georgia. Although I am a muslim,
5	sometimes I can say their religion songs that are beautiful and effective. I mean, I think that
6	I am multicultural. The other reason of it is that I am member of two groups about cultural
7	and I learn English literature in my lesson. As I learn their culture, I want to connect English
8	people whose culture are amazing and effective. I believe some beliefs of their culture
9	because of it. According to me, it is enough to be a multicultural.
10	

Responding to the task prompt, Yesim takes on multiple positionings including a senior student, a Muslim, a migrant from Georgia living in Turkey, a multicultural enthusiast, and a student of English literature. In line 5, she refers to her Muslim identity as a 'no hindrance' to be able to appreciate Georgian religious music, with the word 'although.' In a way, she consolidates her current Muslim identity with her heritage Georgian identity that can align and co-exist. Drawing from her bi-cultural identity and using it as a resource, in lines 6–10, she refers to her English literature student identity and uses the words 'connect, amazing, effective, beautiful' as a blending source and an objective of her multiple positionings. In lines 6–10, she authenticates her multicultural self-positioning using her bicultural and immigrant identity to affirm her claim in line 10.

In the next example, Yesim responds to the question, 'What did you learn from this telecollaboration project?' and engages in interactive positionings by positioning her 'American' partners in multiple ways. In Table 10.3, Tricia responds and comments on some of these positionings and elaborates on her own positionings.

Table 10.3 Interactive positioning

Line	Text
1	**Yesim:** In fact, I experience a lot of somethings from lifes of my American friends.
2	Especially, I notice that my thoughts are mistakes about them. They are really humanistic
3	and understanding people in my opinion. I think that they are very relax and don't
4	experience their religion, completely. After I know them, I really make a mistake about
5	them. They are bound their religion and very humane. I think they are not bound of their
6	family about them. But now, it is not right idea, according to me. In addition that I learn lots
7	of things about them like their accent. I learn some forms from them. Of course, that
8	experience is very useful for me. My point of view is changed thank to this project. I
9	understand that we need to know him/her to think about someone.
10	**Tricia:** We do not share the same religion however religion is extremely important to me,
11	we may have different practices and different beliefs, but like you said we do value our
12	religion just as you value your religion, but in different ways (:
13	**Yesim:** Yes, I understand you thanks to this project.
14	

In lines 1–4, Yesim explains how her previous beliefs about Americans were disproved after her interactions with American partners. In line 3, she likely meant to explain her previous beliefs about Americans, 'They are very relax[ed] and don't experience their religion completely,' which she no longer holds and explains in line 5 that 'they are bound [to] their religion [are religious] and very humane.' It is not clear if Tricia completely understands the positionings offered by Yesim in terms of her previous and current beliefs, and there may have been some confusion. However, Tricia clarifies in lines 11–13 that 'religion is extremely important' to her, and she equates it by creating alignment in line 13 (e.g. 'we do value our religion just as you value your religion, but in different ways.'). The purpose of her clarification becomes further emphasized with the use of 'do' in line 12 'we do value our religion.' Tricia also accepts the moral positioning of being a member of 'American culture' and aligns herself with the use of first-person plural pronouns 'we' and 'our' in lines 11–13, concomitantly positioning Yesim as a Muslim and representing the Muslim community in line 12 (e.g. 'just as you value your religion.'). It is not clear if 'you' here indexes Yesim only and her religion through a personal positioning or Muslims in general through a moral positioning since English does not differentiate between singular you and plural you, but we interpreted this as a plural 'you' since it emerged along with the plural 'we.'

Negotiation of imagined self-communities and other-communities

PTs referred to their imagined communities by aligning with some practices and distancing from others. They used insider and outsider positionings in the subcategories they created in their narrative as it relates to the dominant social, cultural and political discourses in their glocal contexts. In Table 10.4, Tricia discusses gender diversity in her local context.

Table 10.4 Resisting the dominant discourse

Line	Text
1	**Tricia:** Gender roles are based on norms and standards created by society. Most men are
2	associated with strength, aggression and dominance whereas most women are associated
3	with passivity, nurturing and subordination. However, my definition of gender roles differ.
4	For me, gender roles are men and women doing what they desire, whether it is men cooking,
5	or women playing football, they are doing what they desire despite what society thinks. In
6	this day in time women have gained way more privileges than before, for example, there is
7	more women police, firefighters, wrestlers, football players, car advisors, and the list goes
8	on but there is still some discrimination. Unfortunately, society still view women as staying
9	at home, cooking, cleaning and looking after the children, therefore in the workplace and
10	society in general it is hard for women to prove themselves since they are not given the full
11	opportunity due to their sex. I love to play sports, majority of the time just for fun. Me and a
12	group of my friends would meet up and play whatever sport we decided to play that day, and
13	when it came down to picking teams of course the guys wanted all guys on their team and
14	didn't pick any women due to their perception of gender roles. In my opinion women could
15	do anything men could and vice versa.
16	**Esin:** I really liked your comment Tricia. Unfortunately we are still living in a society
17	shaping us according to our sex. We've also experienced such problems with our friends.
18	They say 'Oh, you're a woman so you can't do that.' This is wrong of course. They forget
19	something. Besides being a woman we are human and we can do everything as much as they
20	do.
21	

In this exchange, Tricia starts with explaining her opinions about gender diversity in the US in a rather generic way, and she positions herself as different from and defiant to these norms created by the society. In line 12, her narrative shifts from being a generic explanation to telling a personal narrative. She starts with the present tense (e.g. 'I love to play sports'), and explains a habitual or series of activities in line 13 (e.g. 'me and my group of friends would meet up and play') using 'would' to express the frequency of events in the past. She then shifts to simple past and retrieves a specific past experience in lines 14 and 15 (e.g. 'when it came down to picking teams, of course, the guys wanted all guys on their team and didn't pick any women.'). This seems to be a personal past experience that contributed to Tricia's personal position in terms of gender diversity, and she uses it as a resource and catalyst to position herself in defiance of the gender norms of her glocal context. In her example, she is otherwise qualified and authenticated to play sports with her friends until the moment of selecting teams, and her qualifications did not matter when she was not selected because of her gender. In line 17, Esin responds to Tricia and aligns with her positioning and adequates her own experiences with Tricia's. Both Tricia and Esin create an imagined community of 'friends,' and 'they' associate with discriminative behavior and use the word 'still' in lines 9 and 17 to express how they are tired of the continued gender inequities. They end with hopeful statements in lines 16 and 20, indicating that they may take these positionings to their future classrooms as educators and will act in ways to resist and transform these long-existing inequities with their students.

The following example illustrates alignment with the dominant discourse. In Table 10.5, Esin explains her experiences with religion and positions herself as a Muslim. She presents this positioning as the overarching reality of Turkey but fails to include the experiences of religious minorities in Turkey.

In this conversation, Esin creates an imagined community of Turkish people in which the religion is Islam. Although a majority of Turks identify as Muslim, Turkey is a secular state and houses many religious minorities. In lines 1–2, Esin creates a clearly defined community of Turkish people and positions herself in the community with the first-person plural pronouns 'we' and 'our.' She adds some partitive meaning to this otherwise imagined homogeneous community in line 3 (e.g. 'Most of the people do what is necessary for their religion'), leaving a small minority excluded with this statement. When she talks about this imagined community of 'most of the people,' she excludes herself from the group using third person plural pronouns, thereby adding witnessed objectivity since it is not a personal narrative anymore. In line 6, she equates positive personal qualities with religiosity. She creates an imagined majority community who practices the required pillars of Islam and mentions the minority who do not in line 8. Some of these practices can be observed by others and therefore are

Table 10.5 Alignment with the dominant discourse

Text

Esin: In Turkey, religion is very important and delicate for people. Our religion is Islam and we're Muslims. In our country, Islam occupies a big place in people's lives. Most of the people do what is necessary for their religion. They perform the five pillars of Islam smoothly. Besides the requirements of our religion that can be observed by other people, there are many other qualities that can't be observed such as goodness, ethics, righteousness, honesty etc. which should be found in all human's inside. When we look around, we can easily see; while majority of the people living in our country practise their religion intensely, others practise mildly. We can't make a decision about their outlook on religion and also we shouldn't as we're not decision –makers. The religion is only between God and the person. Nowadays, people have been talking about religion more than previous years. When I was at school, I had religion lessons every year – from primary school to the last year of high school. The students have still been having religion lessons but it occupies bigger place than my school years. Besides religion lessons, Arabic, the life of our prophet 'Hz. Muhammed', Koran lessons are added. This shows that the children who are our future are having an extensive knowledge of religion.

However, this situation brings out a question 'How much is it right to live together with religion as it is only between God and the person?'

Fehime: I think religion is just only between God and person, confidential worship is more sincere.

Jane: Esin, I agree completely that all the qualities that you mentioned should be found in everyone. However, sadly, not everyone does. I find it fascinating that you had religion classes all throughout school. I kind of wish we had had classes on different religions, not just one, when I was in school. I think that would have been so interesting to learn about all the different religions. I love what you have to say about religion being between the individual and God.

visible, while some are not visible such as being righteous or honest. She suspends judgment and does not feel authenticated to make a judgment on this minority in line 10 using the first-person plural pronoun 'we.' Thereby, she differentiates herself from this minority and aligns with the majority who may have the righteous position to make a judgment but shouldn't since 'we are not decision-makers' (i.e. line 10). That is, there is a possibility to decide about this minority, but 'we' do not have the authority. Starting from line 12, she shares her personal experiences taking religion courses and compares to the current curriculum, explaining that there are many more religion courses at schools now. Esin concludes with the question that if religion is something personal and between a person and God, then is it right to institutionalize it? With this question, she goes back and forth between a position of alignment/endorsement and disalignment/questioning, thereby displaying mixed and complex opinions and attitudes in the matter. Fehime, another PT from Turkey, responds to this question saying that 'confidential worship is more sincere,' which indicates her disagreement with the increased intensity of religion courses in schools. In line 21, Jane aligns with Esin's position on the universality of positive qualities (however tied to being religious) mentioned in line 6, but misses the mark on withholding judgment that Esin invited in line 10 and says 'sadly, not everyone does' in line 22. Jane adds that she wishes she would have more religion courses in her schooling but frames them as informative courses on different religions rather than proselytization of a dominant religion.

Constructing cultural identities in relation to discourses

In their exchanges, PTs discursively constructed cultural identities that contested, subverted, or appropriated the dominant social, cultural and political discourses in their glocal contexts. This construction was often apparent when they talked about their own cultural identities explicitly in relation to the dominant discourses by taking on various positionings. For instance, in Table 10.6, Gozde and Leonard use the dining table as a metaphor to explain own positionings in their glocal contexts:

In this exchange, Gozde describes herself through various self-positionings such as being born and living in Bursa for most of her life and having come to [Guzelsehir] to attend college. She uses the dinner table metaphor to appreciate diversity. Leonard takes on this metaphor and equates it to his experiences in his glocal context through his personal narratives. In line 10, he creates an imagined community of people who are closed to experiencing different cultures and differentiates himself with the use of third-person plural pronouns. He also refers to media as the culprit of cultivating such stereotypical depictions of other cultures in lines 12–14. In the next line, he reveals his personal narrative of transformation and explains how he was previously closed-minded. He adds that his opinions have changed after interacting with a variety of people and made 'collaboration' his new

Table 10.6 Resisting dominant discourses

Text

Gozde: Hello! I am Gozde. I am from Bursa\Turkey. I was born in Bursa and except university, I studied in Bursa. For my university education, I live in [Guzelsehir]. I am senior student of English Language Teaching department. In my opinion, multiculturalism is a kind of dinner table. In this table, we can eat desserts, soup, rice etc... We can eat each of them separately but at the same time we can eat them together each of them has different taste and different appearance like cultures. However, when all these food come together. We can see diversity. This has different taste too.

Leonard: The dinner table analogy is a very effective way to describe our multicultural ways of living here as well. Some people just cannot seem to break out of their shell and try something new or adjust their perspective of people due to the news and media blasting us with only the stereotypical mumbo jumbo that they do. With different intents of all the media sources... we can become just as diverse as we are close minded depending on what you follow, watch, enjoy... etc. I was close minded once... then I realized it can be hateful and demeaning to those who did not see my way... now that I have seen many ways that people interact, I see my goals and intents as more of a collaboration of me, those close to me, those I have met, and those I wish to emulate. This makes me who I am culturally, but also individually... I like a little bit of everything at my dinner plate, like Thanksgiving, but with a little Mediterranean zing.

perspective in line 17. In this narrative, Leonard creates a cultural identity that contests and resists the stereotypical depictions portrayed in media. We hope that this personal positioning will translate to some advocacy efforts in PTs' future classrooms, and believe that this emerging awareness is a crucial start for a teacher candidate. In Table 10.7, Leonard contests the dominant discourses in his glocal context in the following post.

In this narrative, Leonard explains his cultural identity and elaborates on how it is different from his family and friends. He constructs two different imagined communities in direct disagreement with each other (e.g. his family and friends on one side and his college friends on the other). He then positions himself in defiance with the values that he grew up with and what his family and friends follow. While his nascent multicultural identity mostly draws from a surface definition of multiculturalism around

Table 10.7 Contesting dominant discourses in the US

Text

I define the multiculturalism in my life in how I try new things often (food, movies, festivals, music, etc.), diversifying when and where I can (out of my comfort zone), trying to view things from alternate perspectives other than my own, and accepting that things will be different for each and every person. My family is not too multicultural in my eyes. They are white-conservatives who live in the back country who are unwilling to accept modern changes outside of their accustomed ways of life. They pretty much resist change. My friends tend to sway the same way as my family. Very closed minded. Our school is fairly diverse and has a niche for anything and everything you want to be. Gay, straight, white, black, Asian, female, transgender... there is something for everyone. I love it...

foods, flags and festivals, he negotiates a critical perspective in line 3 (e.g. 'trying to view things from alternate perspectives'). This perspective gives him a position of flexibility and open-mindedness, contrasting his positioning of his family and friends as closed-minded. A similar example of contesting the dominant discourse comes from Ertugrul, a PT from Turkey in Table 10.8.

In this exchange, Ertugrul shares a similar narrative in which his personal identity emerges in contest with the values his family members taught him and adhere to themselves. Similar to Leonard (Table 10.7), Ertugrul also constructs two different and contrasting imagined communities, his family members and his university community. He uses the keyword 'respect' throughout his narrative, which could be interpreted as a desire to be accepted despite his differences from the dominant social discourse. He reveals how he knows about Islam because he was forced to learn about this religion in schools. Then he imagines two factions of

Table 10.8 Contesting the dominant discourses in Turkey

Text
Ertugrul: Forgive me for past two weeks. I can just attend among you. How do people in Turkey practice and experience religion? First of all, we have an official religion in Turkey. It is Islam. Nearly % 70 of our people are Muslims. I think religion is more sensitive in here than other European countries, since our people (not all of them) have nothing but religion. People's thoughts about religion are too strict. Since thoughts are too strict there is always a disagreement between hard Muslims and the others. For me, this is the reason that makes religion so sensitive. This fact makes things complicated in here but it's about to change. Anyway, we learn Islam from our families at first place. When we grow up enough, government gives us religional courses in our schools. These courses are mainly about Islamic information. They teach us how to practice it in everywhere (in schools, home, Mosque). Some of our important practices are praying and attend to prayers at specific times. But first, one have to believe in God, Hz. Muhammed (prophet of Islam) and Kur'an, which is Muslim's holy book, to become a Muslim. As members of new generation, we show respect to everyone, not only about religion but also every thought. One can practice his religion freely in here. One can go to a Mosque, a Church or where ever you need to go. Nobody interferes to you. But there are some people from old generation they are terrible. In real Islam, you need to respect others. Unfortunately, these old ones never respect to other religions, I am not Muslim. I know the rules of Islam. I know nearly every basic information about Islam because I have to learn (they taught it to me). But I am a Deist. Old ones never likes me, I don't like them too. Even some members of my family show no respect to me. They don't listen to me, they don't want to talk to me. But I am happy with my friend in university they show respect to me.
Leonard: Respectfulness of another's religion is part of the kindness that our religions are based on. Every religion has a purpose to spread the word, but not be mean about it. Wars have been fought over this... but is it justified? Just because we cannot see eye to eye does not mean we should rid the world of the ones who will not conform. There is good in every religion... and with internal conflict, it does not help you to flourish.
Ertugrul: Leonard I agree with you. All religions should be based on respectfulness, but as you said there are bad and good in every religion. Without a new perspective to religions, which contains respect, we can't get any better.

community, using 'the old ones' in line 12, which may be interpreted as the older generation of people authorized by the existing power structures, and the newer generation of people that he frequently interacts with in his college. In this exchange, Ertugrul and Leonard construct similar imagined communities and share similar experiences, in which both of their identities were delegitimized by the dominant power structures. In response, they construct an identity contesting and subverting these power structures. Drawing from their personal experiences, they create an objective to adhere to in their personal and professional lives, using the keywords 'should' in lines 28 and 31, which indexes disagreement, suggestion, and potential subverting action.

Discussion

This telecollaboration project was conducted to afford the PTs a space to reflect on their cultural identities and develop intercultural competence. The PTs engaged in intercultural discussions on a variety of topics, such as language, gender, religion and other educational considerations. Our microanalysis of asynchronous conversations led us to postulate that PTs constructed their identities through complex discursive positionings guided by their imagination and concomitantly (re)negotiated their imagination as they enacted 'socially meaningful identities through language' (Gee, 2018: 145). Their cultural identities were intricately intertwined with their national, ethnic, religious, gender and linguistic identities, which demonstrated the complex and intersectional nature of identities as they are negotiated and enacted in interaction. These identities emerged in interaction through PTs' various acts of positioning in relation to their interlocutors, to Turkish and US contexts, and to the topics being discussed (Bucholtz & Hall, 2005; Davies & Harré, 1999). Some of these positionings were explicitly declared through self-assigned labels and categories, some emerged implicitly and some were discursively assigned by their interlocutors. While some of the positions seemed deliberate and explicitly declared, others were embedded in the linguistic aspects of their interactions, lending further support to the partialness of identity negotiation situated in interactions (Bucholtz & Hall, 2005).

When PTs constructed identities that challenged the dominant discourse and the power structures, they created an imagined community of others through third-person plural pronouns, or a quintessential *other* with generic *they* which may designate the mysterious forces appearing to control the ordinary citizen's life, such as 'the authorities,' 'the media' and 'the government' (Quirk *et al.*, 1985: 354). Sometimes, these opposing forces were as close as one's family and friends, and in other cases were assigned qualities like 'olds' or 'closed-minded' people. In these cases of resistance and defiance, PTs reflected on their marginalization from one community but also being embraced by another, which further supports the relational aspect of identity construction (Bucholtz & Hall, 2005). On the other hand, when some PTs' cultural identities aligned with the dominant discourse, they tended to imagine a homogenized community that conforms with their own cultural identity and neglected the diversity within these communities or the experiences of marginalized others, through the use of universal pronouns such as 'we', 'Turkish people, Americans' and 'everyone' (Quirk *et al.*, 1985; Üzüm *et al.*, 2018; Üzüm *et al.*, 2019). It is possible that the assignment prompts and the wording of the discussion questions might have led to such generic framing in PTs' responses; however, it is still worth noting that generic framing (e.g. Turks, Americans) was more likely to take place when PTs' identities were in alignment with the dominant discourse and the perceived majority of people. Whereas, when PTs' identities were in disalignment with the dominant discourse and perceived majorities, PTs were more likely to enact individual and fragmentary identities that challenge the notion of culture as a nation and create 'multiple, complex, variable, and layered' imagined communities (Jackson, 2014: 68). The use of partitive pronouns, such as 'some people,' indicated a nascent awareness of such diversity, and that people might experience topics like religion and gender differently in their contexts.

Conclusion and Implications

This study implicates that identities emerge in interactions through various complex positionings, and their relational, indexical and partial aspects are prominent in online intercultural exchanges. We believe that participation in telecollaboration has the potential to experience and reflect on the borders between 'self' and 'other,' and it should become commonplace in language teacher education to have PTs self-reflexively engage with their cultural identities in intercultural spaces. In many of the excerpts, the college campuses emerged as a space that provided the necessary conditions for PTs to enact their identities and have a sense of belonging. It is necessary for teacher education curriculum to integrate tasks and activities that promote PTs' reflection on their identities and provide opportunities for PTs to interact with people from different cultural identities and perspectives. Telecollaboration through intercultural partnerships (see http://www.unicollaboration.org for partner institutes) can offer an experiential and discursive space for PTs to reflect on and enact their identities through their interactions with others.

Acknowledgments

We are grateful to the editors of this volume for their comments and suggestions on the earlier versions of this paper, which significantly contributed to improving its quality. We are also thankful to the preservice teachers from the 2015–2016 cohorts in both universities who took part in this telecollaboration project. Lastly, we appreciate Heather Baker and Amanda Giles for their suggestions about the language and content of the article.

Note

(1) PTs' posts were not edited.

References

Blommaert, J. (2010) *The Sociolinguistics of Globalization*. Cambridge: Cambridge University Press.

Bucholtz, M. and Hall, K. (2005) Identity and interaction: A sociocultural linguistic approach. *Discourse Studies* 7 (4–5), 585–614.

Byram, M. (1997) The intercultural dimension in "language learning for European citizenship." In M. Byram and G. Zarate (eds) *The Sociocultural and Intercultural Dimension of Language Learning and Teaching* (pp. 17–20). Strasbourg: Council of Europe.

Canto, S., Jauregi, K. and van den Bergh, H. (2013) Integrating cross-cultural interaction through video-communication and virtual worlds in foreign language teaching programs: Is there an added value? *ReCALL* 25 (1), 105–121.

Chen, W.C. (2012) Professional growth during cyber collaboration between pre-service and in-service teachers. *Teaching and Teacher Education* 28 (2), 218–228.

Chun, D., Kern, R. and Smith, B. (2016) Technology in language use, language teaching, and language learning. *The Modern Language Journal* 100 (S1), 64–80.

Çiftçi, E.Y. and Savaş, P. (2018) The role of telecollaboration in language and intercultural learning: A synthesis of studies published between 2010 and 2015. *ReCALL* 30 (3), 278–298.

Davies, B. and Harré, R. (1999) Positioning and personhood. In R. Harré and L.V. Langenhove (eds) *Positioning Theory* (pp. 32–52). Chichester: Wiley-Blackwell.

Dooly, M.A. (2011) Crossing the intercultural borders into 3rd space culture(s): Implications for teacher education in the twenty-first century. *Language and Intercultural Communication* 11 (4), 319–337.

Dooly, M.A. and Sadler, R. (2013) Filling in the gaps: Linking theory and practice through telecollaboration in teacher education. *ReCALL* 25 (1), 4–29.

Friedman, J. (1994) *Cultural Identity and Global Process*. London: Sage Publication.

Gee, J.P. (2018) *Introducing Discourse Analysis: From Grammar to Society*. New York, NY: Routledge.

Guth, S. and Helm, F. (eds) (2010) *Telecollaboration 2.0.: Language, Literacies and Intercultural Learning in the 21st Century*. Bern: Peter Lang.

Haneda, M. and Alexander, M. (2015) ESL teacher advocacy beyond the classroom. *Teaching and Teacher Education* 49, 149–158.

Harré, R. and Langenhove, L.V. (1991) Varieties of positioning. *Journal for the Theory of Social Behaviour* 21, 393–407.

Helm, F. (2016) Facilitated dialogue in online intercultural exchange. In R. O'Dowd and T. Lewis (eds) *Online Intercultural Exchange: Policy, Pedagogy, Practice* (pp. 150–172). New York, NY: Routledge.

Jackson, J. (2014) *Introducing Language and Intercultural Communication*. New York, NY: Routledge.

Kanno, Y. and Norton, B. (2003) Imagined communities and educational possibilities: Introduction. *Journal of Language, Identity, and Education* 2 (4), 241–249.

Kern, R. (2006) Perspectives on technology in learning and teaching languages. *TESOL Quarterly* 40 (1), 183–210.

Kern, R., Ware, P. and Warschauer, M. (2004) Crossing frontiers: New directions in online pedagogy and research. *Annual Review of Applied Linguistics* 24, 243–260.

Menard-Warwick, J., Heredia-Herrera, A. and Palmer, D.S. (2013) Local and global identities in an EFL internet chat exchange. *The Modern Language Journal* 97 (4), 965–980.

O'Dowd, R. (2016) Emerging trends and new directions in telecollaborative learning. *CALICO Journal* 33 (3), 291–310.

O'Dowd, R. and Lewis, T. (eds) (2016) *Online Intercultural Exchange: Policy, Pedagogy, Practice*. New York, NY: Routledge.

Porto, M. (2014) Intercultural citizenship education in an EFL online project in Argentina. *Language and Intercultural Communication* 14 (2), 245–261.

Quirk, R., Greenbaum, S., Leech, G. and Svartvik, J. (1985) *A Comprehensive Grammar of the English Language*. New York, NY: Longman.

Risager, K. (2007) *Language and Culture Pedagogy: From a National to a Transnational Paradigm*. Clevedon: Multilingual Matters.

Saldaña, J. (2013) *The Coding Manual for Qualitative Researchers*. Thousand Oaks, CA: Sage Publications.

Sercu, L. (2006) The foreign language and intercultural competence teacher: The acquisition of a new professional identity. *Intercultural Education* 17 (1), 55–72.

Tanghe, S. and Park, G. (2016) "Build[ing] something which alone we could not have done": International collaborative teaching and learning in language teacher education. *System* 57, 1–13.

Üzüm, B., Yazan, B. and Selvi, A.F. (2018) Inclusive and exclusive uses of we in four American textbooks for multicultural teacher education. *Language Teaching Research* 22 (5), 625–647.

Üzüm, B., Akayoglu, S. and Yazan, B. (2020) Using telecollaboration to promote intercultural competence in teacher training classrooms in Turkey and the USA. *ReCALL Journal* 32 (2), 162–177.

Üzüm, B., Yazan, B., Avineri, N. and Akayoglu, S. (2019) Preservice teachers' discursive constructions of cultural practices in a multicultural telecollaboration. *International Journal of Multicultural Education* 21 (1), 82–104.

Yazan, B., Rudolph, N. and Selvi, A.F. (2019) Borderland negotiations of identity in language education: Introducing the special issue. *International Multilingual Research Journal* 13 (3), 133–136.

Part 3

Learner Negotiations of Identity in and Beyond the Classroom

11 Meaning-making as a Site of Struggle: One Japanese Language Learner's Negotiation with Identity and Writing

Shinji Kawamitsu

Introduction

A wealth of studies have shown the contribution that post-structuralist approaches to identity can make to language education. The majority of the previous research, however, has primarily focused on the complexity of identity and spoken interaction, and little research has explored said complexity in relation to world language learner *writing*.[1] While such an absence has been addressed by a post-structural perspective to date (e.g. Canagarajah, 2016; Haneda, 2005; Liu & Tannacito, 2013; McKay & Wong, 1996), the absence of writing studies is still acute in the field of world language education, such as Japanese. The purpose of this study is to explore a world language learner's identity and interaction in relation to writing, and further an understanding of complexity in these constructs. More specifically, this study uses the post-structuralist theory of *investment* (Norton, 2013) and *systemic functional linguistics* (Halliday & Hasan, 1989; Rose & Martin, 2012), and explores one elementary Japanese language learner's negotiation with a facilitated writing project. The study suggests the complexity of identity, interaction and writing, and calls for further empirical studies in world language education.

Review of the Relevant Literature

Post-structuralist approach to identity and language education

As an intellectual movement developed in response to the scientific presentations of structuralism, post-structuralist theory has brought various insights into language education. Of particular value are their approaches to identity. In the 1970s and 1980s, a majority of research conceptualized language learners' identities as 'fixed personalities, learning styles and motivations.' However, more recently, identity researchers have drawn on post-structural understandings of identity 'as fluid, context-dependent, and context-producing, in historical and cultural circumstances' (Norton & Toohey, 2011: 419). Moje and Luke (2009) illustrate such a paradigm shift in relation to literacy as follows:

> The move to study identity's relationship to literacy and literacy's relationship to identity ... seems at least partially motivated by an interest in foregrounding the actor or agent in literate and social practices. (2009: 416)

Moje and Luke (2009) explain that this move can be in part 'resistance to a skill-based view of literacy or to a view of literacy as cognitive processes' (2009: 416), which emerged in accordance with the social turn in literacy theory and research.

Of particular significance is Norton's conception of identity. Norton (2013) argues that it is necessary for identity theorists to explore the 'contingent, context-dependent nature of identities' (2013: 5), which includes inequitable relations of power that are changing across time and place or sometimes even co existing in contradictory ways within a single individual (2013: 2). Highlighting that identities are 'not merely given by social structures or ascribed by others, but are also negotiated by agents who wish to position themselves' (2013: 5), Norton conceptualizes *imagined identity* as a transgressive potential that enhances our ways of being that affects language learners' learning trajectories.

Norton further argues that *imagined identities* specify what should be accomplished as a form of *investment* (Kanno & Norton, 2003). Learners invest in a second language with the understanding that the investment will, in turn, give them a range of symbolic and material resources that will increase their capital. Language learners have an expectation and hope for 'a good return on that investment – a return that will give them access to hitherto unattainable resources' (Norton Peirce, 1995: 17). It is a discursive practice to make a meaningful connection between learners' actual language practices in a classroom and their commitment to learn the target language (Norton & Toohey, 2011).

Systemic functional linguistics and its critical instantiations

The present study draws on *systemic functional linguistics* (SFL). SFL is a social semiotic approach to language that explores how people use language and how it is structured for its context. In SFL, language is viewed as a large network of interrelated options, and the user's *choice* of language for meaning-making is emphasized.

SFL has a great interest in the relation between text and context (Martin, 2001: 151), and as such, developed theories of context, such as *context of situation* and *context of culture*. In short, context of situation is an immediate environment where language is used, while context of culture is the cultural and historical environment that informs language use (Malinowski, 1935, as cited in Halliday & Hasan, 1989: 6–7). Both of these contexts are theorized as the necessary constructs for an adequate understanding of a text (Halliday & Hasan, 1989: 7).

To date, the aforementioned SFL notion of text and context has been explored from a post-structural perspective (e.g. Fairclough, 1989, 2003; Janks, 2010; Kamler, 2001), and of particular relevance to the current study is Ivanič's work. Ivanič argues that text is shaped by the institutional and political contexts in which it is embedded. Clark and Ivanič (1997) illustrate that institutional context 'supports particular values, beliefs, associated practices and conventions, and patterns of privileging among them that are specific to the remit of that institution' (1997: 68).

Equally important is their argument for individual writer's agentive negotiation. Clark and Ivanič (1997) argue that the notion of context of situation (i.e. the immediate environment of the text) needs to include learners' agency and commitment:

> We have also been arguing that a narrow view of what constitutes the immediate social context leads to an overly deterministic view of the relationship between language and context. Context of situation must include not only the observable characteristics of participants, but also their interests (in both senses), their values, beliefs, commitments, allegiances, and their sense of self-worth. (1997: 67)

In my study, the above understanding of language learners' commitments and allegiances is incorporated in line with the conception of *investment* (Norton, 2013), for the concept of investment has been theorized and utilized in various educational contexts (for example, see Darvin & Norton, 2015).

'Writing' in Japanese language education

One of the motivations of this study is the oft-perceived educational discourse wherein writing is subordinated to a secondary role (see Byrnes, 2011; Reichelt *et al.*, 2012). To date, although there is such a cross-disciplinary effort to explore social and/or ideological aspects of writing in world language education (e.g. Colombi, 2009; Ryshina-Pankova & Byrnes, 2013), it is fair to say that the subordinated position of writing is still salient in the field.

The subordinated position of writing is particularly acute in Japanese language education. Instructional studies tend to strive for developing learners' oral proficiency, and writing is often downgraded to a space for instructors to monitor learners' understanding of orthography, textbook content and grammar structures (Hirose, 2015; Mizutani, 1997). This static view of writing can be seen in the literature review (Toramaru, 2014: 47), which showcases that the writing/composition studies have a longstanding preference to the view of a classroom as *a space for acquiring language forms* and/or *a space for acquiring language skills*. The static view of writing seems to also be verified, research-methodologically (Ichishima, 2009), which showcases that the positivistic view is understood as the valuable epistemological stance in Japanese language education.

In a sense, this static view of writing is problematic. The current discourse of writing has the potential to conceive of Japanese writers, especially elementary writers, as individuals who have little agency in making meaning. While there are indeed studies that explore elementary Japanese writing, the majority of the studies tend not to question what constructs the writing task (e.g. audience, topic and purpose), how writing is achieved (e.g. genre and register) and how writing relates to the writer's complex identities (with some exceptions such as Hirose, 2015). Such discourse readily leads empirical studies to overlook learners' identities and multilingual resources, despite the fact that language learners bring diverse identities, sets of beliefs and learning resources to the classroom (McKay & Wong, 1996).

The Study

This study is part of the larger study that I conducted for my dissertation research. The purpose of my dissertation study is to explore alternative discourses of writing where elementary Japanese language learners are positioned as *agentive meaning-makers*, which I define as individuals' choice-making in semiotic resources, positionings and identity investments, in a situated context. The study draws on *systemic functional linguistics* that explicitly situates one's meaning-making in a social and institutional context (Clark & Ivanič, 1997; Rose & Martin, 2012) and post-structuralist theory of *investment,* which offers an explanatory potential of learners' learning commitments (Norton, 2013). While my dissertation study includes four Japanese language learners, for the interest of this chapter, I particularly focus on one student, Lapis, and illustrate her agentive negotiation with her identity, interaction and writing.

Research site

The research site is a women's liberal arts college in western Massachusetts, in the United States. The college is highly selective and often described as one of the most competitive colleges in the area in terms of acceptance rates. I taught Japanese in that college for four years, and in one of the academic years, I facilitated this writing project in my elementary-level Japanese language course.

Personal narrative genre

The genre that I selected for this inquiry is the *personal narrative genre*. The social purpose of this genre is illustrated as 'engaging' in the SFL genre tradition (Rose & Martin, 2012: 110), and it aims to engage with readers through narrating the writer's experiences. I selected this genre because of its potential synergies: writing is foregrounded as social practice for learners to make sense of both their lived experiences and the complexity of individual/social relationships (Norton, 2013: 14). With regard to the schooling and selection of genre, Kamler (2001) argues that current competency-based pedagogy attempts to remove the personal from school writing and instead focus on 'the more functional genres students need to master in the "real world"' (2001: 1). Kamler claims that it is essential to position the personal narrative 'in a way that allows a more critical engagement with experiences' (2001: 1), and to treat writing as 'an invitation to identify, analyze and critique, to understand the discursive practices that construct the sense of self – which in turn offer possibilities for social change' (2001: 3).

The selection of personal narrative genre is also attributable to an equally important pedagogical reason. Personal narrative genre is relatively less complex for students to read and write in terms of linguistic features. Registrial variables that are essential to construct narrative genres are mostly introduced in the early stages of an elementary Japanese course.

Pedagogical approach

I integrated the designed pedagogical approach (illustrated below) into the semester's final project. The project started in week 9 in Fall 2016. The grade for this project accounted for 15% of the final grade, and students submitted a portfolio at the end of the final project.

In this project, I primarily used an SFL-based literacy approach, called the *teaching-learning cycle*. This cycle consists of three phases, namely, *deconstruction*, *joint construction* and *independent construction* (Rose & Martin, 2012). To put it succinctly, in the *deconstruction*, I facilitated three reading texts of personal narrative genre. All of the students analyzed rhetorical and linguistic patterns in those texts to understand how meanings are made by the writer's linguistic choices. When those reading texts include grammar structures and vocabulary items that the class does not cover in the semester, I listed such grammar structures and vocabulary items in a footnote with an equivalent meaning in English. In the next *joint construction* phase, students constructed one text as a group. Tasks in this phase included the selection of audience, purpose and goal for the text that they would jointly construct as a group. Students discussed and negotiated their topic, rhetorical organization and linguistic choices.

I provided each group with six days to compose the text, and then they presented their text to the class. In the last *independent construction* phase, students produced three drafts in total (first draft, second draft and final draft). Similar to the previous phase, I gave a writing design sheet to the students before they actually produced their text. I asked them to write their goal, purpose and audience for their individual writing. My intention was to facilitate a learning environment where individual students could *invest*. That is, rather than assigning the audience, goal and purpose for the whole class, I let individual students design such constructs so that they could make choices in accordance with their distinct commitment to learning Japanese. After the writing design, students worked on their drafts. I told my students that they could use outside resources, such as an online dictionary. I told them if they use grammar and vocabulary that they have not learned, put them in a footnote with English translation, as I did in my reading texts. My intention here was not to restrict my students' meaning-making resource to our course textbook – which is admittedly attributed to the static view of writing – but encourage them to go beyond the facilitated learning resource. They had two weeks to complete the three drafts, and they had my feedback, my assessment and two peer response activities in the process.

Research approach

I view my research methodology as an ethnographic case study, particularly informed by a post-structural perspective. I chose this research methodology to understand my students' writing and situated negotiation in the classroom.

Post-structuralism-informed Ethnography

A post-structural ethnography is attributed to the call for moving beyond the imperative of finding 'the real story' (Britzman, 1995). In line with this epistemological alert, Rudolph (2018) conceptualizes post-structural ethnographic inquiry as 'a subjective, sociohistorically situated exploration and *deconstruction* (Derrida, 1976) of the discourses implicated in the "invention," perpetuation and maintenance of essentialized borders of place, identity and knowledge, as well as of individuals' dynamic negotiation of identity and agency – of discursive positioning and being positioned' (2018: 156). With such an understanding of post-structural ethnographic inquiry, an important reminder for the current study is an emphasis that issues of power are never absent (e.g. Edgeworth, 2011). Norton and McKinney (2011: 81–82) ask, 'what kind of research enables scholars to investigate the relationship between language learners as social beings and the frequently inequitable worlds in which learning takes place?' Considering the nature of identity as multiple, a site of struggle and changing over time, they argue that research should be qualitative and critical (Norton & McKinney, 2011). Norton (2013) also highlights the necessity for researchers to understand 'all research studies are understood to be "situated", and the researcher integral to the progress of a research project' (2013: 13).

The above post-structuralist understanding of ethnography is informative for my study because, in this study, I am a teacher who has an institutional power and the only native speaker of Japanese in a Japanese class. My position as a teacher and native speaker partly constitutes my students' meaning-making, and thus, data and interpretation are largely informed by such a relationship with student participants.

Data collection and analysis

The data collection includes texts that students produced in the project (i.e. writing design sheets, three drafts of personal narrative, two peer feedback sheets and two reflective notes about their individual text production). Additional qualitative data were collected through interviews. I conducted a one-hour semi-structured interview with my participant, Lapis. I loosely structured this interview in accordance with the following two aims: (1) to understand Lapis' writing design, linguistic choice and investment and (2) to understand her interaction and negotiation in the independent construction phase. I conducted the interviews in my office at the college in the Spring of 2017. The post-structuralist epistemology in regard to space in part informs the way I interpreted data obtained from interviews (For more on spatiality and unequal power relations, see Tsolidis, 2008.)

Ethnographic accounts of institutional practice and setting, and the text interpretation and production of the student in such an environment are brought together with *critical discourse analysis* (CDA). I followed Fairclough's three stages of CDA (1989, 2003): description of text, interpretation of text and interaction, and explanation of interaction and social context.

Findings

Lapis and her personal narrative text: 'Language and identity'

Lapis identifies herself as 'half' Costa Rican, and in her personal narrative, entitled *Language and Identity*, she narrates her bilingual identity construction. Lapis selected peers/classmates for her audience and designed her goal of writing narrative as 'to talk about how language affects my identity especially learning Spanish vs. learning Japanese.' Her theme was 'the relationship between language and identity in my life.' The connection with learning Japanese was 'Learning Spanish led to me learning Japanese.' Her final draft is given in Figure 11.1.

Figure 11.1 Lapis' personal narrative text

Stage 1: Unaware Childhood

1) 子どもの時、スペイン語をしりませんでした。私はコスタリカ人ですが父と母は私にスペイン語をおしえませんでした。とうしょ私はかまいませんでした。私のきょうだいもスペイン語はなしませんでした。小学校でスペイン語がいりませんでした。えい語は十分でした。

When (I was) a child, (I) did not know Spanish. I am Costa Rican but (my) father and mother did not teach me Spanish. That time I did not care about it. My brother did not speak Spanish either. The elementary school did not require Spanish. English was enough.

Stage 2: Realization with Cousin

2) でも、十一さいの時、私のいとこは私のうちにすんでいました。私といとこはおなじでした。私たちはアメリカでうまれて、コスタリカ人ですから。でも、いとこはスペイン語をはなしましたが私ははなしませんでした。ある日、いとこはリサさんはスペイン語をはなすことができないと言っていました。私はスペイン語がへただとしっていましたがわるくかんじました。しんのコスタリカ人をかんじませんでした。

But, when (I was) eleven, my cousin was living in my house. I and my cousin were the same. Because we were born in the US, and (we are) Costa Rican. But, (my) cousin spoke Spanish, but I did not speak (Spanish). One day, (my) cousin said Lapis was not able to speak Spanish. I knew (I was) poor at Spanish, but (I) felt bad. (I) did not feel true Costa Rican.

Stage 3: Beginning to Study

3) 私は中学校と高校でスペイン語をはなすことをきめました。子どもの時スペイン語を聞きましたから、スペイン語をまなぶことはやさしかったです。私はらんたでした。私はスペイン語のクラスはたんにクラスだと思いました。私はまじめじゃなかったです。

I decided to speak Spanish at middle school and high school. Because (I) heard Spanish when child, learning Spanish was easy. (Not sure what this sentence means). I thought Spanish class is just a class. I was not serious.

(*continued*)

Figure 11.1 (*Continued*)

Stage 4: Death of Uncle

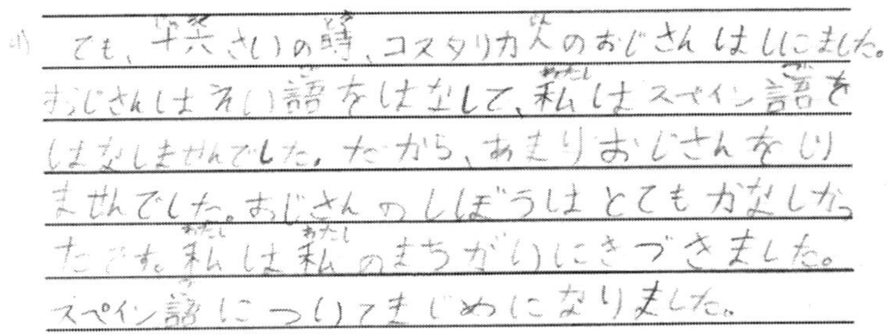
4) でも、十六さいの時、コスタリカ人のおじさんはしにました。おじさんはえい語をはなして、私はスペイン語をはなしませんでした。だから、あまりおじさんをしりませんでした。おじさんのしぼうはとてもかなしかったです。私は私のまちがいにきづきました。スペイン語についてまじめになりました。

But, when (I was) sixteen, Costa Rican uncle passed away. (My) uncle did not speak English[2] and I did not speak Spanish. So, (I) did not know (my) uncle well. The uncle's death was very sad. I realized my misunderstanding. I became serious about Spanish.

Stage 5: Reflections + Lessons

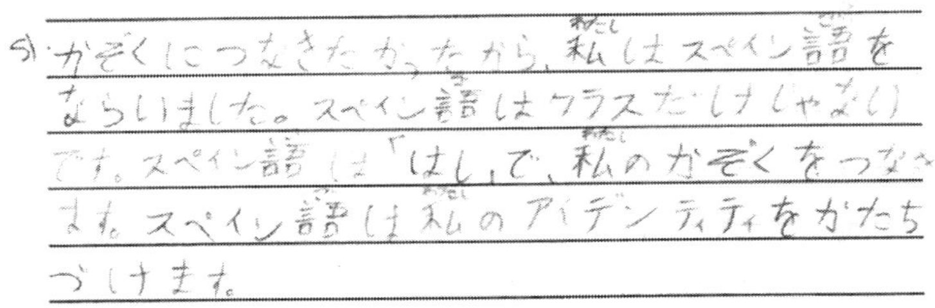
5) かぞくにつなぎたかったから、私はスペイン語をならいました。スペイン語はクラスだけじゃないです。スペイン語は「はし」で、私のかぞくをつなぎます。スペイン語は私のアイデンティティをかたちづけます。

Because (I) wanted to connect with (my) family, I learned Spanish. Spanish is not only a class. Spanish is a 'bridge' and connects my family. Spanish shapes my identity.

Stage 6: Looking to Future

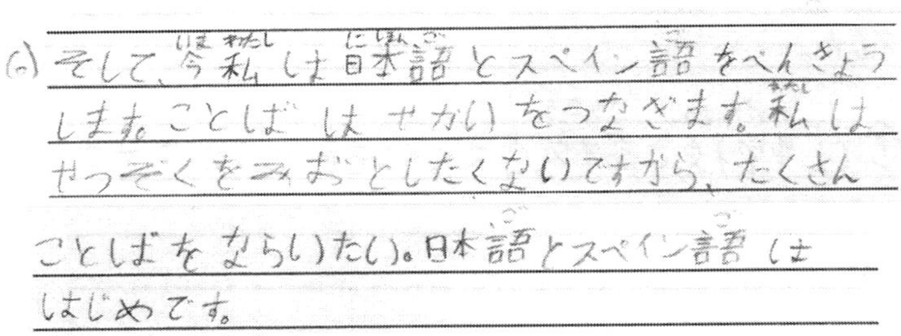
6) そして、今私は日本語とスペイン語をべんきょうします。ことばはせかいをつなぎます。私はせつぞくをみおとしたくないですから、たくさんことばをならいたい。日本語とスペイン語ははじめです。

And, now I study Japanese and Spanish, language connects the world. Because I do not want to miss connection, I want to learn many languages. Japanese and Spanish are the beginning.

Lapis' meaning-making

What I found interesting is Lapis' negotiation with the facilitated writing project. This study found that, although Lapis mostly used learned grammar and vocabulary in her final draft (Figure 11.1), she originally had more non-textbook grammar and vocabulary in her earlier drafts. It is notable that Lapis re-framed her linguistic choice to the learned ones in the process of finalizing her text. For example, in her final draft, she wrote, 'I knew (I **was**) **poor at** Spanish, but (I) felt bad.' However, originally in her first draft, this sentence was 'I knew (I was) **pathetic**, but (I) felt bad.' 'Poor at' is introduced as an important key grammar structure in the semester, whereas 'pathetic' is not introduced in our textbook. The following is a detailed illustration of our interactions that took place around the sentence in question.

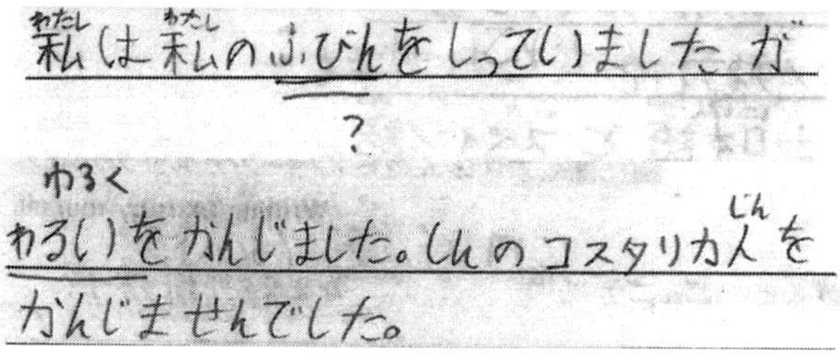
私は私のふびんをしっていましたが
?
わるく
わるいをかんじました。しんのコスタリカ人を
かんじませんでした。

Example 1. First draft: 'I knew (I was) **pathetic**, but (I) felt bad.'

Initially, I did not understand exactly what Lapis meant by 'pathetic,' so I put a question mark in red under 'pathetic' and returned the text to Lapis. The following is what she submitted as her second draft.

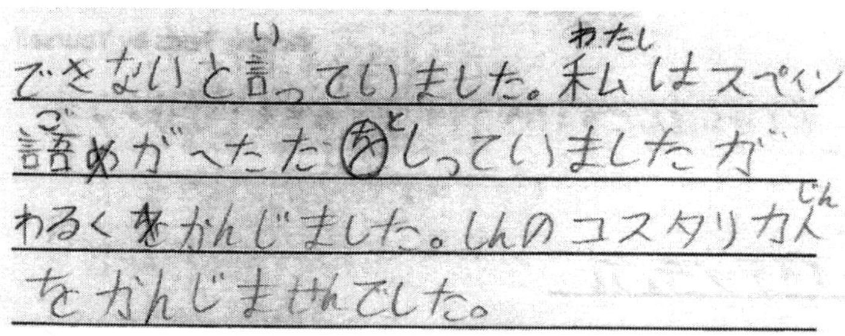
できないと言っていました。私はスペイン
語めがへたたをしっていましたが
わるくをかんじました。しんのコスタリカ人
をかんじませんでした。

Example 2. Second draft: 'I knew (I **was**) **poor at** Spanish, but (I) felt bad.'

The above example shows that Lapis re-framed 'pathetic' to 'poor at.' As I still found some mistakes in her use of 'poor at' in this second draft, I corrected them and returned the corrected text to Lapis. She made a revision and submitted the corrected text as her final draft.

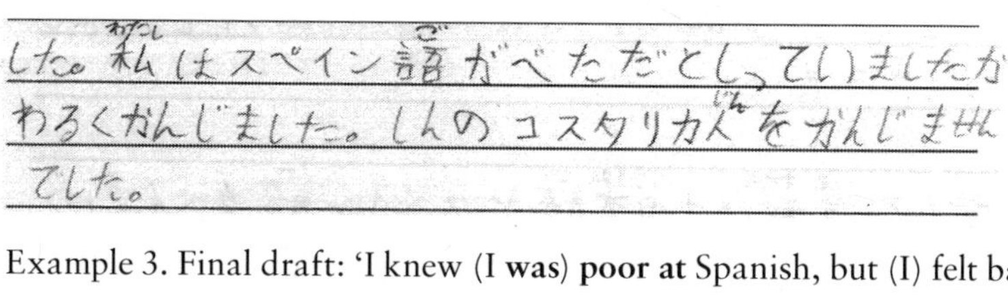
した。私はスペイン語がへただとしっていましたが
わるくかんじました。しんのコスタリカ人をかんじません
でした。

Example 3. Final draft: 'I knew (I **was**) **poor at** Spanish, but (I) felt bad.'

Of significance through this re-framing practice is a change in 'interpersonal' meaning. As can be seen through the examples above, there is a shift from explicit affective emotion ('pathetic') to the implicit judgment of her linguistic ability ('poor at Spanish'). To put it succinctly, her attitude was reformulated from inscribed negative happiness to invoked negative capacity (see Martin & White, 2005 for detail).

Another example is provided below to show a similar shift in such interpersonal meaning. Her first draft had this sentence: 'I **needed to become serious** on Spanish.'

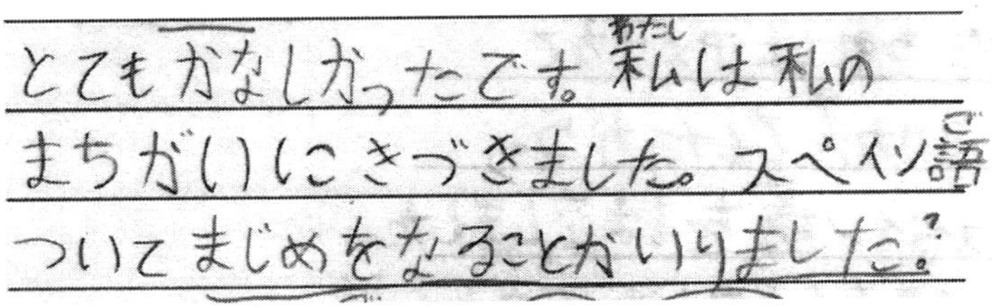
とてもかなしかったです。私は私のまちがいにきづきました。スペイン語ついてまじめをなることがいりました。

Example 4. First draft: 'I **needed to become serious** on Spanish.'

It seemed that Lapis did literal translation for each word, 'needed to,' 'become' and 'serious' from English to Japanese and combined them together to make the sentence. All of those words are non-textbook words and Lapis made several errors when combining them together. Because I did not understand what she meant in this sentence, I put a question mark on 'needed to become serious,' and returned the text to Lapis. The following is her revised second draft.

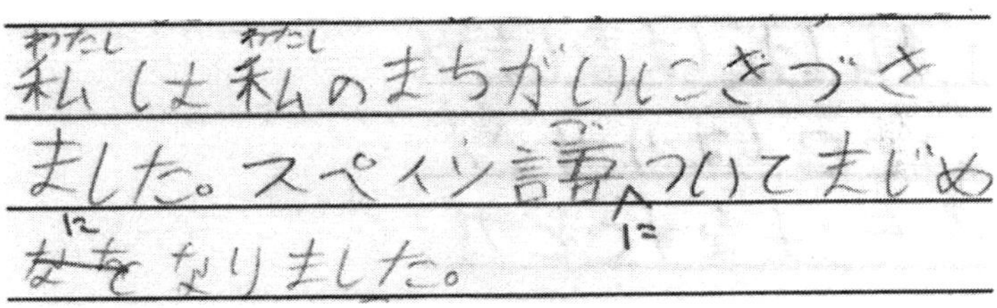
私は私のまちがいにきづきました。スペイン語ついてまじめなをなりました。

Example 5. Second draft: 'I **became serious** on Spanish.'

The above example shows that Lapis changed 'needed to become serious' to 'became serious.' Although 'became' and 'serious' are still something that was not covered in the semester, this re-framing practice showcases that Lapis took out modality ('needed to') and simplified to non-modal verb ('became'). Modality was curtailed through this revision process. As I saw this version still had some mistakes, I corrected them and returned the text to her. She made a revision and submitted the correct text as her final draft:

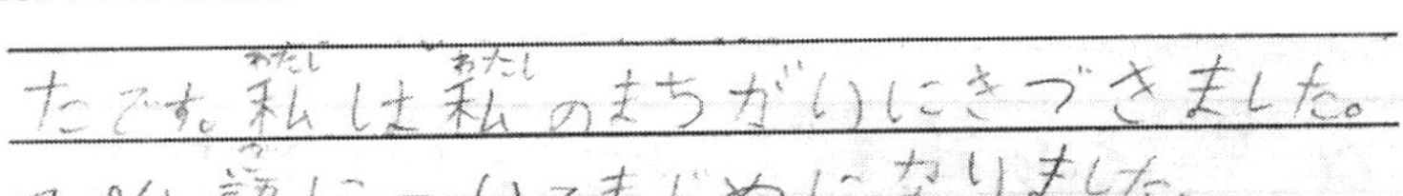
たです。私は私のまちがいにきづきました。スペイン語についてまじめになりました。

Example 6. Final draft: 'I **became serious** on Spanish.'

Overall, this textual analysis informs that Lapis' re-framing practice changed some of her interpersonal meanings. Importantly, the shifts did not occur spontaneously but rather intentionally. The following is her reflection note after her first draft

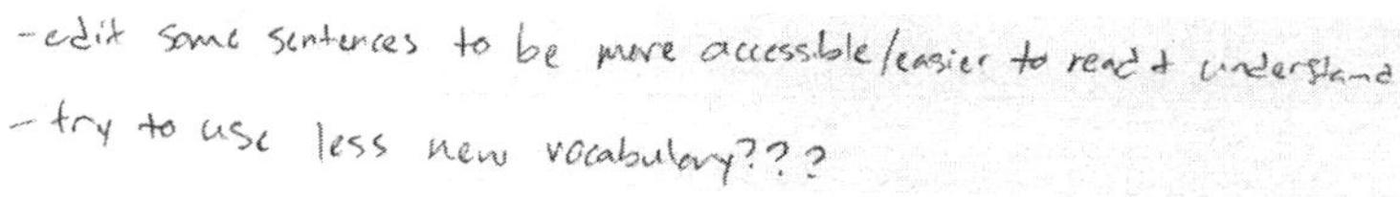
- edit some sentences to be more accessible/easier to read + understand
- try to use less new vocabulary???

Example 7. Lapis' reflection note: 'edit some sentences to be more accessible/easier to read + understand' 'try to use less new vocabulary???'

This reflection note shows that Lapis was aware that she needed to edit some sentences to be more accessible. Although this awareness might not have directly influenced her revision of interpersonal meanings (e.g. 'poor at' and 'became'), it is important to highlight that such revision practice ended up simplifying interpersonal meanings in Lapis' text.

Of relevance to the above finding may be Lapis' maneuvering in meaning-making. As illustrated earlier, Lapis often restricts her linguistic choice to the learned grammar structures in her final draft. Despite such a constraint, however, Lapis' interpersonal meaning seems to resonate throughout the text, particularly through the juxtaposition of herself with other characters (e.g. cousin and uncle). Table 11.1 shows my analysis for such interpersonal meanings construed in Lapis' final draft. For the purpose of illustration, the table has only selected items.

For example, the Table 11.1 showcases that the implicit judgment of Lapis is construed in sentence #10. Lapis implicitly positions herself as

Table 11.1 Text analysis for interpersonal meanings (selected items)

sentc#	Items	appraiser	affect	judgment	appreciation	appraised
10	*Spoke*	(Lapis)		implicit, +capacity		*cousin*
10	*did not speak*	(Lapis)		implicit, neg +capacity		*I* (Lapis)
11	*cannot speak*	cousin		implicit, neg +capacity		*I* (Lapis)
12	*poor at*	'cousin		implicit, -capacity		*I* (Lapis)
12	*felt bad*	(Lapis)	-happiness			*cousin*
20	*did not speak*	(Lapis)		implicit, neg +capacity		*uncle*
20	*did not speak*	(Lapis)		implicit, neg +capacity		*I* (Lapis)

incapable of speaking Spanish, in direct contrast to her cousin, who is capable of speaking Spanish:

But, (my) cousin spoke Spanish,	(implicit positive capability)
but I did not speak (Spanish).	(implicit negative capability)

Example 8. Sentence #10: 'But, (my) cousin spoke Spanish, but I did not speak (Spanish).'

In the subsequent sentence (#11), Lapis' incapability is explicitly evaluated by her cousin. Lapis uses a verb ('said') and projects what her cousin said: 'Lapis is not able to speak Spanish'. This triggers Lapis' negative feelings (explicit negative happiness) in sentence #12:

(my) cousin said Lapis was not able to speak Spanish	(modalization: ability)
I knew I am poor at Spanish, but	(implicit negative capability)
I felt bad.	(explicit negative happiness)

Example 9. Sentence #11&12: '(my) cousin said Lapis was not able to speak Spanish. I knew (I was) poor at Spanish, but (I) felt bad.'

In sentence #20, Lapis again positions herself as incapable. This time, she juxtaposes herself with her uncle, who does not speak English:

(My) uncle did not speak English, and	(implicit negative capability)
I did not speak Spanish.	(implicit negative capability)

Example 10. Sentence #20: '(My) uncle did not speak English, and I did not speak Spanish.'

Taking into account Lapis' revision practice that I illustrated earlier (i.e. simplification), it is possible to interpret that Lapis' juxtaposition with other characters is an instance of her maneuvering in making meaning. That is, Lapis restricted her linguistic choice into an accessible one, and within such a constraint, she made an effort to leave readers with a sense of complex interpersonal meaning that is essential to her story.

Interview with Lapis

The textual analysis above informed three findings: (1) Lapis' re-framing practice from the non-textbook grammar and vocabulary into the ones the class formally covered; (2) her simplification of interpersonal meanings; and (3) her construction of implicit judgment through the textbook grammar. In this section, I will further those findings in reference to an interview with her.

Lapis' re-framing practice

As I illustrated in my textual analysis, Lapis often had grammar and vocabulary that the course did not cover in her earlier drafts, but she ultimately re-framed such meaning-making to the textbook grammar. This shift is, in fact, indicated by her reflection note after her first draft (i.e. 'edit some sentences to be more accessible/easier to read + understand; try to use less new vocabulary???'). During an interview with Lapis, I asked about this shift. A copy of this reflection note was in front of us on a desk.

Shinji: That's your note, like, reflection note. This is what, I think, you produced after first draft, after you receive my feedback and somebody's feedback and then you wrote: 'edit some sentences to be more accessible easier to read + understand. Try to use less new vocabulary' Do you remember what, um, because, let me see. In your first draft, you had more vocabularies and grammars that we have not learned in class, but in final draft, I noticed you kind of reduced such vocabularies and grammars, and in your reflection note, you know, I saw that notes. So, I was wondering if, like um, do you, um, can you share your thought on this?

Lapis: Yeah. Um, so, I remember when I was writing it in the first time, the way I tend to write, um, is like, I think of how I wanna express myself in English, and then I try to translate that to Japanese when I write it. Um, especially, when, like, at that point of time, I wasn't as comfortable with the language as I am now. Um, and so I would think, because, in English, I think of like, kind of more complex sentences than I could make in Japanese at the time, I was like looking at a lot of different grammar to try to, I think it's really important to, like, express exactly. Like, the way you write it is important. Um, and so, I was trying to keep it as close to what I was thinking in English at that time. Um, but then, when we exchanged with Jean[3] and Jean read it the whole time just close reading it, she was like, 'What is this?' 'What does this mean?' 'What is this word?' 'What does that mean?' and like, I'm, it took her long time to even get through it, because I had to, like, keep explaining what I was trying to say to her. Um, and then, these were her suggestions, I think. I was trying to make it more scaled back and make it more accessible, um, and easier to understand. Um, and I agree cuz I was like, one, we haven't been taught these grammar structures and vocabulary and I'm not even one hundred percent sure that I'm using them correctly. Um, because I just sort of found them on my own. And, two, its, I feel like, even though I want to write that way, it's ultimately better for me to understand what I am writing than trying to have it match what I want to say. Um, because for a lot of it, because I wasn't sure if I understood the grammar, I didn't know if what I was saying actually made sense or the words that I was using were actually the words that I could use or should use in the right context. Um, so I scaled it back because that way I was able to understand it myself better, um and it was more in line with my level of Japanese at the time. And um, it was easier for, um, if other people at my level to read it, like other people in class or people taking Japanese in the future, if they had to read it, it would be easier for them to understand.

This excerpt accounts for her shift from the non-textbook grammar to the textbook grammar. At the early stage of writing, Lapis composed her first draft the way she wanted to express herself in English and translated that into Japanese. It was important for Lapis to 'express exactly,' and she was making an effort to keep her writing as close to what she wrote in English as possible. However, through the interactions with her classmate during a peer response activity, Lapis gained an enhanced sense of readership and realized that using grammar and vocabulary that the class did not cover was not an effective way to communicate with readers, especially if they were at the same proficiency level.

Lapis' simplification of interpersonal meanings

The aforementioned shift from the non-textbook to the accessible grammar impacted interpersonal meanings. As I illustrated earlier, an interpersonal meaning was reformulated from explicit affective emotion ('pathetic') to implicit judgment of her linguistic behavior ('poor at'). The following excerpt was her response when I asked about her process of constructing the meaning of 'pathetic' in her first draft.

Lapis: I was trying to say that made me feel, I suppose, probably not pathetic is the right word, but I felt really bad, because, um, it made me feel like less than, um, and made me feel like, because he[4] could speak Spanish he was more Costa Rican than I was. Um, even though we both have the same, like, half Costa Rican heritage. I thought like, I wasn't able to make a claim to that identity because he could speak Spanish, and I couldn't. And he could communicate with our Costa Rican family and I could not.

Shinji: And then, you know, I, so, I put a question mark, you know, under ふびん ('pathetic') and then later, this is your second draft and then the same part says 私はスペイン語をのがへただをしていましたがわるくかんじました。 ('I knew (I was) poor at Spanish, but (I) felt bad.') So in the second draft, you wrote, 'I'm not good at' or 'I'm not good at Spanish, I knew I'm not good at Spanish but I felt bad'. So you changed.

Lapis: Yeah.

Shinji: Is this because of my question? Is this because I put a question mark here?

Lapis: Its, yes, because I saw that and I could tell that whatever I was trying to say, you didn't understand. And it was one of those words where I didn't fully understand it and how to use it. Um, so I took it out as part of my like, simplifying my language, um, and making it writing in a way that I can understand so that other people can understand what I am writing.

Shinji: Okay, that makes sense.

Lapis: Because that, like, that's all, the スペイン語がへた ('poor at Spanish') is all Genki stuff[5] that we had learned.

Shinji: I see.

This excerpt is notable for Lapis' struggle in meaning-making. Due to her enhanced awareness of readership (e.g. a native instructor), Lapis gave up representing her complex feelings about the language ideology she experienced (i.e. fluent speakers have more access to the community). In other words, Lapis' enhanced awareness of readership constrained her not to express her affective emotion, but to simply compare her linguistic behaviors with others.

The same thing can be said of her reformulation from 'I needed to become serious on Spanish' to 'I became serious on Spanish.' The following is our interaction around this topic. A copy of her first draft, second draft and final draft was in front of her.

Shinji: There is similar question, also, um, this is your first draft and then スペイン語ついてまじめをなることかいりました。 I put a question mark, but I think you are saying 'I needed to become serious on Spanish.'
Lapis: Yes.
Shinji: Because you are talking about your uncle's death.
Lapis Hmm-hmm.
Shinji: And that make you super sad.
Lapis Hmm-hmm.
Shinji: And you noticed your own 'mistake'? まちがい.
Lapis: Yeah. I think, I'm pretty sure I'm trying to talk about how, like, um, I had been taking Spanish but I wasn't being super serious about it. I was taking it at that time just because you know, that's the language you take. All my siblings took it, it's my turn to take it, and in class, because it was easy, I wasn't trying very hard. And then, when my uncle died, that kind of is what made me realize that, if don't become serious about Spanish, and if I don't try to, um, learn it and become fluent in it, then I'm going to be losing members of my family that I won't have had a chance to connect to because I can't talk to them cuz they don't speak English.
Shinji: Okay. Yeah, so you know, I again, I highlighted and I put a question mark here and then this is your second draft. スペイン語についてまじめになりました。 ('I became serious on Spanish') You changed to 'I became serious on Spanish'
Lapis: Hmm-hmm.
Shinji: And this is your final draft. It's really similar to the second draft. スペイン語についてまじめになりました ('I became serious on Spanish') Grammatical text production. Um, so do you think this is also the case that you changed to, um, more accessible grammar and vocabulary?
Lapis: Yeah. A simplification. Cuz in that, I was trying to be like, 'I realize that I needed to become serious', um, but in this, I'm just like, 'I became serious' at this point. Cuz both kind of like, this, the first one sort of has more connotations to it about like my feelings, but ultimately the meaning is the same, and because this one is easier to read and understand. Um, cuz I also used, I'm pretty sure I looked up grammar for this one too. Um, I took it out.

Shinji: You took it out.
Lapis: Yeah.

Similar to the first example of reformulating 'pathetic' to 'poor at,' Lapis' account of 'needed to become serious' to 'became serious' shows that the representation of her identity struggle was not accessible to her. Lapis had to give up representing the ideological force she experienced (i.e. she was obliged to become serious in Spanish. otherwise, she would lose access to her community). Lapis was constrained to take out modality ('needed to'), although it 'has more connotations.' She was only enabled to represent it as the fact ('became'). Thus, successful interpretation of the said ideological force may depend on the reader.

Lapis' Construction of Implicit Judgment Through the Textbook Grammar

As illustrated in my textual analysis, Lapis juxtaposed characters (i.e. Lapis, cousin and uncle) and construed the implicit meaning of incapability: who can speak Spanish and who cannot. The interview with Lapis informed her agentive negotiations with the available meaning-making resource. Lapis chose to compare characters because her feelings of inferiority came out by comparing herself with her cousin, and it is natural to write so in her narrative text. However, at the same time, it is true that this comparison was the only way for Lapis to communicate her feelings in Japanese. She was concerned whether those comparison sentences, which just state the facts, would accurately express the way she felt (Interview with Lapis).

Discussion and Implications

Textual analysis and interview with her signal that Lapis negotiated with the two conflicting discourses. More specifically, Lapis negotiated between the meaning-making from outside resources (i.e. the discourse that I intended to create in our classroom through my pedagogical approach) and the meaning-making from the course textbook (i.e. the one Lapis ultimately decided to participate through her enhanced awareness of readership).

On the one hand, Lapis' simplification could be interpreted as a functional approach to achieving the designed goal of her narrative. As illustrated earlier, Lapis selected her classmates as the reader and designed her goal as 'to talk about how language affects my identity especially learning Spanish vs. learning Japanese.' It is admittedly true that she made a conscious effort to communicate with her reader.

On the other hand, behind the aforementioned meaning-making lies Lapis' struggle in writing, identity and interaction. Lapis was holding complex feelings about her multilingual heritage, but most likely, it was not accessible in her elementary Japanese course. Lapis was not able to represent her complex feelings about the language ideology she experienced (fluent speakers have more access to the community) but she was only enabled to compare her linguistic behaviors with others. Similarly, she was not able to position herself as 'someone who needed to become serious on Spanish,' but she was only enabled to a position as 'someone who became serious on Spanish,' which may not display the ideological force and identity struggle she experienced at the time. Given this account, this study argues that certain identity options were not available in the course, and she accommodated herself by simplifying her interpersonal meaning. In other words, Lapis made an effort to achieve the designed goal of her personal narrative (i.e. 'to talk about how language affects my identity especially learning Spanish vs. learning Japanese'), but at the same time, she had to simplify her complex feelings about her identity, ironically, for the sake of achieving the said goal.

The above findings suggest that it is important for writing research to take into account language learners' agentive capacities to negotiate the constraints. World language learners' linguistic choices are not necessarily free choices, but rather, negotiated choices under certain constraints. This perspective is partly attributed to what Darvin and Norton (2015) illustrate. Darvin and Norton (2015) argue that learners may paradoxically contribute to their own subjugation through the performance of hegemonic practices. Individuals may perform counter to their own commitment under certain constraints, and such subjugation is often kept unsaid. Lapis' simplification of interpersonal meaning is most likely such an example.

Conclusion

This study explored writing in relation to meaning-making, identity and interaction in an elementary world language classroom. This study found that meaning-making in world language education could be a goal-oriented functional approach on the one hand, but it could be a site of struggle, on the other hand. This study suggests that it is important to understand that world language learners' linguistic choices are not necessarily to be seen as their free choices, but their negotiated choices under certain constraints. This study contends that such understanding can deconstruct the static, decontextualized view of writing (Mizutani, 1997). Further empirical studies that question the subordinated position of writing and delve into the complexity are surely necessary in world language education.

Notes

(1) I use the term, *world language* rather than *foreign language*, for an ideological assumption of 'who is insider' and 'who is outsider' inherent in the term *foreign language* (see Kubota & Austin, 2007).

(2) In the Japanese sentence, Lapis actually wrote '(My) uncle *spoke* English' but in an interview, I found what she actually meant was '(My) uncle *did not speak* English.'
(3) Jean was a peer response partner.
(4) 'He' refers to Lapis' cousin.
(5) 'Genki' is the course textbook we used in the semester.

References

Britzman, D.P. (1995) 'The question of belief': Writing poststructural ethnography. *International Journal of Qualitative Studies in Education* 8 (3), 229–238.

Byrnes, H. (2011) Beyond writing as language learning or content learning: Construing foreign language writing as meaning-making. In R.M. Manchon (ed.) *Learning to Write and Writing to Learn in an Additional Language*. Amsterdam: John Benjamins Publishing Company.

Canagarajah, S. (2016) Translingual writing and teacher development in composition. *College English* 78 (3), 265–273.

Clark, R. and Ivanič, R. (1997) *The Politics of Writing*. New York, NY: Routledge.

Colombi, C. (2009) A systemic functional approach to teaching Spanish for heritage speakers in the United States. *Linguistics and Education* 20 (1), 39–49.

Darvin, R. and Norton, B. (2015) Identity and a model of investment in applied linguistics. *Annual Review of Applied Linguistics* 35, 36–56.

Derrida, J. (1974) *Of Grammatology* (G.T. Spivak, Trans.). Baltimore: Johns Hopkins University Press.

Edgeworth, K. (2011) Unsettling truth: Post-structural ethnography as a tool to trouble schooling exclusions. In J. Symth and S. Ninetta (eds) *Methodologies for Researching Cultural Diversity in Education: International Perspectives* (pp. 26–41). London: Institute of Education Press.

Fairclough, N. (1989) *Language and Power*. London: Longman.

Fairclough, N. (2003) *Analysing Discourse: Textual Analysis for Social Research*. London: Routledge.

Halliday, M.A.K. and Hasan, R. (1989) *Language, Context, and Text: Aspects of Language in a Social-semiotic Perspective*. Oxford: Oxford University Press.

Haneda, M. (2005) Investing in foreign-language writing: A study of two multicultural learners. *Journal of Language, Identity, and Education* 4 (4), 269–290.

Hirose, W. (2015) *Sogokoui toshiteno yomikakiwo sasaeru jugyo dezain: Nihongogakushusha no sukokateinimiru shosatutekitaiwano igi [Writing as social interaction: The role of reflective dialogue in the learning of Japanese as a second language]*. Coco Publishing Co.

Ichishima, N. (2009) Nihongo kyoikuniokeru Jissen kenkyu ronbunno shitsuteki henka: Gakkaishi "Nihongo kyoiku" wo tegakarini *[The qualitative change of action research theses in Japanese Language teaching: Content analysis on the journals of Japanese Language teaching]*, *Nihongokyoikuronshu* 25, 3–17.

Janks, H. (2010) *Literacy and Power*. New York, NY: Routledge.

Kamler, B. (2001) *Relocating the Personal: A Critical Writing Pedagogy*. Albany, NY: State University of New York Press.

Kanno, Y. and Norton, B. (2003) Imagined communities and educational possibilities: Introduction. *Journal of Language, Identity, and Education* 2 (4), 241–249.

Liu, P. and Tannacito, D. (2013) Resistance by L2 writers: The role of racial and language ideology in imagined community and identity investment. *Journal of Second Language Writing* 22 (4), 355–373.

Martin, J.R. (2001) Cohesion and texture. In D. Schiffrin, D. Tannen and H.E. Hamilton (eds) *The Handbook of Discourse Analysis* (pp. 35–53). Oxford: Blackwell.

Martin, J.R. and White, P.R.R. (2005) *The Language of Evaluation: Appraisal in English*. Basingstoke: Palgrave MacMillan.

McKay, S. and Wong, S. (1996) Multiple discourses, multiple identities: Investment and agency in second-language learning among Chinese adolescent immigrant students. *Harvard Educational Review* 66 (3), 577–608.

Mizutani, N. (1997) Sakubun kyoiku *[Composition education]. Nihongo Kyoiku Journal of Japanese Language Teaching]* 94, 91–95.

Moje, B. and Luke, A. (2009) Literacy and identity: Examining the metaphors in history and contemporary research. *Reading Research Quarterly* 44 (4), 415–437.

Norton Peirce, B. (1995) Social identity, investment, and language learning. *TESOL Quarterly* 29 (1), 9–31.

Norton, B. (2013) *Identity and Language Learning: Extending the Conversation* (2nd edn). Bristol: Multilingual Matters.

Norton, B. and McKinney, C. (2011) An identity approach to second language acquisition. In D. Atkinson (ed.) *Alternative Approaches to Second Language Acquisition* (pp. 73–94). New York: Routledge.

Norton, B. and Toohey, K. (2011) Identity, language learning, and social change. *Language Teaching* 44 (4), 412–446.

Reichelt, M., Lefkowitz, N., Rinnert, C. and Schultz, J. (2012) Key issues in foreign language writing. *Foreign Language Annals* 45 (1), 22–41.

Rose, D. and Martin, J.R. (2012) *Learning to Write, Reading to Learn: Genre, Knowledge and Pedagogy in the Sydney School*. Sheffield: Equinox.

Rudolph, N. (2018) Education for glocal interaction beyond essentialization and idealization: Classroom explorations and negotiations. In A. F. Selvi and N. Rudolph (eds) *Conceptual Shifts and Contextualized Practices in Education for Glocal Interaction: Issues and Implications* (pp. 147–174). Singapore: Springer.

Ryshina-Pankova, M. and Byrnes, H. (2013) Writing as learning to know: Tracing knowledge construction in L2 German compositions. *Journal of Second Language Writing* 22 (2), 179–197.

Toramaru, M. (2014) Nihongokyoikujissenni okeru kyoshitsukanno rekishiteki hensentokadai: Jissennomanabi, sougokoi, kyoshono yakuwarini chumokushite *[Historical change and task regarding view of classroom: Learning, interaction, and teacher's role]*. Waseda Nihongo Kyoikugaku *[Waseda Japanese Language Education]* 17, 41–63.

Tsolidis, G. (2008) The (im)possibility of poststructuralist ethnography: Researching identities in borrowed spaces. *Ethnography and Education* 3 (3), 271–281.

12 Negotiating Complex Identities Through Positionings in Ongoing Interaction: A Case Study in a Foreign Language Teacher Education Program in Colombia

Adolfo Arrieta and Nayibe Rosado

Introduction

Identity has become a major research concern in English as a Second Language (ESL) and and English as a Foreign Language (EFL) contexts due to the role it plays in the teaching and learning of the English language (Norton, 2000; Ushioda, 2009; Varghese *et al.*, 2005). It has been researched from different perspectives: identity and ethnicity, identity and gender, identity and ideology, language learner identity, teacher professional identity, and identity and interaction. Most teacher identity studies (Alsup, 2006; Menard-Warwick, 2011; Norton, 2010) have been carried out mainly from a narrative analysis approach in which teachers reconstruct their identities retrospectively; however, few of them have explored it as it happens in interaction, how teachers' ongoing positioning in classroom discourse contributes to teachers and students' identity co-construction processes from the positionings they enact in ongoing interaction (Anderson, 2009; Montenegro, 2012; Yoon, 2008).

Researchers (Kim, 2012; Tseng, 2011) have stressed that teachers' professional identities contribute to students' investment and agency in learning the English language since the enactment of their positionings provide spaces to develop agency, investment and learning opportunities for their students. Such aspects are of paramount importance in foreign language settings as teachers and students construct their identities through the discourse they co-create in the classroom (Gómez-Lobaton, 2012; Rudolph, 2018).

Traditionally, EFL teachers' identities have been framed within an uncritical stance, which is evidenced in the adoption of replicative EFL didactics derived from hegemonic imperialist ideologies (Pennycook, 2010). Several pre-service and in-service teachers have been trained through pedagogical approaches that emphasize the consumerism of techniques without critical frameworks to help them to assess the pertinence of these techniques for their teaching contexts (González-Moncada, 2010; Guerrero, 2010). The lack of critical frameworks has brought about a technical conception of teaching which has undermined the development of their professional identities as well as the exploration and creation of local pedagogies relevant to the complexities inherent in the teaching and learning of the English language in their contexts (Rudolph *et al.*, 2018). In short, the identities of teachers have traditionally been shaped by external entities such as the Ministry of Education and other regional and local education authorities and instantiated in policies, the National curriculum, the syllabus and prescriptive methodologies. That is to say, teachers' identities have been assigned rather than claimed (Buzzeli & Johnston, 2002).

As documented in the literature, (Kayi-Aydar, 2015; Yoon, 2008), language teacher identities are deployed in their discourse when interacting in the classroom; in consequence, studying teachers' positionings during on-going interactions in the classroom may grant access to some aspects of their complex identity configurations that would otherwise go unnoticed. If we gained an understanding of how these identities are actually being instantiated, we would be better equipped to approach the education of teachers either in pre- or in-service programs.

In language teaching contexts, a growing number of researchers have used positioning as a theoretical framework to disclose the power relations dynamics that constrain or allow meaningful pedagogical processes (i.e. Kayi-Aydar, 2014, 2015). These researchers have unveiled some complex interaction patterns that take place when teachers and students enact power in class (Martin-Beltrán, 2010; Reeves, 2009). They have also explored the relationships between teachers' positionings, agency and classroom participation (Yoon, 2008) or the way native English speakers are positioned by non-native English teachers in terms of pedagogical competence and local cultural awareness. However, most of this research has been done in ESL contexts where the sociocultural aspects influence positioning and identity differently from EFL contexts. This chapter reports part of a larger study that aimed at understanding how a teacher educator and his students negotiated their identities through the positions they assumed in on-going interaction in an EFL class in Colombia.

Positioning, Position and Types of Positions

Positioning is the interplay of positionings and repositionings. Davies and Harré (1990) define positioning as 'a discursive process whereby people are located in conversations as observably and subjectively coherent participants to jointly produce story lines' (1990: 37) or thematic passages. In a classroom, the discursive processes are mainly constructed by the way teachers make use of their privileged authoritative positionings; such positionings may not afford instances of co-constructive collaborative learning spaces and storylines. This concept is key due to its implications for classroom learning and development: its understanding would allow teachers to promote different intersubjective positionings from the students and to open or close the negotiation of meaning and learning opportunities by consciously changing positions during classroom interaction.

Harré and Van Langenhove (1999) propose three elements as the conceptual foundations of positioning and represent their interrelation in what they called a positioning triangle: speech acts, position, storyline. Davies and Harré, (1990) assume an interactive definition of speech act as a joint communicative construction of meaning among individuals. They underline that the meanings of people's actions as social acts determine how people position in a storyline. Positions are 'those momentary clusters of rights and duties to think, act and speak in certain ways that are evident in the flux of everyday life' (Harré & Moghaddam, 2003: 8). They derive from the social practices, rights and duties that entitle individuals to speak and interact according to what they perceive is right to say and to do (Deppermann, 2015) in a storyline. A storyline, in turn, is the thematic passage that portraits positioning acts in a contextualized way.

Davis and Harré (1990) consider two perspectives on positioning: reflexive and interactive. Reflexive, self or first-order positioning occurs when individuals express their personal assumptions and beliefs and '... locate themselves and others within an essentially moral space by using several categories and storylines' (Harré & Van Langenhove, 1991: 393). For instance, some teachers might position themselves as organizers of communicative scenarios and others as linguistics experts, or as entertainers. Interactive or second-order positioning occurs when 'what one person says positions another' (Davis & Harré, 1990: 7) and takes place when someone questions a first-order positioning and, therefore, this positioning has to be negotiated. In interactive positioning, teachers can extend or hinder what their students can say and do as well as impede or favor the choice of speaking forms, actions and thoughts.

Positioning and identity

The relationship between positioning and identity is very close since people continuously construct their identities through the positions that they take up in discourse. Wenger (1998) highlights that identity changes constantly across time and space, and it is negotiated during the ongoing process of construction of the self, with its past and potential futures, incorporating them into the present identity. This notion of identity represents complexities and difficulties, especially in EFL contexts, where teachers and students mainly enact their identities in classroom interactions. In an English class, participants construct their identities through the way they position themselves and others; through their positionings and repositionings, they reshape their identities as current language learners and future teachers. Likewise, the reshaping of their identities also transcends the classroom boundaries affecting the way they negotiate their identities and membership in other social contexts. In other words, whenever human beings are crossing boundaries, there are identities negotiation processes of self and others.

In a similar line to Wenger's, Bucholtz and Hall (2005) state that 'Identity is best viewed as the emergent product rather than the pre-existing source of linguistics and other semiotic practices and therefore as fundamentally a social and cultural phenomenon' (2005: 588). In a class, identity emerges when teachers and students are interacting and making meaning. In connection with this Kayi-Aydar (2015) underlines that 'through the accumulation of positions, positional identities are formed and shaped…Positioning, therefore, closely interacts with who we are, thereby affecting how we behave and communicate' (2015: 688).

Agency

Ahearn (2001: 112) defines agency as 'individuals' sociocultural mediated capacity to act.' It can be both emancipatory and self-benefitting. It is emancipatory when individuals are able to problematize dominant ideological discourses while negotiating their positionings with others. It can also be self-benefiting when they don't problematize hegemonic discourses (Rudolph *et al.*, 2018). In this study, the term agency is considered from the emancipatory perspective; that is, the capacity to act to overcome challenging situations or problematize hegemonic discourses that hamper their ongoing negotiation of discourses and identities.

Context of the Study

The setting of this research was a public university in Colombia. The case study (Duff, 2008) was done with a group of future teachers in their second semester of their Foreign Language Teacher Education Program. The program's main aim is to educate teachers who are communicative and pedagogically competent and who can, in turn, teach their students how to communicate effectively in English and French.

Participants

The participants were an English teacher and his students. At the time of the study, the teacher was 28 years old and had been working for eight years at the secondary level and three years in a private university. He had a diploma in Teaching English as a Foreign Language (TEFL) and a higher intermediate level of English. There were 20 students aged 18 to 22, with an elementary English level; most of them came from low-income households. To keep students' anonymity, students were assigned names according to their level of interactional engagement: names starting with the letter 'E' were students who interacted more in class and those whose names began with 'R' were reactive interactants who only interacted when addressed directly.

An ethnographic case study was used to gain a deeper understanding of how the participants negotiated their positionings and identities in classroom interaction and allowed the exploration of the classroom culture and the values of the whole group. The case favored the bounding of the study at a determined time and space. A post-structural theoretical lens (Derrida, 1976) was considered in this ethnographic case study within which we conceived identity as a dynamic, discursive and contextual process where individuals can negotiate in interaction who they are and who they want to be. Participant's discourses were interpreted from their subjective perspectives located in a specific socio-historical context where individuals could negotiate their complex identities through their ongoing positionings and repositionings in class.

Data collection and analysis

Most of the data gathering process was carried out in the classroom setting. Four sources of data were included to gain deeper insights into the research issue: the teacher's narrative, 20 hours of classroom observation and resulting field notes, three semi-structured interviews with the teacher and two focus group interviews with students.

The classroom observations were video recorded, transcribed and later analyzed to identify the participants' positions, positionings and modes of positionings in moment-by-moment interaction. Using video allowed us to review the data several times and to share it with the participants. The semi-structured interviews helped us explore in-depth aspects concerning the teacher's assumptions in interactions, his pedagogy and his positioning of the students. Similarly, focus group interviews helped to explore how students positioned their teacher. They were done in Spanish to avoid communication limitations, and they are reported in this study in this language in order to highlight how translanguaging (García, 2009) is used to negotiate identities in class.

Data analysis

To analyze data, we used positioning analysis (Bartlett, 2014; Harré & Van Langenhove, 1991). We focused on how the teacher and students enacted their rights and duties through the speech acts and positionings in the storylines they co-constructed based on what they perceived, what they valued, and what they said and did.

The first step was to identify storylines in the data, followed by a careful examination of participants' positionings turn by turn. We analyzed communicative acts in each turn looking for how the right duties and obligations were enacted in the interactions. As we progressed, we created different categories related to the emerging positioning assumed by the participants, the way the participants interpreted their positionings and their social demeanors or behaviors. Afterwards, we analyzed the emergence of positional identities through the accumulation of positionings along and across storylines, as well as the participants' positioning alignments and misalignments in terms of ideological, social, pedagogical affiliations or disaffiliations.

Emerging Storylines

The emerging storylines portray the teacher and students' intersubjective and pedagogical positionings. The resulting misalignments and alignments in their emerging positional identities led to processes of identity co-construction during the semester.

I feel that I fall short teaching to the second-semester students

This storyline shows the pedagogical struggle the teacher was experiencing at the end of the third week of teaching. In this interview, the teacher expressed his feelings towards the group as well as how he thought the group perceived him.

> 'I feel that I fall short teaching to the second-semester students. I sometimes feel that I have used all the teaching strategies that I know, but at the same time, I know that this a dynamic process…With this group, I have to think a lot what I'm going to teach. Maybe, one of the reasons is that they are in the second semester, and they have learned many things… I think that they see me like one of them, a teenager, not like a teacher … I am almost sure of that …I think that they see me like a teenager….' (Storyline 1, Interview 1, February 22)

The use of the 'I' along the storyline shows his self-positioning about the group. He positioned himself as a struggling teacher who was trying to find new strategies to answer the groups' demands. Expressions like, '*I feel that I fall short teaching to the second-semester students, I have used all the teaching strategies, or I have to think a lot what I'm going to teach*' indexes his pedagogical concern and struggle to find a suitable pedagogy for the group. It also shows how the students' demands took him to question and reflect on his pedagogical practices. In addition, the perception he imagined the students had about him affected his self-reliance; he considered the students saw him like another student.

You have created a wall between us

This situation occurred at the beginning of the second week of March, the fourth week of class. The teacher was feeling anxious since most of the students had complained about his teaching methodology; he felt things were not working well, so he started the fourth week telling his students he wanted to have a meeting with them. The storyline shows what happened during the meeting:

T:	*Hoy quiero tener una reunión corta con ustedes acerca lo que está sucediendo en mis clases de inglés.*	T:	Today, I want to have a short meeting with you about what it is happening in my English classes.
Evelio:	*Nosotros también queríamos hablar con usted acerca su de actitud en clases y la metodología de enseñanza que está usando.*	Evelio:	We also wanted to talk to you about your attitude in class and the English teaching methodology you have been using.
Eva:	*Espero un momento, teacher, déjeme tomar nota de lo que se diga. (Eva se levanta de su silla y toma un marcador, divide el tablero con una línea y escribe estudiantes a la izquierda y profesor al derecho. Seguido le pregunta al profesor: ¿Qué le gusta y que le disgusta de nosotros?*	Eva:	Wait a moment, teacher, let me take notes on the board on what we are going to say. (Eva stands up and picks up a marker and goes to the board and draws a line in the middle of the board. Then she writes students on the left side of the board and teacher on the right side (se figure 6). (After, she asked the teacher) What do you like and dislike about us?
T:	*Yo considero que ustedes son buenos estudiantes. Tienen un buen nivel de inglés y sé que les gusta el inglés conversacional. Antes de darles clases a ustedes ya me habían dicho que ustedes eran un buen grupo y que la gran mayoría tenía un buen nivel de inglés. Me he dado cuenta de que llegan con puntualidad a las clases a*	T:	I think you are good students and you have a good English level. I know you like conversational English. The first week of class you told me you don't like the English textbook. I have tried to do different things in class. However, I was demanded to work with the textbook.

pesar de ser a las seis de la mañana. He notado que les gusta participar en clase, sobre todo en las actividades orales. Lo que no me gusta de ustedes es que hablan mucho en clase y no me dejan desarrollar la clase como es debido. Otra cosa que no me gusta es que no les gusta escuchar. Siento que algunas veces no me escuchan y tampoco escuchan a sus compañeros. En las primeras semanas de clase me comentaron que no les gustaba trabajar con el texto guía de inglés y yo he tratado de hacer las clases diferentes. Sin embargo, a mí también me exigen que tengo que trabajar con el libro.

Eva: *¿Eso es todo?*

Teacher: *Si se podría decir que es lo más importante.*

Eva: *Bueno. Ahora es nuestro turno. ¿Quién quiere comenzar? (0.5)*

Rina: *A nosotros nos parece que tiene una buena metodología. Hace muchas actividades interesantes y es muy puntual, siempre llega temprano al salón de clase. Nosotros consideramos que es un buen profesor.*

Erick: *Estoy de acuerdo con Rina. Usted es un buen profesor. Además, he notado que las sugerencias que le hacemos usted las tiene en cuenta.*

Evelio: *Lo que no nos gusta de usted es que parece que ha creado una barrera entre usted y nosotros. Nosotros lo sentimos distante y poco comunicativo.*

Eva: That's all?

T: Yes, I would say it is the most important.

Eva: Well. Now it's our turn. Who wants to start? (0.5)

Rina: We think you have a good methodology. You bring very interesting activities to the class. You are punctual; you are always on time for the class. We think you are a good teacher.

Erick: I agree with Emily. You are a good teacher. Moreover, I have noticed that you have taken into account the suggestions we have made you have

Evelio: What we don't like about you is that you have created a wall between us and you. We feel you scarcely communicate with us.

T: Perhaps, it maybe because there have not been many opportunities to share with you. Our class is at an early hour, then you have another class, and there is no opportunity to share more.

Ramon: Teacher, I would like to ask you to stop nicknaming our classmates. We think it is improper to give the nickname *Kuryko* to Rafael. He doesn't like it.

T: I just do it to play a joke. But I have never done it with the intention to offend him.

Ramon: Yes, but he doesn't feel comfortable with this nickname.

T: Ok. From today on I won't play joke on you.

Teacher:	*Bueno, eso es tal vez porque no ha habido la oportunidad de compartir más. La clase es a primera hora y después ustedes tienen otras clases y no hay ocasión de compartir más*		
Ramón:	*Profesor, también le quiero que pedir el favor de que deje de ponerle sobrenombres a los compañeros. No nos parece bien que a David lo llame con el sobre nombre de Kuryko. A él no le gusta.*		
Teacher:	*Yo lo hago por jugarme con él. En ningún momento lo he hecho para ofenderlo.*		
Ramón:	*Si, pero él no se siente bien.*		
Teacher:	*Bueno. Entonces desde hoy les prometo que no me juego más con ustedes.*		
Enio:	*Profesor no queremos decir eso. Pero es su decisión. No se vaya a los extremos, profesor (la siguiente fotografía muestra la foto de lo que Eva resumió en el tablero el día (Línea de tiempo 2, marzo 10)*	Enio:	Teacher, we did not mean that, but it's up to you. Don't go to extremes, teacher. The following photo shows the summary written by Eva about the meeting. (Storyline 2, March 10)

The teacher started the class announcing he wanted to have a meeting with the students, self-positioning as an individual who was experiencing problems with the students for several weeks. The use of the temporal deictic 'today' at the beginning (turn 1) signals that he wanted to change what was currently happening in his classes. In this first line, the teacher positioned as a concerned person and positioned the students as valid interlocutors to discuss what was happening. The expression 'I want to have a meeting with you' indexes this aspect. Likewise, Evelio used the pronoun 'we' and the verb 'wanted' in the past tense, suggesting the group's collective concern. In his turn, Evelio positioned the teacher as someone who had attitudinal and methodological problems with them (Turn 2). Evelio mentioned the problem directly; in contrast, the teacher used the interrogative pronoun 'what' as if he did not know exactly what was occurring.

In Turn 3, Eva stood up and asked the teacher respectfully to take notes about the meeting, and she started coordinating the meeting by assigning turns, and summarizing the main points of the meeting on the board. She divided the board into two parts one for the teacher and the other one for the students and wrote down on each side the plus and minus signs in parenthesis. Then, she proceeded to inquire with the teacher about what he liked and disliked about the group. The temporal deictic '*wait a minute, teacher*', suggests, the importance it had for her and the group to identify the teacher's perception of the problem. Here, Eva assumed a meeting coordinator positioning and showed agency and leadership among her classmates and the teacher. The way she registered the teacher and her classmates' concerns positioned her as a pedagogic agent and a conflict resolution mediator.

In Turn 4, the teacher evaluated the whole group positively in terms of their linguistic competence and their interest in using English communicatively. Here he was positioning the students not only as individuals empowered with the language but also as valid interlocutors with whom he had to be pedagogically accountable. However, he also underlined he had to be accountable with the coordinator of the program who required him to work with the textbook. Three events seemed to have placed the teacher in a pedagogical conundrum: first, the students' reluctance to work with the book; second, his coordinator demand to use the textbook as the course syllabus, and third, the teacher's pedagogical effort to find a solution for both parties. The use of the discourse marker 'however' indexes the contradictory aims that students and the coordinator wanted to accomplish and that the teacher wanted to reconcile.

In Turns 8 and 9, Rina and Erick evaluated the teacher's pedagogy in a positive way highlighting his good methodology and his punctuality. Both students positioned the teacher as a good teacher who had complied with the group's suggestions. The use of 'the suggestions *we have made you*' shows that the students have granted themselves a power positioning on how they wanted to be taught the English classes. However, Evelio was the only student who addressed the source of the problem directly at the beginning of the meeting, and in turn 10, he stated that the teacher's lack of communication and affective relationship have *created a wall between them*. In the next turn, the teacher justified his attitude by providing an impersonal excuse related to the class schedule and the academic activities in classes failing to acknowledge the intersubjectivity issue. The teacher's answer to Ramon's remarks asking him to stop nicknaming his classmate Rafael also indexed his evasion of the situation. Evelio and Ramon confronted the teacher's attitude in class and positioned him as an affectively disengaged teacher; the teacher assumed a defensive attitude towards their comments. Students showed awareness of what was originating the problem; the teacher did not.

So, what are you doing here?

The following storyline portraits a critical incident between Evelio and the teacher. Before one of the classes, Evelio was talking to some of his classmates outside the room, the teacher was passing by and overheard Evelio saying that he had not learned anything during that semester. When the teacher started the class, whose purpose was to review the present perfect continuous, he told the students they were going to play the game, 'Who wants to be a millionaire?' The teacher projected the questions on the board and assigned one student to identify the right answer; then, he asked the rest if the participant's answer was right or wrong.

96. … This is personal. How long have you been studying English?
97. Eliseo: I have been studying English for two years.
98. Evelio: For ten years
99. T: Ten years! What are you doing here?
100. Evelio: (Unintelligible)
101. Elvia: Since 9th grade
102. Eliseo: For me, he's studying English in the morning only English.
103. T: You said before you didn't see any progress studying here, so I don't know what you say?
104. Evelio: I mean, I have studied it …since …since I was in high school… at high school
105. T: So, what are you doing here?
106. Evelio: (laugh)
107. S: (laugh)
108. Enio: Trying to get the fucking *carton* (diploma)
109. Evelio: I have studied, studied (someone says something, and he looks and stops talking). Maybe I didn't understand the question.
110. T: Thank Mr. No, No, No. It's nice. It's perfect. It's cool. It's nice. Now the thing is that you've been studying for ten years, so why are you here?
111. Evelio: I don't have my {he looks at Nel} certificate.
112. Eliseo: You are here because you want to improve … you don't know all the things.
113. S: Exactly
114. Evelio: To learn something else
115. Enio: I for one… I studied the English only for one year at my English Institute. So, I have been in touch with English since 2011.
116. T: 2011?
117. Enio: Yes. All every day speaking English every day in the world of English
118. T: I like the way you speak English. Very Interesting.
119. Enio: That is the idea, to have your own style (Storyline 3, March 18).

In this storyline, the teacher confronted Evelio about the comment he had made before starting classes by asking the question '*this is personal, how long have you been learning English?* (Turn 96). 'This is personal' could indicate the personalization of the question for learners or index the teacher's discomfort with Evelio's comment and his intention to question him openly. He ignored Roy's answer and focused his attention on Evelio's answer, which he repeated in a sarcastic way, followed by an also sarcastic question (Turn 99) producing in Evelio a nervous smile and a timid answer (Turn 101). Roy tried to save Evelio's face complementing Evelio's short answer, but the teacher ignored Roy's answer once more. He went on questioning Evelio's presence at the University restating Evelio's comment ironically, with the question in Turn 102. Evelio tried to provide a more satisfactory answer; however, the teacher was not questioning his answer, but his derogatory attitude. He questioned his presence not only in class but in the University. This was signaled by the constant repetition of the question, '*What are you doing here?*' Evelio, unable to respond, just projected a nervous laugh. Enio noticed the teacher's nagging questioning to Evelio and disrespectfully replied, '*trying to get the fucking carton* (diploma).' However, the teacher overlooked his disrespectful answer and went on questioning Evelio. Evelio tried to stop the harassing questioning by answering the question he had misunderstood. The teacher evaluated Evelio's answer and attitude with expressions such as *perfect, cool, nice* indexing mordantly Evelio's presence at the University. Eliseo tried to soften the tense situation with a reasonable answer for both parties and Evelio backed up his answer (Turns 112–113). In this part of the storyline, Evelio self-positioned as a competent English language speaker and, in turn, positioned the teacher and the University as insufficient resources to meet his learning expectations. The teacher repeatedly questioned Evelio' presence at the University, positioning him sarcastically as a competent speaker of the language. In contrast, Enio positioned himself as a disrespectful student and Eliseo as a mediator of the tense situation. The contradictory evaluative positionings among Evelio, the teacher, and Enio brought up a tense situation for the whole class, positioning Eliseo as a mediator between the teacher and Evelio.

In Turn 115, Enio intervened to answer the teacher's question and the teacher replied with a question (Turn 116) highlighting Enio's English learning starting date in a sarcastic tone. Enio's continued expanding his answer, but the teacher evaluated Enio's way of speaking sarcastically and Enio retorted sarcastically as well '*That's the idea, to have your own style*' possibly suggesting the teacher had to develop his own teaching style.

In the teacher's interview after these two critical incidents, he expressed that he did not give importance to what the students told him in class. His reaction was originated by Evelio's lack of recognition of his pedagogical efforts to meet the group expectations as the teacher stated:

> 'I did not give any importance either in that moment or in any moment. I don't give importance to those incidents because they can become worse. Maybe, to Evelio because I thought I was giving my best and he, he had said he wasn't learning. It was as if I had not been doing anything. I

> always tell my students I put my professionalism and my disposition on their hands. I tell them I'm here and I know why I'm here, but if you don't engage with what I'm doing, I can't do anything....'(T Interview)

In this excerpt, the teacher assumed two positionings. In one, he overlooked most of the intersubjective incidents that occurred during the semester. This is evident in the emphasis made by the use of the indexical time expression 'in that moment or in any moment'. The only incident he considered important was the one related to Evelio since he felt the student was not recognizing his pedagogical efforts. In the other, he positioned as a professional who was open to students' suggestions. However, during the incident and during the meeting he positioned defensively towards the students. The speech act, *'but if you don't engage with what I'm doing, I can't do anything....'* suggests that the teacher thought his responsibility was setting up activities and engagement was the students' responsibility.

There was a lot of interaction between the teacher and us

In the last focus group interview with the students, many of them considered that the teacher was very creative and had developed a more communicative pedagogy with them after they had *the meeting*. They also acknowledge that the teacher transformed his pedagogy as Raquel explains:

Raquel: 'A mí me parece que el profesor se tomaba el tiempo en preparar la clase. En realizar las actividades no solamente que hiciéramos juegos, sino que le estudiante hiciera algo como que nosotros teníamos que trabajar, teníamos que hablar, que hacer y yo aplaudo eso...' (Línea de tiempo 4, grupo focal 2, junio 2)	Raquel: 'I think that the teacher devoted time to plan the classes; not only in the games, but also in other activities where we had to do and develop speaking through them. And I commend him in this respect. (Storyline 4, Focus Group 2, June 2)

Raquel positioned the teacher as a creator of games and other activities and as someone who gave them the opportunities to express their opinions. Raquel's positioning aligned with some students as well as with the teacher's self-assessment of his pedagogical transformation in this class.

He did not have a good relationship with us, the students

Most of the students highlighted that the teacher was not able to create an affective relationship with them. He scarcely interacted personally with them. In the following storyline, Rosa positioned the teacher as a distant and untactful person. If we compare Rosa's evaluation of the teacher with that of Evelio at the beginning of the course, we can notice how the teacher's affective positioning remained almost the same along the semester and how different students felt that this affected their learning process because it prevented them from participating more confidently and openly in class.

Rosa: 'en lo personal hubo muchos factores que afectaron el aprendizaje en esa clase primero porque él no tenía una buena relación con nosotros los estudiantes, y en mi caso personal yo estaba empezando mi proceso de embarazo, entonces, el no comprendía mi situación. Todos somos seres humanos y como seres humanos sabemos que esa etapa de embarazo no es muy fácil. Entonces esa parte humana le falto a él. Por eso tengo cierto rencor hacia él y le falte mucho a su clase...' (Línea de tiempo 5, grupo focal 2, junio 2)	Rosa: 'Personally, there were many factors that affected the learning process in that class. Firstly, he did not have good relationship with us, the students. In my case, I was in my first months of pregnancy and he did not understand my situation. We are human beings and we know that the pregnancy stage is not easy. He lacks human compassion that's why I dislike him, and I missed many of his classes...' (Storyline 5, Focus Group 2, June 2)

There was consensus among several students that there was not an affective relationship with the teacher; their only relationship was pedagogical. Evelio suggested that the teacher may have assumed this positioning because they were not fair with him when the course began; he felt they were not mature enough to behave more respectfully with the teacher at that time.

Positioning across storylines

The following figure shows how the participants' processes of self-positioning, positioning, and repositioning triggered multiple positional identities along the semester. Since the beginning of the semester, the students positioned themselves as competent language users of the language. They enacted their power demanding the teacher methodological changes. In other words, the students positioned themselves as an agent of their own learning process and subverted the teacher's pedagogical agenda making him reconsider the pedagogical identity he had created. The teacher self-positioned as a pedagogically struggling teacher who was failing to meet the students' learning needs. During the meeting, the teacher was only able to acknowledge his pedagogical problem and the effort he was making to create more meaningful communicative learning opportunities for his students. However, he was averse to recognizing how his disaffected and disrespectful positioning was eroding his emotional relationship with the class.

The teacher experienced different complex, positional identities. On the one hand, he initially assumed a positional identity derived more from an idealized and technical communicative methodology enacted by a lack of pedagogical critique. Then, he underwent a pedagogical identity crisis due to the students' dissatisfaction with his way of teaching. Finally, he experienced a pedagogical transformation in his teacher identity by infusing instances of negotiation of the students' identities in interaction. On the other hand, he was unable to manage his affective relationship with most of the students assuming a distant and confrontational positional identity along the semester. Although the teacher experienced and acknowledged a transformation of his pedagogical identity, he was unable to manage successfully his feelings and emotions with the group, an aspect that affected negatively not only his relationship with the students but also the students' engagement in class.

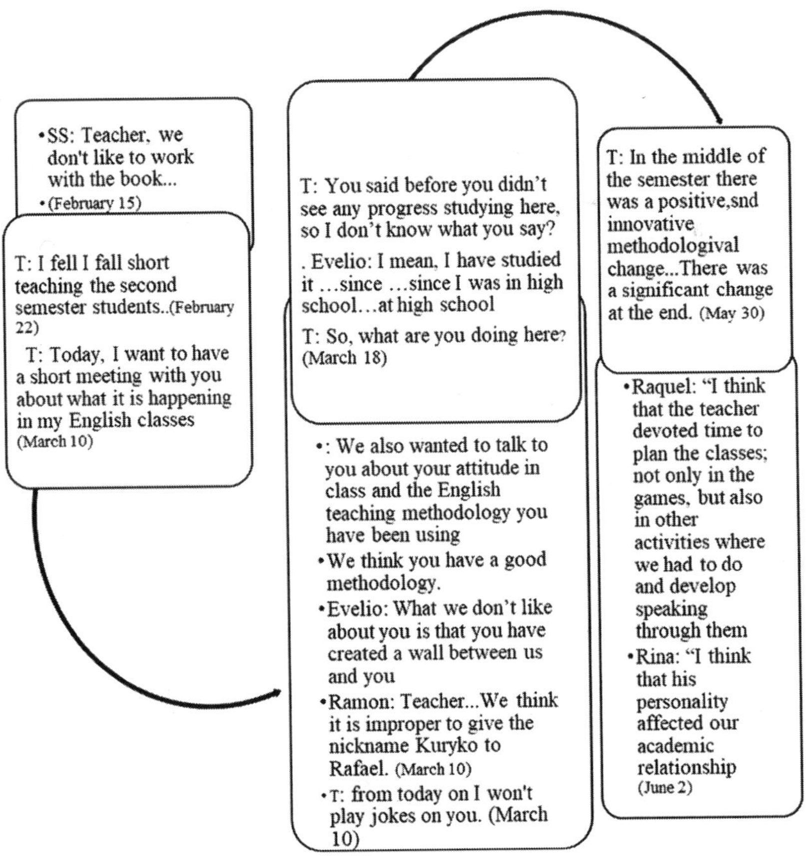

Since the beginning of the semester, the students were able to voice their personal dissatisfaction with the teacher's methodology. They problematized the teacher's lack of dexterity in managing his personal emotions with the group. In short, the students positioned themselves as agents of their learning process, demanding the teacher to fulfill their pedagogical learning agenda. The power that their previous teacher, the coordinator of the program and their current teacher granted to them allowed them to adopt defying positionings towards the program, the content and the teacher in some moments. The different complex positioning and repositioning processes that emerged in interaction along the semester opened spaces of reflexivity for both the teacher and the students creating pedagogical and personal alignments and misalignments for both parties.

Evelio recognized their co-responsibility in the creation of a tense and aloof relationship, by not recognizing the pedagogical efforts the teacher had made. In other words, he took a critical positioning towards their sometimes-improper behavior towards the teacher. In the end, the teacher recognized he had transformed his pedagogical identity as a result of the challenging positioning the students had assumed. That is, the way the students positioned him became learning opportunities for the teacher in terms of pedagogical identity transformation.

Discussion

In this case study, it was possible to see identity as a truly complex construction, configured by the positionings and repositionings of the teacher and his students. We highlight student's enactment of their linguistic and academic rights to ask the teacher to adjust his methodology as well as their positioning as agents of their learning process that entitled them to demand attitudinal and methodological changes. This is an interesting finding as these positional identities might be predictors of future teachers' identities in this context; student teachers who are empowered as English language learners with clear learning expectations might also be empowered teachers.

As shown in the storylines, these students positioned the teacher as someone who did not fulfill their pedagogical expectations. The teacher, in turn, considered that it was his duty to discuss with the students his pedagogical concerns in a meeting. The students took charge of the meeting development, subverting the traditional power relations. In connection with this, Bernstein (1996) states that 'power always acts to provoke ruptures and to produce markers in the social space' (1996: 37). The students' positionings challenged both the teacher's symbolic capital and the coordinator's hegemonic guidelines in relation to the prescribed syllabus and materials. We found that students' voices requesting the teacher to make personal and pedagogical changes opened power-sharing spaces for discourse construction and created productive tensions clashes where teacher and students' voices came together to create instances of third spaces, for instance, in storyline 2 (Bartlett, 2014; Rutherford, 1990).

As discussed earlier, the teacher made some methodological changes implementing what he considered meaningful communicative activities for the group. During the development of these activities, the teacher positioned the students as negotiators of meaning, opinion givers and presenters, allowing them to use their own semiotic resources and to engage in classes. However, the teacher kept a distant attitude and created scarce opportunities to align with the group affectively. In the end, students underlined this attitude affected their participation and learning processes in class. The way our teacher positioned contrasts with a similar case of a novice teacher reported by Reeves (2009): he positioned as a strict teacher, and simultaneously developed a rapport and positioned as a competent affective teacher. In Reeves's case, the teacher's pedagogical success was based on nurturing students' identities. He used their identities as mediational tools to engage them to use and learn the language, thus favoring the construction of narratives and the sharing of positioning in class. Reeves' work suggests that students' narratives and identities should be used intentionally as pedagogical tools to steer students' representations as language learners. Students' narratives and positionings can be used as semiotic tools to shape the students' identities as language learners and as future educators, but they also serve as learning opportunities for the development of teacher educators' identities.

The way participants used the textbook was interesting as well. The textbook was an administrative requirement of the coordinator of the program. The teacher just complied with the coordinators' demands. The students who had been working with the same series from the previous semester considered the book boring because the topics the book presented were irrelevant to their interests. There seems to be that the notion of becoming just consumers of functional bites of language was not relevant for the students; they wanted to use the English language to create meaningful and 'glocal' discourses. The coordinator and the teacher assumptions about using the textbook suggest an essentialized and idealized notion of textbooks as the main tool to model English and learn English in the classroom; however, the students did not want to be textbooks consumers, they wanted to be producers of more complex discourses in the classroom where they could voice their ideas.

The teacher perceived his pedagogical concern as a pedagogical identity crisis that made him reflect on his teaching beliefs and principles as well as on how meaningful his teaching practice was for the students. He mainly focused on what he taught and how he taught the class, narrowing his teaching approach to the deployment of teaching techniques without any emotional engagement with the students. He seemed to have assumed a more technical and essentialized world view of the English language teaching ideology (Rudolph, 2018) widespread in many language undergraduate programs in Colombia. Likewise, the students positioned themselves as individuals who were more interested in developing their oral skills, devoid of critical positionality about the discourses they enacted in class. In other words, the notions of concern and suitable for the participants was permeated by the hegemonic ideology of English language teaching that essentialized English as an interpersonal communication skill.

Teachers who do not align both affectively and pedagogically with students may hinder their agency to negotiate meaning in creating complex relationships in class (Yoon, 2008). Student teachers, in our study, contingently developed agency and empowerment in the midst of conflict in classroom interaction. We agree with Yoon (2008) in that 'teachers should pay more scrupulous attention to the students' acceptance and interactions by viewing them as complex, cultural, social beings, more than simply language learners' (2008: 516) and expand this to in-service teachers. They should also be viewed as complex cultural, social beings, more than simply language teachers. For instance, the teacher should transcend the boundaries of the classroom since there are life experiences that went beyond, namely, Rosa's pregnancy state and Evelio's previous English studies. These two examples suggest that teachers should always be crossing borderlines in time and space to co-construct more meaningful and humane learning experiences with their students. In spite of the lack of intersubjectivity and interactional awareness, the teacher in our study experienced a pedagogical identity change due to the evaluative positioning the students assumed in his classes; changes were also transferred to other courses he was teaching. All in all, this represented a learning opportunity for him too.

Conclusion

In this chapter, we have discussed how students' empowerment and agency as language learners have functioned as triggers of a teacher's identity transformation. We have also discussed the way the teacher and his learners' positioning in ongoing interaction, as well as the alignments and misalignments they experienced, helped to construct learning opportunities which configured their identities. An aspect to highlight is the need for teacher education programs to provide opportunities for student teachers to develop ideological and interactional awareness to enhance their pedagogical positioning. This awareness could favor teachers' intersubjectivity and their creation of engaging learning opportunities for learners. Another important aspect is the potential that positioning analysis has as a tool to unveil power relations that bring about identity transformation in an ongoing interaction.

To conclude, it is important for teachers to understand the classroom as a complex system, where what is not prescribed counts. They also need to understand that intersubjective relationships and interactional awareness are part of the complex, dynamic and non-linear processes that intersect and interplay in the development of learners' identity construction, especially if the learners are future teachers. We hope this research opens discussion spaces to reconsider how teacher educators and in-service teachers need to develop consciousness about how they mediate their communicative intentions and feelings in the classroom. Teacher educators and program administrators need to create dialogical spaces where students can negotiate power relations and position themselves as agents of their own ongoing identity construction processes.

References

Ahearn, L.M. (2001) Language and agency. *Annual Review of Anthropology* 30 (1), 109–137.

Alsup, J. (2006) *Teacher Identity Discourses: Negotiating Personal and Professional Spaces*. Mahwah, NJ: Lawrence Erlbaum.

Anderson, K. (2009) Applying positioning theory to the analysis of classroom interactions: Mediating micro-identities, macro-kinds, and ideologies of knowing. *Linguistics and Education* 20 (4), 291–310.

Bartlett, T. (2014) *Analyzing Power in Language: A Practical Guide*. London: Routledge.

Bernstein, B. (1996) *Pedagogy, Symbolic Control and Identity: Theory, Research, Critique*. London and New York: Taylor and Francis.

Bucholtz, M. and Hall, K. (2005) Identity and interaction: A socio-cultural linguistic approach. *Discourse Studies* 7 (4–5), 585–614.

Buzzeli, C. and Johnston, B. (2002) *The Moral Dimensions of Teaching: Language, Power, and Culture in Classroom Interaction*. New York: Routledge.

Davies, B. and Harré, R. (1990) Positioning the discursive production of selves. *Journal for the Theory of Social Behavior* 20 (1), 43–63.

Deppermann, A. (2015) Positioning. In A. De Fina and A. Georgakopoulou (eds) *The Handbook of Narrative Analysis* (pp. 369–387). Malden, MA: Wiley-Blackwell.

Derrida, J. (1976) *Of Grammatology* (G.C. Spivak, trans.). Baltimore: John Hopkins University Press (original work published 1967).

Duff, P. (2008) *Case Study in Applied Linguistics*. New York: Taylor and Francis.

García, O. (2009) *Bilingual Education in the 21st Century: A Global Perspective*. Malden, MA: Wiley-Blackwell.

Gómez-Lobaton, J.C. (2012) Language learners' identities in EFL settings: Resistance and power through discourse. *Colombian Applied Linguistics Journal* 14 (1), 60–76.

González-Moncada, A. (2010) English and English teaching in Colombia tensions and possibilities in the expanding circle. In A. Kirkpatrick (ed.) *The Routledge Handbook of World Englishes* (pp. 332–351). New York: Routledge.

Guerrero, C.H. (2010) The portrayal of EFL teachers in official discourse: The perpetuation of disdain. *Profile Issues in Teachers Professional Development* 12 (2), 33–49.

Harré, R. and Moghaddam, F.M. (2003) Introduction: The self and others in traditional psychology and in positioning theory. In R. Harré and F. M. Moghaddam (eds) *The Self and Others: Positioning Individuals and Groups in Personal, Political and Cultural Context* (pp. 1–11). Westport, CT: Greenwood Publishing Group.

Harré, R. and van Langenhove, L. (1991) Variety of positioning. *Journal for the Theory of Social Behavior* 21 (4), 393–407.

Harré, R. and van Langenhove, L. (1999) *Positioning Theory: Moral Contexts of Intentional Action*. Malden, MA: Blackwell.

Kayi-Aydar, H. (2014) Social positioning, participation, and second language learning: talkative students in an academic ESL classroom. *TESOL Quarterly* 48 (4), 686–714.

Kayi-Aydar, H. (2015) Teacher agency, positioning and English language learners: Voices of pre-service classroom teachers. *Teaching and Teacher Education* 45, 94–103.

Kim, H.-K. (2012) Understanding the interplay between language, power, and ideology in the identity formation of Asian English teachers. Unpublished PhD thesis, Indiana University, USA.

Martin-Beltrán, M. (2010) Positioning proficiency: How students and teachers (de)construct language proficiency at school. *Linguistics and Education* 21 (4), 257–281.

Menard-Warwick, J. (2011) Chilean English teacher identity and popular culture: Three generations. *International Journal of Bilingual Education and Bilingualism* 4 (3), 261–277.

Montenegro, A. (2012) Analyzing EFL university learners' positioning and participation structures in collaborative learning environment. *Colombian Applied Linguistics Journal* 14 (1), 127–145.

Norton, B. (2000) *Identity and Language Learning*. Essex: Pearson Education.

Norton, B. (2010) Identity, literacy, and English-language teaching. *TESL Canada Journal* 8 (1), 1–13.

Pennycook, A. (2010) *Language as a Local Practice*. New York, NY: Routledge.

Reeves, J. (2009) Teacher investment in learner identity. *Teaching and Teacher Education* 25 (1), 34–41.

Rudolph, N. (2018) Essentialization, idealization, and apprehensions of local language practice in the classroom. In B. Yazan and N. Rudolph (eds) *Criticality, Teacher Identity, and (In)equity in English Language Teaching: Issues and Implications* (pp. 275–302). Dordrecht: Springer.

Rudolph, N., Yazan, B. and Rudolph, J. (2018) Negotiating 'ares,' 'cans,' and 'shoulds' of being and becoming in English language teaching: two teacher accounts from one Japanese university. *Asian Englishes* 21 (1), 1–16.

Rutherford, J. (1990) The third space: Interview with Homi Bhabha. In J. Rutherford (ed.) *Identity, Community, Culture, Difference* (pp. 207–221). London: Lawrence and Wishart.

Tseng, S.C. (2011) Understanding non-native English-speaking teachers' identity construction and transformation in the English-speaking community: A closer look at past, present, and future. Unpublished PhD thesis, Indiana State University, USA.

Ushioda, E. (2009) A person-in-context relational view of emergent motivation, self and identity. In Z. Dörnyei and E. Ushioda (eds) *Motivation, Language Identity and the L2 Self* (pp. 215–228). Bristol: Multilingual Matters.

Varghese, M., Morgan, B., Johnston, B. and Johnson, K.A. (2005) Theorizing language teacher identity: Three perspectives and beyond. *Journal of Language, Identity, and Education* 4 (1), 21–44.

Wenger, E. (1998) *Communities of Practice: Learning, Meaning, and Identity*. New York: Cambridge University Press.

Yoon, B. (2008) Uninvited guests: The influence of teachers' role and pedagogies on positioning of English language learners in the regular classroom. *American Educational Research Journal* 45 (2), 496–520.

13 Dancing between English and Arabic: Complexities in Emirati Cultural Identities

Sarah Hopkyns

Introduction

There has long been a tendency to use 'culture' and 'country' as synonyms. Even in well-known International English exams, questions in the speaking part often have a slash between the two terms. For example, candidates are asked, 'Is this common in your country/culture?' In today's globalized and highly mobile world, however, people living in one country rarely share one culture. From a transnational perspective, 'languages spread across cultures, and cultures spread across languages' (Risager, 2007: 2). This especially applies to highly diverse and transient contexts, such as the Arabian Gulf countries where transnational workers and residents often outnumber local citizens. Such demographics as well as rapid globalization, especially in terms of using English, lead to a plethora of complexities in identity construction. In the United Arab Emirates (UAE), where English Medium Instruction (EMI) dominates higher education, the majority of university students obtain their degrees in a second language. Viewed by some as a microcosm of the country's multicultural and multilingual society, a complex mix of cultures and languages are present in EMI higher education contexts. This is, therefore, a fascinating setting for a study on identity construction and interaction in language learning. The following section of this chapter will hold a microscope to the UAE with a focus on the 'ordinariness' of linguistic and cultural hybridity. Complexities in modern cultural identities will then be explored by defining the key concepts of culture and identity and explaining the theory of interculturality. Following this, the study's methodology will be described, and key findings will be analysed. The chapter will end with a discussion of themes arising from the findings and the resulting implications for interaction in language education.

A Microscope on the United Arab Emirates

The UAE is nestled between conservative oil giant Saudi Arabia to its West and the calm desert paradise of Oman to its East. Although the UAE is small in size, ranking 115th globally in terms of population (Harris, 2013: 87), as the world's fourth-largest exporter of oil, it has a powerful economy. The UAE has unusual demographics, with only 13% of the population being citizens (Harris, 2013: 87). The rest of its inhabitants are transnationals from over 200 countries (Solloway, 2018: 459), usually drawn to the country for work opportunities, which come with comparatively enticing salaries and benefits. As citizens of a rentier state (Gray, 2011), Emiratis enjoy additional privileges such as free housing, free education, subsidized food and fuel, as well as governmental support for starting businesses.

Such wealth and demographic diversity are relatively new phenomena for the young country, which only became an official nation in 1971. The pre-oil-era lives of the grandparents of the Emirati Millennials participating in this study were starkly different from the lives of Emirati youth today. The nation then referred to as the Trucial States was thinly populated with desert dwellers, traders and pearl-divers, who spoke mainly local dialects and were relatively untouched by globalization and its accompanying language of English. With the discovery of oil in the late 1950s, fast-paced and dynamic globalization and development enveloped the UAE, and this continues to the present day. Just like a Shinkansen ride (Japanese bullet-train), for those witnessing even a short part of the UAE's journey, one's eyes cannot easily keep up with the changing infrastructure and ever-developing cityscapes.

Due to the UAE's high number of foreign workers, who speak over 100 languages, it is an undeniably 'superdiverse' nation (Vertovec, 2007). The language with the largest influence is English, which is the '*de facto* lingua franca' (Nickerson, 2015: 240) and the medium of instruction for core subjects at all levels of education. In terms of visibility, despite the multitude of languages spoken, English, in conjunction with the official language of the country, Arabic, dominates public spaces. Permanent signs (e.g. road signs, shop signs, etc.), event-related signs (e.g. posters and announcements) and 'noise' (readable objects left by accident such as a note on a door) (Blommaert, 2013: 53) show that English is highly conspicuous. In fact, as Solloway (2018: 459) states, 'a visitor to the country could be forgiven for believing that the E in the acronym UAE stood for English.' In private spheres, too, the majority of Emiratis have hired help, which is the topic of an acclaimed UAE-based documentary named 'Nanny Culture' (*The National*, 11 July 2017). Although the nanny followed in the documentary is British, most nannies in the UAE are from the Philippines, Sri Lanka and Ethiopia and also use mainly English with the children.

For the past decade, there have been frequent debates in public discourse, scholarly circles and in the media over the effects of such an all-encompassing presence of English on Emiratis' cultural identities. In the media, English tends to be dressed as a powerhouse or a dominating force, whereas Arabic is very much portrayed as 'a victim in need of saving' (Hopkyns, 2016: 87). In terms of how the languages are viewed by Emiratis, previous studies (Findlow, 2005, 2006; Hopkyns, 2016, 2017) have found that English is associated with the wider world, the future, jobs and education. Arabic, on the other hand, is associated with the home, local life, religion, tradition and family. Thus, the languages are polarized and seen as representing different spheres of life. Previous studies (Al-Bataineh & Gallagher, 2018; Palfreyman & Al-Bataineh, 2018) indicate that local language ideologies (system of ideas and ideals) often center around 'double monolingualism' (Al-Bataineh & Gallagher, 2018: 9) where there is a preference for keeping English and Arabic separate rather than mixing them. However, this ideology clashes quite dramatically with what is seen 'on the ground.' As Dovchin and Lee (2019) point out in their introduction to a special issue of the *Journal of Multilingualism* on 'the ordinariness of translinguistics,' translanguaging in many contexts is 'quite normal' (Blommaert, 2013) and 'ordinary' (Dovchin, 2017). This is certainly the case in the UAE where, when walking down university corridors, one hears a complex mix of languages, often within one conversation or one sentence. Such languages are the local Khaleeji or Gulf Arabic dialect, Modern Standard Arabic (MSA), English, as well as a smattering of other languages such as Tagalog, Urdu, Turkish and Korean often acquired through conversations with maids or drivers as well as through watching popular drama series in the latter two languages (Hopkyns *et al.*, 2018). Students naturally code-switch by alternating between two or more languages in the same stretch of discourse (Bullock & Toribio, 2009, xii), and use translanguaging, which is the use of 'multilingual oral interaction and use of different languages in written texts' (Conteh, 2018) with an emphasis on aiding understanding. When asked about feelings towards such language practices, however, mixing of the languages is generally frowned upon (Al-Bataineh & Gallagher, 2018), especially by older Emiratis. Such a disparity between dominant language ideologies and actual practice serves to deepen complexities within local identities.

Complexities in Modern Cultural Identities

As stated in the introductory section of this chapter, modern cultural identities are far from synonymous with physical spaces, especially in superdiverse contexts such as the UAE. Rather than a nation sharing a culture, individuals tend to create cultures through multiple smaller social groupings such as families, colleagues, friendship circles, special interest groups, contemporaries, etc. Holliday (1999) identifies such 'cohesive social groupings' as 'small cultures' (1999: 237). Whereas notions of large culture divide the social world into 'hard,' essentially different ethnic, national or international cultures, the notion of small culture 'leaves the picture open, finding "softer cultures" in all types of social grouping, which may or may not have significant ethnic, national or international qualities' (Holliday, 1999: 240). In this sense, rather than viewing cultures as monolithic, the small culture approach focuses on social processes as they emerge and explores cultures 'from the bottom up' (Atkinson & Sohn, 2013: 671) with an emphasis on individuals within cultural groups.

Just as understandings of the term 'culture' have expanded and become increasingly multifaceted, definitions of the term 'identity' have followed a similar pattern of complexity in scholarly discourse. In recent years, there has been a paradigm shift moving away from 'inter-group approaches' to identity (Pavlenko & Blackledge, 2004: 5), which tended to over-simplify and essentialize differences between large groups such as nationality or language. Although there has not been a full-scale replacement of essentialist views (Lytra, 2016), identities in recent times are generally recognized as plural, rich, complex and sometimes contradictory (Block, 2007; Kramsch, 1998; Mercer, 2011; Norton, 2000; Zhu, 2014, 2017). Many aspects of identity are accepted as highly changeable due to social, linguistic and personal factors, making them fluid and dynamic over time and space.

Pavlenko and Blackledge (2004: 21) recognize the plurality of identities by distinguishing between *imposed identities* (unnegotiable in a particular time and space, such as one's name or nationality at birth), *assumed identities* (accepted and not negotiated due to being legitimized by traditionally dominant discourses, such as being heterosexual or white) and *negotiable identities* (contested by groups and individuals). The latter are arguably the most interesting types to investigate as they refer to all identity options which can be contested and resisted by individuals and groups. Examples include race, ethnicity, nationality, religious affiliation and 'linguistic competence and ability to claim a "voice" in a second language' (Pavlenko & Blackledge, 2004: 22). It is the latter which is investigated in the current study.

Pavlenko and Blackledge's (2004) categories of *imposed, assumed* and *negotiable* identities were influenced by *positioning theory*, which can traditionally be defined as 'the process by which selves are located in conversation as observably and subjectively coherent participants in jointly produced storylines, informed by particular discourses' (Davies & Harre, 1990: 48). While Davies and Harre (1990) saw positioning as mainly a conversational phenomenon, Pavlenko and Blackledge (2004) expanded and built upon the traditional meaning of positioning to include 'all discursive practices which may position individuals in particular ways or allow individuals to position themselves' (2004: 20). In this sense, how individuals see themselves (*reflective positioning*) or are seen by others (*interactive positioning*) affects identities in a variety of settings and in multiple ways. Based on the combination of *reflexive* and *interactive positioning*, identity becomes a process of analyzing and reanalyzing, reflecting and re-reflecting, negotiating and renegotiating; it is not something one *has*, rather it is 'something which people *use* to justify, explain, and make sense of themselves in relation to other people and to the contexts in which they operate' (MacLure, 1993: 312). It is important to realize that reflective positioning is often contested by others, causing 'perpetual tension between self-chosen identities and others attempts to position them' (Pavlenko & Blackledge, 2004: 20). As Emiratis in the study participate in discourses related to a range of roles such as *university student, daughter/son, sister/brother, shopper, traveler, etc.*, various identities are co-constructed, and at times contested. The complex interplay between reflective and interactive positioning, in this sense, is shaped to serve specific purposes, affiliations, contexts and spaces.

The Theory of Interculturality (IC)

Considering the UAE's dynamic and diverse linguistic landscape and current understandings of plurality in culture and identity, the theoretical perspective of 'interculturality' (IC), which originates in Nishizaka's seminal work (1995) and was extended by Mori (2003), Higgins (2007) and Zhu (2010, 2014) is a useful lens for analyzing complexities existing in identity construction. The theory of IC has traditionally been used in two different ways: *IC as being* and *IC as doing*. The first way of viewing IC is as a state *of being* 'intercultural'. In this sense, people have cultural values and cultural differences, which are part of their state of being. By taking this view, previous studies have tended to concentrate on the search for cultural values that underlie cultural differences, and theories and models that bridge differences in communication (Zhu, 2010: 192). Although popular between the 1970s and 1990s with Hofstede's often-cited work (1980) exemplifying this approach, recently criticisms have been launched against 'IC as being' due to it being seen as 'essentialist' (Holliday, 2010), 'reductionist' (Kubota & Lehner, 2004) and lacking problematization.

In contrast, IC *as doing* views cultural identities as multidimensional and socially constructed. According to this perspective, an individual has a number of identities and belongs to many membership categories, but not all identities are equally salient or relevant at a given point in different social interactions (Zhu, 2014: 209). Instead of seeing cultural identity as static or given, the theoretical lens of *IC as doing* 'problematizes the notion of cultural identities and emphasizes the emergent, discursive and inter- nature of interactions' (Zhu, 2014: 209).

IC is particularly useful in analysing the many complexities which often go hand in hand with superdiverse study contexts. For example, previous studies using IC as a lens include Zhu's (2010) study which investigated the process of language socialization in Chinese diasporic families in the United Kingdom. Tensions within communities, especially between different generations, were frequently found where adolescent children of immigrant parents were exposed to conflicting sets of cultural values and practices. This led to challenges when constructing their own sociocultural identities. Further challenges surrounding language ideologies were identified where older generations viewed the L2 (English) as the 'they-code' (Gumperz, 1982) and therefore preferred to use their mother-tongue language for family interaction, whereas the younger generation often considered English as a 'we-code' and prefer it to ethnic languages.

The Study

The study, which is part of a larger project, aimed to explore language use and the effects of English on Emirati identities. While the larger study included three groups of participants (Emirati university students, Emirati primary school teachers and foreign university teachers), the focus of this chapter is one of those groups which comprises 100 Emirati university students. The study combines the case study approach with phenomenology. As the study aims to explore opinions, insights and perceptions on the effects of English on Emirati cultural identities from multiple angles, and by using multiple data collection methods, the case study approach was appropriate. The 'bounded nature' (Creswell, 2009: 61) of the case study approach also fits the study as participants are bound by both place and time. It is descriptive in nature as the aim was to provide a rich thick description (Merriam, 1998) and to present a complete description of the phenomenon within its context (Yin, 2003: 5). The phenomenon being investigated is 'English in the UAE and its effects on Emirati cultural identities', and the cases or units of analysis are the three participant groups, of which one participant group (Emirati university students) will be the focus of this chapter. The phenomenological approach was appropriate as the study investigates participants' perceptions of a particular phenomenon. Phenomenology, which was founded in the early 20th century by Edmund Hesserl and furthered by Berger and Luckman (1966) concentrates on 'people's perceptions or meanings; people's attitudes and beliefs; people's feelings and emotions' (Denscombe, 2010: 93) with an emphasis on the existence of multiple realities.

Open-response questionnaires, semi-structured focus groups and a research journal were used as data collection tools (in English and Arabic). These tools were designed to collect in-depth qualitative data, exploring opinions and experiences. The content of the questionnaires and focus group schedules focused on language use, attitudes towards English and Arabic, and perceptions of the effects of English on cultural identities. The study's main research questions include:

(RQ1) In which domains do Emirati university students use English and Arabic?

(RQ2) What are Emirati university students' attitudes towards English?

(RQ3) How does English affect local cultural identities in the view of Emirati university students?

Of the 100 participants, 80 were female and 20 were male. This gender imbalance is representative of the university's student body due to males often studying abroad or completing military service. All the students completed the questionnaires, and 18 were focus group members.

The questionnaires, which took approximately 20 minutes to complete, were given to the students in their classrooms with the permission of their teachers. The focus groups, which were audio-recorded and later transcribed verbatim, were approximately one hour in length. They took place in a reserved meeting room outside class time. For the student questionnaires, 'cluster sampling' (Kelly, 2006: 29) was used as the research population had been divided into random classes or 'clusters' at the start of the semester. From a total of 14 classes (clusters), nine were used in the study (seven female and two male classes). For the focus groups (two female groups of 6, one male group of 6), 'purposive sampling' was used, where participants were 'hand-picked' (Denscombe, 2010: 35) to obtain the most detailed and valuable insights on the research topic. The participants were aged 18–30 and had all attended state schools. Prior to collecting data, ethical approval was granted by the university in which the study took place.

Thematic analysis (TA), which involves identifying, analyzing and reporting patterns in the data (Braun & Clarke, 2006), was used to approach the data. By focusing on three different methods of data collection within a phenomenological case study, the aim was to reveal a deeper and increased understanding of participants' attitudes, which allowed for *methodological triangulation* (within-methods).

Findings

In terms of languages spoken by the Emirati participants (RQ1), all the university students named Arabic as their first language, and 96% named English as their second. Only 13% of the undergraduate students spoke an additional language (Turkish (4%), Indian/Hindi (4%), Korean (3%), Spanish (1%) and French (1%)). Table 13.1 shows the areas in which participants used English. Additional areas mentioned included: '*while driving, restaurants, cafes while reading books, speaking with other nationalities.*'

Table 13.1 supports the omnipresence of English as well as a tendency for students to use mainly Arabic with friends and at home. When

Table 13.1 Domains in which Emirati participants use English

	%		%
For travelling	98	Email/texting	73
In shopping malls	97	Listening to music	61
In hospitals	97	Outside class time at university	60
Internet	91	Talking with friends outside the university	34
Movies	90	At home with family members	33

participants were asked if they felt English was important in the UAE (RQ2), 97% stated 'yes.' The most common reasons for the importance of English can be seen in Figure 13.1. These reasons reflected utilitarian and pragmatic goals, such as global communication, self-development and career ambitions.

Students were then asked to comment on whether they felt English affected three categories: (1) their lives, (2) culture in the UAE and (3) their identities. It was felt these categories together represented various layers of cultural identity (RQ3). While participants initially responded with 'yes', 'no' or 'partly' (Figure 13.2), when giving reasons and examples, there was considerable overlap and blurring of the categories and similar themes arose across the layers.

We can see from Figure 13.2 that most participants felt English affected their lives and culture, whereas, in terms of English affecting identities, participants were divided. This could be due to the category of *identity* being deeper and more personal than the categories of *life* and *culture*. In this sense, the latter categories tend to be associated with what happens around us, whereas the former category is more closely tied to what happens inside us. It could be, therefore, less comfortable to discuss changes to identity due to its highly personal connotation. Connected to this is the notion that one can exercise control over one's identity, whereas culture and life are concepts we can observe but not necessarily control to the same degree.

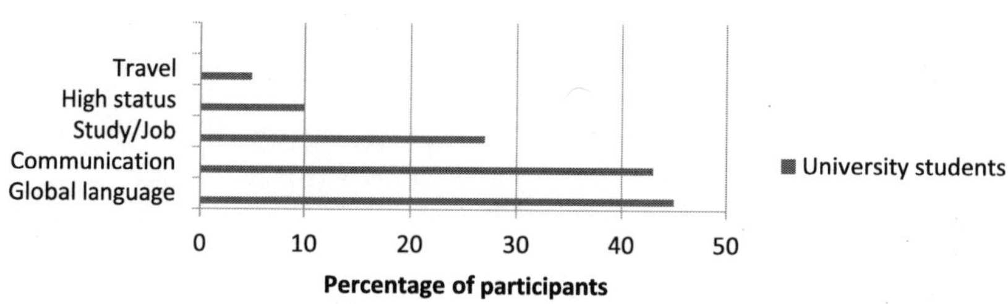

Figure 13.1 Factors contributing to the importance of English

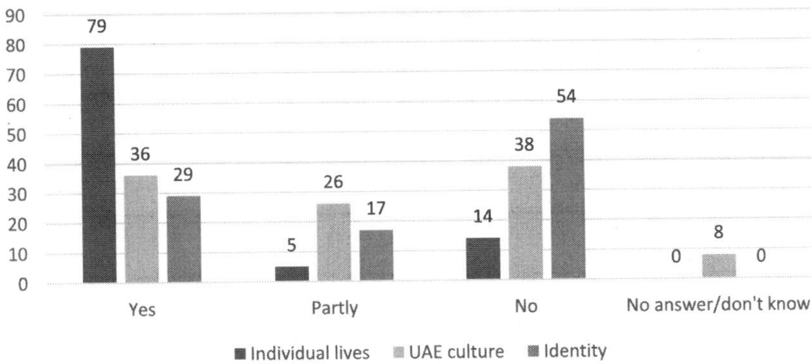

Figure 13.2 Emirati university students' views on the effects of English on layers of cultural identity

Moving on to look at the reasons behind the initial responses shown in Figure 13.2, the most commonly mentioned positive effects of English related to individual lives and identities, in terms of personal growth, confidence levels, increased knowledge and future study/career goals. A selection of quotes from participants, relating to these themes can be seen in Table 13.2.

From Table 13.2, Abdul's reflective positioning (how he sees himself) is affected by the context in which he refers to (public space). Being bilingual allowed him to help others and resulted in feelings of pride. However, in other contexts, such as a home with parents, his English-speaking self may not induce the same levels of self-worth. This demonstrates how not all aspects of identity (e.g. English-speaking self) are equally salient or relevant during any given social interaction.

Table 13.2 Areas in which English has positively affected layers of cultural identities

Increased confidence	It affects the way I think. English language makes me happy when I use it. It makes me confident. **(Sultan)**
Increased knowledge	You start thinking out of the circle and start knowing new stuff **(Taif)**
Education and career	It has made me an educated person in society, so in the future I could get my dream job and I hope so. **(Fakhera)**
Helping others	I do feel different from other people. For example, once I was in a restaurant and a guy only speaks English, the waiters, and the guy who wants to order, he doesn't know English so he called me and I started translating, that's the moment when I feel different than, because I have studied English. **(Abdul)**

Note: All names are pseudonyms

Unwanted effects of global English on culture

While the positive effects of English were discussed mainly in relation to the participants themselves (reflective positioning), negative effects tended to be discussed in relation to observations of others (interactive positioning). The negative cultural changes participants mentioned can be seen in Table 13.3.

Through the lens of IC, Fahad and Abdul's comments indicate that identity shifts according to interaction patterns and membership categories. Being a competent English speaker around those who are less proficient, can lead to arrogant reflective positioning and condescending or snobbish interactive positioning towards those who speak mainly in Arabic. Abdul stresses that this attitude is only present in contexts where English is being spoken. Nadia's comment illustrates that for her generation Arabic is still the 'we code' at home, and English is the 'they code.' However, she raises concerns over the reverse being true for the next generation, thus resulting in tensions within families and communities. This is a concern echoed in Rajwa's comment about Arabic loss.

Further tensions between generations and within families are exemplified through personal stories participants voiced during the focus group sessions. Here, differing language ideologies and language use caused rifts inside and outside the home. Older generations such as grandparents and parents disapproved of English at home, whereas younger generations such as the participants' younger siblings often naturally used English in the home, despite excluding family members from some conversations due to their lack of English proficiency. This was also found in studies by Johannsen (1996), Hassall (2004) and O'Neill (2016), where younger Emirati family members used English to communicate 'secretly' with each other despite the disapproval of older relatives. Even in public spaces, tensions surrounding English between family members were present and

Table 13.3 Areas in which English has negatively affected layers of cultural identities

Personality changes	When a person uses English, his personality changes. He expresses different views, a different side of himself. Some people, when they start using English, think that anyone who only uses Arabic is ignorant. Sometimes. **(Fahad)** Some people speaks English just for show off. Oh, look at me, I know English! **(Abdul)**
Arabic loss	There are some Emirati people don't speak Arabic and that hurt me a lot. **(Rajwa)**
English as all-powerful for the next generation	At school now they speak in English, all of the subjects are in English now, so I think in the future it will affect our language. For us we learned Arabic more than English and now we are learning more but to them, they only speak, or learn English, more than Arabic. So, I think, we will not feel it now, the effect will not be nowadays. **(Nadia)**

Table 13.4 Generational tensions caused by English

Tensions at home	My brother he doesn't know how to write in Arabic, so he's lost that. (He's) seven. He just writes in English. But he speaks Arabic but he doesn't know how to write in Arabic. He doesn't know the letters. When my mother teaches him, she feels she will die. She wants to kill him (laughs). **(Nadia)** My baby brother, he all the time speaks English, even in the home. I tell him, 'no, now you have to speak Arabic, you have to know that in school you will speak English but in our home you will speak just Arabic'. So, he said 'no, I want to know, I love to speak English'. I said, 'okay but in my home, you have to speak Arabic'. So, I think in school they all focus on English. **(Tahani)**
Tensions outside	**Alya:** My grandmother takes me to hospital. She has appointment because nothing Arabic in the hospital. **Researcher:** So, she needs you because you speak English? **Alya:** A little. Yes. I help her. **Researcher:** How do you feel about that? **Alya:** Happy, yeah for me, but bad for her.

caused traditional power relations (e.g. seniority) to be reversed, in some cases. Participant experiences of such tensions can be seen in Table 13.4.

We can see in Alya's case, that she has mixed feelings. On the one hand, she feels proud to be able to help her non-English-speaking grandmother (positive reflective positioning). This feeling was also found in female Emirati university students in Palfreyman's study (2006) where participants stated that acting as 'English brokers' (2006: 365) for the family added to feelings of prestige in the traditional role of 'helpful daughter.' Alya, however, also feels uncomfortable or 'bad' seeing her grandmother being forced to rely on her in this way due to the dominance of English in the UAE. Alya's sense of identity is evidently plural, complex and contradictory. Tahani and Nadia's comments analysed through the lens of IC, also show plurality in identity construction. Whereas Tahani and Nadia may accept the use of English at their EMI university, they show discomfort hearing their younger siblings using it at home.

Linguistic dualism: Two loyalties in two spaces

In addition to the participants who felt English had affected layers of cultural identity both positively and negatively, a sizable percentage of participants stated that English had not affected their lives (14%), culture (38%), and identity (54%), as seen in Figure 13.2. The most common reasons for this response included the fact that local culture and the Arabic language were in their hearts and minds and could not be easily affected, English was additive rather than subtractive, and the two languages operated in different spheres and therefore did not affect each other. Here we see English and Arabic are viewed as 'two solitudes' (Cummins, 2007). Responses relating to these perspectives can be seen in Table 13.5.

Table 13.5 Reasons for English not affecting local cultural identities

Arabic hearts and minds	Our culture will stay in our heads, nothing will change. English will improve us and develop us but we will not forget our culture. **(Reem)**
English is not subtractive	I think it adds something in me but it doesn't change a person. Like a skill, new language it's a benefit to me to speak to other people and interact. But not in my personality. It doesn't affect my personality. **(Marwa)** It adds something nice to our culture or Emirati culture. **(Sultan)**
Double monolingualism or 'two solitudes'	For me I separate my Arabic language from English. Everything has its own time. **(Fatima)** In our family, we speak English outside but in my home we should speak Arabic, only Arabic. **(Alya)**

Despite voicing ideologies related to linguistic dualism, as indicated most obviously in Fatima's comment 'I separate my Arabic language from English,' when analysing the focus group transcripts it was noted in the research journal that many participants switched languages midway through sentences. English sentences were punctuated with Arabic words such as 'yani' (it means), 'hatha' (this and that), or 'khalas' (finished). Arabic sentences often contained English words such as 'okay,' 'lap' (laptop), and 'culture.' This indicates a clear mismatch between language ideology and actual practice.

Discussion

The findings showed that English was by far the most dominant second language used amongst the Emirati participants at the expense of any other language. Given the UAE's multilingual environment, one might expect a wider range of languages to be mentioned. Van den Hoven and Carroll (2016) speak of Abu Dhabi's 'rich linguistic context' (2016: 37) stating that the Emirati pre-service teacher participants in their study recognized English and Arabic as the primary languages but also spoke of using four peripheral languages: 'Indian,' 'Persian,' 'Filipino' and 'Korean.' In the present study, however, only 13% of the university students mentioned a language other than English as a 'second or other' language (Turkish, Indian/Hindi, Korean, Spanish, French), demonstrating the wide gap in terms of scope and power between English and the 'peripheral languages.'

With regard to the effects of English on participants' cultural identities, complexities were unveiled mainly in terms of global/local or pragmatism/heritage pulls. Such complexities were also seen in Patent's (2016) study with female Emirati university students, where local linguistic identities were described, in the words of one participant, as 'English is the half of life.' However, this 'half' was far from a neat fraction but rather 'a nexus of powerful and often contradictory discourses of the modern and traditional' (Patent, 2016: 166). Further complexities can be seen in how participants' English-speaking selves are reflected upon in different ways according to social context and interaction patterns. For example, English is embraced as a positive part of participants' identities in terms of personal growth and self-esteem (increased confidence and open-mindedness) and the domain of education. Here, being an English-speaker positively affected the way most participants saw themselves (reflective positioning). However, there appeared to be a fine line, for some, between self-confidence and arrogance with regard to English ability. Male participants, in particular, spoke of English being a language used to 'show off' leading to changes in personality and a tendency to look down on Arabic speakers. Seymour (2016: 8) states that in the UAE, such feelings are commonplace, with the local nickname 'Bresteej boy' meaning 'prestigious guy,' being used for those using mainly English. Complexities around embracing English-speaking parts of identities arose in situations where lack of acceptance was felt (e.g. with older generations, at home). For example, Nadia's story of her little brother choosing to use English at home and being unable to complete his Arabic homework may arouse personal feelings of pride over English proficiency but negative positioning by parents due to his loss of Arabic. Here we see that identities continuously shift according to context and relationships.

The findings also revealed 'they-code versus we-code' tensions between generations. Rather than there being a general feeling of comfort in embracing both languages or using both languages naturally in all contexts, participants described situations of differentiated bilingualism or 'linguistic dualism' (Findlow, 2006). In postmodern societies, especially in the case of the UAE, languages often serve as sites of solidarity, empowerment, resistance, disempowerment or discrimination. How one positions oneself depends upon 'the level of inclusion, acceptance, and equality' one feels among certain communities (Pavlenko & Blackledge, 2004: 17). Undoubtedly, the level of acceptance in various contexts affects language choices and how one feels about those language choices.

Conclusion

In the context of the UAE where English is used as the lingua franca as well as in education, cultural identity tends to display itself in what Baker (2009) describes as 'a hybrid, mixed and liminal manner, drawing on and moving between global, national, local, and individual orientations' (2009: 567). Such hybridity leads to the phenomenon of 'togetherness-in-difference' (Ang, 2001), 'double belonging' (Lam & Warriner, 2012), or 'dancing between languages.' As Kramsch (2002) stresses, in such cases distinguishing 'the dancer from the dance' can be difficult. Recognizing complex individual identities in the language classroom requires an extra level of awareness from teachers. It is important to consider the implications of such complexities in both the areas of language interaction and policymaking.

In language classrooms in the UAE and other superdiverse contexts, it is firstly important for teachers to be aware of the web of complexities frequently existing within students' identity construction. As Zhu (2010: 191) states, discrepancies in language ideologies (as found in the current study) can challenge language maintenance and result in 'conflict and tension regarding what language to use, when and to what extent.' In this sense, students may feel negatively positioned (both reflectively and interactively) in the EMI university context when using Arabic or when mixing English and Arabic through translanguaging. Even though in daily life, Emiratis often use both languages within a conversation, alternating between two languages to support learning is often considered a taboo in the UAE (Carroll & Van den Hoven, 2017). Awareness needs to be raised among stakeholders (management, teachers and learners) on the benefits of translanguaging in bilingual education in terms of students being comfortable with using their full linguistic repertoires to support learning and embracing bilingual identities in the classroom. Acceptance of translanguaging as a learning resource has proven to work well in other contexts such as in Puerto Rican universities (Carroll & Mazak, 2017) and South African higher education (Hornberger & Link, 2012).

In terms of policymaking, strict 'English only' policies in EMI universities are undoubtedly contributing to the separation of languages. For example, currently, at the university in which the study takes place, students who wish to utilize their full linguistic repertoires through translanguaging are not encouraged to do so. On assessment criteria, 'using Arabic' is often cause for lowering the grade. Even for bilingual teachers, there is an expectation that only English will be used in the EMI context. Wong *et al.* (2016) describe this as 'linguistic muzzling,' where students and teachers feel pressure to refrain from using their knowledge of other languages in the classroom to abide by the 'English only' policies (2016: 225). Active reflection on how such policies jar with natural language use is necessary.

Looking at education in general, it is important for Arabic, as well as English, to also be viewed as a language of education and future workplaces. This can be achieved if greater emphasis is placed on the language in both public and private schools. Steps towards this are already taking place. For example, Arabic language lessons have been made compulsory in all private schools (Kapiszeski, 2007), and private schools also offer a range of foreign languages in addition to Arabic (Calafato & Tang, 2018). Encouraging translanguaging in the classroom and the mixing of languages in multiple contexts would do much to 'encourage avenues of belonging which are not exclusionary or segregated, and the promotion of identity which values hybridity, not purity' (Davies, 2006: 1037).

References

Al-Bataineh, A. and Gallagher, K. (2018) Attitudes towards translanguaging: How future teachers perceive the meshing of Arabic and English in children's story books. *International Journal of Bilingual Education and Bilingualism*. https://doi.org.10.1080/13670050.2018.1471039

Ang, I. (2001) *On Not Speaking Chinese: Living Between Asia and the West*. London: Routledge.

Atkinson, D. and Sohn, J. (2013) Culture from the bottom up. *TESOL Quarterly* 47 (4), 669–693.

Baker, W. (2009) The cultures of English as a lingua franca. *TESOL Quarterly* 43 (4), 567–592.

Berger, P.L. and Luckmann, T. (1966) *The Social Construction of Reality*. London: Penguin.

Block, D. (2007) *Second Language Identities*. New York: Continuum.

Blommaert, J. (2013) *Ethnography, Superdiversity and Linguistic Landscapes: Chronicles of Complexity*. Bristol: Multilingual Matters.

Bullock, B. and Toribio, A. (2009) *The Cambridge Handbook of Linguistic Codeswitching*. Cambridge: Cambridge University Press.

Braun, V. and Clarke, V. (2006) Using thematic analysis in psychology. *Qualitative Research in Psychology* 3 (2), 77–101.

Calafato, R. and Tang, F. (2018) The status of Arabic, superdiversity, and language learning motivation among non-Arab expats in the Gulf. *Lingua* 219, 24–38.

Carroll, K. and Mazak, C. (2017) Language policy in Puerto Rico's higher education: Opening the door for translanguaging practices. *Anthropology and Education Quarterly* 48 (1), 4–22.

Carroll, K. and van den Hoven, M. (2017) Translanguaging within higher education in the United Arab Emirates. In K. Carroll and C. Mazak (eds) *Translanguaging in Higher Education: Beyond Monolingual Ideologies* (pp. 139–154). Bristol: Multilingual Matters.

Conteh, J. (2018) Translanguaging. *ELT Journal* 72 (4), 445–447

Creswell, J.W. (2009) *Research Design: Qualitative, Quantitative, and Mixed Methods Approaches* (3rd edn). Thousand Oaks, CA: Sage Publications.

Cummins, J. (2007) Rethinking monolingual instructional strategies in multilingual classrooms. *Canadian Journal of Applied Linguistics* 10 (2), 221–240.

Davies, L. (2006) Education for positive conflict and interruptive democracy. In H. Lauder, P. Brown, L. Dillabough and A.H. Halsey (eds) *Education, Globalization and Social Change* (pp. 1029–1037). Oxford: Oxford University Press.

Davies, B. and Harré, R. (1990) Positioning: The discursive production of selves. *Journal for the Theory of Social Behaviour* 20 (1), 43–63.

Denscombe, M. (2010) *The Good Research Guide: For Small-scale Social Research Projects*. New York: Open University Press.

Dovchin, S. (2017) The ordinariness of youth linguascapes in Mongolia. *International Journal of Multilingualism* 14 (2), 144–159.

Dovchin, S. and Lee, J.W. (2019) Introduction to special issue: 'The ordinariness of translinguistics'. *International Journal of Multilingualism* 16 (2), 105–111.

Findlow, S. (2005) International networking in the United Arab Emirates higher education: Global-local tension. *Compare* 35 (3), 285–302.

Findlow, S. (2006) Higher education and linguistic dualism in the Arab Gulf. *British Journal of Sociology of Education* 27 (1), 19–36.

Gray, M. (2011) A Theory of 'Late Rentierism' in the Arab states of the Gulf. *Georgetown University School of Foreign Service in Qatar Occasional Papers* 7, 1–44.

Gumperz, J. (1982) *Discourse Strategies*. Cambridge: Cambridge University Press.

Harris, J. (2013) Desert dreams in the Gulf: Transnational crossroads for the global elite. *Race and Class* 54 (4), 86–99.

Hassall, P.J. (2004) World Englishes and English for global communications. In P. Davidson *et al.* (eds) *Proceedings of the 9th TESOL Arabia Conference* (pp. 224–244). Dubai, UAE.

Higgins, C. (2007) A closer look at cultural difference: 'Interculturality' in talk-in-interaction. *Pragmatics* 17 (1), 1–8.

Hofstede, G. (1980) *Culture's Consequences: International Differences in Work-related Values*. London: Sage Publications.

Holliday, A. (1999) Small cultures. *Applied Linguistics* 20 (2), 237–264.

Holliday, A. (2010) Complexity in cultural identity. *Language and Intercultural Communication* 10 (2), 165–177.

Hopkyns, S. (2016) Emirati cultural identity in the age of 'Englishization': Voices from an Abu Dhabi university. In L. Buckingham (ed.) *Language, Identity and Education on the Arabian Peninsula* (pp. 87–115). Bristol: Multilingual Matters.

Hopkyns, S. (2017) A conflict of desires: Global English and its effects on cultural identity in the United Arab Emirates. Unpublished PhD thesis, University of Leicester, UK.

Hopkyns, S., Zoghbor, W. and Hassall, P. (2018) Creative hybridity over linguistic purity: The status of English in the United Arab Emirates. *Asian Englishes* 20 (2), 158–169.

Hornberger, N.H. and Link, H. (2012) Translanguaging in today's classrooms: A biliteracy lens. *Theory into Practice* 51 (4), 239–247.

Johannsen, K.L. (1996) Errors and identity: A World English perspective. In A. Holbrook, C. Coombe and S. Troudi (eds) *TESOL Arabia: Conference Proceedings Selected Papers 1995 and 1996* (pp. 76–86). Dubai: TESOL Arabia.

Kapiszeski, A. (2007) De-Arabization in the Gulf: Foreign labor and the struggle for local culture. *Georgetown Journal of International Affairs* 8 (2), 87–102.

Kelly, A. (2006) Cluster Sampling. In V. Jupp (ed.) *The SAGE Dictionary of Social Research Methods* (pp. 20–21). London: Sage.

Kramsch, C. (1998) *Language and Culture*. Oxford: Oxford University Press.

Kramsch, C. (2002) Introduction: "How can we tell the dancer from the dance?". In C. Kramsch (ed.) *Language Acquisition and Language Socialization* (pp. 1–30). London: Continuum.

Kubota, R. and Lehner, A. (2004) Toward critical contrastive rhetoric. *Journal of Second Language Writing* 13 (1), 7–27.

Lam, W.S.E. and Warriner, D.S. (2012) Transnationalism and literacy: Investigating the mobility of people, languages, texts, and practices in contexts of migration. *Reading Research Quarterly* 47 (2), 191–215.

Lytra, V. (2016) Language and ethnic identity. In S. Preece (ed.) *Handbook of Language and Identity* (pp. 131–145). New York: Routledge.

MacLure, M. (1993) Arguing for your self: Identity as an organizing principle in teachers' jobs and lives. *British Educational Research Journal* 19 (4), 311–323.

Mercer, S. (2011) Language learner self-concept: Complexity, continuity and change. *System* 39 (3), 335–346.

Merriam, S.B. (1998) *Qualitative Research and Case Study Applications in Education*. San Francisco, CA: Jossey-Bass.

Mori, J. (2003) The construction of interculturality: A study of initial encounters between Japanese and American students. *Research on Language and Social Interaction* 36 (2), 143–184.

Nickerson, C. (2015) Unity in diversity: The view from the (UAE) classroom. *Language Teaching* 48, 235–49.

Nishizaka, A. (1995) The interactive constitution of interculturality: How to be Japanese with words. *Human Studies* 18, 301–326.

Norton, B. (2000) *Identity and Language Learning*. Harlow: Longman.

O'Neill, G.T. (2016) Heritage, heteroglossia and home: Multilingualism in Emirati families. In L. Buckingham (ed.) *Language, Identity and Education on the Arabian Peninsula* (pp. 13–38). Bristol: Multilingual Matters.

Palfreyman, D. (2006) Social context and resources for language learning. *System* 34 (3), 352–370.

Palfreyman, D. and Al-Bataineh, A. (2018) 'This is my life style, Arabic and English': Students' attitudes to (trans)languaging in a bilingual university context. *Language Awareness* 27 (1–2), 79–95.

Patent, D. (2016) "English is the half of life": The language learner identity of female Emiratis. In W. Zoghbor, C. Coombe, S. Al-Alami and S. Abu-Rmaileh (eds) *Proceedings of the 22nd TESOL Arabia Conference* (pp. 164–181). Dubai: TESOL Arabia.

Pavlenko, A. and Blackledge, A. (2004) Introduction: New theoretical approaches to the study of negotiation of identities in multilingual contexts. In A. Pavlenko and A. Blackledge (eds) *Negotiation of Identities in Multilingual Contexts* (pp. 1–33). Clevedon: Multilingual Matters.

Risager, K. (2007) *Language and Culture Pedagogy*. Clevedon: Multilingual Matters.

Seymour, J. (2016) Supporting bi-literacy among Emiratis in Dubai's private schools: An analysis of current Arabic language policy. Doctoral module assignment, University of Bath, UK, https://bath.academia.edu/JoanneSeymour

Solloway, A. (2018) 'Make them take an "IELTS test" in Arabic'! Resentment of and resistance towards English and English-medium instruction in the UAE. *Arab World English Journal* 9 (3), 458–478.

The National (2017) *Emirati documentary Nanny Culture is on a festival roll*. https://www.thenational.ae/arts-culture/film/emirati-documentary-nanny-culture-is-on-a-film-festival-roll-1.484561

van den Hoven, M. and Carroll, K.S. (2016) Emirati pre-service teachers' perspectives of Abu Dhabi's rich linguistic context. In L. Buckingham (ed.) *Language, Identity and Education on the Arabian Peninsula* (pp. 39–58). Bristol: Multilingual Matters.

Vertovec, S. (2007) Super-diversity and its implications. *Ethnic and Racial Studies* 30 (6), 1024–1054.

Wong, M.S., Lee, I. and Gao, X. (2016) Problematising the paradigm of 'nativeness' in the collaboration of local (NNEST) and foreign (NEST) teachers: Voices from Hong Kong. In F. Coupland, S. Garton and S. Mann (eds) *LETs and NESTs: Voices, Views and Vignettes* (pp. 217–232). London: British Council.

Yin, R.K. (2003) *Applications of Case Study Research*. London: Sage Publications.

Zhu, H. (2010) Language socialization and interculturality: Address terms in intergenerational talk in Chinese diasporic families. *Language and Intercultural Communication* 10 (3), 189–205.

Zhu, H. (2014) *Exploring Intercultural Communication: Language in Action*. Abingdon: Routledge.

Zhu, H. (2017) New orientations to identities in mobility. In S. Canagarajah (ed.) *Routledge Handbook of Migration and Language* (pp. 117–132). London: Routledge.

14 The Story of Tabasum: An Exploration of a Refugee Student's Developing Identities

Eliana Hirano and Caroline Payant

Introduction

Language learner identity has been the focus of increasing scholarly interest in the past 20 years. This growing body of research views identity as multiple; a site of struggle; socially, historically and discursively constructed; and continually changing over time and space (Fenton-O'Creevy *et al.*, 2015; Norton, 2013; Pavlenko & Blackledge, 2004b). The exploration of second language (L2) learner identity in higher education settings has included L2 learners from a variety of backgrounds, including international (e.g. Morita, 2004), generation 1.5 (e.g. Schwartz, 2010), immigrant (e.g. Prior, 2011) and refugee (e.g. Perry & Mallozzi, 2011) students. These categories sometimes overlap, and scholars often foreground one aspect of the students' life over others, grouping participants as, for example, linguistic minority students or immigrant students. Although refugees do not form a homogeneous group, there is general consensus that they have been through specific experiences that set them apart from other immigrants (e.g. trauma and the resettlement process), and that it is important to gain a better understanding of how these experiences affect the educational paths of this population (e.g. McBrien, 2005; Shapiro *et al.*, 2018). Refugees are defined by international law as unable to return to their country of origin without fear of being 'persecuted for reasons of race, religion, nationality, membership in a particular social group or political opinion' (United Nations High Commissioner for Refugees, 1951/1967). Until recently, studies investigating refugee students in educational settings, especially in higher education, were scarce.

In the past ten years, the topic of educating refugee-background students has received more attention, and a few edited volumes have been published exploring this issue (e.g. Dryden-Peterson & Giles, 2010;

Shapiro *et al.*, 2018). Ramsay and Baker (2019) reviewed articles on refugee-background students in higher education and found that these students face challenges to access higher education, and when they do attend college, several factors hinder their successful participation. In addition, they claimed that student identity has been overlooked in this literature. Intending to contribute knowledge to this gap, we explore the negotiation of identity experienced by a refugee-background student with interrupted education during her first year of college. In particular, we are interested in analyzing how interactions promoted by faculty members affect the student's identity as a college student.

Theoretical Framework

In order to explore the relationship between a refugee-background college student's identity development and the interactions in college courses, we draw on Bakhtin's dialogic approach (Bakhtin, 1981; Holquist, 1990). This framework helps explain how 'we, as humans, are always intimately connected to the spatial and temporal contexts in which we live, and these connections are how we articulate who we are' (Hallman, 2015: 4). In addition, it highlights that 'identity creation is, at its core, a response to others' (Hallman, 2015: 13), helping dispel the myth that identity is purely about 'self.' Students' identities, therefore, are constructed partially in response to interactions with instructors and peers in the various courses they take. In higher education, individual courses form distinct communities of practice (Lave & Wenger, 1991; Wenger, 1998): each course entails mutual engagement of participants, a joint enterprise and a shared repertoire – the three constitutive dimensions of a community of practice (Wenger, 1998). Each time a learner begins a new course, their access, participation and membership in this new community afford them the possibility to negotiate his or her identity anew as they engage in a shared practice (Fenton-O'Creevy *et al.*, 2015).

While viewing identity as a negotiated experience, it is important to consider the power relations that mediate relationships between teachers and students and among students (Pavlenko & Blackledge, 2004a). In discussing research on L2 learners and communities of practice, Higgins (2011) explains:

> Learners' engagement with new [communities of practice] is usually dependent on degrees of access and acceptance by the L1 speakers in these communities, and newcomers often struggle to find ways to legitimize their own forms of participation, often because of the failure of L1 speakers to create inclusive atmospheres for them to operate in as legitimated participants. (2011: 5)

For refugee-background students whose English proficiency is still developing, access to communities of practices in higher education may be limited due to their L2 status. Moreover, unlike international students with advanced literacy practices in their home countries, refugee-background learners may experience unique struggles that are not limited to their target language proficiency (Kanno & Varghese, 2010). According to Ramsay and Baker (2019), some of the challenges these learners face in higher education include 'interrupted education; continuing [...] effects of experiences of trauma; lack of familiarity with the dominant language and writing and literacy demands, and social conventions around higher education [...]; and difficulties connecting with other students' (2019: 66–67). In a college class, various experiences ultimately mediated by the instructor play an important role in the identity construction of students. These experiences may involve face-to-face interactions between the instructor and a student in and out of the classroom, student-to-student interaction in the classroom and feedback on assignments in the form of grades or comments, and, while these may affect all college students, refugee-background students may be more susceptible to them given their distinct needs.

The formation of individual identities is a never-ending process resulting from the interaction of complex factors. Gee (2001) proposes an analytical framework to view identities from four different angles, namely the nature, the institutional, the discursive and the affinity perspectives. These are not separate from each other or discrete categories. Rather, these are ways to 'focus our attention on different aspects of how identities are formed and sustained' (2001: 101). Considering the multi-faceted life experiences most refugees have had, Gee's taxonomy is particularly useful to capture the various factors influencing their identity development. A nature perspective (N-identity) can, for example, highlight one's refugee-background status, seen as a state the student is in, and not something she has done or accomplished. As Gee cautions, 'natural identities can only become identities because they are recognized [...] as meaningful' (2001: 102). A natural identity, just like other types of identities, can thus collapse into the other perspectives. An example of an institutional identity (I-identity) would be being a college student. As a consequence of being admitted into a college and registering for classes, a person becomes a college student. This identity is sanctioned by an institution of higher education. From a discursive perspective, however, the institutional label does not suffice for one to be a college student. A discursive identity (D-identity) would require other people to treat, talk about and interact with this person as a college student. According to Gee, discursive identities can be seen as an achievement, in the sense that they are constructed and negotiated in social interaction between members with various degrees of legitimacy. Finally, the fourth perspective is the affinity perspective (A-identity). This identity derives from participation in specific practices that are part of an affinity group. In educational settings, each class can be viewed as an affinity group.

Communities of practice are akin to affinity groups in that levels of participation affect a member's identity. Participation, however, is contingent upon social positioning, and access may not always be granted by the more legitimate members who typically hold a position of power. The Bakhtinian dialogic nature of identity construction, in turn, focuses on the discursive practices that take place between the self and the other, allowing for an exploration of the roles played by interaction and power relations, which are especially visible in faculty–learner relationships. In this chapter, we explore how interactions in first-year college created a site for struggle in the identity (re-)construction of a refugee-background college student.

Methodology

In this chapter, we present the qualitative longitudinal case study of Tabasum, a refugee-background student from Afghanistan, focusing on her identity (re-)construction as she transitioned from high school to her first year of college. We note that all names are pseudonyms in the study. Tabasum was resettled in the United States as a teenager, having attended school for less than one year in her home country. Between fleeing Afghanistan and arriving in the US, Tabasum lived in Pakistan for six years, during which time she did not attend school and spent her days weaving carpets to help her widowed mother. Upon arrival in the US, she was placed in 7th grade, and to avoid reaching the maximum age allowed in her school district, she skipped 8th grade so that she could complete high school. After only five years of education in the US, she was admitted to Hope College, a small, private, liberal arts college in the US Southeast. Born to uneducated parents, Tabasum was the first in her family to go to college. Because Hope College did not offer any specific support for language learners, Tabasum continued learning English as a regular student in college classes.

The data used for this chapter were taken from a larger multiple case study that examined how seven refugee-background students coped with academic literacies in college (see, e.g. Hirano, 2014, 2015). The data subset used for this study includes eight monthly hour-long face-to-face interviews with Tabasum during her first year of college, writing samples, and class observations. To explore how the identity of a refugee-background student can be affected by interactions promoted by college professors, we also analyzed one interview each with two professors that Tabasum had in her first year of college: Dr Spark, who taught a Speech class; and Dr Ellis, who taught a Rhetoric and Writing class. We selected these two professors because, taken together, they promoted a range of interactions that affected Tabasum's identity construction in various ways.

A qualitative approach to this inquiry (Creswell, 2003) allowed us to investigate Tabasum's identity construction as it was unfolding in college, using various data collection tools. In addition, the use of a longitudinal case study (Harklau, 2008) enabled us to 'document the interaction of individual and context and to document how [identity construction] is mediated by participants' understanding of and interactions with context over time' (2008: 26). Analysis of the data was on-going, recursive, inductive, and data-driven (Duff, 2008; Taylor & Bogdan, 1998) through a process of open coding to identify emergent themes (Mackey & Gass, 2005). Both researchers discussed themes they separately identified in Tabasum's interviews and then analyzed her professors' interviews to locate excerpts that were pertinent to Tabasum's identity construction. Findings from the analysis of the interviews were complemented by insights gleaned from the written documents and class observations.

Results

From active participant in high school to emotional and physical peripheries in college

In describing her academic performance and interactions with college professors, Tabasum repeatedly questioned her academic abilities. The analysis suggests that she attributed her low self-esteem as a college student to various aspects of her identity. In a first instance, she expressed the belief that socialization is an important factor leading to academic success, and that her interrupted educational path negatively affected her ability to interact with peers and gain access to classroom networks. She explained:

> When you are in a school you are socialized and you know people can communicate easily. But I have not been in a school, I've been at home like all the time like before I came to the U.S., and it's very hard to communicate with people and be socialized. (Interview 4)

Tabasum also struggled with her freshman status. In two of her courses, she reported that a majority of her peers were sophomore and junior (Year 2 and Year 3, respectively) students who already had, at least from her perspective, an understanding of college-level expectations and benefited from existing relationships with classmates. On repeated occasions, Tabasum expressed frustration as she attempted to become an active participant in her classrooms, a struggle she had not sensed in high school:

> In high school, I participated a lot, I was very active, I was like always in class discussion, I was involved [...] I wasn't shy [...], but now, no. [...] cause I'm in that class with so many different people and like upper classmates, so [...] I want to, but I can't [...] I don't wanna take classes with upper classmates anymore. (Interview 4)

Finally, in describing her experiences, she positioned herself at an inferior level, compared to her peers, which she attributed to her non-native speaker status:

> Also my speech class, [...] when I have to give a speech [...] I make mistakes on my speech and I feel bad because all of them are not at the same level as I am. And plus, English is not my native language, I mean there's still pressure on me. (Interview 1)

In summary, Tabasum perceived that her ability to successfully join these new college communities was adversely impacted by her limited social skills, her interrupted education and her freshman and non-native speaker statuses.

Besides feeling that she was on the periphery of the communities of practice that her courses comprised, it became evident that she also positioned herself physically on the periphery, potentially increasing the distance between herself and her peers and instructors. She opted to stay at the back of the classroom to avoid having to contribute to class discussions. Her positioning appears to have made her invisible and safe. In referencing her World Religion class, for example, she explains:

> In high school, I was always in the front seat, but now [...] I don't feel comfortable sitting in the front because there, people are asking question and the professor, and I don't know the answers so I'd better sit behind I mean back. (Interview 2)

Class observations confirmed her seating towards the back of the classroom. In addition, even when there was group work, she would sit quietly in the group circle and avoid interacting with her peers. In summary, her transition from high school to college may have destabilized her identity as a successful student and instilled doubt in her own potential.

Classroom practices that promoted integration

Learning is a fluid and social process, and interactions with professors and peers are central. Some of Tabasum's professors noted changes in her participation as the semester progressed. Dr Spark, the instructor for the speech class, noticed Tabasum's preference for sitting in the back of the room and worried that this precluded her from engaging and participating. She stated: 'Part of me wants her to sit closer. You know, because she sits way in the back, and I worry that she's not getting that same connection.' Sitting in the back of the room was not the only way Tabasum positioned herself in the periphery in her speech class. Students were given the option to collaborate and discuss current issues among themselves in preparation for quizzes. Despite having opportunities to discuss with classmates, Tabasum worked individually. She explained how she was shy and 'I didn't know what to ask [...] I didn't know anything about the quiz' (Interview 3).

As the semester progressed, however, we see changes in her positioning, and one contributing factor resulted from her instructor's practices. Teachers can play an important role in creating classroom communities that support and facilitate students' integration, and Dr Spark was intentional in contributing to this. She described her efforts to increase opportunities for peer interaction and task preparation by having students practice their speeches in small groups. In reflecting on their behaviors, she was reminded of the importance of learner-learner collaboration for knowledge development and for social integration. She explained:

> I've done more work in the last couple of weeks of getting them to interact with the other students. [...]. I did something where they had to, kind of, practice their speech in a smaller group. And I think they gave her some really good suggestions. [...] I forget how much students can learn from other students [...]. And it also allowed her to interact more with students than she had before.

Becoming a legitimate member in any social context requires mutual engagement and also recognition by other members, including peers, which did not always happen. While Tabasum was becoming more engaged and participated in small group discussions, she shared that some students were not respectful of her participation. This unwillingness to recognize her as a legitimate member was frustrating. For instance, near the end of the semester, her peers offered some feedback on her speech. And while she received constructive feedback from some, she felt that others were simply too critical. In her words:

> One of them was like fair, cause she thought I had to practice more and I had to work on my transition, like move from one point to another point, should be like smooth and connected, and the other person said like you are still weak, your voice is not clear and your points are not clear and you are making me confused. I was like that's not right. You wrote everything negative about me. (Interview 3)

In this class, Tabasum highlighted, on numerous occasions, how her freshman status placed her on the periphery and she tended to gravitate towards learners with shared experiences. In particular, she expressed a preference for working with one classmate who, like her, was not from the US, which facilitated interactions. She explained: 'cause he's not from American, so he understands, because I'm the only person like I don't speak English in that class, and he is also, he's not from United States so he understands' (Interview 3).

Changes in Tabasum's engagement with her peers were noted by Dr Spark, who explained:

> She really seems to have opened up a little more in class. And I think the real catalyst was when I had them do the little practice in front of other group members. I think she found them to be supportive. And like when

> she got up to do her speech, she did something that they were like 'she did it, she did it.' [...] I don't know what it was that she had done, but I heard the whispering and they were so proud of her. And it was really pretty cool.

Creating these opportunities for explicit collaboration partly supported Tabasum's success in this course. Tabasum became more engaged, but, despite her teacher's efforts, she felt as though her contributions were not always recognized by her peers.

While teachers can play an important role in creating supportive learning environments, it can be of equal importance to carefully identify which students can be grouped together to ensure emotionally supportive learning environments. In this particular case, the status (freshman and senior) and linguistic background (native and non-native) appeared to be crucial dimensions that mediated the quality of the interactions. Learning about students' individual needs and preferences may help educators make more informed decisions about collaboration, even in higher education contexts.

Instructor–student interaction outside the classroom

Interactions that unfold within the classroom can impact the learning experience and influence one's identity construction. Likewise, getting to know students individually outside the classroom is critical for professors to foster a sense of belonging, help students understand course expectations, and create a space for negotiating roles and contributions within a community. In higher education, in the US, professors are required to indicate their availability for office hours on their syllabus. These are times when professors are in their office, available for students who come to discuss their performance in the course, to ask for guidance, and other such matters. These individual conversations are an opportunity for instructors to provide the necessary scaffolding to support students' learning. This practice, however, places the onus of communication on the student, rather than on the instructor, and students often do not take the initiative to see their instructors in their office. Tabasum was no exception.

Tabasum expressed some discomfort in approaching Dr Spark even after a two-month period and felt that her instructor was not interested in her. She then asked the researcher to help facilitate communication: 'I was wondering [...] if you could come to my speech class and talk to her because I don't think she, she is not interested to learn about me, because I tried to talk to her, but, so that's why I don't go and talk to her, cause I don't want to' (Interview 2). The speech instructor was not part of the initial pool of faculty participants, but, after Tabasum's request, the researcher reached out to Dr Spark, who agreed to participate in the study. Tabasum's perception of Dr Spark's helpfulness changed after the researcher spoke to Dr Spark. Of her initial interaction with Dr Spark, prior to the researcher's intervention, she said: 'I thought this is not gonna help because she didn't know anything about me [...] and I don't think she's gonna listen to me.' In contrast, when talking about a meeting with the instructor after the intervention, she said: 'I asked her about the quiz, what's going on, I have no idea, I don't know how to study and my grades are bad. And she gave some clues how to study [...]. That helped and this time she said talk to your partner' (Interview 3). The perceived distance eventually disappeared with the support of the researcher, increasing Tabasum's sense of belonging in that class. At the end of the first semester, Tabasum had clearly learned the importance of reaching out to professors, as this gave them the opportunity to get to know her. When asked what advice she would give to students transitioning from high school to college, Tabasum said:

> Talk to your professors all the time and get them to know [you], because it's helpful because it's important for us if they know us because in the beginning, in my speech class, she didn't know me, [...] and I thought she was not nice to me and at the end when she got, I mean, she know me, she was so nice to me. (Interview 4)

For Tabasum, knowing that teachers understood her and her past was key. This created a pathway to move away from the periphery and become a more integral part of the classroom community.

Establishing personal connections impacted not only Tabasum's identity. In light of Tabasum's experiences in the classroom, we see how Dr Spark began to evaluate her own role in initiating communication with students. She realized that an instructor must have individual conversations with students, especially with those who are struggling to adapt to new learning situations. She explained:

> I want to do more of that. I think I need to do more of encouraging her to come in and talk to me. And I do that, and I try to do that with a lot of students who struggle. [...] I think she needs to get more comfortable doing that. [...] She needs to know she can come in and talk to her professors and say 'help'. You know, and I encourage all the students who are struggling in class to go in and talk to the professor because then the professor sees you as someone who cares.

In summary, while Tabasum assumed some of the responsibility by scheduling meetings with her professor, we notice that this experience was transformative for the professor as well.

Challenging interactions

As the interactions with Dr Spark above illustrate, Tabasum believed that teachers who knew about her unique story demonstrated greater empathy and were more willing to work with her to help her reach her academic goals. Conversely, those she perceived as not being interested in her story were felt as being less caring and supportive. In the first semester, she trusted her Religions instructor, who was also a mentor to her and the cohort of refugee-background students, her English 095 instructor, who knew all the students in the cohort from the college admissions process and had all of them in her remedial English class, and eventually came to trust Dr Spark. In her second semester, Tabasum was to find out that knowledge of her life story did not automatically translate into positive connections.

At the beginning of her second semester in college, Tabasum felt confident about starting new courses, especially since she now had some college experience and had registered for two classes she was very excited about: 'My favorite classes are Psychology and English' (Interview 5). She felt particularly optimistic about her English 101 class since she had briefly met the instructor, Dr Ellis, the previous semester: 'Cause I talked to her, like before, and she said that she teaches English 101, so I thought maybe, cause I talked to her, and I said maybe she's nice, I'll take her cause she seems like fun' (Interview 5). However, her first written assignment experience in this class quickly led her to reconsider her initial beliefs about this instructor. She soon realized that Dr Ellis followed a strict policy for late assignments, and it would appear as though there were no exceptions to this rule. After being penalized, as per the teacher's grading policy, Tabasum revisited the positive impression she had of her English instructor: 'I got a C [and], because I turned in late, [...] she gave me D [...] So I don't like her. Because she doesn't excuse like anything. She's like "There's no excuse for anything, you have to follow [the rules]"' (Interview 6). As a result, Tabasum was not interested in meeting with this instructor to discuss her writing process (drafting, going to the writing center, revisions), as she said: 'So I think it's not helpful to talk to her, so I'm not' (Interview 6). She felt that her teacher was ignoring her needs: 'She didn't listen to me, what I was saying, that I need help, I need some time, and she was not listening to me' (Interview 7). Her first-semester success negotiating membership in the speech class, while important, did not ensure immediate success in other courses, even when the instructor knew about her background. And while Tabasum had begun to understand the importance and value of meeting with teachers, she realized that with each new professor, she would have to build a relationship.

Although frustrated by this experience, Tabasum continued to demonstrate investment in her learning and took each assignment seriously. Rather than giving up or withdrawing from that class, she persevered and sought help from literacy brokers (Lillis & Curry, 2006). She did not, however, go to Dr Ellis for assistance given that she perceived her instructor to be unwilling to provide her with the necessary scaffolding that she had previously received from other instructors. Tabasum explained:

> I thought she's not gonna help me [...], so I never went to her and ask her for help. But I told her that I have problems so 'can I either turn in late or send?' and she was like 'you should do the same thing like other students'.

> So she seems that she never understand like my other teachers. My other teachers are nice and they help me and they never take points for late or for any kinds of small mistake. (Interview 7)

As a result, Tabasum did not follow her own advice of regularly talking to professors. Learning to negotiate membership in each course is a complex process that can be challenging for students.

A strategy that Tabasum would often employ to cope with college writing was to seek help from tutors in the writing center and from Mr Raymond, a retired linguist who had assisted Tabasum since her arrival in the US. This strategy had worked well for her until she experienced an upsetting incident. On her second assignment, Dr Ellis felt that Tabasum's paper was too strong and did not represent her own writing. Upon being confronted by the instructor, Tabasum explained her writing approach:

> I was honest. I told her I went to writing center and Mr. Raymond revised my paper. Then she said 'I'm not gonna give you any grade because you didn't write your paper'. And I did, I mean, I worked so hard, I was about to cry, like it was the hardest paper ever. (Interview 7)

Dr Ellis gave Tabasum an opportunity to re-write the paper in her presence. Tabasum complied and performed quite well on the task. Her teacher recognized that it was a B paper, but, given the circumstances, penalized her for initially not performing ethically and for submitting it late. On her paper, the professor wrote: 'This is C+/B- paper (grade of 80). I am taking off 10 points for turning it in late +20 points for cheating by turning in work that was not yours. Grade = 50.' Tabasum was labeled a cheater, lacking academic integrity. A deflating effect of this experience was reflected in Tabasum not wanting to talk about this class anymore, showing her positioning on the periphery of that course. After explaining what had happened, she said: 'That's why I don't want to talk about it. Cause I was so excited about that class, and I thought I had the best teacher' (Interview 7).

The instructor's perspective on this incident, unfortunately, was not captured in this study. After this incident, Tabasum reported she did not seek Mr Raymond's help again during that semester, and she felt that Dr Ellis showed more understanding of her situation, giving her extended time to turn in her essays. The reason the instructor changed her attitude and became more flexible is not clear, although it is possible that she was encouraged to do so by other faculty and administration that heard of the incident.

Discussion

Tabasum's interactions with the Speech and the Rhetoric and Writing professors are interesting in that they illustrate somewhat opposite trajectories concerning her identity development. Tabasum had never met Dr

Spark before the Speech course began, and she initially had difficulty establishing a relationship with the instructor, placing herself in the periphery of that class. As the semester progressed, Tabasum became a legitimate member of that course community, gradually increasing her participation. Her experience with the ENG 101 class, conversely, started with her intentionally choosing the section taught by Dr Ellis. She initially felt confident and optimistic, only to find out that the professor was not willing to accommodate her needs. Several interactions with the instructor, ranging from strict deadlines to an accusation of plagiarism, pushed Tabasum to the periphery of that class.

Tabasum's ongoing identity construction in her first year of college is evident. The transition from high school to college and from semester to semester illustrates how in each community of practice, Tabasum constructed strikingly different student identities. While she perceived herself as being a full participant in high school, her identity in college was somewhat more precarious. As a newcomer to higher education, Tabasum faced many challenges to assert herself as a college student. It is likely that Tabasum's recollection of high school refers specifically to her senior year and that her self-esteem had not always been so high. In any case, her student identity in her first year of college contrasted sharply from the way she remembered herself as a high school student. The transition from high school to college can be challenging for many students and, language learners, in particular, have been shown to have a difficult time coping with the shift in academic literacy expectations from one educational setting to the other (Harklau, 2000). Beyond the transition, research has also shown that English learners in college typically lag behind English proficient peers in terms of attainment and graduation rates (Kanno & Harklau, 2012).

Tabasum's student identity in college was influenced by many different forces, and the struggle that ensued is almost palpable. To closely examine these forces, we draw on Gee's (2001) framework, namely, the nature (N), the institutional (I), the discursive (D) and the affinity (A) perspectives to one's identity. Applying this analytical lens, we are better able to understand how her identities are tied to her past and present experiences and to tease apart the conflicting forces acting on her overall identity construction.

In a first instance, an N-identity that played an important role in college was her refugee-background status and, more specifically, her years of interrupted education. Tabasum had no control over this positioning. From her viewpoint, people learn to socialize in school settings, so she attributed her difficulty conversing with peers to her lack of education while living in Pakistan. She also believed that her non-native speaker status and her still-developing English proficiency made her stand out in a negative way in a community that is composed mostly of native speakers. Despite the fact that Tabasum attributed these difficulties to

N-identities, it is the discourses and interactions surrounding those identities that gave them meaning and made Tabasum feel at a disadvantage. To cite Gee (2001), 'N-Identities must always gain their force as identities through the work of institutions, discourse, and dialogue, or affinity groups, that is, the very forces that constitute our other perspectives on identity' (2001: 102). To illustrate, during the speech group practice, when Tabasum's peer only provided her with negative feedback, she seems to have taken it as an attack on her language proficiency, although the student never explicitly said so. The incident in her English course provides further evidence. Her L2 status was highlighted when Dr Ellis accused her of using the work of others, questioning her writing abilities, despite subsequent evidence that Tabasum was, in fact, able to write quality work. In these cases, the discursive practices of her peers and instructor reinforced her N-identity, from her perspective. In addition, these incidents exemplify Higgins' (2011) claim that language learners might face difficulty engaging and participating in communities of practice when the L1 members fail to create 'inclusive atmospheres for them to operate in as legitimated participants' (2011: 5).

From an I-identity perspective, Tabasum was a freshman college student. She had been admitted, had registered for college classes and was participating in sanctioned activities that align with this I-identity. This was a de jure identity. For her I-identity to be sanctioned discursively and become a de facto identity; however, complex and intricate negotiations needed to take place. At the end of her first year, her D-identity as a college student was still in flux, with interactions provided by her instructors deeply affecting how she perceived herself and her legitimacy as a college student. Throughout her first year, Tabasum had to negotiate a socioacademic relationship with her professors where each individual actor contributes to the forging of this social relation in an academic setting (Leki, 2006), but she was not always successful. Specifically, we found that while the Speech instructor attempted to provide interactions that pulled Tabasum towards the center of that community, thus boosting her D-identity, the discursive practices of the Rhetoric and Writing instructor pushed her towards the periphery. As Leki (2006) argues, however, students can manipulate social situations to their advantage. Although Tabasum had limited parental guidance, which can be crucial in academic socialization (McCarron & Inkelas, 2006), she actively sought out support from her developing academic network (e.g. writing mentors, peers, researchers) to resist the negative discursive forces.

The fluctuating nature of her identity as a college student may have prevented her from fully developing an A-identity as a college student. Each course can be viewed as an 'institutionally sanctioned' affinity group (Gee, 2001: 107) because of its set of distinctive experiences. However, because Tabasum's 'allegiance to, access to, and participation in specific practices' (Gee, 2001: 105) pertaining to these courses were somewhat constrained, her A-identity as a college student was still in flux. On the other hand, throughout her first year, Tabasum worked closely with expert writers and was a regular member of the writing center. Her active participation in the specific activities of this affinity group contributed to her A-Identity as a developing writer. Tabasum chose to join and participate regularly in the activities of the writing center, which supported her I-Identity as a college student as well as her D-identity.

The application of Gee's framework allows us to better understand Tabasum's multiple identities and the forces that influenced how she perceived herself in her first year as a college student. More broadly, this identity work highlights how 'self' and 'other' are always intricately related and influencing each other as posited by Bakhtin's dialogic approach. From this stance, individuals' positioning across social settings can impact access to new communities. In the context of her English class, Tabasum was positioned on the periphery and struggled to find her voice. This position, however, was context-dependent, and Tabasum, rather than accepting her position, challenged it. She negotiated a new position by seeking support from her network of mentors, empowering her to challenge her N-identity as a non-native English learner with a refugee background and interrupted education. In sum, by adopting a Bakhtinian lens to her process of academic socialization, we can see more clearly the changes in her identity in the first year of college, drawing attention to the fact that, while identity construction happens in response to 'others,' this process is not deterministic and 'can also be negotiated by agents who wish to position themselves' (Norton & Toohey, 2011: 418). Tabasum's already complex background coupled with the conflicting interactions she received from her instructors made the construction of her college student identity particularly taxing and a site of struggle but also afforded her opportunities to challenge a deficient student identity.

Conclusion

This chapter contributes to the growing body of evidence that individual identities are multiple and subject to moment-to-moment interactions over time and space (Fenton-O'Creevy *et al.*, 2015; Norton, 2013; Pavlenko & Blackledge, 2004b). Students and educators engage in activities that influence who they are and who they are becoming. Our detailed analysis of Tabasum's experiences as a first-year college student reveals her ongoing efforts to negotiate her identity. Her background as a refugee with years of interrupted education may have exacerbated the challenges for the construction of a solid identity as a college student with full access and membership to the academic communities of practice that her classes constituted. Even though in Tabasum's case her identity as a refugee with interrupted education was an important lens through which she understood her experiences in college, students from other backgrounds may experience similar issues with their identity in college, perhaps as a result of having limited socioacademic knowledge (Leki, 2006). Tabasum's later experiences in college likely led to further (re-)construction of her identity, which eventually contributed to her identity as a college graduate. It is also worth noting that interviews with instructors represent a single point in time; thus, interactions they had with Tabasum over a longer time were not captured in this study and constitute, therefore, an avenue for future research with instructors.

Before concluding this discussion, another point that is notable concerns the impact that her presence had on her instructors' identities. As a result of her interactions with Tabasum, Dr Spark became more aware of her cultural biases and became cognizant that her materials favored American values that her American students possessed, that her classroom activities limited the amount of interaction between learners, which may have inadvertently kept Tabasum on the periphery, and that her teaching style supported students with native or native-like comprehension abilities. Less information is available on Dr Ellis and whether her becoming more responsive to Tabasum's needs towards the end of the semester was the result of a change in her own identity. As Hallman (2015) states, 'teachers form their narratives of self as responses, in part, to the students they teach, the administrators they work with, [...] among others' (2015: 3). It is therefore plausible that either the experience with Tabasum itself or conversations with the administration prompted Dr Ellis to adopt more flexible policies and, perhaps, her identity was also touched in this process. In closing, teachers working within homogenous settings may seldom challenge their own assumptions. The fast-changing cultural and linguistic landscapes in higher education afford them the opportunity to work with students who are not always considered legitimate members of academic communities of practice, which can prompt deep reflection and a re-construction of the instructors' identities.

References

Bakhtin, M.M. (1981) *The Dialogic Imagination* (C. Emerson and M. Holquist, Trans.). Austin: University of Texas Press.

Creswell, J.W. (2003) *Research Design: Qualitative, Quantitative, and Mixed Methods approaches* (2nd edn). Thousand Oaks, CA: Sage Publications.

Dryden-Peterson, S. and Giles, W. (2010) Higher education for refugees [special issue]. *Refuge* 27 (2).

Duff, P.A. (2008) *Case Study Research in Applied Linguistics*. New York, NY: Lawrence Erlbaum.

Fenton-O'Creevy, M., Dimitriadis, Y. and Scobie, G. (2015) Failure and resilience at boundaries: The emotional process of identity work. In E. Wenger-Trayner, M. Fenton-O'Creevy, S. Hutchinson, C. Kubiak and B. Wenger-Trayner (eds) *Learning in Landscapes of Practice: Boundaries, Identity, and Knowledgeability in Practice-based Learning* (pp. 33–42). New York, NY: Routledge.

Gee, J.P. (2001) Identity as an analytic lens for research in education. *Review of Research in Education* 25, 99–125.

Hallman, H.L. (2015) Teacher identity as dialogic response: A Bakhtinian perspective. In Y.L. Cheung, S.B. Said and K. Park (eds) *Advances and Current Trends in Language Teacher Identity Research* (pp. 3–15). London: Routledge.

Harklau, L. (2000) From the "good kids" to the "worst": Representations of English language learners across educational settings. *TESOL Quarterly* 34 (1), 35–67.

Harklau, L. (2008) Developing qualitative longitudinal case studies of advanced language learners. In L. Ortega and H. Byrnes (eds) *The Longitudinal Study of Advanced L2 Capacities* (pp. 22–35). New York: Routledge.

Higgins, C. (2011) The formation of L2 selves in a globalizing world. In C. Higgins (ed.) *Identity Formation in Globalizing Contexts: Language Learning in the New Millenium* (pp. 1–17). Berlin: Walter de Gruyter.

Hirano, E. (2014) Refugees in first-year college: Academic writing challenges and resources. *Journal of Second Language Writing* 23 (1), 37–52.

Hirano, E. (2015) 'I read, I don't understand': Refugees coping with academic reading. *ELT Journal* 69 (2), 178–187.

Holquist, M. (1990) *Dialogism*. New York: Routledge.

Kanno, Y. and Harklau, L. (eds) (2012) *Linguistic Minority Students Go to College: Preparation, Access, and Persistence*. New York: Routledge.

Kanno, Y. and Varghese, M.M. (2010) Immigrant and refugee ESL students' challenges to accessing four-year college education: From language policy to educational policy. *Journal of Language, Identity and Education* 9 (5), 310–328. doi:10.1080/15348458.2010.517693

Lave, J. and Wenger, E. (1991) *Situated Learning: Legitimate Peripheral Participation*. Cambridge: Cambridge University Press.

Leki, I. (2006) Negotiating socioacademic relations: English learners' reception by and reaction to college faculty. *Journal of English for Academic Purposes* 5 (2), 136–152. doi:https://doi.org/10.1016/j.jeap.2006.03.003

Lillis, T. and Curry, M.J. (2006) Professional academic writing by multilingual scholars: Interactions with literacy brokers in the production of English-medium texts. *Written Communication* 23 (1), 3–35.

Mackey, A. and Gass, S. (2005) *Second Language Research: Methodology and Design*. Mahwah, NJ: Lawrence Erlbaum.

McBrien, J.L. (2005) Educational needs and barriers for refugee students in the United States: A review of the literature. *Review of Educational Research* 75 (3), 329–364.

McCarron, G.P. and Inkelas, K.K. (2006) The gap between educational aspirations and attainment for first-generation college students and the role of parental involvement. *Journal of College Student Development* 47 (5), 534–549.

Morita, N. (2004) Negotiating participation and identity in second language academic communities. *TESOL Quarterly* 38 (4), 573–603.

Norton, B. (2013) *Identity and Language Learning: Extending the Conversation* (2nd edn). Bristol: Multilingual Matters.

Norton, B. and Toohey, K. (2011) Identity, language learning, and social change. *Language Teaching* 44 (4), 412–446.

Pavlenko, A. and Blackledge, A. (2004a) Introduction: New theoretical approaches to the study of negotiation of identities in multilingual contexts. In A. Pavlenko and A. Blackledge (eds) *Negotiation of Identities in Multilingual Contexts* (pp. 1–33). Clevedon: Multilingual Matters.

Pavlenko, A. and Blackledge, A. (eds) (2004b) *Negotiation of Identities in Multilingual Contexts*. Clevedon: Multilingual Matters.

Perry, K.H. and Mallozzi, C.A. (2011) 'Are you able... to learn?': Power and access to higher education for African refugees in the USA. *Power and Education* 3 (3), 249–262.

Prior, M.T. (2011) "I'm two pieces inside of me": Negotiating belonging through narratives of linguistic and ethnic hybridity. In C. Higgins (ed.) *Identity Formation in Globalizing Contexts: Language Learning in the New Millenium* (pp. 27–47). Berlin: Walter de Gruyter.

Ramsay, G. and Baker, S. (2019) Higher education and students from refugee backgrounds: A meta-scoping study. *Refugee Survey Quarterly* 38, 55–82.

Schwartz, G.G. (2010) Subtexting mainstream generation 1.5 identities: Acculturation theories at work. In M. Cox, J. Jordan, C. Ortmeier-Hooper and G.G. Schwartz (eds) *Reinventing Identities in Second Language Writing* (pp. 29–50). Urbana, IL: National Council of Teachers of English.

Shapiro, S., Farrelly, R. and Curry, M.J. (eds) (2018) *Educating Refugee-Background Students: Critical Issues and Dynamic Contexts*. Bristol: Multilingual Matters.

Taylor, S.J. and Bogdan, R. (1998) *Introduction to Qualitative Research Methods: A Guidebook and Resource*. New York, NY: John Wiley.

United Nations High Commissioner for Refugees (1951/1967) *Convention and protocol relating to the status of refugees*. Retrieved from http://www.unhcr.org/3b66c2aa10.html

Wenger, E. (1998) *Communities of Practice: Learning, Meaning, and Identity*. Cambridge: Cambridge University Press.

Afterword

Glenn Toh

In a book rich with accounts of identity negotiations and struggles, candidness in storytelling is of axiomatic essence. I wish in this Afterword to consider how a book like this one draws attention to the way identities are staked and negotiated interactively and how struggles and relations of power thereof can be surfaced for critical observation.

If the contingency and precariousness of human identity and subjectivity are sometimes hidden or taken for granted, neither my wife Sakiko, who comes from Japan, nor I, would have thought that returning to my homeland, Singapore, was going to be as challenging as it turned out to be. Plying my trade as an English teacher, I had left Singapore soon after the millennium bug, not expecting to be away for longer than a short interim, returning 15 years later.

In the course of my work in various locations in the Asia-Pacific including Thailand, Hong Kong, New Zealand and Japan, I have encountered a fair share of challenges implicating language, ideology, power relations and different ways in which they influence the construction, constitution and contestation of identity. Such matters in turn bear heavily on ways in which individual actors are able to invest personally and agentively, ultimately, in their own humanness. The range of interactive experiences that life has to offer epitomize the fact that issues of identity (and as has been seen throughout this book, both their personal and professional aspects) and sense making are actually imbrications of larger concerns over humanity and humanization. Such concerns are those for which people have to stake out their own vested, negotiated positionings, while drawing on their own human praxis. For most people, encounters with a fluidity of discourses and ideologies influencing identity positioning and investment make it necessary to develop a deepening consciousness of existential struggles with different ways of being, bearing, behaving and becoming in situ. Such a consciousness is not apart from a much-needed understanding that agency, strategy and investment are vital aspects of being and remaining human(ized), not least as historical subjects who are supposed to be 'capable of transforming their own lived realities' (Dale & Hyslop-Margison, 2010: 110). In this connection, if one's ontology is about one's 'freedom to be' (Freire, 2000: 146), this freedom should in no way suggest an absence of struggle against forces of regulation, control, and in certain cases, oppression, in any quest for such a possibility to materialize. Still less can 'attitudes, values, or self-claims' which are staked expressions of claims to this freedom be understood on a 'cognitively given, either/or' basis (Bamberg, 2005: 222).

As may be seen in the following story, one of many told in this volume, attitudes, values and claims 'are partial and shifting devices' that 'spring up in ... *constantly shifting interaction*' (Bamberg, 2005: 222, italics added). The possibility of presenting different 'Is' at 'different times and places' can go some way toward constructing a particular understanding of the 'me' (Bamberg, 2005: 223). In the following instance, the story will not only help to illustrate an 'I' in flux as a new returnee encountering 'interactive trouble' (Bamberg, 2005: 222), but it will also bear out the fact that 'the sequence of I-positions in the story world' can provide a way of apprehending the 'me', in the midst of identity negotiations. In all of these, the self that is enacted 'as character in the story' and the self that one occupies 'as speaker (animator and/or author)' (Bamberg, 2005: 223) help to foreground hopeful possibilities for understanding identity struggles in the richer and more generative manner that a book like this aims to achieve.

In so appropriating identity, I highlight the manner in which circumstances, contexts, interactions and stories of identities and positionings waiting here to be told, can be given their deserved attention for the ways in which ideologies become legitimated, and power relations reified. Such relations, while naturalizing particularized epistemologies, beliefs and relationships, can also dissimulate not so obvious ways in which people are categorized taxonomically (Manan *et al.*, Wernicke), marginalized or self-marginalized (Toker, Mohamed, Hopkyns, Hirano and Payant). In this regard, forms of overreliance on fixed or prefabricated understandings of identity are liable to be generally unhelpful, not least due to the over-simplicities they can perpetuate.

Before our relocation to Singapore, Sakiko and I lived in Japan's Kanto region where I taught English before becoming part of a daring initiative to launch an English as a Lingua Franca program in almost incorrigibly 'native-speakerist' Japan (see Rivers, 2013; Toh, 2016a). This was before we came to the conclusion/realization that our two children would benefit from opportunities to experience interaction in more trans(multi)lingual settings that would be more supportive of the generation of new meanings or significations and conducive to creative or reflexive interactional and learning engagements (Manan *et al.*, Asadi, *et al.*). For us, Singapore was an exciting proposition, alas to be somewhat dampened by the fact that our children, then aged eight and nine, having been schooled monolingually in Japanese, knew hardly enough English to be schooled in Singapore's bi/multilingual system. Faced with the only realistic choice, which was to have them enrolled in a Japanese-medium school, we made enquiries to this end.

Over one preliminary visit, the English-speaking Singaporean office staff explained the enrolment procedures. Before we left Japan, we were instructed to go to the education ministry in Tokyo to avail ourselves of the recommended textbooks (all in Japanese) as the school's curriculum was based entirely on the Japanese state system. There was, however, one exception, which was that English would be taught, something unheard of in our experience of the monolingual Japanese system. Our curiosity about how English classes would be taught and administered was in part aroused by a doubtfulness that came about through my own documented experience of the manner in which English was generally taught and treated in Japan (see Toh, 2012, 2016b; see Gombin-Sperling and Baker Robbins for laudable attempts at developing multi-layered values, approaches and carefully nuanced attitudes towards English). The fact that English continues to be linked inextricably and reductively to its White native speakers (see e.g. Kubota & Fujimoto, 2013; Rudolph *et al.*, 2018) in no insignificant way caused me to wonder how the language would be taught to school-going Japanese children in cosmopolitan multicultural Singapore. The English textbook turned out to be an edition of Oxford's *Family and Friends*, the contents of which were all-too-apparent reflections of English used in stultifyingly monolingual culturalist terms (chapters by Manan *et al.*, Asadi *et al.*, Lemoine-Bresson, discuss the idealization of a monolingual English-only perspective and its supposed links with 'good and true English' and pedagogical orthodoxy) as if language, culture and country corresponded in a non-complex manner (Hopkyns). In one unit, three young characters, Holly, Amy and Leo, are seen asking each other how much money each happened to have, with the amounts denominated in pounds. Places mentioned index the likes of Oxford, Cornwall and London. In an abridged excerpt from Jonathan Swift's novel, the main character, Gulliver, is seen speaking to the Lilliputians in English ('only'), only becoming 'bilingual' over his extended stay. Static representations of identity, common as they are in reality, hardly attempt to position learners as agentive meaning makers in English let alone include the 'personal' as a dimension of their learning (Kawamitsu). Neither do they help learners imaginatively develop a sense of who they are in a globalized world (Gombin-Sperling and Robbins) nor engender a sense of the complexities of language learning experiences (Salerno and Andrei) or cultural identity relations (Akayoglu *et al.*).

Meanwhile, English teacher turnover was high. Over three terms, our children were subjected to a total of seven changes. The sudden departure of one teacher took place just four weeks before the end of term. This particular teacher was well-liked by the pupils for her engaging lessons. The lack of an announcement (let alone explanation) left the children with little closure. When I sought to enquire about the matter, a conference call was arranged with two teachers in attendance, Teacher A (TA) and Teacher B (TB). TA was the department head, a Japanese, and TB, from a country in the northern hemisphere, was in charge of English Conversation. TA spoke first, repeatedly asserting that she could not hear me, while entreating that I should speak louder. Her glib answer to my question about the teacher's departure was an equivocating 'she-is-absent' comment before TB's non-committal answers came in the vein of 'medical-leave', 'yet-to-be-confirmed-resignation' and other evasive equivocations. When I enquired about how or whether an announcement would be made, TB said that the question would be handled by someone from the school administration, who would contact us presently.

At that stage of the conversation, there was little indication that the situation was going to develop (or mutate) into one in which my role identities and praxes as parent and teacher (or as person and professional – cf. Lemoine-Bresson's chapter for discussion of struggles therein) would be put to the sorts of duress that one would rarely expect out of parent–teacher interaction. To cut short the story, I was to receive an undated handwritten note from TA the next day, through my daughter. The note was written on absorbent color paper, the sort that some people might use in informal communication, complete with floral designs. The note began with the following apology: 'I'd like to apologize your for inconvenience of informing the issue about the left teacher (sic). I could only say that she was absent to any parents or students until the principal announces officially. I am sorry to make you unconfortable (sic). (Also I've been scared of a raised voice of males recently, I couldn't continue the conversation ...)'.

The writer goes on to say that she had observed our children's classes and noted that they were enjoying English. Moreover, she added that she lived very close to where we were and since her children and ours commuted on the same school bus, offered gladly to reach out to my wife about the matter. Concluding her message, she had the following to say: 'I hope you'll understand the differences of the ways (in various cases) between Japanese school and other international schools, regarding how to announce information of anything in school to parents. Thank you.'

In her naturalization of the existence of a *Japanese way* of 'announc[ing] information', TA's claims to the uniqueness of such a way (which is supposedly different from 'other international schools') betrays the legitimation of a social-moral order that is pegged (endemically, indexically) to a particularized manner of Japaneseness (see Befu, 2001). In strategically seeking to manage intersectional identities and positionings in this exchange, TA resorts to invocations of gender and nationality (by implication race-ethnicity, see Befu, 2001; cf. Asadi *et al.*, Hirano and Payant) which are deployed as strategies both to exclude and disqualify, thereafter to denigrate and disenfranchise. By first claiming my inaudibility, TA manages to set up a situation by which she would then be able to say in her written note that she was 'scared of a raised voice of males (sic)'. By way of thereby saying that she 'couldn't continue the conversation', she then steers (hints) in the direction of having my (Japanese) wife deal with the matter, in so readily offering to communicate with her. Her construction of a loud-voiced Singaporean male (father was incidental or positionally inconsequential) became an (identity) project(ion) directed at finding a way of indexing marginality and disfavor (cf. Lemoine-Bresson for a parallel case of people being locked into categories of origin and culture, using what in effect is a 'national' argument; and Salerno and Andrei for the privileging and repudiation of certain identities, and pretentions to others). Voice was precisely wielded, *figuratively* and *literally*, with a view to its very silencing.

Subtle playing-off of paternity and maternity is then achieved through highlighting the matter of children on the same bus. As Japanese parents (practically speaking, mothers, as expatriate fathers go to work) are required by rule to wait for their offspring to come home after each school day, the matter of similar bus route is used to insinuate Japanese and motherhood role identities, and the fact that the matter can or should be solved between people who inhabited these role identities. Japaneseness becomes technology, project and symbolic space, three-in-one. TA's claims from her classroom observations of our children's enjoyment of English revealed her bid to reassume (reassert) her position of watch as 'Head', from which role-positioning she is then able to imply that parental concerns over (yet another) teacher's departure were quite unnecessary. This latter attempt was accomplished using the ruse of a reassuring you-need-not-worry demurral, once again seeking to disqualify another party's right to register concern and parental (paternal) opinion.

As Bamberg (2005) would helpfully observe, TA assumes simultaneous positions (mother-of-kids-on-the-same-bus, 'Head' etc.) while seeking to 'hold the floor by ... blocking off interruptions and objections' (2005: 231; see Wernicke for interesting treatment of the exercising of identity authentications, situational, transportable and self-ascribed identities, emerging actions and extra-situational agendas; Toker for multiple, shifting and contradictory identity constructions and trajectories; and Mohamed for treatment of professional self-understanding informing teachers' personal interpretive frameworks). Concerning the matter of right-to-speak, Pittway (2004) notes too that shifts in power relations take place from moment to moment in interactions where one party's right to speak can be quickly facilitated, or forfeited. The silencing of an opposing voice, and symbolically, the silencing-of-voice itself, becomes literal.

Notwithstanding the egregiousness of these putative paternity/maternity, Japanese/non-Japanese insinuations, a keener positioning analysis (Korobov, 2001; cf. chapters by Mohamed, Arrieta and Rosado for discussions on positioning; Salerno and Andrei for critical events in the shaping and appropriation of identity) would lead one to further conclude that the matter of paternity and maternity was actually an insinuation of deeper bigotry – over the fact that a non-Japanese parent did not possess the

Japaneseness (or normalcy) to rightfully raise matters with (about) the school (see earlier section discussing categorizations of people). Amusingly, the school in question is located in cosmopolitan Singapore, with its many sites for intercultural exchange (Lemoine-Bresson) and plurilingual hybridities. A particularized rendition (or caricaturing) of maleness served as a back-handed way of indexing non-Japaneseness. Ironically, characterizations of Japaneseness by the Japanese themselves attest to their being the gentle, tolerant and malleable progeny of a 'soft, moist, humid climate' (see Rudolph *et al.*, 2018: 10).

I am not unaware that the above narrative might be read (quite pointlessly) as a complaint or the like. To do so would be to overlook the kinds of storying (and the practicing of small-stories – Bamberg, 2005) that signal the manner in which instances of friction and discontinuity are recognizably as much betrayers of ideological orientation for some as they can be opportunities for identity praxis for others. For teachers, they can be a reminder of the resonant importance of the more humanizing aspects of self-exploration as a personal identity theme (Connelly & Clandinin, 1999; Leeferink *et al.*, 2019; also Urzúa's chapter). In seeking to write this Foreword as more than just a platitude of generalities or niceties, the above story allows me to identify with the multi-levelled, multi-faceted landscape in which claims to identity are made immanently and performatively. My own respect for the editors of this volume makes necessary a commitment to recognizing the harsher reality that interactive activities and moments are the very sites in which identity and belongingness are instantiated, negotiated or (con)tested as the case may be (Davies & Harré, 1990; Korobov, 2001). One resonates with Connelly and Clandinin (1999) whose valuing of the stories that teachers live by stems from honest appreciation of the ways in which teacher identities are linked to professional knowledge, background (Asadi *et al.*, Toker, Mohamed), storied compositions and dialogues (Salerno and Andrei) and negotiated reflections (Urzúa), which are necessarily personal yet social in nature. Such linkage must be the case if due recognition is given to the porousness and mutually informing quality of teachers' personal and professional identities. Indeed, the matter of teacher identity as it must be tied fundamentally to ontological and epistemological beliefs, self-perceptions, self-definitions, personal biographies and professional knowledge landscapes, speaks of the multiple social roles teachers inhabit (not to be mistaken for TA's chary double-dealings), be they as colleagues, scientists or parents (Beijaard, 2019; Connelly & Clandinin, 1999). Ontologically, existentially and substantially, Connelly and Clandinin (1999) are helpful in pointing out that the who-am-I aspect of a personal-professional encounter is probably just as (if not more) crucial as the what-I-know aspect of the same. Insofar as who-I-am is fought for in intersectional and interstitial spaces which mark out the fluidity and precariousness of real-life, especially border-crossing, interactions, the issues raised here are ones of current moral concern (cf. Asadi *et al.*, Mohamed). Moreover, superstructural discourses need to be recognized (and owned up to) as being liable to weigh on discourses of identity and ways of negotiating inclusion, identification and affiliation, with attendant implications for matters of humanization and dehumanization. Identity, or phrased another way, the meanings and positionings that are claimed and fought-for at any interactive moment, are worth contending for, as part of one's human praxis (Freire, 2000). In the manner in which agency finds enactment and expression in self-reflection and self-assertion, a better understanding of the positioning of self, as well as the discursive resources, rights and repertoires available or not available to this end, are enabled by examinations of these domains of praxis (Freire, 2000; Bamberg, 2005).

One must therefore laud the commitment that one sees in efforts to view identity in its full range of discursive, representational, interactional and intersectional fluidities towards a hopefulness of outcomes. Reductionist aspects of language teaching can be dehumanizing in their categorizations of speakerhood and marginalization of learners, quite inanely, as *speakers* of *other* languages. Holliday's (2005) caricaturizing of English-speaking Western Teaching English to the Speakers of Other Languages (TESOL) ensures that an element of burlesque puts to rest any thought that TESOL can remotely be ideologically (let alone benignly) neutral. In a day and age when even critical scholarship is taken to task for detachment or aloofness (see Rudolph, invited, under review), in this case from contextualized and historicized negotiations of identity (on pain of the loss of descriptive power), English-speaking Western TESOL's smugness in its native speakerist personas must stand out for notice (Wernick, Asadi *et al.*, offer their respective elaborations; Gombin-Sperling and Baker Robbins provide a self-reflexive critique, of this concern). Holliday's (2005) burlesque, seen in his native speakerist personas' collusiveness with their respective patrons and protectors, speaks perhaps of a yet culpable manner in which TESOL invokes categorizing subjectivities among its teachers and students, the monologic assumptions behind which are seen problematized in Salerno and Andrei's chapter. The non-native speaker learner is a reified artefact of TESOL's rough-and-ready (or cold-blooded) codification or commodification of an alienated and culturally deficient (deprived) Other, by dint of malnourishment or infelicity in English or English-only, while translanguaging is regarded as a problematic aberration (cf. Asadi *et al.* and Hopkyns). TESOL's reification of such an artefact is not outshone by reifications of the native speaker who is not spared the same caricaturing, TESOL's beloved and potent icon of its globalist expansionist exploitative ambitions, albeit (re)cast benignly as 'English-speaking Western TESOL "philanthropists"' (Holliday, 2005: 165). These philanthropists, so identified for their personification (or impersonation) of magnanimity in their eagerness to '"give" more to "those" "nonnative speakers"' (Holliday, 2005: 165), are said to be impositions (transpositions) of particularized cultural constructions on hapless nonnative speaker learners. While it remains possible to carefully negotiate oneself away from the pitfalls of this role as shown in Gombin-Sperling and Robbins, such philanthropic impositions, Holliday (2005) argues, are a way for 'the West to satisfy its own needs' (2005: 165) both 'to dominate and [to] control' through 'cultural correction' (2005: 157). Elsewhere in those brutally impassioned Second Language Acquisition (SLA) debates (see Firth & Wagner, 1997; Gass, 1998; Long, 1997), one is reminded that reference to primatologists' interest in primates (Gass, 1998) as an analogy of the vested interest which SLA researchers have in leaners, does not reflect complimentarily on both learners nor humans in sympathy with the analogy, however much unintended (or Freudian). In all of these ideological machinations, the inner workings of vested interests mean that certain identity projects representing and mobilizing powerful interests are not easily destabilized, on pain of violent objection – asymmetries in power relations notwithstanding.

Indeed, the fact that one is still able to write relevantly about enduring forms of stereotyping, silencing and marginalization suggests that voices of resistance and contestation on the ground (or in the margins) remain materially weak and muted. It is in this connection that the challenge to criticality remains not just in problematizing and exposing inequities and asymmetries as such, which it is wont to do, but also to ensure that it too is energized by a reflexive element (Rudolph, 2019) which will ensure its relevance in such discussions as those seen in this book.

References

Bamberg, M. (2005) Narrative discourse and identities. In J. C. Meister, T. Kindt and W. Schernus (eds) *Narratology Beyond Literary Criticism: Mediality, Disciplinarity* (pp. 214–235). Berlin: Walter de Gruyter.

Befu, H. (2001) *Hegemony of Homogeneity*. Melbourne: Transpacific.

Beijaard, D. (2019) Teacher learning as identity learning: Models, practices, and topics. *Teachers and Teaching* 25(1), 1–6.

Connelly, F.M. and Clandinin, D.J. (1999) *Shaping a Professional Identity: Stories of Educational Practice*. New York: Teachers College Press.

Dale, J. and Hyslop-Margison, E. (2010) *Paulo Freire: Teaching For Freedom and Transformation: The Philosophical Influences on the Work of Paulo Freire*. Dordrecht: Springer.

Davies, B. and Harré, R. (1990) Positioning: The discursive production of selves. *Journal for the Theory of Social Behavior* 20 (1), 43–63.

Firth, A. and Wagner, J. (1997) On discourse, communication, and (some) fundamental concepts in SLA research. *Modern Language Journal* 81 (3), 285–300).

Gass, S. (1998) Apples and oranges: Or, why apples are not orange and don't need to be: A response to Firth and Wagner. *Modern Language Journal* 82 (1), 83–94.

Freire, P. (2000) *Pedagogy of the Oppressed* (30th anniversary edition). New York: Continuum.

Holliday, A. (2005) *The Struggle to Teach English as an International Language*. Oxford: Oxford University Press.

Korobov, N. (2001) Reconciling theory with method: From conversation analysis and critical discourse analysis to positioning analysis. *Forum: Qualitative Social Research* 2 (3), 11.

Kubota, R. and Fujimoto, D. (2013) Racialized native speakers: Voices of Japanese American English language professionals. In S.A. Houghton and D.J. Rivers (eds) *Native-Speakerism in Japan: Intergroup Dynamics in Foreign Language Education* (pp. 196–207). Bristol: Multilingual Matters.

Leeferink, H., Koopman, M., Beijaard, D. and Schellings, G. (2019) Overarching professional identity themes in student teacher workplace learning. *Teachers and Teaching* 25 (1), 69–89.

Long, M.H. (1997) Construct validity in SLA research: A response to Firth and Wagner. *The Modern Language Journal* 81 (3), 318–323.

Rivers, D.J. (2013) Institutionalized native-speakerism: Voices of dissent and acts of resistance. In S.A. Houghton and D.J. Rivers (eds) *Native-Speakerism in Japan: Intergroup Dynamics in Foreign Language Education* (pp. 75–91). Bristol: Multilingual Matters.

Rudolph, N. (2019) Native Speakerism (?!): (Re) considering critical lenses and corresponding implications in the field of English Language Teaching. *Indonesian Journal of English Language Teaching* 14 (1), 89–113.

Rudolph, N., Yazan, B. and Rudolph, J. (2018) Negotiating 'ares,' 'cans,' and 'shoulds' of being and becoming in English language teaching: Two teacher accounts from one Japanese university. *Asian Englishes* 21 (1), 22–37.

Toh, G. (2012) Having English as a resource for multicultural understanding: Exploring possibilities in Japanese ELT. *Journal of Multilingual and Multicultural Development* 33 (3), 301–311.

Toh, G. (2016a) Doing justice to an English as a lingua franca paradigm. *Journal of English as a Lingua Franca* 5 (2), 355–367.

Toh, G. (2016b) *English as Medium of Instruction in Japanese Higher Education: Presumption, Mirage or Bluff?* London: Palgrave Macmillan.

Index